TAKING SIDES

Clashing Views in

World Politics

FIFTEENTH EDITION

Selected, Edited, and with Introductions by

John T. Rourke
University of Connecticut

TAKING SIDES: CLASHING VIEWS IN WORLD POLITICS,
FIFTEENTH EDITION

1 2 3 4 5 6 7 8 9 0 DOC/DOC 1 0 9 8 7 6 5 4 3 2 1

MHID: 0-07-805010-3
ISBN: 978-0-07-805010-7
ISSN: 1094-754X (print)
ISSN: 2158-1452 (online)

Managing Editor: *Larry Loeppke*
Senior Developmental Editor: *Jill Meloy*
Permissions Coordinator: *Rita Hingtgen*
Senior Marketing Communications Specialist: *Mary Klein*
Senior Project Manager: *Jane Mohr*
Design Coordinator: *Brenda A. Rolwes*
Cover Graphics: *Rick D. Noel*
Buyer: *Nicole Baumgartner*
Media Project Manager: *Sridevi Palani*

Compositor: MPS Limited, a Macmillan Company
Cover Image: Brand X Pictures/Jupiter Images

Editors/Academic Advisory Board

Members of the Academic Advisory Board are instrumental in the final selection of articles for each edition of TAKING SIDES. Their review of articles for content, level, and appropriateness provides critical direction to the editors and staff. We think that you will find their careful consideration well reflected in this volume.

TAKING SIDES: Clashing Views in WORLD POLITICS

Fifteenth Edition

EDITOR

John T. Rourke
University of Connecticut

ACADEMIC ADVISORY BOARD MEMBERS

Editors/Academic Advisory Board continued

Preface

In the first edition of *Taking Sides: Clashing Views in World Politics,* I wrote of my belief in informed argument: [A] book that debates vital issues is valuable and necessary. . . . [It is important] to recognize that world politics is usually not a subject of absolute rights and absolute wrongs and of easy policy choices. We all have a responsibility to study the issues thoughtfully, and we should be careful to understand all sides of the debates.

It is gratifying to discover, as indicated by the success of *Taking Sides* over 14 editions, that so many of my colleagues share this belief in the value of a debate-format text.

The format of this edition follows a formula that has proved successful in acquainting students with the global issues that we face and in generating discussion of those issues and the policy choices that address them. This book addresses 19 issues on a wide range of topics in international relations. Each issue has two readings, one pro and one con. Each is also accompanied by an issue *introduction,* which sets the stage for the debate, provides some background information on each author, and generally puts the issue into its political context. Each issue concludes with a *postscript* that summarizes the debate, gives the reader paths for further investigation, and suggests additional readings that might be helpful. I have also provided relevant Internet site addresses (URLs) in each postscript and on the *Internet References* page that accompanies each part opener. At the back of the book is a listing of all the *contributors to this volume,* which will give you information on the political scientists and other commentators whose views are debated here.

I have continued to emphasize issues that are currently being debated in the policy sphere. The authors of the selections are a mix of practitioners, scholars, and noted political commentators.

Changes to this edition The dynamic, constantly changing nature of the world political system and the many helpful comments from reviewers have brought about significant changes to this edition. Nearly half (47 percent) of the issues are new. They are: Is Capitalism a Failed Model for a Globalized Economy? (Issue 2); Is the United States a Declining Power? (Issue 4); Should the Jackson–Vanik Amendment Targeting Russia Be Repealed? (Issue 5); Is U.S. Policy Toward Latin American on the Right Track? (Issue 9); Does China's Currency Manipulation Warrant International and National Action? (Issue 10); Should Export Controls on High Technology Be Eased Substantially? (Issue 12); Is U.S. Strategic Nuclear Weapons Policy Ill-Conceived? (Issue 13); Should U.S. Forces Continue to Fight in Afghanistan? (Issue 14); and Does Using Drones to Attack Terrorists Globally Violate International Law? (Issue 15). All these use readings new to this edition, and because of the kaleidoscopic dynamism of the international system, 40 percent of the issues that have been carried over also have new readings.

These include the eight issues (42 percent) that were included in the last edition but have one or more new readings: Is Economic Globalization Good for Both Rich and Poor? (Issue1); Does Globalization Threaten Cultural Diversity? (Issue 3); Is U.S. Refusal to Join the International Criminal Court Wise? (Issue17); and Should the United States Ratify the Convention to Eliminate All Forms of Discrimination Against Women? (Issue 18). Thus, 68 percent of issues are new or have at least one new reading.

It is important to note that the changes to this edition from the last should not disguise the fact that most of the issues address enduring human concerns, such as global political organization, arms and arms control, justice, development, and the environment. Also important is the fact that many of the issues have both a specific and a larger topic. For instance, Issue 16 is about the specific topic of the performance of United Nations peacekeeping, but it is also about more general topics. These include the proper role of international organizations in the global system and the degree to which countries should subordinate their sovereignty to them.

A word to the instructor An *Instructor's Manual with Test Questions* (multiple-choice and essay) is available through the publisher for instructors using *Taking Sides* in the classroom. A general guidebook, *Using Taking Sides in the Classroom,* which discusses methods and techniques for integrating the pro–con approach into any classroom setting, is also available. An online version of *Using Taking Sides in the Classroom* and a correspondence service for *Taking Sides* adopters can be found at http://www.mhhe.com/cls. *Taking Sides: Clashing Views in World Politics* is only one title in the *Taking Sides* series. If you are interested in seeing the table of contents for any of the other titles, please visit the *Taking Sides* Web site at http://www.mhhe.com/cls.

A note especially for the student reader You will find that the debates in this book are not one-sided. Each author strongly believes in his or her position. And if you read the debates without prejudging them, you will see that each author makes cogent points. An author may not be "right," but the arguments made in an essay should not be dismissed out of hand, and you should work to remain tolerant of those who hold beliefs that are different from your own. There is an additional consideration to keep in mind as you pursue this debate approach to world politics. To consider divergent views objectively does not mean that you have to remain forever neutral. In fact, once you are informed, you ought to form convictions. More important, you should try to influence international policy to conform better with your beliefs. Write letters to policymakers; donate to causes you support; work for candidates who agree with your views; join an activist organization. *Do* something, whichever side of an issue you are on!

Acknowledgments I received many helpful comments and suggestions from colleagues and readers across the United States and Canada. Their suggestions have markedly enhanced the quality of this edition of *Taking Sides*. If as you read this book you are reminded of a selection or an issue that could be included in a future edition, please write to me in care of McGraw-Hill/ Contemporary Learning Series with your recommendations or e-mail them to me at john.rourke@uconn.edu.

My thanks go to those who responded with suggestions for the 15th edition. I would also like to thank Jill Meloy, my editor for this volume, for her help in refining this edition.

John T. Rourke
University of Connecticut

For my son and friend—John Michael

Contents In Brief

Contents

Staff members of the International Monetary Fund conclude on the basis of experiences across the world that unhindered international economic interchange, the core principle of globalization, seems to underpin greater prosperity. Ravinder Rena, an associate professor of economics at the Eritrea Institute of Technology, contends that globalization creates losers as well as winners and the losers are disproportionately found among the world's poorer countries.

Walden Bello, the president of the Freedom from Debt Coalition, examines on the part played by events in the United States in creating the global financial crisis beginning in 2008 and argues that capitalism is failing as a national and global model. Dani Rodrik, a professor of political economy at Harvard University's John F. Kennedy School of Government, concedes that various aspects of capitalism caused the crisis, but contends that capitalism can be reformed and remain as the prevailing economic model across the globe.

Allan Brian Ssenyonga, a Ugandan freelance writer for *The New Times,* an English daily in Rwanda, claims that one of the negative effects of globalization is cultural assimilation via cultural imperialism. Philippe Legrain, the chief economist of Britain in Europe, an organization supporting the adoption by Great Britain of the euro as its currency, counters that it is a myth that globalization involves the imposition of Americanized uniformity, rather than an explosion of cultural exchange.

John J. Tkacik, Jr., a senior research fellow in China policy at the Asian Studies Center of the Heritage Foundation in Washington, DC, contends that the evidence suggests instead that China's intent is to challenge the United States as a military superpower. Samuel A. Bleicher, principal in his international consulting firm, The Strategic Path LLC, argues that while China has made some remarkable economic progress, the reality is that the Chinese "Communist" central government and Chinese economic, social, political, and legal institutions are quite weak.

Patricia Berlyn, an author of studies on Israel, primarily its ancient history and culture, refutes 12 arguments supporting the creation of an independent state of Palestine, maintaining that such a state would not be wise, just, or desirable. Rosemary E. Shinko, who teaches in the department of political science at the University of Connecticut, contends that a lasting peace between Israelis and Palestinians must be founded on a secure and sovereign homeland for both nations.

Christopher Hemmer, an associate professor in the Department of International Security Studies at the Air War College, Maxwell Air Force Base, Montgomery, Alabama, writes that while a nuclear-armed Iran will pose challenges for the United States, they can be met through an active policy of deterrence, containment, engagement, and the reassurance of America's allies in the region. Norman Podhoretz, editor-at-large of the opinion journal *Commentary,* argues that the consequences of Iran acquiring nuclear weapons will be disastrous and that there is far less risk using whatever measures are necessary, including military force, to prevent that than there is in dealing with a nuclear-armed Iran.

Arturo A. Valenzuela, the U.S. assistant secretary of state for Western Hemisphere affairs, describes the views and policies of the Obama administration regarding the Western Hemisphere, as focused on three priorities critical to everyone in the region: promoting social and economic opportunity, ensuring safety, and strengthening effective institutions of democratic governance. Otto J. Reich, the U.S. assistant secretary of state for Western Hemisphere affairs during the administration of President George H. W. Bush, tells Congress that he believes the U.S. government today is underestimating the security threats in the Western Hemisphere.

UNIT 3 ECONOMIC ISSUES 161

C. Fred Bergsten, the director of the Peterson Institute for International Economics and former (1977–1981) assistant secretary of the treasury for international affairs, argues that China is manipulating the value of its currency in a way that is harming the U.S. international economic position and that it is time to use international and, if necessary, national pressure to remedy the situation. Pieter Bottelier, the senior adjunct professor of China studies at the School of Advanced International Studies at Johns Hopkins University and the former chief of the World Bank's resident mission in Beijing, and Uri Dadush, the director of the International Economics Program at the Carnegie Endowment for International Peace and former (2002–2008) World Bank's director of international trade, contend that dangerous myths about China's currency may unwisely touch off a strong U.S. reaction while more effective solutions will be overlooked.

Dan Siciliano, executive director, Program in Law, Business, and Economics, and research fellow with the Immigration Policy Center at the American Immigration Law Foundation, Stanford Law School,

Barack Obama, the 44th president of the United States, tells the cadets at West Point and, beyond them, the American people that the United States did not ask for a war in Afghanistan but must successfully wage it. Dennis Kucinich, a member of the U.S. House of Representatives from Ohio's 10th Congressional District, explains to members of the House why he sponsored a resolution demanding the president to withdraw U.S. military forces from Afghanistan by December 31, 2010, and urges the members to pass the legislation.

Mary Ellen O'Connell, a research professor at the Kroc Institute, University of Notre Dame, and the Robert and Marion Short Professor of Law at the School of Law, University of Notre Dame, tells a congressional committee that the United States is failing more often than not to follow the most important single rule governing drones: restricting their use to the battlefield. Michael W. Lewis, a professor of law at Ohio Northern University's Pettit College of Law, disagrees, contending that there is nothing inherently illegal about using drones to target specific terrorists or groups of terrorists on or away from the battlefield.

foreign policy interests, including the security and advancement of women around the globe.

UNIT 6   THE ENVIRONMENT   333

James Inhofe, a Republican member of the U.S. Senate from Oklahoma, tells the Senate that objective, evidence-based science is beginning to show that the predictions of catastrophic humanmade global warming are overwought. Barbara Boxer, a Democratic member of the U.S. Senate from California, responds that Senator Inhofe's is one of the very few isolated and lonely voices that keeps on saying we do not have to worry about global warming, while, in reality, it is a major problem that demands a prompt response.

Correlation Guide

The *Taking Sides* series presents current issues in a debate-style format designed to stimulate student interest and develop critical thinking skills. Each issue is thoughtfully framed with an issue summary, an issue introduction, and a postscript. The pro and con essays—selected for their liveliness and substance—represent the arguments of leading scholars and commentators in their fields.

Taking Sides: Clashing Views in World Politics, 15/e is an easy-to-use reader that presents issues on important topics such as *globalization, economics, armaments and violence, the environment,* and *international law.* For more information on *Taking Sides* and other *McGraw-Hill Contemporary Learning Series* titles, visit www.mhhe.com/cls.

This convenient guide matches the issues in **Taking Sides: World Politics, 15/e** with the corresponding chapters in two of our best-selling McGraw-Hill Political Science textbooks by Rourke and Boyer.

Taking Sides: World Politics, 15/e	International Politics on the World Stage, 12/e by Rourke	International Politics on the World Stage, Brief, 8/e by Rourke/Boyer
Issue 1: Is Economic Globalization Good for Both Rich and Poor?	**Chapter 5:** Globalism: The Alternative Orientation **Chapter 12:** National Economic Competition: The Traditional Road **Chapter 13:** International Economic Cooperation: The Alternative Road	**Chapter 5:** Globalization and Transnationalism: The Alternative Orientation **Chapter 10:** Globalization in the World Economy
Issue 3: Does Globalization Threaten Cultural Diversity? **Issue 4:** Is the United States a Declining Power?	**Chapter 5:** Globalism: The Alternative Orientation **Chapter 8:** National Power and Statecraft: The Traditional Approach	**Chapter 5:** Globalization and Transnationalism: The Alternative Orientation **Chapter 6:** Power and the National tates: The Traditional Structure
Issue 5: Should the Jackson–Vanik Amendment Targeting Russia Be Repealed?	**Chapter 4:** Nationalism: The Traditional Orientation **Chapter 14:** Prospective Human Rights	**Chapter 8:** International Law and Human Rights: An Alternative **Chapter 12:** Preserving and Enhancing the Global Commons
Issue 6: Will China Soon Become a Threatening Superpower?	**Chapter 8:** National Power and Statecraft: The Traditional Approach	**Chapter 6:** Power and the National States: The Traditional Structure
Issue 7: Would It Be an Error to Establish a Palestinian State?	**Chapter 4:** Nationalism: The Traditional Orientation **Chapter 6:** National States: The Traditional Structure	**Chapter 7:** International Organization: An Alternative Structure
Issue 10: Does China's Currency Manipulation Warrant International and National Action?	**Chapter 9:** International Law and Justice: An Alternative Approach **Chapter 11:** International Security: The Alternative Road **Chapter 13:** International Economic Cooperation: The Alternative Road	**Chapter 8:** International Law and Human Rights: An Alternative Approach **Chapter 11:** Global Economic Competition and Cooperation

(Continued)

Taking Sides: World Politics, 15/e	International Politics on the World Stage, 12/e by Rourke	International Politics on the World Stage, Brief, 8/e by Rourke/Boyer
Issue 11: Is Immigration an Economic Benefit to the Host Country? **Issue 12:** Should Export Controls on High Technology Be Eased Substantially?	**Chapter 4:** Nationalism: The Traditional Orientation **Chapter 5:** Globalism: The Alternative Orientation **Chapter 12:** National Economic Competition: The Traditional Road **Chapter 13:** International Economic Cooperation: The Alternative Road	**Chapter 5:** Globalization and Transnationalism: The Alternative Orientation **Chapter 10:** Globalization in the World Economy **Chapter 11:** Global Economic Competition and Cooperation
Issue 8: Is Patient Diplomacy the Best Approach to Iran's Nuclear Program? **Chapter 13:** Is U.S. Strategic Nuclear Weapons Policy Ill-Conceived?	**Chapter 3:** Levels of Analysis and Foreign Policy **Chapter 10:** National Security: The Traditional Road **Chapter 11:** International Security: The Alternative Road **Chapter 12:** National Economic Competition: The Traditional Road	**Chapter 9:** Pursuing Security
Issue 14: Should U.S. Forces Continue to Fight in Afghanistan? **Issue 15:** Does Using Drones to Attack Terrorists Globally Violate International Law?	**Chapter 10:** National Security: The Traditional Road **Chapter 11:** International Security: The Alternative Road	**Chapter 9:** Pursuing Security **Chapter 8:** International Law and Human Rights: An Alternative Approach
Issue 16: Is UN Peacekeeping Seriously Flawed?	**Chapter 11:** International Security: The Alternative Road	**Chapter 9:** Pursuing Security
Issue 17: Is U.S. Refusal to Join the International Criminal Court Wise?	**Chapter 9:** International Law and Justice: An Alternative Approach	**Chapter 8:** International Law and Human Rights: An Alternative Approach
Issue 18: Should the United States Ratify the Convention to Eliminate All Forms of Discrimination Against Women?	**Chapter 14:** Prospective Human Rights	**Chapter 8:** International Law and Human Rights
Issue 19: Are Warnings About Global Warming Unduly Alarmist?	**Chapter 15:** Preserving and Enhancing the Biosphere	**Chapter 12:** Preserving and Enhancing the Global Commons

Topic Guide

This topic guide suggests how the selections in this book relate to the subjects covered in your course. You may want to use the topics listed on these pages to search the Web more easily. On the following pages, a number of Web sites have been gathered specifically for this book. They are arranged to reflect the units of this *Taking Sides* reader. You can link to these sites by going to http://www.mhhe.com/cls. **All issues and their articles that relate to each topic are listed below in the bold-faced term.**

Introduction

World Politics and the Voice of Justice

John T. Rourke

Some years ago, the Rolling Stones recorded "Sympathy with the Devil." If you have never heard it, go find a copy. It is worth listening to. The theme of the song is echoed in a wonderful essay by Marshall Berman, "Have Sympathy for the Devil" (*New American Review,* 1973). The common theme of the Stones' and Berman's works is based on Johann Goethe's *Faust.* In that classic drama, the protagonist, Dr. Faust, trades his soul to gain great power. He attempts to do good, but in the end he commits evil by, in contemporary paraphrase, "doing the wrong things for the right reasons." Does that make Faust evil, the personification of the devil Mephistopheles among us? Or is the good doctor merely misguided in his effort to make the world better as he saw it and imagined it might be? The point that the Stones and Berman make is that it is important to avoid falling prey to the trap of many zealots who are so convinced of the truth of their own views that they feel righteously at liberty to condemn those who disagree with them as stupid or even diabolical.

It is to the principle of rational discourse, of tolerant debate, that this reader is dedicated. There are many issues in this volume that appropriately excite passion—for example, Issue 7 on whether or not Israel should agree to an independent Palestinian state.

As you will see, each of the authors in all the debates strongly believes in his or her position. If you read these debates objectively, you will find that each side makes cogent points. They may or may not be right, but they should not be dismissed out of hand. It is important to repeat that the debate format does not imply that you should remain forever neutral. In fact, once you are informed, you *ought* to form convictions, and you should try to act on those convictions and try to influence international policy to conform better with your beliefs. Ponder the similarities in the views of two very different leaders, a very young president in a relatively young democracy and a very old emperor in a very old country: In 1963 President John F. Kennedy, in recalling the words of the author of the epic poem *The Divine Comedy* (1321), told a West German audience, "Dante once said that the hottest places in hell are reserved for those who in a period of moral crisis maintain their neutrality." That very same year, while speaking to the United Nations, Ethiopia's emperor Haile Selassie (1892–1975) said, "Throughout history it has been the inaction of those who could have acted, the indifference of those who should have known better, the silence of the voice of justice when it mattered most that made it possible for evil to triumph."

The point is: Become Informed. Then *do* something! Write letters to policymakers, donate money to causes you support, work for candidates with whom you agree, join an activist organization, or any of the many other things that you can do to make a difference. What you do is less important than that you do it.

Approaches to Studying International Politics

As will become evident as you read this volume, there are many approaches to the study of international politics. Some political scientists and most practitioners specialize in *substantive topics,* and this reader is organized along topical lines. Unit 1 (Issues 1 through 3) features debates on the evolution of the international system in the direction of greater globalization. In Issue 1, members of the staff of the International Monetary Fund and Ravinder Rena, an associate professor of economics at the Eritrea Institute of Technology, debate the general topic of economic globalization. The IMF staff members argue that economic globalization has generally brought prosperity. Rena counters that globalization is not benefiting all and that the process needs to be regulated in order to alleviate persistent and unjust inequality. Issue 2 explores capitalism's interface with economic globalization. Dani Rodrik, a professor of political economy at Harvard University, concedes that various aspects of capitalism caused the crisis, but contends that capitalism can be reformed and remain as the prevailing economic model across the globe. Walden Bello of the Philippines argues that capitalism is failing as a national and global model. Issue 3 addresses the accompanying phenomenon of cultural globalization. Ugandan journalist Allan Brian Ssenyonga fears that American culture is wiping away cultural diversity in the world, while British analyst Philippe Legrain rejects these charges and points to the positive aspects of cultural diversity.

Unit 2 (Issues 4 through 9) focuses on regional and country-specific issues, including the U.S. positions in the world trends in Russian domestic and foreign policy, whether China should be considered a growing threat, the possibility of a Palestinian state, if patient dilplomacy is the best way to address Iran's alleged nuclear weapons program, and the pros and cons of U.S. policy toward Latin America.

Unit 3 (Issues 10 through 12) deals with economic issues. Issue 10 debates the question of whether China's currency manipulation warrants international and national action. C. Fred Bergsten, who heads the Peterson Institute for International Economics, argues that China is manipulating the value of its currency in a way that is harming the U.S. international economic position and it is time to use international and, if necessary, national pressure to remedy the situation. Pieter Bottelier, former chief of the World Bank's resident mission in Beijing, and Uri Dadush, former director of international trade at the World Bank, contend that dangerous myths about China's currency may unwisely touch off an strong U.S. reaction while more effective solutions will be overlooked. In Issue 11, the debate turns to the impact of immigration on host countries. The flow of both legal and illegal immigration is a contentious topic in many countries, and here the debate focuses on the United States as an example of the controversy. Issue 12 takes up how far national security considerations should go in the restriction of free trade.

Unit 4 (Issues 13 through 15) examines violence and the attempts to limit it in the international system. Issue 13 finds scholar Ariel Cohen and Robert Farley disagreeing over the wisdom of President Barack Obama's approach to nuclear weapons policy. Issue 14 focuses toward the other end of the arms spectrum by asking whether U.S. troops should soon exit Afghanistan. On a related topic, Issue 15 explores whether the use of drones to attack terrorists outside Afghanistan in Pakistan and elsewhere around the world violates international law.

Unit 5 (Issues 16 through 18) addresses controversies related to international law and organizations. The ability of the United Nations to deploy effective peacekeeping forces is severely constrained by a number of factors, and in Issue 16, Brett D. Schaefer and William J. Durch, analysts from two private research and advocacy organizations (think tanks), debate whether UN peacekeeping is fundamentally flawed or is on the way to overcoming its internal problems and deserved renewed and increased global support. Issue 17 evaluates the wisdom of establishing a permanent international criminal court to punish those who violate the law of war. It is easy to advocate such a court as long as it is trying and sometimes punishing alleged war criminals from other countries. But one has to understand that one day a citizen of one's own country could be put on trial. The third debate in Unit 5 takes up the convention to eliminate all forms of discrimination against Women. The United States is nearly the only country that has not ratified the treaty and this issue inquires whether that is a laudable U.S. stand.

Unit 6, which consists of Issue 19, addresses the environment. Over the past few decades there has been a growing concern about global warming. Many people believe that it is mostly being caused by human activities, especially the burning of petroleum and other fossil fuels that discharges carbon dioxide into the atmosphere. There is also widespread belief that global warming will bring increasingly catastrophic results and that strong measures should be quickly taken to greatly reduce the emission of carbon dioxide and similar gases. U.S. Senator James Inhofe rejects this view in the first reading, and his view is directly contested in the second reading by U.S. Senator Barbara Boxer.

Political scientists also approach their subject from differing *methodological perspectives*. You will see, for example, that world politics can be studied from different *levels of analysis*. The question is, What is the basic source of the forces that shape the conduct of politics? Possible answers are world forces, the individual political processes of the specific countries, or the personal attributes of a country's leaders and decision makers. Various readings will illustrate all three levels.

Another way for students and practitioners of world politics to approach their subject is to focus on what is called the realist versus the idealist (or liberal) debate. Realists tend to assume that the world is permanently flawed and therefore advocate following policies in their country's narrow self-interests. Idealists take the approach that the world condition can be improved substantially by following policies that, at least in the short term, call for some risk or self-sacrifice. This divergence is an element of many of the debates in this book. Issue 17 is one example. In the first reading, Brett Schaefer and

Steven Groves from the Heritage Foundation, a conservative think tank, write that there are a number of reasons to be wary about how ratification of the Rome Statute would affect U.S. sovereignty and how ICC action could affect politically precarious situations around the world. Jonathan F. Fanton, head of one of the world's largest foundations promoting world peace, disagrees, arguing that the ICC is a major step toward a more just world and does not pose any threat to the United States.

Dynamics of World Politics

The action on the global stage today is vastly different from what it was a few decades ago, or even a few years ago. *Technology* is one of the causes of this change. Technology has changed communications, manufacturing, health care, and many other aspects of the human condition. Technology has given humans the ability to create biological, chemical, and nuclear compounds and other material that in relatively small amounts have the ability to kill and injure huge numbers of people. Another negative by-product of technology may be the vastly increased consumption of petroleum and other natural resources and the global environmental degradation that has been caused by discharges of waste products, deforestation, and a host of other technology-enhanced human activities. Technology has also changed warfare in many ways. Some of these, like the use of drones to attack enemies away from the immediate battlefield covered in Issue 15, raise new matters of law and morality that need to be addressed.

Another dynamic aspect of world politics involves the *changing axes* of the world system. For about 40 years after World War II ended in 1945, a bipolar system existed, the primary axis of which was the *East-West* conflict, which pitted the United States and its allies against the Soviet Union and its allies. Now that the Cold War is over, one broad debate is over what role the United States should play. In Issue 4 national security scholar Christopher Layne argues that the United States is declining in its power and increasingly unable to play a dominant role on the world stage. Alan W. Dowd, a scholar at the Sagamore Institute for Policy Research, contends that there have been previous pronouncements of the end of U.S. dominance on the world stage that have proved to be incorrect and the current ones may well be wrong also. Then Issue 6 deals with Russia by taking up whether in any case, and particularly given Russia's growing autocratic tendency, the United States should finally repeal a trade restraint, the Jackson–Vanik Amendment, which dates back to the cold war era.

Technological changes and the shifting axes of international politics also highlight the *increased role of economics* in world politics. Economics has always played a role, but traditionally the main focus has been on strategic-political questions—especially military power. This concern still strongly exists, but now it shares the international spotlight with economic issues. One important change in recent decades has been the rapid growth of regional and global markets and the promotion of free trade and other forms of international economic interchange. As Issue 1 on economic interdependence indicates, many people support these efforts and see them as the wave of the future. But there are others who believe that free economic globalization and interdependence undermine sovereignty and the ability of governments to control their destinies. In part because of the dominance of the United States, capitalism is the prevailing economic globalization model for domestic economic systems, and Issue 3 debates whether that will and should continue.

Another change in the world system has to do with the main *international* actors. At one time states (countries) were practically the only international actors on the world stage. Now, and increasingly so, there are other actors. Some actors are regional. Others, such as the United Nations, are global actors. Turning to the most notable international organization, Issue 16 examines the UN peacekeeping and, by extension, the role of that world organization and the proper approach of member countries to it and to global cooperation. Issue 17 focuses on whether or not a supranational criminal court should be established to take over the prosecution and punishment of war criminals from the domestic courts and ad hoc tribunals that have sometimes dealt with such cases in the past.

Perceptions Versus Reality

In addition to addressing the general changes in the world system outlined above, the debates in this reader explore the controversies that exist over many of the fundamental issues that face the world.

One key to these debates is the differing *perceptions* that protagonists bring to them. There may be a reality in world politics, but very often that reality is obscured. Many observers, for example, are alarmed by the seeming rise in radical actions by Islamic fundamentalists. However, the image of Islamic radicalism is not a fact but a perception; perhaps correct, perhaps not. In cases such as this, though, it is often the perception, not the reality, that is more important because policy is formulated on what decision makers *think*, not necessarily on what *is*. Thus, perception becomes the operating guide, or *operational reality,* whether it is true or not. Perceptions result from many actors. One factor is the information that decision makers receive. For a variety of reasons, the facts and analyses that are given to leaders are often inaccurate or represent only part of the picture. The conflicting perceptions of Israelis and Palestinians, for example, make the achievement of peace in Israel very difficult. Many Israelis and Palestinians fervently believe that the conflict that has occurred in the region over the past 50 years is the responsibility of the other. Both sides also believe in the righteousness of their own policies. Even if both sides are well-meaning, the perceptions of hostility that each holds means that the operational reality often has to be violence. These differing perceptions are a key element in the debate in Issue 7.

A related aspect of perception is the tendency to see oneself differently than some others do. Specifically, the tendency is to see oneself as benevolent and to perceive rivals as sinister. This reverse image is part of Issue 8, the debate over Iran's nuclear program. Many Americans and others see Iran as a rogue nation intent on developing nuclear weapons to use to threaten or attack other countries. But Iran claims that its intentions are only to develop nuclear energy plants, as many other countries have, and that even if it does choose to develop nuclear weapons, they would only for defense against such hostile nuclear powers as the United States and Israel. Which view is the reality and which is the perception? Perceptions, then, are crucial to understanding international politics. It is important to understand objective reality, but it is also necessary to comprehend subjective reality in order to be able to predict and analyze another country's actions.

Levels of Analysis

Political scientists approach the study of international politics from different levels of analysis. The most macroscopic view is *system-level analysis*. This is a top-down approach that maintains that world factors virtually compel countries to follow certain foreign policies. Governing factors include the number of powerful actors, geographic relationships, economic needs, and technology. System analysts hold that a country's internal political system and its leaders do not have a major impact on policy. As such, political scientists who work from this perspective are interested in exploring the governing factors, how they cause policy, and how and why systems change.

After the end of World War II, the world was structured as a *bipolar* system, dominated by the United States and the Soviet Union. Furthermore, each superpower was supported by a tightly organized and dependent group of allies. For a variety of reasons, including changing economics and the nuclear standoff, the bipolar system has faded. Some political scientists argue that the bipolar system is being replaced by a *multipolar* system. In such a configuration, those who favor *balance-of-power* politics maintain that it is unwise to ignore power considerations. Or it may be that something like at least a limited one-power (unipolar) system exists, with the United States as that power. Whatever exists, its future will depend in part on the willingness of the United States to take an actively global role, a topic taken up in Issue 4.

State-level analysis is the middle and most common level of analysis. Social scientists who study world politics from this perspective focus on how countries, singly or comparatively, make foreign policy. In other words, this perspective is concerned with internal political dynamics, such as the roles of and interactions between the executive and legislative branches of government, the impact of bureaucracy, the role of interest groups, and the effect of public opinion. This level of analysis is very much in evidence in Issue 11 and the debate over immigration to the United States, a topic that has cultural, as well as economic, ramifications. Whatever the international ramifications, whether U.S. troops in Afghanistan should or should not be soon withdrawn, as Issue 14 debates, the decision will be heavily rooted in public opinion and other domestic political factors in the United States. The dangers to the global environment, which are debated in Issue 19, extend beyond rarified scientific controversy to important issues of public policy. For example, should the United States and other industrialized countries adopt policies that are costly in terms of economics and lifestyle to significantly reduce the emission of carbon dioxide and other harmful gases? This debate pits interest groups against one another as they try to get the governments of their respective countries to support or reject the steps necessary to reduce the consumption of resources and the emission of waste products.

A third level of analysis, which is the most microscopic, is *human-level analysis*. This approach focuses, in part, on the role of individual decision makers. This technique is applied under the assumption that individuals make decisions and that the nature of those decisions is determined by the decision makers' perceptions, predilections, and strengths and weaknesses. A great deal of Issue 9 on U.S. Latin America policy is based on the question of who had wiser foreign policy views: President Geroge W. Bush or Barack Obama.

The Political and Ecological Future

Future *world alternatives* are discussed in many of the issues in this volume. Abraham Lincoln once said, "A house divided against itself cannot stand." One suspects that the sixteenth president might say something similar about the world today if he were with us. Issue 1, for example, debates whether growing globalization is a positive or negative trend. The world has responded to globalization by creating and strengthening the UN, the IMF, the World Bank, the World Trade Organization, and many other international organizations to try to regulate the increasing number of international interactions. There can be little doubt that the role of global governance is growing, and this reality is the spark behind specific debates about the future that are taken up in many of the selections. Far-reaching alternatives to a state-centric system based on sovereign countries include international organizations' (Issue 16) taking over some (or all) of the sovereign responsibilities of national governments, such as the prosecution of international war criminals (Issue 17). The global future also involves the ability of the world to prosper economically while not denuding itself of its natural resources or destroying the environment. This is the focus of Issue 19 on the environment.

Increased Role of Economics

Economics has always played a part in international relations, but the traditional focus has been on strategic political affairs, especially questions of military power. Now, however, political scientists are increasingly focusing on the international political economy, or the economic dimensions of world politics. International trade, for instance, has increased dramatically, expanding from an annual world export total of $20 billion in 1933 to $13 trillion in 2009. The impact has been profound. The domestic economic health of most countries is heavily affected by trade and other aspects of international economics. Since World War II there has been an emphasis on expanding free trade by decreasing tariffs and other barriers to international commerce. In recent years, however, a downturn in the economies of many of the industrialized countries has increased calls for more protectionism. Yet restrictions on trade and other economic activity can also be used as diplomatic weapons. The intertwining of economies and the creation of organizations to regulate them, such as the World Trade

Organization, is raising issues of sovereignty and other concerns. This is a central matter in the debate in Issue 1 over whether or not the trend toward global economic integration is desirable, in Issue 2 on the role of capitalism as the prevailing economic model on democracy, in Issue 11 on the benefits of free trade, and in Issue 12 on export controls.

Conclusion

Having discussed many of the various dimensions and approaches to the study of world politics, it is incumbent on this editor to advise against your becoming too structured by them. Issues of focus and methodology are important both to studying international relations and to understanding how others are analyzing global conduct. However, they are also partially pedagogical. In the final analysis, world politics is a highly interrelated, perhaps seamless, subject. No one level of analysis, for instance, can fully explain the events on the world stage. Instead, using each of the levels to analyze events and trends will bring the greatest understanding.

Similarly, the realist-idealist division is less precise in practice than it may appear. As some of the debates indicate, each side often stresses its own standards of morality. Which is more moral: defeating a dictatorship or sparing the sword and saving lives that would almost inevitably be lost in the dictator's overthrow? Furthermore, realists usually do not reject moral considerations. Rather, they contend that morality is but one of the factors that a country's decision makers must consider. Realists are also apt to argue that standards of morality differ when dealing with a country as opposed to an individual. By the same token, most idealists do not completely ignore the often dangerous nature of the world. Nor do they argue that a country must totally sacrifice its short-term interests to promote the betterment of the current and future world. Thus, realism and idealism can be seen most accurately as the ends of a continuum—with most political scientists and practitioners falling somewhere between, rather than at, the extremes. The best advice, then, is this: think broadly about international politics. The subject is very complex, and the more creative and expansive you are in selecting your foci and methodologies, the more insight you will gain. To end where we began, with Dr. Faust, I offer his last words in Goethe's drama, *"Mehr licht,"* . . . More light! That is the goal of this book.

Internet References . . .

The Ultimate Political Science Links Page

Under the editorship of Professor P. S. Ruckman, Jr., at Rock Valley College in Rockford, Illinois, this site provides a gateway to the academic study of not just world politics but all of political science. It includes links to journals, news, publishers, and other relevant resources.

http://upslinks.net/

Poly-Cy: Internet Resources for Political Science

This is a worthwhile gateway to a broad range of political science resources, including some on international relations. It is maintained by Robert D. Duval, director of graduate studies at West Virginia University.

http://www.polsci.wvu.edu/polycy/

The WWW Virtual Library: International Affairs Resources

Maintained by Wayne A. Selcher, professor of international studies at Elizabethtown College in Elizabethtown, Pennsylvania, this site contains approximately 2,000 annotated links relating to a broad spectrum of international affairs. The sites listed are those that the Webmaster believes have long-term value and that are cost-free, and many have further links to help in extended research.

http://www.etown.edu/vl/

The Globalization Web Site

The goals of this site are to shed light on the process of globalization and contribute to discussions of its consequences, to clarify the meaning of globalization and the debates that surround it, and to serve as a guide to available sources on globalization.

http://www.sociology.emory.EDU/globalization/

Globalization Issues

*T*he most significant change that the international system is experiencing is the trend toward globalization. Countries are becoming interdependent, the number of international organizations and their power are increasing, and global communications have become widespread and almost instantaneous. As reflected in the issues that make up this unit, these changes and others have led to considerable debate about the value of globalization and what it will mean with regard to human governance.

- Is Economic Globalization Good for Both Rich and Poor?
- Is Capitalism a Failed Model for a Globalized Economy?
- Does Globalization Threaten Cultural Diversity?

ISSUE 1

Is Economic Globalization Good for Both Rich and Poor?

YES: International Monetary Fund Staff, from "Globalization: A Brief Overview," *Issues Brief* (May 2008)

NO: Ravinder Rena, from "Globalization Still Hurting Poor Nations," *Africa Economic Analysis* (January 2008)

ISSUE SUMMARY

YES: Staff members of the International Monetary Fund conclude on the basis of experiences across the world that unhindered international economic interchange, the core principle of globalization, seems to underpin greater prosperity.

NO: Ravinder Rena, an associate professor of economics at the Eritrea Institute of Technology, contends that globalization creates losers as well as winners and the losers are disproportionately found among the world's poorer countries.

Globalization is a process that is diminishing many of the factors that divide the world. Advances in travel and communication have made geographical distances less important; people around the world increasingly resemble one another culturally; and the United Nations and other international organizations have increased the level of global governance. Another aspect, economic integration, is the most advanced of any of the strands of globalization. Tariffs and other barriers to trade have decreased significantly since the end of World War II. As a result, all aspects of international economic exchange have grown rapidly. For example, global trade, measured in the value of exported goods and services, has grown about 2000 percent since the mid-twentieth century and now comes to over $15 trillion annually. International investment in real estate and stocks and bonds in other countries, and in total, now exceeds $25 trillion. The flow of currencies is so massive that there is no accurate measure, but it certainly is more than $1.5 trillion a day.

In this liberalized atmosphere, huge multinational corporations (MNCs) have come to dominate global commerce. Just the top 500 MNCs have combined annual sales of over $15 trillion. The impact of all these changes is that the economic prosperity of almost all countries and the individuals within them is heavily dependent on what they import and export, the flow of investment in and out of each country, and the exchange rates of the currency of each country against the currencies of other countries.

The issue here is whether this economic globalization and integration is a positive or negative trend. For more than 60 years, the United States has been at the center of the drive to open international commerce. The push to reduce trade barriers that occurred during and after World War II was designed to prevent a recurrence of the global economic collapse of the 1930s and the war of the 1940s. Policymakers believed that protectionism caused the Great Depression, that the ensuing human desperation provided fertile ground for the rise of dictators who blamed scapegoats for what had occurred and who promised national salvation, and that these fascist dictators had set off World War II. In sum, policymakers thought that protectionism caused economic depression, which caused dictators, which caused war. They believed that free trade, by contrast, would promote prosperity, democracy, and peace.

Based on these political and economic theories, American policymakers took the lead in establishing a new international economic system, including helping to found such leading global economic organizations as the International Monetary Fund (IMF), the World Bank, and the World Trade Organization (WTO). During the entire latter half of the twentieth century, the movement toward economic globalization was strong, and there were few influential voices opposing it.

In the following selection, members of the IMF staff contend that there is substantial evidence, from countries of different sizes and with different regions, that suggests that as nations globalize, their citizens benefit because they gain "access to a wider variety of goods and services, lower prices, more and more better-paying jobs, improved health, and higher overall living standards." Not everyone agrees, though, and in recent years the idea that globalization is necessarily beneficial has come under increasing scrutiny and has met with increasing resistance. Within countries, globalization has benefited some, whereas others have lost jobs to imports and suffered other negative consequences. Similarly, some countries, notably those in sub-Saharan Africa, have not prospered. Reflecting this uneven impact, one line of criticism of globalization comes from those who believe that the way global politics work is a function of how the world is organized economically. These critics contend that people within countries are divided into "haves" and "have-nots" and that the world is similarly divided into have and have-not countries. Moreover, these critics believe that, both domestically and internationally, the wealthy haves are using globalization to keep the have-nots weak and poor in order to exploit them. Representing this view, Ravinder Rena argues in the second selection that globalization is not a panacea for world economic development because it broadens the gap between rich and poor and creates other distortions in the global economy.

Globalization: A Brief Overview

A perennial challenge facing all of the world's countries, regardless of their level of economic development, is achieving financial stability, economic growth, and higher living standards. There are many different paths that can be taken to achieve these objectives, and every country's path will be different given the distinctive nature of national economies and political systems. The ingredients contributing to China's high growth rate over the past two decades have, for example, been very different from those that have contributed to high growth in countries as varied as Malaysia and Malta.

Yet, based on experiences throughout the world, several basic principles seem to underpin greater prosperity. These include investment (particularly foreign direct investment) [owning foreign companies or real estate], the spread of technology, strong institutions, sound macroeconomic policies, an educated workforce, and the existence of a market economy. Furthermore, a common denominator which appears to link nearly all high-growth countries together is their participation in, and integration with, the global economy.

There is substantial evidence, from countries of different sizes and different regions, that as countries "globalize" their citizens benefit, in the form of access to a wider variety of goods and services, lower prices, more and better-paying jobs, improved health, and higher overall living standards. It is probably no mere coincidence that over the past 20 years, as a number of countries have become more open to global economic forces, the percentage of the developing world living in extreme poverty—defined as living on less than $1 per day—has been cut in half.

As much as has been achieved in connection with globalization, there is much more to be done. Regional disparities persist: while poverty fell in East and South Asia, it actually rose in sub-Saharan Africa. The UN's Human Development Report notes there are still around 1 billion people surviving on less than $1 per day—with 2.6 billion living on less than $2 per day. Proponents of globalization argue that this is not because of too much globalization, but rather too little. And the biggest threat to continuing to raise living standards throughout the world is not that globalization will succeed but that it will fail. It is the people of developing economies who have the greatest need for globalization, as it provides them with the opportunities that come with being part of the world economy.

These opportunities are not without risks—such as those arising from volatile capital movements. The International Monetary Fund works to help economies manage or reduce these risks, through economic analysis and policy advice and through technical assistance in areas such as macroeconomic policy, financial sector sustainability, and the exchange-rate system.

The risks are not a reason to reverse direction, but for all concerned—in developing and advanced countries, among both investors and recipients—to embrace policy changes to build strong economies and a stronger world financial system that will produce more rapid growth and ensure that poverty is reduced.

The following is a brief overview to help guide anyone interested in gaining a better understanding of the many issues associated with globalization.

What Is Globalization?

Economic "globalization" is a historical process, the result of human innovation and technological progress. It refers to the increasing integration of economies around the world, particularly through the movement of goods, services, and capital across borders. The term sometimes also refers to the movement of people (labor) and knowledge (technology) across international borders. There are also broader cultural, political, and environmental dimensions of globalization.

The term "globalization" began to be used more commonly in the 1980s, reflecting technological advances that made it easier and quicker to complete international transactions—both trade and financial flows. It refers to an extension beyond national borders of the same market forces that have operated for centuries at all levels of human economic activity—village markets, urban industries, or financial centers.

There are countless indicators that illustrate how goods, capital, and people have become more globalized.

- The value of trade (goods and services) as a percentage of world GDP [gross domestic product: the value of all goods and services produced within an economic unit] increased from 42.1 percent in 1980 to 62.1 percent in 2007.
- Foreign direct investment increased from 6.5 percent of world GDP in 1980 to 31.8 percent in 2006.
- The stock of international claims (primarily bank loans), as a percentage of world GDP, increased from roughly 10 percent in 1980 to 48 percent in 2006.
- The number of minutes spent on cross-border telephone calls, on a per-capita basis, increased from 7.3 in 1991 to 28.8 in 2006.
- The number of foreign workers has increased from 78 million people (2.4 percent of the world population) in 1965 to 191 million people (3.0 percent of the world population) in 2005.

The growth in global markets has helped to promote efficiency through competition and the division of labor—the specialization that allows people and economies to focus on what they do best. Global markets also offer greater opportunity for people to tap into more diversified and larger markets around the world. It means that they can have access to more capital, technology, cheaper imports, and larger export markets. But markets do not necessarily ensure that the benefits of increased efficiency are shared by all. Countries must be prepared to embrace the policies needed, and, in the case of the poorest countries, may need the support of the international community as they do so. The broad reach of globalization easily extends to daily choices of personal, economic, and political life. For example, greater access to modern technologies, in the world of health care, could make the difference between life and death. In the world of communications, it would facilitate commerce and education, and allow access to independent media. Globalization can also create a framework for cooperation among nations on a range of non-economic issues that have cross-border implications, such as immigration, the environment, and legal issues. At the same time, the influx of foreign goods, services, and capital into a country can create incentives and demands for strengthening the education system, as a country's citizens recognize the competitive challenge before them.

Perhaps more importantly, globalization implies that information and knowledge get dispersed and shared.

Innovators—be they in business or government—can draw on ideas that have been successfully implemented in one jurisdiction and tailor them to suit their own jurisdiction. Just as important, they can avoid the ideas that have a clear track record of failure. Joseph Stiglitz, a Nobel laureate and frequent critic of globalization, has nonetheless observed that globalization "has reduced the sense of isolation felt in much of the developing world and has given many people in the developing world access to knowledge well beyond the reach of even the wealthiest in any country a century ago."

International Trade

A core element of globalization is the expansion of world trade through the elimination or reduction of trade barriers, such as import tariffs. Greater imports offer consumers a wider variety of goods at lower prices, while providing strong incentives for domestic industries to remain competitive. Exports, often a source of economic growth for developing nations, stimulate job creation as industries sell beyond their borders. More generally, trade enhances national competitiveness by driving workers to focus on those vocations where they, and their country, have a competitive advantage. Trade promotes economic resilience and flexibility, as higher imports help to offset adverse domestic supply shocks. Greater openness can also stimulate foreign investment, which would be a source of employment for the local workforce and could bring along new technologies—thus promoting higher productivity.

Restricting international trade—that is, engaging in protectionism—generates adverse consequences for a country that undertakes such a policy. For example, tariffs raise the prices of imported goods, harming consumers, many of which may be poor. Protectionism also tends to reward concentrated, well-organized and politically-connected groups, at the expense of those whose interests may be more diffuse (such as consumers). It also reduces the variety of goods available and generates inefficiency by reducing competition and encouraging resources to flow into protected sectors.

Developing countries can benefit from an expansion in international trade. Ernesto Zedillo, the former president of Mexico, has observed that, "In every case where a poor nation has significantly overcome its poverty, this has been achieved while engaging in production for export markets and opening itself to the influx of foreign goods, investment, and technology."

And the trend is clear. In the late 1980s, many developing countries began to dismantle their barriers to international trade, as a result of poor economic performance under protectionist polices and various economic crises. In the 1990s, many former Eastern bloc countries integrated into the global trading system and developing Asia—one of the most closed regions to trade in 1980—progressively dismantled barriers to trade. Overall, while the average tariff rate applied by developing countries is higher than that applied by advanced countries, it has declined significantly over the last several decades.

The Implications of Globalized Financial Markets

The world's financial markets have experienced a dramatic increase in globalization in recent years. Global capital flows fluctuated between 2 and 6 percent of world GDP during the period 1980–95, but since then they have risen to 14.8 percent of GDP, and in 2006 they totaled $7.2 trillion, more than tripling since 1995. The most rapid increase has been experienced by advanced economies, but emerging markets and developing countries have also become more financially integrated. As countries have strengthened their capital markets they have attracted more investment capital, which can enable a broader entrepreneurial class to develop, facilitate a more efficient allocation of capital, encourage international risk sharing, and foster economic growth. Yet there is an energetic debate underway, among leading academics and policy experts, on the precise impact of financial globalization. Some see it as a catalyst for economic growth and stability. Others see it as injecting dangerous—and often costly—volatility into the economies of growing middle-income countries.

A recent paper by the IMF's Research Department takes stock of what is known about the effects of financial globalization. The analysis of the past 30 years of data reveals two main lessons for countries to consider.

First, the findings support the view that countries must carefully weigh the risks and benefits of unfettered capital flows. The evidence points to largely unambiguous gains from financial integration for advanced economies. In emerging and developing countries, certain factors are likely to influence the effect of financial globalization on economic volatility and growth: countries with well-developed financial sectors, strong institutions, sound macroeconomic policies, and substantial trade openness are more likely to gain from financial liberalization and less likely to risk increased macroeconomic volatility and to experience financial crises. For example, well-developed financial markets help moderate boom-bust cycles that can be triggered by surges and sudden stops in international capital flows, while strong domestic institutions and sound macroeconomic policies help attract "good" capital, such as portfolio equity flows and FDI.

The second lesson to be drawn from the study is that there are also costs associated with being overly cautious about opening to capital flows. These costs include lower international trade, higher investment costs for firms, poorer economic incentives, and additional administrative/monitoring costs. Opening up to foreign investment may encourage changes in the domestic economy that eliminate these distortions and help foster growth.

Looking forward, the main policy lesson that can be drawn from these results is that capital account liberalization should be pursued as part of a broader reform package encompassing a country's macroeconomic policy framework, domestic financial system, and prudential regulation. Moreover, long-term, non-debt-creating flows, such as FDI, should be liberalized before short-term, debt-creating inflows. Countries should still weigh the possible risks involved in opening up to capital flows against the efficiency costs associated with controls, but under certain conditions (such as good institutions, sound domestic and foreign policies, and developed financial markets) the benefits from financial globalization are likely to outweigh the risks.

Globalization, Income Inequality, and Poverty

As some countries have embraced globalization, and experienced significant income increases, other countries that have rejected globalization, or embraced it only tepidly, have fallen behind. A similar phenomenon is at work within countries—some people have, inevitably, been bigger beneficiaries of globalization than others.

Over the past two decades, income inequality has risen in most regions and countries. At the same time, per capita incomes have risen across virtually all regions for even the poorest segments of populations, indicating that the poor are better off in an absolute sense during this phase of globalization, although incomes for the relatively well off have increased at a faster pace. Consumption data from groups of developing countries reveal the striking inequality that exists between the richest and the poorest in populations across different regions.

As discussed in the October 2007 issue of the *World Economic Outlook*, one must keep in mind that there are many sources of inequality. Contrary to popular belief, increased trade globalization is associated with a decline in inequality. The spread of technological advances and increased financial globalization—and foreign direct investment in particular—have instead contributed more to the recent rise in inequality by raising the demand for skilled labor and increasing the returns to skills in both developed and developing countries. Hence, while everyone benefits, those with skills benefit more.

It is important to ensure that the gains from globalization are more broadly shared across the population. To this effect, reforms to strengthen education and training would help ensure that workers have the appropriate skills for the evolving global economy. Policies that broaden the access of finance to the poor would also help, as would further trade liberalization that boosts agricultural exports from developing countries. Additional programs may include providing adequate income support to cushion, but not obstruct, the process of change, and also making health care less dependent on continued employment and increasing the portability of pension benefits in some countries.

Equally important, globalization should not be rejected because its impact has left some people unemployed. The dislocation may be a function of forces that have little to do with globalization and more to do with inevitable technological progress. And, the number of people who "lose" under globalization is likely to be outweighed by the number of people who "win."

Martin Wolf, the *Financial Times* columnist, highlights one of the fundamental contradictions inherent in those who bemoan inequality, pointing out that this charge amounts to arguing "that it would be better for everybody to be equally poor than for some to become significantly better off, even if, in the long run, this will almost certainly lead to advances for everybody."

Indeed, globalization has helped to deliver extraordinary progress for people living in developing nations. One of the most authoritative studies of the subject has been carried out by World Bank economists David Dollar and Aart Kraay. They concluded that since 1980, globalization has contributed to a reduction in poverty as well as a reduction in global income inequality. They found that in "globalizing" countries in the developing world, income per person grew three-and-a-half times faster than in "non-globalizing" countries, during the 1990s. In general, they noted, "higher growth rates in globalizing developing countries have translated into higher incomes for the poor." Dollar and Kraay also found that in virtually all events in which a country experienced growth at a rate of two percent or more, the income of the poor rose.

Critics point to those parts of the world that have achieved few gains during this period and highlight it as a failure of globalization. But that is to misdiagnose the problem. While serving as Secretary-General of the United Nations, Kofi Annan pointed out that "the main losers in today's very unequal world are not those who are too much exposed to globalization. They are those who have been left out."

A recent BBC World Service poll found that on average 64 percent of those polled—in 27 out of 34 countries—held the view that the benefits and burdens of "the economic developments of the last few years" have not been shared fairly. In developed countries, those who have this view of unfairness are more likely to say that globalization is growing too quickly. In contrast, in some developing countries, those who perceive such unfairness are more likely to say globalization is proceeding too slowly. As individuals and institutions work to raise living standards throughout the world, it will be critically important to create a climate that enables these countries to realize maximum benefits from globalization. That means focusing on macroeconomic stability, transparency in government, a sound legal system, modern infrastructure, quality education, and a deregulated economy.

Myths about Globalization

No discussion of globalization would be complete without dispelling some of the myths that have been built up around it.

Downward pressure on wages: Globalization is rarely the primary factor that fosters wage moderation in low-skilled work conducted in developed countries. As discussed in a recent issue of the *World Economic Outlook,* a more significant factor is technology. As more work can be mechanized, and as fewer people are needed to do a given job than in the past, the demand for that labor will fall, and as a result the prevailing wages for that labor will be affected as well.

The "race to the bottom": Globalization has not caused the world's multinational corporations to simply scour the globe in search of the lowest-paid laborers. There are numerous factors that enter into corporate decisions on where to source products, including the supply of skilled labor, economic and political stability, the local infrastructure, the quality of institutions, and the overall business climate. In an open global market, while jurisdictions do compete with each other to attract investment, this competition incorporates factors well beyond just the hourly wage rate.

According to the UN Information Service, the developed world hosts two-thirds of the world's inward foreign direct investment. The 49 least developed countries—the poorest of the developing countries—account for around 2 percent of the total inward FDI stock of developing countries. Nor is it true that multinational corporations make a consistent practice of operating sweatshops in low-wage countries, with poor working conditions and substandard wages. While isolated examples of this can surely be uncovered, it is well established that multinationals, on average, pay higher wages than what is standard in developing nations, and offer higher labor standards.

Globalization is irreversible: In the long run, globalization is likely to be an unrelenting phenomenon. But for significant periods of time, its momentum can be hindered by a variety of factors, ranging from political will to availability of infrastructure. Indeed, the world was thought to be on an irreversible path toward peace and prosperity in the early 20th century, until the outbreak of Word War I. That war, coupled with the Great Depression, and then World War II, dramatically set back global economic integration. And in many ways, we are still trying to recover the momentum we lost over the past 90 years or so.

That fragility of nearly a century ago still exists today—as we saw in the aftermath of September 11th, when U.S. air travel came to a halt, financial markets shut down, and the economy weakened. The current turmoil in financial markets also poses great difficulty for the stability and reliability of those markets, as well as for the global economy. Credit market strains have intensified and spread across asset classes and banks, precipitating a financial shock that many have characterized as the most serious since the 1930s.

These episodes are reminders that a breakdown in globalization—meaning a slowdown in the global flows of goods, services, capital, and people—can have extremely adverse consequences.

Openness to globalization will, on its own, deliver economic growth: Integrating with the global economy is, as economists like to say, a necessary, but not sufficient, condition for economic growth. For globalization to be able to work, a country cannot be saddled with problems endemic to many developing countries, from a corrupt political class, to poor infrastructure, and macroeconomic instability.

The shrinking state: Technologies that facilitate communication and commerce have curbed the power of some despots throughout the world, but in a globalized world governments take on new importance in one critical respect, namely, setting, and enforcing, rules with respect to contracts and property rights. The potential of globalization can never be realized unless there are rules and regulations in place, and individuals to enforce them. This gives economic actors confidence to engage in business transactions. Further undermining the idea of globalization shrinking states is that states are not, in fact, shrinking. Public expenditures are, on average, as high or higher today as they have been at any point in recent memory. And among OECD [Organization of Economic Cooperation and Development is composed of 30 mostly high-income countries] countries, government tax revenue as a percentage of GDP increased from 25.5 percent in 1965 to 36.6 percent in 2006.

The Future of Globalization

Like a snowball rolling down a steep mountain, globalization seems to be gathering more and more momentum. And the question frequently asked about globalization is not whether it will continue, but at what pace.

A disparate set of factors will dictate the future direction of globalization, but one important entity—sovereign governments—should not be overlooked. They still have the power to erect significant obstacles to globalization, ranging from tariffs to immigration restrictions to military hostilities.

Nearly a century ago, the global economy operated in a very open environment, with goods, services, and people able to move across borders with little if any difficulty. That openness began to wither away with the onset of World War I in 1914, and recovering what was lost is a process that is still underway. Along the process, governments recognized the importance of international cooperation and coordination, which led to the emergence of numerous international organizations and financial institutions (among which the IMF and the World Bank, in 1944).

Indeed, the lessons included avoiding fragmentation and the breakdown of cooperation among nations. The world is still made up of nation states and a global marketplace. We need to get the right rules in place so the global system is more resilient, more beneficial, and more legitimate. International institutions have a difficult but indispensable role in helping to bring more of globalization's benefits to more people throughout the world. By helping to break down barriers—ranging from the regulatory to the cultural—more countries can be integrated into the global economy, and more people can seize more of the benefits of globalization.

Ravinder Rena  **NO**

Globalization Still Hurting
Poor Nations

Globalization is a buzzword gaining increasing importance all over the world. Today, the world appears radically altered. A very significant feature of the global economy is the integration of the emerging economies in world markets and the expansion of economic activities across state borders. Other dimensions include the international movement of ideas, information, legal systems, organizations, people, popular globetrotting cuisine, cultural exchanges, and so forth.

However, the movement of people, even in this post-1970s era of globalization, is restricted and strictly regulated in the aftermath of the 9/11 attacks. More countries are now integrated into a global economic system in which trade and capital flow across borders with unprecedented energy. Nonetheless, globalization has become painful, rather than controversial, to the developing world. It has produced increasing global economic interdependence through the growing volume and variety of cross-border flows of finance, investment, goods, and services, and the rapid and widespread diffusion of technology.

A World Bank study, "Global Economic Prospects: Managing the Next Wave of Globalization," succinctly discusses the advantages of globalization. Driven by 1974-onward globalization, exports have doubled, as a proportion of world economic output, to over 25 percent, and, based on existing trends, will rise to 34 percent by 2030.

World income has doubled since 1980, and almost half-a-billion people have climbed out of poverty since 1990. According to current trends, the number of people living on less than 1-purchasing power-dollar-a-day will halve from today's 1 billion by 2030. This will take place as a result of growth in Southeast Asia, whose share of the poor will halve from 60 percent, while Africa's will rise from 30 percent to 55 percent.

The scale, benefits, and criticism of globalization are often exaggerated. On the contrary, compared to the immediate post-war period, the average rate of growth has steadily slowed during the age of globalization, from 3.5 percent per annum in the 1960s to 2.1 percent, 1.3 percent, and 1.0 percent in the 1970s, 1980s, and 1990s, respectively.

The growing economic interdependence is highly asymmetrical. The benefits of linking and the costs of de-linking are not equally distributed.

Industrialized countries—the European Union, Japan, and the United States—are genuinely and highly interdependent in their relations with one another. The developing countries, on the other hand, are largely independent from one another in terms of economic relations, while being highly dependent on industrialized countries. Indeed, globalization creates losers as well as winners, and entails risks as well as opportunities. An International Labor Organization blue-ribbon panel noted in 2005 that the problems lie not in globalization per se but in the deficiencies in its governance.

Some globalization nay-sayers have vouched that there has been a growing divergence, not convergence, in income levels, both between countries and peoples. Inequality among, and within, nations has widened. Assets and incomes are more concentrated. Wage shares have fallen while profit shares have risen. Capital mobility alongside labor immobility has reduced the bargaining power of organized labor. The rise in unemployment and the accompanying "casualization" of the workforce, with more and more people working in the informal sector, have generated an excess supply of labor and depressed real wages.

Globalization has spurred inequality—both in the wealthiest countries as well as the developing world. China and India compete globally, yet only a fraction of their citizens prosper. Increasing inequality between rural and urban populations, and between coastal and inland areas in China, could have disastrous consequences in the event of political transition. Forty of the poorest nations, many in Africa, have had zero growth during the past 20 years. Their governments followed advice from wealthy nations and World Bank consultants on issues ranging from privatization to development, but millions of people suffer from poverty. Ironically, the wealthiest people benefit from the source of cheap labor. Western policies reinforce the growing divide between rich and poor.

Nearly three-quarters of Africa's population live in rural areas in contrast with less-than-10-percent in the developed world. Globalization has driven a wedge between social classes in the rich countries, while among the world's poor, the main divide is between countries—those that adapted well to globalization and, in many areas, prospered, and those that maladjusted and, in many cases, collapsed.

As the Second World [the Soviet Union and the communist countries of Eastern Europe] collapsed and globalization took off, the latter rationale evaporated and a few countries, notably India and China, accelerated their growth rates significantly, enjoying the fruits of freer trade and larger capital flows. Although the two countries adapted well to globalization, there is little doubt that their newfound relative prosperity opened many new fissure lines. Inequality between coastal and inland provinces, as well as between urban and rural areas, skyrocketed in China.

Another large group of Third World countries in Latin America, Africa, and former Communist countries experienced a quarter-century of decline, or stagnation, punctuated by civil wars, international conflicts, and the onslaught of AIDS. While rich countries grew on average by almost 2 percent per capita annually from 1980 to 2002, the world's poorest 40 countries had a combined growth rate of zero. For large swaths of Africa, the income level today is less than 1-dollar-per-day.

For these latter countries, the promised benefits of globalization never arrived. Social services were often taken over by foreigners. Western experts and technocrats arrived on their jets, stayed in luxury hotels, and hailed the obvious worsening of economic and social conditions as a step toward better lives and international integration.

Indeed, for many people in Latin America and Africa, globalization was merely a new, more attractive label, for the old imperialism, or worse—for a form of re-colonization. The left-wing reaction sweeping Latin America, from Mexico to Argentina, is a direct consequence of the fault lines opened by policies designed to benefit Wall Street, not the people in the streets of Asmara [capital of Eritrea] or Kampala [capital of Uganda].

The rapid growth of global markets has not seen the parallel development of social and economic institutions to ensure their smooth and efficient functioning; labor rights have been less diligently protected than capital and property rights; and the global rules on trade and finance are unfair to the extent that they produce asymmetric effects on rich and poor countries.

The deepening of poverty and inequality has implications for the social and political stability among, and within, nations. It is in this context that the plight and hopes of developing countries have to be understood in the Doha Round of trade talks. Having commenced in 2001, the Doha Round was supposed to be about the trade-led and trade-facilitated development of the world's poor countries. After five years of negotiations, the talks collapsed because of unbridgeable differences among the EU [European Union], the US, and developing countries led by India, Brazil, and China. [The Doha Round is the latest and continuing series of negotiations under the aegis of the World Trade Organization to reduce restrictions on trade and other forms of international economic interchange. The Doha Round began in 2001 and is at a virtual standstill because of, among other things, disagreements between the wealthier and poorer countries.]

From the developing world's perspective, the problem is that the rich countries want access to poor countries' resources, markets, and labor forces at the lowest possible price. Some rich countries were open to implementing deep cuts in agricultural subsidies, but resisted opening their markets, others wanted the reverse. Developing countries like India, China, and Eritrea, among other[s], are determined to protect the livelihood of their farmers. In countries like India, farmer suicide has been a terrible human cost and a political problem for India's state and central governments for some time, as well as a threat to rural development. Protecting farmers' needs, therefore, is essential for social stability as well as the political survival of governments in the developing world.

The rich countries' pledges of flexibility failed to translate into concrete proposals during the Doha negotiations. Instead, they effectively protected the interests of tiny agricultural minorities. By contrast, in developing countries, farming accounts for 30 to 60 percent of the Gross Domestic Product [GDP] and up to 70 percent of the labor force. This is why labor rights protection is at least as critical for developing countries as intellectual property rights protection is for the rich.

Developing countries were promised a new regime that would allow them to sell their goods and trade their way out of poverty through undistorted market openness. This required generous market access by the rich for the products of the poor, and also reduction-cum-elimination of market-distorting producer and export subsidies, with the resulting dumping of the rich world's produce on world markets.

Thus, Europe launched its "Everything but Arms" initiative whereby it would open its markets to the world's poorest countries. The initiative foundered on too many non-tariff barriers, for example in the technical rules of origin. The US seemed to offer so-called EBP—Everything But what they Produce. Under its proposals, developing countries would have been free to export jet engines and supercomputers to the US, but not textiles, agricultural products, or processed foods.

Elimination of rich country production and export subsidies, and the opening of markets, while necessary, would not be sufficient for developing countries to trade their way out of underdevelopment. They also have a desperate need to institute market-friendly incentives and regulatory regimes and increase their farmers' productivity, and may require technical assistance from international donors to achieve this through investment in training, infrastructure, and research.

The failure of the Doha Round is also, finally, symptomatic of a much bigger malaise, namely the crisis of multilateral governance in security and environmental matters, as well as in trade. In agriculture, as in other sectors, problems-without-passports require solutions-without-borders.

To convince Africans about the benefits of globalization, we must take a more enlightened view of liberalizing trade, services, and labor-intensive manufacturing in which African countries are competitive. Trade is not only a means to prosperity, but also a means of peace-building. We need to devise an enlightened approach in negotiations over the reduction of harmful gas emissions, intellectual property rights, lifesaving drugs, and the transfer of technologies toward combating poverty. Ultimately, globalization broadens the gap between rich and poor. It also creates distortions in the global economy. Therefore, it is not a panacea for world economic development.

POSTSCRIPT

Is Economic Globalization Good for Both Rich and Poor?

Globalization is both old and new. It is old in that the efforts of humans to overcome distance and other barriers to increased interchange have long existed. The first canoes and signal fires are part of the history of globalization. The first event in true globalization occurred between 1519 and 1522, when Ferdinand Magellan circumnavigated the globe. MNCs have existed at least since 1600 when a group of British merchants formed the East India Company. In the main, though, globalization is mostly a modern phenomenon. The progress of globalization until the latter half of the 1800s might be termed "creeping globalization." There were changes, but they occurred very slowly. Since then, the pace of globalization has increased exponentially. A brief introduction to globalization is available in Jürgen Osterhammel, Niels P. Petersson, and Dona Geyer, *Globalization: A Short History* (Princeton University Press, 2005). A contemporary look at globalization is Thomas L. Friedman's updated and expanded *The World Is Flat: A Brief History of the Twenty-First Century* (Picador, 2007).

The recent rapid pace of globalization has sparked an increasing chorus of criticism against many of its aspects including economic interdependence.

Now it is not uncommon for massive protests to occur when the leaders of the world countries meet to discuss global or regional economics or when the WTO, IMF, or World Bank holds important conferences.

One of the oddities about globalization, economic or otherwise, is that it often creates a common cause between those of marked conservative and marked liberal views. More than anything, conservatives worry that their respective countries are losing control of their economies and, thus, a degree of their independence. Echoing this view, archconservative political commentator Patrick J. Buchanan has warned that unchecked globalization threatens to turn the United States into a "North American province of what some call The New World Order."

Some liberals share the conservatives' negative views of globalization but for different reasons. This perspective is less concerned with sovereignty and security; it is more concerned with workers and countries being exploited and the environment being damaged by MNCs that shift their operations to other countries to find cheap labor and to escape environmental regulations. During the 2008 campaign for the Democratic presidential nomination, both Barack Obama and Hillary Clinton expressed concern about the impact that U.S. free trade agreements were having both on American and foreign workers and on their environments. One widely read critique of economic globalization is Joseph E. Stiglitz, *Making Globalization Work* (W. W. Norton, 2006). Taking the opposite view is Jagdish N. Bhagwati, *In Defense of Globalization* (Oxford University Press, 2007).

Questions for Critical Thinking and Reflection

1. Are the poor being harmed by globalization or modernization—with robotics, the high value of technology, the importance of education, and related factors?
2. Would it be better to reform or reduce globalization?
3. Is it possible to significantly reform and regulate globalization without creating binding international law and authoritative international enforcement agencies that will diminish national sovereignty?

ISSUE 2

Is Capitalism a Failed Model for a Globalized Economy?

YES: Walden Bello, from "Capitalism in an Apocalyptic Mood" *Foreign Policy In Focus* (February 20, 2008)

NO: Dani Rodrik, from "Coming Soon: Capitalism 3.0," *The Taipei Times* (February 11, 2009)

ISSUE SUMMARY

YES: Walden Bello, the president of the Freedom from Debt Coalition, examines on the part played by events in the United States in creating the global financial crisis beginning in 2008 and argues that capitalism is failing as a national and global model.

NO: Dani Rodrik, a professor of political economy at Harvard University's John F. Kennedy School of Government, concedes that various aspects of capitalism caused the crisis, but contends that capitalism can be reformed and remain as the prevailing economic model across the globe.

The intersection of politics and economics is called the study of *political economy* or, at the global level, *international political economy* (IPE). How to structure either a national economy or the global economy can be divided into three main categories. The first is capitalism, which is the focus of this debate. Capitalism is referred to as economic liberalism, free enterprise, or laissez-faire economics.

Each of the other two economic approaches features considerable political control of the economy. One favors manipulating the economy to improve a country's power and to promote its political goals. This idea is variously called economic nationalism, mercantilism, and economic statecraft. The other theory of political intervention in the economy favors manipulating in such way as having a minimum wage to achieve social ends. One name for this approach is economic structuralism, because its adherents believe that the very economic structure must be dramatically changed to improve the system. Socialism and Marxism and, at the IPE level, dependency/neoimperialism theory all also represent variations of this third approach. These closely related views hold that within countries, richer classes dominate and exploit the poor and that globally richer countries dominate and exploit poor ones.

In the "bible" of capitalist theory, Adam Smith argued in *The Wealth of Nations* (1776) that people are inspired to work hard and to innovate by striving to improve their own fortunes, not those of their country or their society. Smith theorized that this self-interest, some would call it "greed," of individuals collectively constitutes an "invisible hand" of competition that creates the most efficient economies and that political interference lessens economic efficiency and therefore prosperity. On the international level, for instance, Smith would oppose having tariffs to protect jobs from international competition. He believed it was better to benefit from the low-cost imports and to train workers for industries that produce items that other countries need to import from you.

It is important to note that at the national or international level, none of these approaches is utilized in a pure sense. For example, the United States is basically a capitalist country, but it still has many policies, such as a minimum wage, that manipulate the economy to improve equity. Other U.S. policies are mercantilist, such as not selling some high-tech products with a potential military application to potentially hostile countries (see Issue 12).

The current international system has aspects of all three economic approaches, but capitalism is the most prominent. At the center of the capitalist approach to IPE is free economic interchange, the notion that trade, investment, and currencies should flow across international borders with as few restrictions as possible. Whatever the relative advantages of the three approaches, an important reason that free economic interchange is such a prominent approach is because the United States has been the world's most powerful country for nearly three-quarters of a century. Based on their philosophical beliefs and U.S. interests, American diplomats were the driving force behind the current, mostly capitalistic, global economic model.

When Walden Bello and Dani Rodrik wrote the two issues in this debate, the global economy had gone into a decline that was the worst since the Great Depression of the 1930s and so severe that some have begun to call it the Great Recession. Global trade plunged 12.2% between 2008 and 2009, unemployment shot up in many countries (including the United States, where it grew from 4.6% in late 2007 to an average 9.3% in 2009), and many other economic woes surfaced. Many observers, including Bello, blame the capitalist system, especially its largely unregulated banking and investment system, for the Great Recession. Others, including Dani Rodrik, concede that there are problems in global capitalism, but are convinced that capitalism is the best economic model and its flaws can be fixed.

YES

Walden Bello

Capitalism in an Apocalyptic Mood

Skyrocketing oil prices, a falling dollar, and collapsing financial markets are the key ingredients in an economic brew that could end up in more than just an ordinary recession. The falling dollar and rising oil prices have been rattling the global economy for sometime. But it is the dramatic implosion of financial markets that is driving the financial elite to panic.

And panic there is. Even as it characterized [U.S.] Federal Reserve Board Chairman Ben Bernanke's deep cuts amounting to a 1.25 [percentage] points off the prime [lending] rate in late January [2008] as a sign of panic, the *Economist* admitted that "there is no doubt that this is a frightening moment." The losses stemming from bad securities tied up with defaulted mortgage loans by "sub-prime" [below the prime rate] borrowers are now estimated to be in the range of about $400 billion. But as the *Financial Times* warned, "the big question is what else is out there" at a time that the global financial system "is wide open to a catastrophic failure." . . . The globalization of finance was, from the beginning, the cutting edge of the globalization process, and it was always an illusion to think that the subprime crisis could be confined to U.S. financial institutions, as some analysts had thought.

Some key movers and shakers sounded less panicky than resigned to some sort of apocalypse. At the global elite's annual week-long party at Davos in late January [at the World Economic Forum], George Soros sounded positively necrological, declaring to one and all that the world was witnessing "the end of an era." World Economic Forum host Klaus Schwab spoke of capitalism getting its just desserts, saying, "We have to pay for the sins of the past." He told the press, "It's not that the pendulum is now swinging back to Marxist socialism, but people are asking themselves, 'What are the boundaries of the capitalist system?' They think the market may not always be the best mechanism for providing solutions."

Ruined Reputations and Policy Failures

While some appear to have lost their nerve, others have seen the financial collapse diminish their stature.

As chairman of President [George W.] Bush's Council of Economic Advisers in 2005, Ben Bernanke attributed the rise in U.S. housing prices to "strong

From *Foreign Policy In Focus,* February 20, 2008. Copyright © 2008 by The Institute for Policy Studies. Reprinted by permission. www.fpif.org.

economic fundamentals" instead of speculative activity. So is it any wonder why, as Federal Reserve chairman, he failed to anticipate the housing market's collapse stemming from the subprime mortgage crisis? His predecessor, Alan Greenspan, however, has suffered a bigger hit, moving from iconic status to villain in the eyes of some. They blame the bubble on his aggressively cutting the prime rate to get the United States out of recession in 2003 and restraining it at low levels for over a year. Others say he ignored warnings about aggressive and unscrupulous mortgage originators enticing "subprime" borrowers with mortgage deals they could never afford.

The scrutiny of Greenspan's record and the failure of Bernanke's rate cuts so far to reignite bank lending has raised serious doubts about the effectiveness of monetary policy in warding off a recession that is now seen as all but inevitable. Nor will fiscal policy or putting money into the hands of consumers do the trick, according to some weighty voices. The $156 billion stimulus package recently approved by the White House and Congress consists largely of tax rebates, and most of these, according to *New York Times* columnist Paul Krugman, will go to those who don't really need them. The tendency will thus be to save rather than spend the rebates in a period of uncertainty, defeating their purpose of stimulating the economy. The specter that now haunts the U.S. economy is Japan's experience of virtually zero annual growth and deflation despite a succession of stimulus packages after Tokyo's great housing bubble deflated in the late 1980s.

The Inevitable Bubble

Even with the finger-pointing in progress, many analysts remind us that if anything, the housing crisis should have been expected all along. The only question was when it would break. As progressive economist Dean Baker of the Center for Economic Policy Research noted in an analysis several years ago, "Like the stock bubble, the housing bubble will burst. Eventually, it must. When it does, the economy will be thrown into a severe recession, and tens of millions of homeowners, who never imagined that house prices could fall, likely will face serious hardship."

The subprime mortgage crisis was not a case of supply outrunning real demand. The "demand" was largely fabricated by speculative mania on the part of developers and financiers that wanted to make great profits from their access to foreign money that flooded the United States in the last decade. Big ticket mortgages were aggressively sold to millions who could not normally afford them by offering low "teaser" interest rates that would later be readjusted to jack up payments from the new homeowners. These assets were then "securitized" with other assets into complex derivative products called "collateralized debt obligations" (CDOs) by the mortgage originators working with different layers of middlemen who understated risk so as to offload them as quickly as possible to other banks and institutional investors. The shooting up of interest rates triggered a wave of defaults, and many of the big name banks and investors—including Merrill Lynch, Citigroup, and Wells Fargo—found themselves with billions of dollars worth of bad assets that had been given the green light by their risk assessment systems.

The Failure of Self-Regulation

The housing bubble is only the latest of some 100 financial crises [around the world] that have swiftly followed one another ever since the lifting of Depression-era capital controls at the onset of the neoliberal era in the early 1980s. The calls now coming from some quarters for curbs on speculative capital have an air of déjà vu. After the Asian Financial Crisis of 1997, in particular, there was a strong clamor for capital controls, for a "new global financial architecture." The more radical of these called for currency transactions taxes such as the famed Tobin Tax, which would have slowed down capital movements, or for the creation of some kind of global financial authority that would, among other things, regulate relations between northern creditors and indebted developing countries. [In 1972, James Tobin, a recipient of the Nobel Prize in economics, proposed levying a 0.5% tax on all exchanges of one currency for another as a way of curbing short-term currency speculation.]

Global finance capital, however, resisted any return to state regulation. Nothing came of the proposals for Tobin taxes. The banks killed even a relatively weak "sovereign debt restructuring mechanism" akin to the U.S. Chapter Eleven to provide some maneuvering room to developing countries undergoing debt repayment problems, even though the proposal came from Anne Krueger, the conservative American deputy managing director of the IMF [International Monetary Fund]. Instead, finance capital promoted what came to be known as the Basel II process, described by political economist Robert Wade as steps toward global economic standardization that "maximize [global financial firms'] freedom of geographical and sectoral maneuver while setting collective constraints on their competitive strategies." The emphasis was on private sector self-surveillance and self-policing aimed at greater transparency of financial operations and new standards for capital. Despite the fact that it was finance capital from the industrialized countries that triggered the Asian crisis, the Basel process focused on making developing country financial institutions and processes transparent and standardized along the lines of what Wade calls the "Anglo-American" financial model.

Calls to regulate the proliferation of these new, sophisticated financial instruments, such as derivatives placed on the market by developed country financial institutions, went nowhere. Assessment and regulation of derivatives were left to market players who had access to sophisticated quantitative "risk assessment" models.

Focused on disciplining developing countries, the Basel II process accomplished so little in the way of self-regulation of global financial from the North that even Wall Street banker Robert Rubin, former secretary of treasury under President [Bill] Clinton, warned in 2003 that "future financial crises are almost surely inevitable and could be even more severe."

As for risk assessment of derivatives such as the "collater[al]ized debt obligations" (CDOs) and "structured investment vehicles" (SIVs)—the cutting edge of what the *Financial Times* has described as "the vastly increased complexity of hyper-finance"—the process collapsed almost completely. The most sophisticated quantitative risk models were left in the dust. The sellers of securities priced risk by one rule only: underestimate the real risk and pass it on to the suckers down the line. In the end, it was difficult to distinguish what was fraudulent, what was poor judgment, what was plain foolish, and what was out of anybody's control. "The U.S. subprime mortgage market was marked by poor underwriting standards and 'some fraudulent practices,'" as one report on the conclusions of a recent meeting of the Group of Seven's Financial Stability Forum put it. "Investors didn't carry out sufficient due diligence when they bought mortgage-backed securities. Banks and other firms managed their financial risks poorly and failed to disclose to the public the dangers on and off their balance sheets. Credit-rating companies did an inadequate job of evaluating the risk of complex securities. And the financial institutions compensated their employees in ways that encouraged excessive risk-taking and insufficient regard to long-term risks."

The Specter of Overproduction

It is not surprising that the G-7 report sounded very much like the postmortems of the Asian financial crisis and the dot-com bubble. [The G-7 includes the leading developed countries: Canada, France, Germany, Italy, Japan, the United Kingdom, and the United States.] One financial corporation chief writing in the *Financial Times* captured the basic problem running through these speculative manias, perhaps unwittingly, when he claimed that "there has been an increasing disconnection between the real and financial economies in the past few years. The real economy has grown but nothing like that of the financial economy, which grew even more rapidly—until it imploded." What his statement does not tell us is that the disconnect between the real and the financial is not accidental, that the financial economy expanded precisely to make up for the stagnation of the real economy.

The stagnation of the real economy is related to the condition of overproduction or over-accumulation that has plagued the international economy since the mid-1970s. Stemming from global productive capacity outstripping global demand as a result of deep inequalities, this condition has eroded profitability in the industrial sector. One escape route from this crisis has been "financialization," or the channeling of investment toward financial speculation, where greater profits could be had. This was, however, illusory in the long run since, unlike industry, speculative finance boiled down to an effort to squeeze out more "value" from already created value instead of creating new value.

The disconnect between the real economy and the virtual economy of finance was evident in the dot-com bubble of the 1990s. With profits in the real economy stagnating, the smart money flocked to the financial sector. The workings of this virtual economy were exemplified by the rapid rise in the stock values of Internet firms that, like Amazon.com, had yet to turn a profit. The dot-com phenomenon probably extended the boom of the 1990s by about two years. "Never before in U.S. history," Robert Brenner wrote, "had the stock market played such a direct, and decisive, role in financing non-financial corporations, thereby powering the growth of capital expenditures and in this way the real economy. Never before had a U.S. economic expansion become so dependent upon the stock market's ascent." But the divergence between momentary financial indicators like stock prices and real values could only proceed to a point before reality bit back and enforced a "correction." And the correction came savagely in the dot-com collapse of 2002, which wiped out $7 trillion in investor wealth.

A long recession was avoided, but only because another bubble, the housing bubble, took the place of the dot-com bubble. Here, Greenspan played a key role by cutting the prime rate to a 45-year low of one percent in June 2003, holding it there for a year, then raising it only gradually, in quarter-percentage-increments. As Dean Baker put it, "an unprecedented run-up in the stock market propelled the U.S. economy in the late nineties and now an unprecedented run-up in house prices is propelling the current recovery."

The result was that real estate prices rose by 50% in real terms, with the run-ups, according to Baker, being close to 80% in the key bubble areas of the West Coast, the East Coast north of Washington, DC, and Florida. Baker estimates that the run-up in house prices "created more than $5 trillion in real estate wealth compared to a scenario where prices follow their normal trend growth path. The wealth effect from house prices is conventionally estimated at five cents to the dollar, which means that annual consumption is approximately $250 billion (2 per cent of gross domestic product [GDP]) higher than it would be in the absence of the housing bubble."

The China Factor

The housing bubble fueled U.S. growth, which was exceptional given the stagnation that has gripped most of the global economy in the last few years. During this period, the global economy has been marked by underinvestment and persistent tendencies toward stagnation in most key economic regions apart from the United States, China, India, and a few other places. Weak growth has marked most other regions, notably Japan, which was locked until very recently into a one percent GDP growth rate, and Europe, which grew annually by 1.45% in the last few years.

With stagnation in most other areas, the United States has pulled in some 70% of all global capital flows. A great deal of this has come from China. Indeed, what marks this current bubble period is the role of China as a source not only of goods for the U.S. market but also capital for speculation. The relationship between the United States and Chinese economies is what I have characterized elsewhere as chain-gang economics. On the one hand, China's economic growth has increasingly depended on the ability of American consumers to continue their debt-financed spending spree to absorb much of the output of China's production. On the other hand, this relationship depends on a massive financial reality: the dependence of U.S. consumption on China's lending the U.S. Treasury and private sector dollars from the reserves it accumulated from its yawning trade surplus with the United States, one trillion dollars so far, according to some estimates. Indeed, a great deal of the tremendous sums China—and other Asian countries—lent to American institutions went to finance middle-class spending on housing and other goods and services, prolonging the fragile U.S. economic growth but only by raising consumer indebtedness to dangerous, record heights.

The China–U.S. coupling has had major consequences for the global economy. The massive new productive capacity by American and other foreign investors moving to China has aggravated the persistent problem of overcapacity and overproduction. One indicator of persistent stagnation in the real economy is the aggregate annual global growth rate, which averaged 1.4% in the 1980s and 1.1% in the 1990s, compared to 3.5% in the 1960s and 2.4% in the 1970s. Moving to China to take advantage of low wages may shore up profit rates in the short term. But as it adds to overcapacity in a world where a rise in global purchasing power is constrained by growing inequalities, such capital flight erodes profits in the long term. And indeed, the profit rate of the largest 500 U.S. transnational corporations fell drastically from 4.9% from 1954–59, to 2.04% from 1960–69, to −5.30% from 1989–89, to −2.64% from 1990–92, and to −1.92% from 2000–2002. Behind these figures, notes Philip O'Hara, was the specter of overproduction: "Oversupply of commodities and inadequate demand are the principal corporate anomalies inhibiting performance in the global economy."

The succession of speculative manias in the United States has had the function of absorbing investment that did not find profitable returns in the real economy and thus not only artificially propping up the U.S. economy but also "holding up the world economy," as one IMF document put it. Thus, with the bursting of the housing bubble and the seizing up of credit in almost the whole financial sector, the threat of a global downturn is very real.

Decoupling Chain-Gang Economics?

In this regard, talk about a process of "decoupling" regional economies, especially the Asian economic region, from the United States has been without substance. True, most of the other economies in East and Southeast Asia have been pulled along by the Chinese locomotive. In the case of Japan, for instance, a decade-long stagnation was broken in 2003 by the country's first sustained recovery, fueled by exports to slake China's thirst for capital and technology-intensive goods. Exports shot up by a record 44%, or $60 billion. Indeed, China became the main destination for Asia's exports, accounting for 31% while Japan's share dropped from 20 to 10%. As one account in the *Strait Times* in 2004 pointed out, "In country-by-country profiles, China is now the overwhelming driver of export growth in Taiwan and the Philippines, and the majority buyer of products from Japan, South Korea, Malaysia, and Australia."

However, as research by C.P. Chandrasekhar and Jayati Ghosh has underlined, China is indeed importing intermediate goods and parts from these countries but only to put them together mainly for export as finished goods to the United States and Europe, not for its domestic market. Thus, "if demand for Chinese exports from the United States and the EU slow down, as will be likely with a U.S. recession, this will not only affect Chinese manufacturing production, but also Chinese demand for imports from these Asian developing countries." Perhaps the more accurate image is that of a chain-gang linking not only China and the United States but a host of other satellite economies whose fates are all tied up with the now-deflating balloon of debt-financed middle-class spending in the United States.

New Bubbles to the Rescue?

Do not overestimate the resiliency of capitalism. After the collapse of the dot-com boom and the housing boom, a third line of defense against stagnation owing to overcapacity may yet emerge. For instance, the U.S. government might pull the economy out of the jaws of recession through military spending. And, indeed, the military economy did play a role in bringing the United States out of the 2002 recession, with defense spending in 2003 accounting for 14% of GDP growth while representing only 4% of the overall U.S. GDP. According to estimates cited by Chalmers Johnson, defense-related expenditures will exceed $1 trillion for the first time in history in 2008.

Stimulus could also come from the related "disaster capitalism complex" so well studied by Naomi Klein: the "full fledged new economy in homeland security, privatized war and disaster reconstruction tasked with nothing less than building and running a privatized security state both at home and abroad." Klein says that, in fact, "the economic stimulus of this sweeping initiative proved enough to pick up the slack where globalization and the dot-com booms had left off. Just as the Internet had launched the dot-com bubble, 9/11 launched the disaster capitalism bubble." This subsidiary bubble to the real-estate bubble appears to have been relatively unharmed so far by the collapse of the latter.

It is not easy to track the sums circulating in the disaster capitalism complex. But one indication of the sums involved is that InVision, a General Electric affiliate producing high-tech bomb-detection devises used in airports and other public spaces, received an astounding $15 billion in Homeland Security contracts between 2001 and 2006.

Whether or not "military Keynesianism" and the disaster capitalism complex can in fact fill the role played by financial bubbles is open to question. To feed them, at least during the Republican administrations, has meant reducing social expenditures. A Dean Baker study cited by Johnson found that after an initial demand stimulus, by about the sixth year, the effect of increased military spending turns negative. After 10 years of increased defense spending, there would be 464,000 fewer jobs than in a scenario of lower defense spending.

A more important limit to military Keynesianism and disaster capitalism is that the military engagements to which they are bound to lead are likely to create quagmires such as Iraq and Afghanistan. And these disasters could trigger a backlash both abroad and at home. Such a backlash would eventually erode the legitimacy of these enterprises, reduce their access to tax dollars, and erode their viability as sources of economic expansion in a contracting economy. Yes, global capitalism may be resilient. But it looks like its options are increasingly limited. The forces making for the long-term stagnation of the global capitalist economy are now too heavy to be easily shaken off by the economic equivalent of mouth-to-mouth resuscitation.

Coming Soon: Capitalism 3.0

Capitalism is in the throes of its most severe crisis in many decades. A combination of deep recession, global economic dislocations and effective nationalisation of large swathes of the financial sector in the world's advanced economies has deeply unsettled the balance between markets and states. Where the new balance will be struck is anybody's guess.

Those who predict capitalism's demise have to contend with one important historical fact: capitalism has an almost unlimited capacity to reinvent itself. Indeed, its malleability is the reason it has overcome periodic crises over the centuries and outlived critics from Karl Marx on. The real question is not whether capitalism can survive—it can—but whether world leaders will demonstrate the leadership needed to take it to its next phase as we emerge from our current predicament.

Capitalism has no equal when it comes to unleashing the collective economic energies of human societies. That is why all prosperous societies are capitalistic in the broad sense of the term: they are organized around private property and allow markets to play a large role in allocating resources and determining economic rewards. The catch is that neither property rights nor markets can function on their own. They require other social institutions to support them.

So property rights rely on courts and legal enforcement, and markets depend on regulators to rein in abuse and fix market failures. At the political level, capitalism requires compensation and transfer mechanisms to render its outcomes acceptable. As the current crisis has demonstrated yet again, capitalism needs stabilising arrangements such as a lender of last resort and a counter-cyclical fiscal policy. In other words, capitalism is not self-creating, self-sustaining, self-regulating or self-stabilising.

The history of capitalism has been a process of learning and re-learning these lessons. Adam Smith's idealised market society required little more than a 'night-watchman state.' All that governments needed to do to ensure the division of labour was to enforce property rights, keep the peace and collect a few taxes to pay for a limited range of public goods.

Through the early part of the twentieth century, capitalism was governed by a narrow vision of the public institutions needed to uphold it. In practice, the state's reach often went beyond this conception (as, say, in the case of Bismarck's introduction of old-age pensions in Germany in 1889). But governments continued to see their economic roles in restricted terms.

This began to change as societies became more democratic and labour unions and other groups mobilised against capitalism's perceived abuses. Anti-trust policies were spearheaded in the Unites States. The usefulness of activist monetary and fiscal policies became widely accepted in the aftermath of the Great Depression.

The share of public spending in national income rose rapidly in today's industrialised countries, from below 10 per cent on average at the end of the nineteenth century to more than 20 per cent just before World War II. And, in the wake of WWII, most countries erected elaborate social-welfare states in which the public sector expanded to more than 40 per cent of national income on average.

This 'mixed-economy' model was the crowning achievement of the twentieth century. The new balance that it established between state and market set the stage for an unprecedented period of social cohesion, stability and prosperity in the advanced economies that lasted until the mid-1970s.

This model became frayed from the 1980s on, and now appears to have broken down. The reason can be expressed in one word: globalization.

The postwar mixed economy was built for and operated at the level of nation-states and required keeping the international economy at bay. The Bretton Woods-GATT regime entailed a 'shallow' form of international economic integration that implied controls on international capital flows, which Keynes and his contemporaries had viewed as crucial for domestic economic management. Countries were required to undertake only limited trade liberalisation, with plenty of exceptions for socially sensitive sectors (agriculture, textiles, services). This left them free to build their own versions of national capitalism, as long as they obeyed a few simple international rules.

The current crisis shows how far we have come from that model. Financial globalisation, in particular, played havoc with the old rules. When Chinese-style capitalism met American-style capitalism, with few safety valves in place, it gave rise to an explosive mix. There were no protective mechanisms to prevent a global liquidity glut from developing and then, in combination with US regulatory failings, from producing a spectacular housing boom and crash. Nor were there any international roadblocks to prevent the crisis from spreading from its epicentre.

The lesson is not that capitalism is dead. It is that we need to reinvent it for a new century in which the forces of economic globalisation are much more powerful than before. Just as Smith's minimal capitalism was transformed into Keynes' mixed economy, we need to contemplate a transition from the national version of the mixed economy to its global counterpart.

This means imagining a better balance between markets and their supporting institutions at the global level. Sometimes, this will require extending institutions outward from nation-states and strengthening global governance. At other times, it will mean preventing markets from expanding beyond the reach of institutions that must remain national. The right approach will differ across country groupings and among issue areas.

Designing the next capitalism will not be easy. But we do have history on our side: capitalism's saving grace is that it is almost infinitely malleable.

POSTSCRIPT

Is Capitalism a Failed Model for a Globalized Economy?

Between 2008 and mid-2010 when this issue was being written, world economic problems persisted. After a 12.2% decline in the world trade between 2008 and 2009, the WTO was projecting a 9.5% increase in 2010, but that would still leave trade below its 2008 record highs. The Great Recession hit the economically developed countries (EDCs) the hardest, with 2008–2009 export declines of 13.9% for the United States and 14.8% for the European Union (EU). The EDCs were also the slowest to recover. The IMF projected that in 2010, the export of less developed countries (LDCs) would grow by 11%, whereas those of more developed countries would grow only by 7.5%. Unemployment also persisted in the EDCs, with the June 2010 U.S. rate at 9.5% and the EU's rate at 10.0%. Massive budget deficits added to the EDCs' economic woes. Greece required an intervention by the EU to avoid bankruptcy, and several other EU members teetered on the edge of insolvency.

The United States took several measures including passing a massive financial regulation reform bill in 2010 to further restrict capitalism internally, but there was little consensus about what, if anything, should be done at a global level to regulate the largely unrestrained areas of currency trading, investments, and other financial flows. Even if there were a consensus, international regulatory reform would be quite difficult in a world where international governance institutions like the United Nations, IMF, World Bank, and WTO have relatively little ability to enforce global rules.

Although it is now about a decade old, Johan Norberg's *In Defense of Global Capitalism* (originally in Swedish by Timbro (2001), but now also available in English and a dozen other languages) is something of a classic. Information is also available at Norberg's Web page at http://www.johannorberg .net. For a good historical review of global capitalism and a critical view of it in today's globalizing world, read Jeffrey A. Freiden, *Global Capitalism: Its Fall and Rise in the Twentieth Century* (W. W. Norton, 2006). A reform-minded look at the future of the international economic system can be found in Leila Simona Talani (ed.), *The Global Crash: Towards a New Global Financial Regime?* (Palgrave Macmillan, 2010). For a specific look at international regulation, consult Eric Helleiner, Stefano Pagliari, and Hubert Zimmermann (eds.), *Global Finance in Crisis: The Politics of International Regulatory Change* (Routledge, 2010). The Web site of an organization, Third World Traveler, that is an unstinting critic of global capitalism is http://www.thirdworldtraveler .com/. Equally dedicated to capitalism is the Cato Institute at http://www .cato.org/.

Questions for Critical Thinking and Reflection

1. Opponents of capitalism argue that it is based on greed and the economic oppression of many in the interests of the few. Supporters of capitalism depict it as based in the liberty to profit from your work and talent and to succeed as far as your talents and efforts allow. Which is correct?

2. The only way to institute effective financial reform at the global level is to create international organizations of governance that have real authority to tell countries, not just corporations, what policies are acceptable and to impose penalties for noncompliance. Are you willing to have your country subject to such international control?

3. Bello writes, "The forces making for the long-term stagnation of the global capitalist economy are now too heavy to be easily shaken off." Why do you agree or disagree?

ISSUE 3

Does Globalization Threaten Cultural Diversity?

YES: Allan Brian Ssenyonga, from "Americanization or Globalization," *Global Envision* (October 2, 2006)

NO: Philippe Legrain, from "In Defense of Globalization," *The International Economy* (Summer 2003)

ISSUE SUMMARY

YES: Allan Brian Ssenyonga, a Ugandan freelance writer for *The New Times,* an English daily in Rwanda, claims that one of the negative effects of globalization is cultural assimilation via cultural imperialism.

NO: Philippe Legrain, the chief economist of Britain in Europe, an organization supporting the adoption by Great Britain of the euro as its currency, counters that it is a myth that globalization involves the imposition of Americanized uniformity, rather than an explosion of cultural exchange.

Globalization is often thought of in terms of economic integration, but it is a much broader phenomenon. Another important aspect of globalization is the spread of national cultures to other countries, regions, and, indeed, the world. One impetus for cultural globalization is economic globalization, as products spread around the world and as huge multinational corporations establish global operations. Additionally, cultural globalization is a product of advances in transportation that allow an increasing number of people to travel to other countries and of radio, television, the Internet, and other advances in communications that permit people to interact passively or actively with others around the world.

To a degree, the culture of many nations is spreading, with Japanese sushi bars now a common site in the United States, Europe, and elsewhere. Cultural globalization also involves a certain amount of cultural amalgamation, with influences merging to create new cultural realities. A third possibility, and the one that is at the heart of this debate, is when the spread of one culture is far greater than the spread of others. Arguably, that is what is currently occurring, with American "cultural exports" much greater than those of any other country.

There is significant evidence of the spread of Western, particularly American, culture. Casual dress around the world is more apt to include jeans, T-shirts, and sneakers than traditional dress. Young people everywhere listen to music by artists ranging from Lady Gaga to Susan Boyle, and fast-food hamburgers, fries, and milk shakes are consumed around the world. Adding to the spread of American culture, U.S. movies are everywhere, earning the majority of all film revenues in Japan, Europe, and Latin America, and U.S. television programming is increasingly omnipresent, with, for instance, about two-thirds of the market in Latin America.

Another indication of the spread of American culture is that English is increasingly the common language of business, diplomacy, communications, and even culture. Among Europeans, for instance, nearly all schoolchildren receive English instruction, and two-thirds of younger Europeans speak at least some English compared to less than 20 percent of retirement-age Europeans.

It is important to not trivialize cultural globalization even though it involves, in part, fast food, sneakers, rock music, and other elements of pop culture. Some scholars argue the elimination of culture differences will help reduce conflicts as people become more familiar with one another and, indeed, more similar to each other.

Others, however, believe the cultural globalization has negative aspects. One argument is that it is causing a backlash as people face the loss of their own cultures. Some analysts contend that the growth of religious fundamentalism and even terrorism is a reaction to cultural threats. Other analysts believe that defense of cultural traditionalism could even lead to culture wars in the future, with the world dividing itself into antagonist cultural groups. A third worry is represented by Allan Brian Ssenyonga in the first reading, who worries that "the rest of the world seems to be following Uncle Sam . . . and leaving behind its authentic ways of life." He suggests that the spread of American culture is a product of American economic and other forms of power, rather than the result of the superiority of American culture. Philippe Legrain is much more at ease with cultural globalization. He contends that it reflects new realities and is making many contributions, such as giving people the freedom to adopt whatever language, style of dress, or other cultural aspect that they find most compatible with their tastes and needs.

YES

Allan Brian Ssenyonga

Americanization or Globalization?

Global socio-political issues never cease to fascinate any interested soul. From the times of civilization came the era of colonialism then independence. This was followed by the cold war era where the Soviets were slowly but surely out-smarted by the more versatile capitalists of the day.

The post cold war era led to the increasing influence of what some people these days call quasi-governments (such as the International Monetary Fund and the World Bank).

The IMF and World Bank consequently took on the role of the world's economic 'police,' telling particularly poorer nations how to spend their money. In order to receive more aid, these Bretton Woods institutions demanded that countries open up their economies to liberalization under Structural Adjustment Programmes that encouraged governments to fund privatization programmes, ahead of welfare and public services. Concurrently we had the influence of multinational organisations like the United Nations Organisation also greatly formatting global issues.

Fast-forward to the new millennium—things took a different path. All of a sudden we were being pumped with rhetoric titled globalization. Globalization is an umbrella term for a complex series of economic, social, technological, and political changes seen as increasing interdependence and interaction between people and companies in disparate locations. In general use within the field of economics and political economy, it refers to the increasing integration of economies around the world, particularly through trade and financial flows. The term sometimes also refers to the movement of people (labour) and knowledge (technology) across international borders. There are also broader cultural, political and environmental dimensions of globalization. For the common man it was always argued that the world had become like a global village of sorts.

At its most basic, there is nothing mysterious about globalization. But not so fast; some people are now arguing that globalization has mainly benefited the already strong economies of the world and it has given them leverage to not only trade with the rest of the world but to also influence their general lifestyles and politics. Proponents of the school of thought contend that countries like U.S.A. are using globalization as an engine of "corporate imperialism"; one which tramples over the human rights of developing societies, claims to bring prosperity, yet often simply amounts to plundering and profiteering.

Another negative effect of globalization has been cultural assimilation via cultural imperialism. This can be further explained as a situation of exporting of artificial wants, and the destruction or inhibition of authentic local cultures. This brings me to the gist of my submission. At a closer look, globalization is slowly shifting towards Americanization. Have you heard the word "Americanization"? Well in the early 1900's Americanization meant taking new immigrants and turning them into Americans . . . whether they wanted to give up their traditional ways or not. This process often involved learning English and adjusting to American culture, customs, and dress.

Critics now say globalization is nothing more than the imposition of American culture on the entire world. In fact, the most visible sign of globalization seems to be the spread of American hamburgers and cola (Pepsi and Coca Cola products) to nearly every country on earth. The song "Amerika" by the German rock band Rammstein is often seen as a satire of Americanization. It has received mixed reviews: some perceive it as anti-American, others as being opposed to globalization. The band views it as a satirical commentary on "cocacolonization".

According to information from Globalisation.about.com, even globalization champions like Thomas Friedman see it. In a recent column describing why terrorists hate the United States, Friedman wrote: ". . . globalization is in so many ways Americanization: globalization wears Mickey Mouse ears, it drinks Pepsi and Coke, eats Big Macs, does its computing on an IBM laptop with Windows 98. Many societies around the world can't get enough of it, but others see it as a fundamental threat."

The rest of the world seems to be following Uncle Sam (U.S.A.) and leaving behind its authentic ways of life. This has not spared even the 'air tight' Chinese society. Americanization is the contemporary term used for the influence the United States of America has on the culture of other countries, substituting their culture with American culture. When encountered unwillingly, it has a negative connotation; when sought voluntarily, it has a positive connotation.

How Are We Being Americanized?

U.S.A, which has the world's biggest economy and strongest known army, has taken gigantic steps in persuading the rest of the world to think and act like them. Many people, especially the Europeans, have often despised Americans, saying they have no culture. But as any sociologist will tell you, even having no culture is a culture in itself. So for many years, the land of immigrants has been on a process of creating an identity and hence a culture. Now they seem to be selling their culture to the rest of the world as a new and improved product of what we all have as culture.

As far as fashion is concerned, the casual 'American' style of wearing jeans, T-shirts and sports shoes is now common and acceptable in many places. For the office it is not rare to see someone wearing tight jeans with a long-sleeved shirt plus a tie. His defence is, of course, that it is the American style (read modern). Cowboy hats, boots and large silver belt buckles are also a common imitation of the dress style of Americans, especially those from Texas and Arizona. The American music industry has also gone a long way in influencing the dress culture of other people around the world. What about the example youths have picked up from famous American rap artists like 50-cent, Eminem, Tupac Shakur (R.I.P) and Snoop Dogg with their flashy fashions characterized by what is commonly known as "bling bling" (expensive shiny jewellery and watches). Look at the music played in the Nyamirambo-bound taxis and you will be amazed at how it matches with the dress style of the passengers!

Around the world the United States is perhaps best known for its numerous and successful fast food franchises. Such chains, including McDonald's, Burger King, and Kentucky Fried Chicken, are known for selling simple, pre-prepared meals of foods such as hamburgers, French fries (chips), soft drinks, fried chicken, and ice cream. Though undeniably popular, such food, with its emphasis on deep-frying, has been criticized by dietitians in recent decades for being unhealthy and a cause of obesity. It has thus become somewhat of a stereotype to associate American cuisine with obesity and junk food. The whole world now is full of similar eating joints. In Africa many are referred to as take-aways.

Popular Culture

This transmission of American culture has been mainly through several conduits, with the number one medium being the electronic media. Television in particular has done a lot in Americanizing those who view images especially from Hollywood. The guys in Hollywood have made us adore the tough cigar-smoking guys in the Casinos, the thin shapely long-legged women, and to dream about rags-to-riches stories that are a common tag line of the movies. We now adore jazz, hip-hop, rap music, [and] country music as well as gospel music, all of which were pioneered by the United States.

And trust us in following Uncle Sam; many countries now have equivalents of the American awards of Oscars for the movies and Grammys for the music. Just check out the PAM awards in Uganda or the Kisima awards in Kenya, not forgetting the continental Kora awards held annually in South Africa. Many countries have also gone ahead to construct theme parks based on the American Disney World model. Americanization has also led to the popularity and acceptability of what is known as American English. I have seen many posters here in Rwanda of schools claiming to teach American English. Many youths are now using this type of English, considering it 'modern'.

We ought not to ignore the heavy influence that the United States has demonstrated in the development of the Internet and its subsequent control. Remember the conference that was held at the beginning of this year in Tunisia where nations were complaining about the control the US has over the Internet? They were proposing that instead an international body should take over, but the conference ended in defeat of this line of argument. The iPod, the most popular gadget for portable digital music, is also [an] American invention.

American sports, especially basketball, have now become famous world-wide, especially among college students. However other games like baseball and American football have not been easily adopted by other people in the world, as has been the case with basketball. Soccer, which is known to be the world's most popular sport, is not so popular in the US. However the US women's soccer team is one the of the world's premier women's sides.

War on Terrorism

Americans have also been known to spearhead the spread of the Pentecostal, Charismatic, Evangelical or born-again religious movements worldwide. American preachers are always globetrotting all in the name of spreading the word of 'God'. We should not ignore the fact that the United States Constitution enshrined individual freedom of religious practice, which courts have since interpreted to mean that the government is a secular institution, an idea called "separation of church and state". This notion of separating religion from the state is one of the controversial aspects of exporting American culture. This is embedded in the Bush administration's "War on Terror" which some have gone ahead to read as a war on Islam. This controversial American policy is what inspired Prof. Mamdani to write a book titled, *Good Muslim, Bad Muslim.*

America, which has thousands of military servicemen around the world, has of late been preoccupied with fighting terror in Afghanistan, Iraq, and it is getting ready to deal with the Iran problem soon. Actually some people are already speculating that the current crisis between Israel and Hezbollah is a precursor to America's war with Iran—that [the] US is supporting the Olmert government to keep bombing Lebanon until Iran, which is said to be the Godfather of Hezbollah, gets angry enough to join the war. At this point it is argued that the US will join hands with Israel and fight the Iran government because "they have weapons of mass destruction". At the end of the war, as usual [the] US will be expected by many viewers to have conquered another oil-producing country.

Many see the War on Terror as a veil for acquiring cheap oil to run the US economy. Returning to the Israeli conflict with Hezbollah, one cannot fail to see an American tone in the whole conflict. Do you remember the first people to use the words "collateral damage"? This was what Americans first used to describe the death of innocent civilians and destruction of infrastructure by 'precision' missiles during the Afghan war after 9/11. This was an excuse used for having bombed the Chinese Embassy and a Red Cross facility during the war. Now compare it with the death of thousands of Lebanese civilians and the destruction of hundreds of buildings. The death of UN officers and the recent Qana massacre can be accurately referred to as collateral damage by the Israeli government.

This notion of separating religion from the state is one of the controversial aspects of exporting American culture. This is embedded in the Bush administration's "War on Terror" which some have gone ahead to read as a war on Islam.

The apparent determination by the US to appoint itself "Mr. Fix it all" is a somewhat naive but optimistic belief among Americans that all problems can be fixed with enough commitment and effort. This sometimes leads America into problematic situations such as Vietnam and Iraq. In some cases though, [the] American fix-it-all attitude has positively led to [a] large out-pouring of humanitarianism. This is clearly evidenced by the enormous aid that Americans, especially at the individual level, are sending to poor nations. Americans like Bill Gates and CNN's Ted Turner are some of the world's biggest donors.

In conclusion, therefore, the global stage is at a period of American conquest in many [more] different ways than you can imagine. Globalization seems to be hijacked by the Americans. The world also seems to be clamouring for more of the Yankee lifestyle. However simply dismissing—or demonizing—globalization as mere Americanization is misleading. Globalization has the ability to alter much more than just the movies or food consumed by a society. And the results can be powerfully positive, devastatingly negative, or (more often) something in between.

Philippe Legrain  **NO**

In Defense of Globalization

Fears that globalization is imposing a deadening cultural uniformity are as ubiquitous as Coca-Cola, McDonald's, and Mickey Mouse. Many people dread that local cultures and national identities are dissolving into a crass all-American consumerism. That cultural imperialism is said to impose American values as well as products, promote the commercial at the expense of the authentic, and substitute shallow gratification for deeper satisfaction.

Thomas Friedman, columnist for the *New York Times* and author of *The Lexus and the Olive Tree,* believes that globalization is "globalizing American culture and American cultural icons." Naomi Klein, a Canadian journalist and author of *No Logo,* argues that "Despite the embrace of polyethnic imagery, market-driven globalization doesn't want diversity; quite the opposite. Its enemies are national habits, local brands, and distinctive regional tastes."

But it is a myth that globalization involves the imposition of Americanized uniformity, rather than an explosion of cultural exchange. And although—as with any change—it can have downsides, this cross-fertilization is overwhelmingly a force for good.

The beauty of globalization is that it can free people from the tyranny of geography. Just because someone was born in France does not mean they can only aspire to speak French, eat French food, read French books, and so on. That we are increasingly free to choose our cultural experiences enriches our lives immeasurably. We could not always enjoy the best the world has to offer.

Globalization not only increases individual freedom, but also revitalizes cultures and cultural artifacts through foreign influences, technologies, and markets. Many of the best things come from cultures mixing: Paul Gauguin painting in Polynesia, the African rhythms in rock 'n' roll, the great British curry. Admire the many-colored faces of France's World Cup-winning soccer team, the ferment of ideas that came from Eastern Europe's Jewish diaspora, and the cosmopolitan cities of London and New York.

Fears about an Americanized uniformity are overblown. For a start, many "American" products are not as all-American as they seem; MTV in Asia promotes Thai pop stars and plays rock music sung in Mandarin. Nor are American products all-conquering. Coke accounts for less than two of the 64 fluid ounces that the typical person drinks a day. France imported a mere $620 million in food from the United States in 2000, while exporting to America three times

From *The International Economy* by Philippe Legrain, vol. 17, no. 3, Summer 2003, pp. 62–65.

that. Worldwide, pizzas are more popular than burgers and Chinese restaurants sprout up everywhere.

In fashion, the ne plus ultra is Italian or French. Nike shoes are given a run for their money by Germany's Adidas, Britain's Reebok, and Italy's Fila. American pop stars do not have the stage to themselves. According to the IFPI, the record-industry bible, local acts accounted for 68 percent of music sales in 2000, up from 58 percent in 1991. And although nearly three-quarters of television drama exported worldwide comes from the United States, most countries' favorite shows are homegrown.

Nor are Americans the only players in the global media industry. Of the seven market leaders, one is German, one French, and one Japanese. What they distribute comes from all quarters: Germany's Bertelsmann publishes books by American writers; America's News Corporation broadcasts Asian news; Japan's Sony sells Brazilian music.

In some ways, America is an outlier, not a global leader. Baseball and American football have not traveled well; most prefer soccer. Most of the world has adopted the (French) metric system; America persists with antiquated British Imperial measurements. Most developed countries have become intensely secular, but many Americans burn with fundamentalist fervor—like Muslims in the Middle East.

Admittedly, Hollywood dominates the global movie market and swamps local products in most countries. American fare accounts for more than half the market in Japan and nearly two-thirds in Europe. Yet Hollywood is less American than it seems. Top actors and directors are often from outside America. Some studios are foreign-owned. To some extent, Hollywood is a global industry that just happens to be in America. Rather than exporting Americana, it serves up pap to appeal to a global audience.

Hollywood's dominance is in part due to economics: Movies cost a lot to make and so need a big audience to be profitable; Hollywood has used America's huge and relatively uniform domestic market as a platform to expand overseas. So there could be a case for stuffing subsidies into a rival European film industry, just as Airbus was created to challenge Boeing's near-monopoly. But France's subsidies have created a vicious circle whereby European film producers fail in global markets because they serve domestic demand and the wishes of politicians and cinematic bureaucrats.

Another American export is also conquering the globe: English. By 2050, it is reckoned, half the world will be more or less proficient in it. A common global language would certainly be a big plus—for businessmen, scientists, and tourists—but a single one seems far less desirable. Language is often at the heart of national culture, yet English may usurp other languages not because it is what people prefer to speak, but because, like Microsoft software, there are compelling advantages to using it if everyone else does.

But although many languages are becoming extinct, English is rarely to blame. People are learning English as well as—not instead of—their native tongue, and often many more languages besides. Where local languages are dying, it is typically national rivals that are stamping them out. So although, within the United States, English is displacing American Indian tongues, it is not doing away with Swahili or Norwegian.

Even though American consumer culture is widespread, its significance is often exaggerated. You can choose to drink Coke and eat at McDonald's without becoming American in any meaningful sense. One newspaper photo of Taliban fighters in Afghanistan showed them toting Kalashnikovs—as well as a sports bag with Nike's trademark swoosh. People's culture—in the sense of their shared ideas, beliefs, knowledge, inherited traditions, and art—may scarcely be eroded by mere commercial artifacts that, despite all the furious branding, embody at best flimsy values.

The really profound cultural changes have little to do with Coca-Cola. Western ideas about liberalism and science are taking root almost everywhere, while Europe and North America are becoming multicultural societies through immigration, mainly from developing countries. Technology is reshaping culture: Just think of the Internet. Individual choice is fragmenting the imposed uniformity of national cultures. New hybrid cultures are emerging, and regional ones re-emerging. National identity is not disappearing, but the bonds of nationality are loosening.

Cross-border cultural exchange increases diversity within societies—but at the expense of making them more alike. People everywhere have more choice, but they often choose similar things. That worries cultural pessimists, even though the right to choose to be the same is an essential part of freedom.

Cross-cultural exchange can spread greater diversity as well as greater similarity: more gourmet restaurants as well as more McDonald's outlets. And just as a big city can support a wider spread of restaurants than a small town, so a global market for cultural products allows a wider range of artists to thrive. If all the new customers are ignorant, a wider market may drive down the quality of cultural products: Think of tourist souvenirs. But as long as some customers are well informed (or have "good taste"), a general "dumbing down" is unlikely. Hobbyists, fans, artistic pride, and professional critics also help maintain (and raise) standards.

A bigger worry is that greater individual freedom may undermine national identity. The French fret that by individually choosing to watch Hollywood films they might unwittingly lose their collective Frenchness. Yet such fears are overdone. Natural cultures are much stronger than people seem to think. They can embrace some foreign influences and resist others. Foreign influences can rapidly become domesticated, changing national culture, but not destroying it. Clearly, though, there is a limit to how many foreign influences a culture can absorb before being swamped. Traditional cultures in the developing world that have until now evolved (or failed to evolve) in isolation may be particularly vulnerable.

In *The Silent Takeover,* Noreena Hertz describes the supposed spiritual Eden that was the isolated kingdom of Bhutan in the Himalayas as being defiled by such awful imports as basketball and Spice Girls T-shirts. But is that such a bad thing? It is odd, to put it mildly, that many on the left support multiculturalism in the West but advocate cultural purity in the developing world—an attitude they would tar as fascist if proposed for the United States. Hertz appears to want people outside the industrialized West preserved in unchanging but supposedly pure poverty. Yet the Westerners who want this supposed paradise preserved in aspic rarely feel like settling there. Nor do most people in developing countries want to lead an "authentic" unspoiled life of isolated poverty.

In truth, cultural pessimists are typically not attached to diversity per se but to designated manifestations of diversity, determined by their preferences. Cultural pessimists want to freeze things as they were. But if diversity at any point in time is desirable, why isn't diversity across time? Certainly, it is often a shame if ancient cultural traditions are lost. We should do our best to preserve them and keep them alive where possible. Foreigners can often help, by providing the new customers and technologies that have enabled reggae music, Haitian art, and Persian carpet making, for instance, to thrive and reach new markets. But people cannot be made to live in a museum. We in the West are forever casting off old customs when we feel they are no longer relevant. Nobody argues that Americans should ban nightclubs to force people back to line dancing. People in poor countries have a right to change, too.

Moreover, some losses of diversity are a good thing. Who laments that the world is now almost universally rid of slavery? More generally, Western ideas are reshaping the way people everywhere view themselves and the world. Like nationalism and socialism before it, liberalism is a European philosophy that has swept the world. Even people who resist liberal ideas, in the name of religion (Islamic and Christian fundamentalists), group identity (communitarians), authoritarianism (advocates of "Asian values") or tradition (cultural conservatives), now define themselves partly by their opposition to them.

Faith in science and technology is even more widespread. Even those who hate the West make use of its technologies. Osama bin Laden plots terrorism on a cellphone and crashes planes into skyscrapers. Antiglobalization protesters organize by e-mail and over the Internet. China no longer turns its nose up at Western technology: It tries to beat the West at its own game.

Yet globalization is not a one-way street. Although Europe's former colonial powers have left their stamp on much of the world, the recent flow of migration has been in the opposite direction. There are Algerian suburbs in Paris, but not French ones in Algiers. Whereas Muslims are a growing minority in Europe, Christians are a disappearing one in the Middle East.

Foreigners are changing America even as they adopt its ways. A million or so immigrants arrive each year, most of them Latino or Asian. Since 1990, the number of foreign-born American residents has risen by 6 million to just over 25 million, the biggest immigration wave since the turn of the 20th century. English may be all-conquering outside America, but in some parts of the United States, it is now second to Spanish.

The upshot is that national cultures are fragmenting into a kaleidoscope of different ones. New hybrid cultures are emerging. In "Amexica" people speak Spanglish. Regional cultures are reviving. The Scots and Welsh break with British monoculture. Estonia is reborn from the Soviet Union. Voices that were silent dare to speak again.

Individuals are forming new communities, linked by shared interests and passions, that cut across national borders. Friendships with foreigners met on holiday. Scientists sharing ideas over the Internet. Environmentalists campaigning together using e-mail. Greater individualism does not spell the end of community. The new communities are simply chosen rather than coerced, unlike the older ones that communitarians hark back to.

So is national identity dead? Hardly. People who speak the same language, were born and live near each other, face similar problems, have a common experience, and vote in the same elections still have plenty in common. For all our awareness of the world as a single place, we are not citizens of the world but citizens of a state. But if people now wear the bonds of nationality more loosely, is that such a bad thing? People may lament the passing of old ways. Indeed, many of the worries about globalization echo age-old fears about decline, a lost golden age, and so on. But by and large, people choose the new ways because they are more relevant to their current needs and offer new opportunities.

The truth is that we increasingly define ourselves rather than let others define us. Being British or American does not define who you are: It is part of who you are. You can like foreign things and still have strong bonds to your fellow citizens. As Mario Vargas Llosa, the Peruvian author, has written: "Seeking to impose a cultural identity on a people is equivalent to locking them in a prison and denying them the most precious of liberties—that of choosing what, how, and who they want to be."

POSTSCRIPT

Does Globalization Threaten Cultural Diversity?

Cultural globalization, dominated by the spread of Western, primarily American, culture is likely to continue into the foreseeable future. For example, English may not be a common global language, but the possibility of that occurring is given some credence by a survey of people in 42 countries that recorded the vast majority in every region agreed with the statement, "Children need to learn English to succeed in the world today."

Attitudes toward cultural globalization are less clear-cut and are even contradictory. A global survey found that, on average, three-quarters of all people thought culture imports were good. Regionally, that favorable response ranged from 61 percent in the Middle East to 86 percent in western Europe. At the same time, though, an approximately equal percentage of people thought cultural imports were eroding their traditional way of life, with Africans, at 86 percent, the most likely to think so. Not surprisingly, this sense of cultural threat also leads to a desire to protect traditional cultures. The survey found that about 70 percent of its respondents felt that their way of life needed protection from foreign influence. At 79 percent each, people in Africa and the Middle East were most likely to feel their traditional cultures needed protection; western Europeans (56 percent) were the least insecure. Whether this sense of cultural loss is all due to globalization is unclear. It may well be that the changes that are unsettling most people worldwide are also part of the even broader phenomenon of rapid technological modernization that is spurring globalization.

An oddity of the cultural globalization phenomenon is that American attitudes are not much different from those of other people, despite the worry that American culture is becoming dominant. The poll showed that the overwhelming majority of Americans were favorable to the increased availability of goods, music, films, and other cultural imports. Yet two-thirds of all Americans replied to the survey that their traditional way of life was being lost, and a similar percentage responded that they believed that their way of life needed to be protected against foreign influences.

For more on the progress of globalization, visit the British Broadcasting Corporation's Web site at http://www.bbc.co.uk/worldservice/programmes/globalisation/ and Randolph Kluver and Wayne Fu, "The Cultural Globalization Index," an annual posted on the Web site of *Foreign Policy* at http://www.foreignpolicy.com. An overview of cultural globalization focusing on its sociological aspects is Bryan S. Turner and Habibul H. Khondker, *Globalization East and West* (Sage, 2010). F. Jan Nederveen Pieterse, *Globalization and Culture: Global Melange* (Rowman &

Littlefield, 2009) views the process as a cultural hybridization rather than Americanization. A study focusing on the spread of American culture is Lane Crothers, *Globalization and American Popular Culture* (Rowman & Littlefield, 2009).

Questions for Critical Thinking and Reflection

1. What do you make of the argument that worldwide cultural homogeneity (one culture) would be a force for peace by reducing the degree to which "others" appear different and, therefore, threatening?
2. Other than diversity for diversity's sake, what important losses result from diminished cultural diversity or even complete cultural homogeneity?
3. Is a substantial, perhaps complete, loss of cultural diversity inevitable given advances in travel, communications, and other forms that facilitate global interactions among people?

Internet References . . .

Country Indicators for Foreign Policy (CIFP)

Hosted by Carlton University in Canada, the Country Indicators for Foreign Policy project represents an ongoing effort to identify and assemble statistical information conveying the key features of the economic, political, social, and cultural environments of countries around the world.

http://www.carleton.ca/cifp/

U.S. Department of State

The information on this site is organized into categories based on countries, topics, and other criteria. "Background Notes," which provide information on regions and specific countries, can be accessed through this site.

http://www.state.gov/index.cfm
http://www.state.gov/countries/

WorldAtlas.com

The world may be "getting smaller," but geography is still important. This organization's site contains a wide variety of maps and a range of other useful information.

http://www.worldatlas.com/aatlas/world.htm

UNIT 2

Regional and Country Issues

*T*he issues in this section deal with countries that are major regional powers. In this era of interdependence among nations, it is important to understand the concerns that these issues address and the actors involved because they will shape the world and will affect the lives of all people.

- Is the United States a Declining Power?
- Should the Jackson–Vanik Amendment Targeting Russia Be Repealed?
- Will China Soon Become a Threatening Superpower?
- Would It Be an Error to Establish a Palestinian State?
- Is Patient Diplomacy the Best Approach to Iran's Nuclear Program?
- Is U.S. Policy Toward Latin America on the Right Track?

ISSUE 4

Is the United States a Declining Power?

YES: Christopher Layne, from "Graceful Decline: The End of Pax Americana," *The American Conservative* (May 1, 2010)

NO: Alan W. Dowd, from "Declinism," *Policy Review* (August 1, 2007)

ISSUE SUMMARY

YES: Christopher Layne, who holds the Robert M. Gates chair in National Security in the George H. W. Bush School of Government and Public Service at Texas A&M University, argues that the United States is declining in its power and increasingly unable to play a dominant role on the world stage.

NO: Alan W. Dowd, a senior fellow at the Sagamore Institute for Policy Research, contends that there have been previous pronouncements of the end of U.S. dominance on the world stage that have proved to be incorrect and the current ones may well be wrong also.

The emergence of the United States as a world power began in the late 1800s. Rapid industrialization was one factor. By 1900, for example, U.S. steel production was equal to that of the British and French combined. A rapidly growing population, largely due to high immigration, also added to U.S. power, with the U.S. population in 1890 equal to the combined populations of Great Britain and France. A third factor, which is the willingness of Americans to be involved in world affairs, also began to change. One indicator of declining isolation is U.S. involvement in the Spanish–American War (1898), World War I beginning in 1917, World War II beginning in 1941, and a range of minor conflicts.

World War II devastated most of the existing major powers. However, U.S. industrial capacity and infrastructure survived untouched, and in 1946 the U.S. gross national product (GNP) was a stunning 50% of the GNP of the entire world. Militarily, U.S. air and naval power were the world's best, and the United States was the only country with atomic weapons. Furthering U.S. power even more, Americans were willing to be active in world affairs. Symbolizing this, the United States joined the United Nations (UN) (1945), whereas the country had refused to be part of the League of Nations after World War I. In 1946, the United States was not only the world's most powerful country, but in its own class, that of superpower.

This sole superpower status soon changed with the emergence of the Soviet Union as a rival superpower. While the United States had rapidly demobilized most of its army after 1945, the Soviets had maintained an immense ground force, one that could threaten Western Europe. The Soviets also had a hostile ideology, communism, and became even more potent in 1949 when they acquired atomic weapons.

What ensued for the next several decades was the cold war with two superpowers in a bipolar confrontation. Then for reasons that are still debated, the Soviet Union collapsed in 1991. Just a year before amid the decay of Soviet power, analyst Charles Krauthammer had heralded the prediction of the coming of a "unipolar moment" with the United States at "the center of world power" as "the unchallenged superpower." He was right, and in 1992 the United States once again, as had occurred in the late 1940s, stood alone as the world's only superpower.

Still, the moment was different than it had been in 1946. Europe had long ago recovered economically, and many of its countries had joined in an economic powerhouse, the European Union. Japan had also become an economic power, and China was fast approaching that status. The United States was still by far the world's largest economy, but its share of the world GDP had declined from about 50% in 1946 to 23% in 1991. The U.S. share of the world economy remained at 23% in 2008, but there were numerous signs of trouble in the U.S. economy beyond the immediate impacts of the Great Recession. The U.S. trade deficit had become huge ($842 billion), as has the measure of the overall flow of money into and out of the country—the balance of payments. It had yielded a slight surplus in 1991; in 2008 it saw a $7.0-trillion deficit. The United States was also troubled by increasingly large budget deficits ($438 billion in 2008). As a result, the country was increasingly living on borrowed money: borrowed from foreign countries, borrowed from Americans in treasury notes, and borrowed from the future by using surpluses in Social Security and other trust fund accounts to pay current expenses.

U.S. military power remains beyond that of any other country, but the extent to which it is stretched has been demonstrated by the difficulty of maintaining U.S. global commitment while fighting in Iraq and Afghanistan. Those two wars also showed how difficult it is to apply conventional military strength to irregular warfare, much less terrorism. At the other end of the military spectrum from guerilla warfare, there was one atomic power in 1946, six in 1991, nine in 2010, with a tenth, Iran, about to join the nuclear club (see Issue 8).

What does all of this mean for the United States? In the first reading, Christopher Layne depicts the United States as a fading superpower and argues that the country will suffer if it does not accept its new, less than hegemonic (dominant) status. Alan Dowd disagrees. He contends that the United States is resilient, that repeated declarations of its decline have proven inaccurate, and that it remains the world's dominant power.

Graceful Decline: The End of Pax Americana

The United States emerged from World War II in a position of global dominance. From this unparalleled military and economic power came a Pax Americana that has endured for more than six decades. It seemed the sun would never set on the U.S. empire. [Pax Americana borrows from the Latin term *Pax Romana,* which refers to the approximately two hundred years of relative peace during the first and second centuries A.D. within the boundaries of the empire dominated by Rome.]

But America is increasingly unable to play the hegemon's [dominant power] assigned role. Militarily, a hegemon is responsible for stabilizing key regions and guarding the global commons. Economically, it offers public goods by opening its domestic market to other states, supplying liquidity for the world economy, and providing the reserve currency. A hegemon is supposed to solve international crises, not cause them. It is supposed to be the lender of last resort, not the biggest borrower. Faced with wars it cannot win or quit and an economy begging rescue, the United States no longer fits the part.

Still, many in the mainstream foreign-policy community see these as temporary setbacks and believe that U.S. primacy will endure for years to come. The American people are awakening to a new reality more quickly than the academy. According to a December 2009 Pew survey, 41 percent of the public believes that the U.S. plays a less important and powerful role as a world leader than it did a decade ago.

The epoch of American dominance is drawing to a close, and international politics is entering a period of transition: no longer unipolar [one dominant power] but not yet fully multipolar. President Barack Obama's November 2009 trip to China provided both substantive and emblematic evidence of the shift. As the *Financial Times* observed, "Coming at a moment when Chinese prestige is growing and the U.S. is facing enormous difficulties, Mr. Obama's trip has symbolized the advent of a more multi-polar world where U.S. leadership has to co-exist with several rising powers, most notably China." In the same Pew study, 44 percent of Americans polled said that China was the leading economic power; just 27 percent chose the United States.

Much of America's decline can be attributed to its own self-defeating policies, but as the U.S. stumbles, others—notably China, India, and Russia—are rising. This shift in the global balance of power will dramatically affect international politics: the likelihood of intense great-power security competitions—and even war—will increase; the current era of globalization will end; and the post-1945 Pax Americana will be replaced by an international order that reflects the interests, values, and norms of emerging powers.

China's economy has been growing much more rapidly than the United States over the last two decades and continues to do so, maintaining audacious 8 percent growth projections in the midst of a global recession. Leading economic forecasters predict that it will overtake the U.S. as the world's largest economy, measured by overall GDP, sometime around 2020. Already in 2008, China passed the U.S. as the world's leading manufacturing nation—a title the United States had enjoyed for over a century—and this year China will displace Japan as the world's second-largest economy. Everything we know about the trajectories of rising great powers tells us that China will use its increasing wealth to build formidable military power and that it will seek to become the dominant power in East Asia.

Optimists contend that once the U.S. recovers from what historian Niall Ferguson calls the "Great Repression"—not quite a depression but more than a recession—we'll be able to answer the Chinese challenge. The country, they remind us, faced a larger debt–GDP ratio after World War II yet embarked on an era of sustained growth. They forget that the postwar era was a golden age of U.S. industrial and financial dominance, trade surpluses, and persistent high growth rates. Those days are gone. The United States of 2010 and the world in which it lives are far different from those of 1945.

Weaknesses in the fundamentals of the American economy have been accumulating for more than three decades. In the 1980s, these problems were acutely diagnosed by a number of writers—notably David Calleo, Paul Kennedy, Robert Gilpin, Samuel Huntington, and James Chace—who predicted that these structural ills would ultimately erode the economic foundations of America's global preeminence. A spirited late-1980s debate was cut short, when, in quick succession, the Soviet Union collapsed, Japan's economic bubble burst, and the U.S. experienced an apparent economic revival during the Clinton administration. Now the delayed day of reckoning is fast approaching.

Even in the best case, the United States will emerge from the current crisis with fundamental handicaps. The Federal Reserve and Treasury have pumped massive amounts of dollars into circulation in hope of reviving the economy. Add to that the $1 trillion-plus budget deficits that the Congressional Budget Office (CBO) predicts the United States will incur for at least a decade. When the projected deficits are bundled with the persistent U.S. current-account deficit, the entitlements overhang (the unfunded future liabilities of Medicare and Social Security), and the cost of the ongoing wars in Iraq and Afghanistan, there is reason to worry about the United States' fiscal stability. As the CBO says, "Even if the recovery occurs as projected and the stimulus bill is allowed to expire, the country will face the highest debt/GDP ratio in 50 years and an increasingly unsustainable and urgent fiscal problem."

The dollar's vulnerability is the United States' geopolitical Achilles' heel. Its role as the international economy's reserve currency ensures American preeminence, and if it loses that status, hegemony will be literally unaffordable. As Cornell professor Jonathan Kirshner observes, the dollar's vulnerability "presents potentially significant and underappreciated restraints upon contemporary American political and military predominance."

Fears for the dollar's long-term health predated the current financial and economic crisis. The meltdown has amplified them and highlighted two new factors that bode ill for continuing reserve-currency status. First, the other big financial players in the international economy are either military rivals (China) or ambiguous allies (Europe) that have their own ambitions and no longer require U.S. protection from the Soviet threat. Second, the dollar faces an uncertain future because of concerns that its value will diminish over time. Indeed, China, which has holdings estimated at nearly $2 trillion, is worried that America will leave it with huge piles of depreciated dollars. China's vote of no confidence is reflected in its recent calls to create a new reserve currency.

In coming years, the U.S. will be under increasing pressure to defend the dollar by preventing runaway inflation. This will require it to impose fiscal self-discipline through some combination of budget cuts, tax increases, and interest-rate hikes. Given that the last two options could choke off renewed growth, there is likely to be strong pressure to slash the federal budget.

But it will be almost impossible to make meaningful cuts in federal spending without deep reductions in defense expenditures. Discretionary non-defense domestic spending accounts for only about 20 percent of annual federal outlays. So the United States will face obvious "guns or butter" choices. As Kirshner puts it, the absolute size of U.S. defense expenditures is "more likely to be decisive in the future when the U.S. is under pressure to make real choices about taxes and spending. When borrowing becomes more difficult, and adjustment more difficult to postpone, choices must be made between raising taxes, cutting non-defense spending, and cutting defense spending." Faced with these hard decisions, Americans will find themselves afflicted with hegemony fatigue.

The United States will be compelled to overhaul its strategy dramatically, and rather than having this adjustment forced upon it suddenly by a major crisis, the U.S. should get ahead of the curve by shifting its position in a gradual, orderly fashion. A new American global posture would involve strategic retrenchment, burden-shifting, and abandonment of the so-called "global counterinsurgency" being waged in Afghanistan and Iraq.

As a first step, the U.S. will need to pull back from its current security commitments to NATO [North Atlantic Treaty Organization], Japan, and South Korea. This is not isolationism. The United States undertook the defense of these regions under conditions very different from those prevailing today. In the late 1940s, all were threatened by the Soviet Union—in the case of South Korea and Japan, by China as well—and were too weak to defend themselves. The U.S. did the right thing by extending its security umbrella and "drawing a line in the sand" to contain the Soviet Union. But these commitments were never intended to be permanent. They were meant as a temporary shield to enable Western Europe, Japan, and South Korea to build up their own economic and military strength and assume responsibility for defending themselves.

There are several explanations for why the U.S. did not follow through with this policy. Fundamentally, during the Pax Americana there was no need. As the U.S. declines, however, it will be compelled to return to its original intent. If we remember that an eventual pullback was the goal of U.S. policy, strategic retrenchment in the early 21st century looks less like a radical break than a fulfillment of strategic goals adopted in the late 1940s.

Burden-shifting—not burden-sharing—is the obvious corollary of strategic retrenchment. American policy should seek to compel our allies to assume responsibility for their own security and take the lead role in providing security in their regions. To implement this strategic devolution, the U.S. should disengage gradually from its current commitments in order to give an adequate transition period for its allies to step up to the plate. It should facilitate this transition by providing advanced weapons and military technology to friendly states in Europe and Asia.

With respect to Islamic terrorism, we need to keep our priorities straight. Terrorism is not the most pressing national-security threat facing the United States. Great powers can be defeated only by other great powers—not by non-state terrorists or by minor powers. The U.S. needs to be careful not to pay more attention to Islamic terrorists than to emerging great powers. Here the Obama administration and Defense Secretary Robert M. Gates are getting it wrong.

Although many in the U.S. foreign-policy community—especially the counterinsurgency lobby, based at the Center for a New American Security, and the American Enterprise Institute—call for the U.S. to "win" the war on terror, there can be no decisive victory over terrorism. The trick is finding the right strategy to minimize its effects on American security. The strategy of the Bush and Obama administrations—invading and occupying Iraq and Afghanistan—is exactly the wrong approach. The U.S. is bad at counterinsurgency. Foreign occupying powers seldom are good at it, which is the main reason big powers usually lose these kinds of small wars. The U.S. also is not good at nation-building. Rather than quelling terrorism, a long-term foreign military presence in places like Iraq and Afghanistan inflames nationalism and anti-Americanism.

The Nobel Prize–winning Columbia University economist Joseph Stiglitz and his coauthor Linda Bilmes have estimated that the direct and indirect costs of the Iraq War will exceed $3 trillion. No similar projection of the Afghanistan war's costs exists. But the Obama administration's fall 2009 internal debate about whether to increase troop levels in Afghanistan offered a preview of coming attractions. During these deliberations, some officials argued that the U.S. needed to limit its commitment because the cost of the war effort has serious budgetary implications. According to the *New York Times*, when presented with an OMB projection that showed existing troop deployments and nation-building expenses combined with the cost of sending an additional 40,000 troops to Afghanistan for a decade would total $1 trillion, "the president seemed in sticker shock, watching his domestic agenda vanishing in front of him."

That the United States needs a post-Pax Americana foreign policy should be obvious. But there is no guarantee that the U.S. will adjust to a transforming world. Even as the globe is being turned upside down by material factors, the foreign policies of individual states are shaped by the ideas leaders hold about their own nations' identity and place in world politics. More than most, America's foreign policy is the product of such ideas, and U.S. foreign-policy elites have constructed their own myths of empire to justify the United States' hegemonic role. To move successfully to a post-Pax Americana foreign policy, Americans will need to move beyond these myths.

The foundational American myth of empire is exceptionalism, the belief, dating back to the Puritans, that the U.S. is different, better, and morally superior to the rest of the world. Americans have always looked at the outside world suspiciously and viewed it as a source of contagion: war, imperialism, militarism, religious intolerance, non-democratic forms of governance, and latterly totalitarianism, genocide, and terrorism. All these bad things, we believe, come from "over there."

We have long thought that we cannot live safely in a world of such imperfections and that it is therefore our national duty to cure these ills by using American power to construct a world order based on our values. U.S. foreign-policy elites have extrapolated from our national experience and concluded, as Edmund Stillman and William Pfaff wrote some 45 years ago, that the United States is a model for the world and "America's wants and values are universal"—a point George W. Bush made repeatedly in justifying his policy of exporting democracy at the point of a bayonet. Americans believe that our political and economic systems provide "a prototypical solution for the world's disorders." If we could just give the rest of the world a makeover so it looked like the United States, all would be well.

These assumptions invest American foreign policy with a tendency to see the world in terms of good versus evil. And because the U.S. looks through this prism, it believes it has the obligation to prevail in this global struggle. America's security and way of life are purportedly endangered by the existence of hostile ideologies anywhere in the world because peace and freedom are allegedly indivisible. Intervention is thus the United States' default in foreign policy.

We attempt to tame the world by exporting democracy because—we are told—democracies do not fight each other. We export our model of free-market capitalism because—we are told—states that are economically interdependent do not fight each other. We work multilaterally through international institutions because—we are told—these promote cooperation and trust among states. None of these propositions is self-evident. Indeed, there is overwhelming evidence that they are wrong. But they are illusions that "express the deepest beliefs which Americans, as a nation, hold about the world." So we cling to the idea that our hegemony is necessary for our own and everyone else's security. The consequence has been to contribute to the very imperial overstretch that is accelerating the United States' decline.

Because that U.S. enjoyed such vast superiority for such a long time, it had the luxury of acting on its delusions without paying too high a price. (That is, if you discount the 58,000 names on the Vietnam Memorial or the tens of thousands of U.S. military personnel who have suffered disfiguring wounds or been killed in Iraq and Afghanistan.) But as my graduate school mentor, Kenneth Waltz, one of the towering figures in the study of international politics, used to tell us about American foreign policy, "When you are big, strong, and powerful, you can afford to make the same dumb mistakes over and over again. But when your power declines, you begin to pay a price for repeating your mistakes."

U.S. decline means that in the 21st century, the United States will pay a high price if it endlessly repeats its mistakes. To change our foreign policy—to come to grips with the end of the Pax Americana—we first need to change the way we see the world.

Alan W. Dowd    **NO**

Declinism

The worries and warnings come from across the political spectrum and across the oceans. [*The*] *New York Times* critic Nicolai Ouroussoff calls America "an empire enthralled with its own power and unaware that it is fading." Former Clinton administration official Charles Kupchan concludes that "American primacy is already past its peak." According to Joseph Nye, who served under Presidents [Jimmy] Carter and [Bill] Clinton, America's "soft power—its ability to attract others by the legitimacy of U.S. policies and the values that underlie them—is in decline."

Peggy Noonan, speechwriter for the most optimistic of presidents, Ronald Reagan, asserts that "in some deep fundamental way things have broken down and can't be fixed." Ivan Eland of the Independent Institute warns that America's military "overextension could hasten the decline of the United States as a superpower."

Matthew Parris of the London *Sunday Times* reports that the United States is "overstretched," romantically recalling the [John F.] Kennedy presidency, when "America had the best arguments" and could use moral suasion rather than force to have its way in the world. From his vantage point in Shanghai, the *International Herald Tribune's* Howard French worries about "the declining moral influence of the United States" over an emergent China.

Are the declinists right about America's impending demise? Perhaps. But perhaps they're wrong: After all, declinism has a long history and a strange way of rearing its head when the U.S. is riding the waves of what [British Prime Minister Winston S.] Churchill called the "primacy of power." Indeed, it is during periods of U.S. ascendance—or perhaps better said, periods that subsequently are recognized as having been ascendant—that the declinists usually start sounding the (false) alarms. The "decline and fall of America" mantra has become an almost-decennial prophecy.

By the mid-eighteenth century, the University of Virginia's James Ceaser has written, it was widely accepted in Europe that "due chiefly to atmospheric conditions, in particular excessive humidity, all living things in the Americas were not only inferior to those found in Europe but also in a condition of decline." Not surprisingly, the men who forged the American republic took issue with this early form of declinism. In fact, Ceaser notes, Alexander Hamilton rebutted Europe's pseudoscientific slander in *Federalist*

No. 11. Pointing to "the arrogant pretensions" of Europe, Hamilton observed that "men admired as profound philosophers have in direct terms attributed to her inhabitants a physical superiority and have gravely asserted that all animals, and with them the human species, degenerate in America." He called on his countrymen to "vindicate the honor of the human race" by building "one great American system superior to the control of all transatlantic force or influence, able to dictate the terms of the connection between the old and the new world!"

Descending and Ascending

The 13 colonies hugging the Atlantic seaboard would rally behind Hamilton's vision and redefine the nature of their connection with the Old World, but the revolutionary moment was short-lived. After defeating the British Empire in a brutal war for independence, the young republic was soundly swatted back into its place less than 30 years later during the War of 1812. The war saw U.S. forces routed in Canada, U.S. sailors captured and impressed into duty on British warships, U.S. ports blockaded, and the U.S. Capitol and White House set ablaze by a British invasion force. When measured against Great Britain—and against its own position just a generation earlier—it appeared that the United States had declined drastically.

Two generations later, the Civil War would decapitate the national government and deform the nation. As Jay Winik's *April 1865* (HarperCollins, 2001) reminds us, the war not only called into question almost a hundred years of independent self-government, but also embodied decline in its purest sense. Winik recounts savage episodes of murder, mayhem, guerilla warfare, terrorism, vigilantism, and state-sanctioned brutality on a par with anything we condemn today—innocent civilians rounded up and summarily executed; cities burned to the ground; entire counties depopulated; mutilations and beheadings; all manner of torture. After Lincoln's murder, General Sherman openly feared America's slipping into anarchy. The Union general wondered "who was left on this continent to give order and shape to the now disjointed elements of the government." The war had rolled back American civilization, and recovery of what was lost was anything but certain. America had declined immeasurably—or perhaps better said, descended.

Of course, Americans on both sides of the war would rebuild. By the early twentieth century, the United States would claim an empire of its own, with President Theodore Roosevelt using U.S. warships to flex American muscle in the Caribbean, Mediterranean, and Pacific and President Woodrow Wilson deploying American troops to Russia and Europe. Indeed, the rise of the United States in the global pecking order was aided by the economic and military devastation visited upon Europe by the Great War. Yet as historian Benjamin Rhodes has observed, America's "image abroad sank disastrously" during the [Calvin] Coolidge presidency, mainly due to European resentment over how the U.S. handled the role of global creditor. Washington's mishandling of its newfound status as an economic–military power yielded a United States weaker than the nation that had tipped the balance in the Great War.

The U.S. failed to respond to the threats posed by the rise of power-projecting dictatorships in Europe and the Pacific—threats punctuated by Japan's attack on the USS *Panay* in December 1937 and numerous German attacks in the Atlantic and the Red Sea. As if to underscore American weakness, President Franklin Roosevelt famously sent word to Hitler in 1938 that "the United States has no political involvements in Europe." The German dictator got the message. Washington's diplomatic deference and military meekness, says Gerhard Weinberg in *A World At Arms* (Cambridge, 1994), confirmed Hitler's "assessment that this was a weak country, incapable, because of its racial mixture and feeble democratic government, of organizing and maintaining strong military forces."

Losing the Postwar Peace, Losing the Cold War

In 1945, notes Derek Leebaert in *The Fifty Year Wound* (Little Brown, 2002), America had the "strut and swagger of a confident nation beating back tyrants. . . . The country was alive with strength and purpose." But by 1946, less than an eye-blink in the lifespan of a great power, everything had changed. The swagger was gone, replaced by uncertainty and worry.

Consider John Dos Passos's gloomy analysis of postwar Germany, which appeared in the January 7, 1946, *Life*. The U.S. had just flattened Imperial Japan and plowed into the heart of Hitler's Thousand Year Reich, yet Dos Passos could say "We've lost the peace. . . . Friend and foe alike look you accusingly in the face and tell you how bitterly they are disappointed in you as an American."

Pointing to the postwar division of Europe, which left half of the continent free and the other under Soviet domination, historian Michael Hunt has noted that "American policymakers opened this period of ostensible dominance by 'losing' Eastern Europe." Leebaert adds texture to the portrait of postwar decline. "Ten months after the war's end," he writes, "not one U.S. Army division or Air Force group could be rated ready for combat." General Marshall himself called the postwar force "a hollow shell." In fact, as late as 1949, the U.S. had just 12 battle-ready tanks in Germany. Likewise, the evidence in occupied Japan pointed to America's virtual collapse as an enduring military power. Each division of the Eighth Army, Leebaert reports, was a thousand rifles short, the Fifth Air Force still had no jet fighters in 1949, and there were just 500 U.S. soldiers based in Korea. Thus, as world war gave way to Cold War, "The United States neither looked nor felt ready to contain anybody."

As the Cold War began in earnest, accusations over "Who lost China?" rang out across the U.S. Worries about America's decline soon spiked when communist forces rolled through Korea. General [Douglas] MacArthur's daring amphibious landing at Inchon would lead not to victory over the invaders but stalemate. Against a global backdrop of communist revolution, U.S. power seemed to be ebbing—and Washington seemed to be expending the power it had at an unsustainable clip.

Between the Potsdam Conference [1945] and the Berlin airlift [1948–1949], President Harry Truman committed the American people to support any nation "resisting attempted subjugation by armed minorities or by outside pressures." He poured unheard-of sums into a standing peacetime army and oversaw the creation of the Department of Defense, National Security Agency, Joint Chiefs of Staff, and NATO [North Atlantic Treaty Organization] to wage a new kind of war. He signed on to permanent defense treaties in Western Europe and the Pacific, opened the door to scores of other entangling alliances, repackaged war as police action, and justified it all because of the nature of the enemy and the omnipresent threat it posed. "If we falter in our leadership," he warned, "we may endanger the peace of the world—and we shall surely endanger the welfare of our own nation."

Truman's doctrine wasn't a ready-made road map for waging the Cold War, according to Leebaert. Instead, the Cold War's first four years—which coincided with Truman's first four years as president—"were filled with starts and stops rather than any considered policy or long-range goals." The result: "a patched-together postwar order."

Nor did Americans immediately rally around Truman's battle plan. As historian Walter LaFeber recalls, Truman's critics "tore apart" his doctrine and policies. They warned that Truman would weaken the Constitution, overinflate the presidency, militarize U.S. foreign policy and destroy the UN [United Nations].

Still others argued that, despite all its spending, deployments and pronouncements, America's Cold War battle plan was not working. "Even in the early 1950s," as Barry Goldwater recalled in *The Conscience of a Conservative* (Victor Publishing, 1960), "it was clear that we were losing the Cold War." Lamenting "the deterioration of America's fortunes," the arch-conservative worried about an enemy with the will and capacity to "dominate absolutely every square mile of the globe" and warned that "a craven fear of death is entering the American consciousness." Indeed, Washington's nonreaction to the Soviet invasion of Hungary [1956] just three years after the armistice in Korea seemed to trace the outer limits of America's will, if not its power. "As the bloody tragedy played itself out on the streets of Budapest, America watched, waited and did nothing," Patrick Buchanan bitterly recounts in his introduction. "The sense of frustration and failure was all the greater because Moscow had taken the risk of war, and Moscow had won."

U.S. political power and prestige suffered yet another blow when Sputnik rocketed into orbit in 1957 and Moscow took the high ground in the space race. Senator Henry Jackson [D-WA] called it "a national week of shame and danger." Senator Lyndon Johnson [D-TX] warned that "control of space means control of the world."

Of course, the U.S. faced terrestrial problems as well. "The Soviet Union increasingly appeared to be a triumphal industrial giant," Leebaert says. *The New York Times,* he notes, predicted that Soviet industrial output would exceed America's by the end of the twentieth century, and the CIA [Central Intelligence Agency] surmised that the Soviet economy would be three times larger than America's by 2000. "The overwhelming question," Leebaert writes of the 1950s, "was whether an apparently soft, even hedonistic American consumer society had the stamina for a long, inconclusive contest with communism."

Senator John Kennedy [D-MA] was worried about the answer to that question. Running for president in 1960, he pointed to a "missile gap" with the Soviet Union as evidence of America's weakening defenses. "We are . . . gambling with our survival," he warned. "This year's defense budget is our last chance to do something about it," he added for dramatic effect. Among those echoing Kennedy was his Democratic colleague Joseph Clark [D-PA]. Under the headline "U.S. Decline Seen in Eisenhower Era," *The New York Times* reported on a May 1960 speech in which Clark derided "timid leadership in both foreign and domestic affairs." Like Goldwater, he expressed worries that "America's world role had shrunk" and called for a "build-up in American military muscle."

Yet even after Kennedy had swooped in to save America from decline, it continued to look as if the U.S. had fallen fast and hard from its World War II perch. Ineptitude at the Bay of Pigs and irresolute responses to earlier communist challenges would conspire to invite the very thing Churchill had warned against in his Cold War preamble: "temptations to a trial of strength." [The Bay of Pigs in Cuba was the site of a failed invasion of Cuba in 1961 by Cuban exiles backed by the CIA.]

In fact, by building missile bases and airstrips on Cuba, Moscow was exploiting a gaping hole in America's veneer of invincibility. The ensuing Cuban missile crisis [1962] merely exposed that gap to the rest of the world and prompted some governments to develop alternative sources of deterrence: Shaken by the notion that, in LaFeber's clever phrase, Washington had dragged them "uncomfortably close to annihilation without representation," the French and others grew ever more independent.

The trial of strength over Cuba would precede a trial by fire in Vietnam. In *Modern Times* (HarperCollins, 1983), Paul Johnson calls Vietnam and the consequent crisis of confidence "America's suicide attempt." During the Vietnam War, Washington entered into 16 bombing pauses and 72 peace initiatives. These self-imposed restraints, as Johnson observes, were "interpreted by friend and foe alike as evidence not of humanity, but of guilt and lack of righteous conviction"—and decline. The war's final chapter, which saw North Vietnam violated the peace accords with impunity and Washington beat a hasty retreat out of Saigon, would be "the gravest and most humiliating defeat in American history."

In the midst of this macro-humiliation, there were countless smaller humiliations, each serving as a piece in the dark mosaic of American decline:

- French leader Charles de Gaulle withdrew from NATO's military structure in 1966 and afterwards pursued a separate peace with Moscow.
- Western Europe averted its gaze from the agony of its patron and protector. Not even Britain would lend a hand in Vietnam.
- When Israel called for help and the U.S. answered during the 1973 war, NATO turned its back. Only Portugal would grant overflight rights to U.S. supply planes.
- North Korea openly challenged and mocked U.S. power during the Vietnam debacle. Pyongyang [capital of North Korea] seized the USS *Pueblo* [in 1968] in international waters and tortured its crew for 11 months, shot down a U.S. plane in international airspace, and,

according to Leebaert, "hacked to death two U.S. officers in the 38th parallel's demilitarized zone."

- In the American sphere, Venezuela sided with OPEC [Organization of Petroleum Exporting Countries] and nationalized U.S. firms; left-wing forces ousted a U.S.-backed government in Nicaragua; and Argentina broke ranks and shipped grain to Moscow.

After Vietnam, the United States appeared to be in a geopolitical free fall. Amid recession, oil embargoes and assassinations, Johnson says, Soviet leaders referred to "the deepening general crisis" in the United States, and Beijing dismissed America as a power in decline. Even Washington seemed to believe America's best days were behind it. Leebaert records an exchange between Admiral Elmo Zumwalt and Henry Kissinger in which Kissinger concluded the United States had "passed its high point like so many other civilizations," adding that he was trying "to persuade the Russians to give us the best deal we can get."

It wasn't a very good deal. Coming on the heels of Vietnam, détente was an expression of American weakness. A 1976 report by [then Secretary of Defense] Donald Rumsfeld conceded that in the event of war, America's ability to reinforce NATO or come to the aid of Japan or Israel was in doubt. Indeed, according to Johnson, "America's decline in the Seventies seemed even more precipitous in contrast with the apparent solidity and self-confidence of the Soviet regime." By 1971, he notes, Moscow had bypassed Washington in numbers of land-based and sub-based nuclear missiles. The USSR [Union of the Soviet Socialist Republics] built some 1,300 warships between 1962 and 1977, the U.S. just 302; and while Washington retracted and retreated, Moscow's proxies established themselves across the Third World.

"We've become fearful to compete with the Soviet Union," one presidential candidate concluded in a campaign speech. "I want to see our nation return to a posture and an image and a standard to make us proud once again . . . we ought to be a beacon for nations who search for peace and who search for freedom." The words could have been spoken by Ronald Reagan, but in fact it was Jimmy Carter, who three years later would deliver a sermon to the American people essentially blaming them for American decline. Johnson takes note of Carter's conclusion that America's capacity to shape global events was "very limited." This was never more apparent than during Iran's unchallenged violation of the U.S. embassy in Tehran [capital of Iran], which would mark the postwar nadir of American power and, it appeared, the fulfillment of declinist prophecies.

Bipolar Disorder

"The country did not elect [President Ronald] Reagan out of serious belief that he would change things," Derek Leebaert argues, "but because it felt cornered. If embassies could be seized with impunity, if OPEC could gear up to new heights of effrontery, if the United States was behaving as if its liberties depended on the People's Republic of China, then America was indeed looking like a 'pitiful giant' and perhaps well on the way to becoming one."

As a candidate, Reagan ticked off a seemingly endless list of U.S. vulnerabilities and outright defeats in the global conflict with Moscow: Soviet troops in Afghanistan, failure in the arms race, American hostages languishing in Iran, propaganda defeats at the UN, faltering leadership in Europe. Reagan's solution was simple. Rather than accommodating Moscow through détente or containing it behind curtains and parallels, the United States would defeat the Soviet system once and for all: "We win," he said. "They lose."

Even as Reagan was reformulating America's grand strategy, those in the declinist school clung tenaciously to their arguments. In his treatise on decline, *The Rise and Fall of the Great Powers* (Random House, 1987), Paul Kennedy wondered whether the country's electoral and political system had the capacity to allow policymakers to reformulate the "grand strategy in light of the larger, uncontrollable changes taking place in world affairs." His implication was not just that the U.S. political system was outmoded, but that American power was outmatched.

The book laid out in grim detail how the United States was tumbling toward the same fate that had felled the dominant powers of earlier centuries; how "the American share of world power has been declining relatively faster than Russia's over the past few decades"; and how U.S. defense outlays and commitments were unsustainable and were pushing the United States toward the same "imperial overstretch" that had undone earlier powers.

From Kennedy's perspective, U.S. interests were too numerous, too widespread and too expensive to sustain. The bipolar system, he said, was giving way to a multipolar one. Thus, he reasoned, "there was a need to manage affairs so that the relative erosion of the United States takes place slowly and smoothly."

Kennedy's requiem was representative of a chorus of declinist predictions in the mid- to late 1980s.

- Writing just a few years ahead of Kennedy, Richard Barnet declared that the American Century had "lasted about 26 years." He mocked the Reagan administration for promising to reverse "the stunning decline of American power that marked the 1970s," for "alarming millions in the United States and Europe," and, finally, for retreating from its hard line with Moscow.
- In 1988, Flora Lewis sighed that "Talk of U.S. decline is real in the sense that the U.S. can no longer pull all the levers of command or pay all the bills."
- Even in trying to deflect the declinists, James Schlesinger conceded in 1988 that the U.S. was "no longer economically the preponderant power . . . no longer militarily the dominant power . . . no longer can achieve more or less whatever it desires."
- "The signs of decline are evident to those who care to see them," declared Peter Passell in 1990, noting that the U.S. had lost its competitive edge and was losing its battle with the Japanese juggernaut.
- "Europeans and Asians," wrote Anthony Lewis in 1990, "are already finding confirmation of their suspicion that the United States is in decline."
- Citing America's dependence on foreign sources for energy and "crucial weaknesses" in the military, Tom Wicker concluded "that maintaining

superpower status is becoming more difficult—nearly impossible—for the United States."

Other declinists of the late 1980s and early 1990s, as Leebaert recalls, were predicting that the last decade of the twentieth century would be when "the American empire ran out of gas" and "took the British route to second-class economic status."

Moreover, says Samuel Huntington, American decline dominated academic discussions in 1988. By 1990, political scientists and pundits were borrowing Kennedy's premise and quipping that the U.S. and USSR had waged the Cold War, but Japan and Germany had won it. In 1993, historian William Pfaff looked back upon America's "soaring national ascent, and descent, between 1900 and the century's end" and concluded that "superpowerdom" had deformed the United States and delivered "better results for others than for itself."

Of course, it was the Soviet Union that had declined and collapsed under the weight of empire. In an unfortunate stroke of timing for Kennedy, his analysis hit bookstores not long before the United States emerged as the unrivaled, unchallenged leader of something not known since the days of Rome—a unipolar world. Leebaert calls it "a world unrecognizable from Professor Kennedy's one-dimensional perspective," noting that Kennedy "overlooked inconvenient facts, as information technologies forced decentralization and demanded the sort of adaptivity made for America."

Impotent or Imperial?

Indeed, the U.S. surged into the 1990s, its global primacy punctuated by the military rout of Iraq in 1991, the collapse of Soviet communism, and a mastery of the Information-Age economy. Yet, as President George H.W. Bush expressed it in *A World Transformed* (Knopf, 1998), the U.S. was forced to defend its relevance in post-Cold War Europe in the same way an aging employee on the verge of being downsized might defend his job: "In our discussion about NATO," Bush wrote, "I explained why it was important for the United States to stay in Europe."

He succeeded in convincing the Europeans, but Americans remained unsure about the proper place of a superpower with no rival. This uncertainty was accentuated by Washington's increasingly allergic reaction to post-Cold War challenges:

- Two successive U.S. administrations seemed helpless to stop the vivisection of Bosnia. As Pfaff notes, the West's failure to stanch the bleeding in Yugoslavia "dealt a brutal blow to the idea that democracies possessed the capacity, or the will, to enlarge that zone of pacification and cooperation created inside the western political community. It even raised the question of whether that achievement would last." As the leader of the West, the U.S. was weakened and scarred by that failure.

- Disorganized clans were able to chase the mighty U.S. military out of Somalia, and the U.S. then averted its gaze from Rwanda's machete massacre.
- North Korea crashed into the nuclear club; India and Pakistan shook the subcontinent with a spasm of nuclear tests; and China conducted a reckless foreign policy of gunboat diplomacy in the Taiwan Straits.
- Even in America's backyard, Washington dithered over how to remove a scrawny junta in Haiti. "Rarely," recalled David Halberstam in *War in a Time of Peace* (Scribner, 2001), "had the United States looked so impotent."

In each instance, the U.S. played the role of spectator or prisoner of events. Friend and foe took notice. As the Balkans hemorrhaged, French President Jacques Chirac concluded that "the position of leader of the free world is vacant." Even after U.S. forces intervened, questions lingered about America's strength and stomach for global leadership. After the 78-day war from 30,000 feet over Kosovo, wrote Halberstam, Army Secretary Louis Caldera worried that Americans were more willing to take casualties when training for war than when waging it.

Osama bin Laden came to the same conclusion. From his perspective, America's retreat from Beirut [capital of Lebanon] in the 1980s, Mogadishu [capital of Somalia] in the 1990s, and Yemen in 2000 was evidence of decline. "America exited dragging its tail in failure, defeat, and ruin, caring for nothing," bin Laden preached. "The extent of your impotence and weaknesses became very clear."

Decline and Conquer

To be sure, the U.S. faces challenges, competitors and threats that could erode its global position: China and India are ascending economically; the world abounds with asymmetrical threats that have the capacity to undermine the liberal order that Washington has sought to spread for generations; and Americans find themselves in the midst of yet another "great ideological conflict," in the words of the president's most recent security strategy document.

Today as in the past, U.S. primacy is neither inevitable nor a birthright. It is a burden that must be justified and shouldered anew by each generation in its own way. Even so, and notwithstanding Iraq, this is an unusual moment to diagnose the United States as a nation in decline. Just as the past is littered with unfulfilled predictions by the declinists, the present is teeming with evidence of unprecedented U.S. power.

From peace-keeping to war-fighting, deterrence to disaster relief, it is the U.S. military that the world turns to when in need. Johns Hopkins professor Fouad Ajami has noted, "The world rails against the United States, yet embraces its protection, its gossip and its hipness." Especially its protection: More than half the globe enjoys overt defense and security treaties with the United States. The U.S. military is the last (and first) line of defense for most of the rest.

Of course, the U.S. military does more than protect and defend: In the span of about 23 months, it overthrew two enemy regimes located on the other side of the planet and replaced them with popularly supported govern-ments. Even as American forces deployed to Iraq and Afghanistan, they kept watch on the Korean peninsula and kept the sea-lanes open for the oil and goods that feed a truly global economy; did the dirty work of counterterrorism from Tora Bora to Timbuktu; and responded to disasters of biblical proportion in places as disparate as Louisiana and Sumatra.

This does not seem to be the handiwork of a faltering empire. Indeed, no other military could attempt such a feat of global multitasking. "The British empire," writes Niall Ferguson in *Colossus* (Allen Lane, 2004), "never enjoyed this kind of military lead over the competition . . . [and] never dom-inated the full spectrum of military capabilities the way the United States does today."

Yet the declinists say America's overseas commitments and consequent deployments are an indication of waning. Paul Kennedy warned in the 1980s that the U.S. was susceptible to "imperial overstretch" due to its overseas com-mitments. Later, Thomas Paterson maintained that military interventions in Central America during the latter stages of the Cold War "attested not to U.S. strength but to the loosening of its imperial net." Today, Matthew Parris argues that "America's might is draining away" by listing some of the disparate places U.S. troops are deployed.

As to the charge that the U.S. is overstretched, Ferguson reminds us that the United States had 3.4 million men on active duty in the 1950s, which rep-resented a sizable 2.1 percent of America's population (around 160 million at the time). By 1963, Leebaert adds, the U.S. had a million troops "stationed at more than 200 foreign bases." Today, by comparison, the U.S. has 1.4 million men and women on active duty (out of a population of 300 million). Even when activated reserve and National Guard components are factored in, only a fraction of a percent of the U.S. population is under arms today—and just 350,000 U.S. troops are deployed overseas.

Moreover, while the declinists claim that the U.S. military is too expen-sive, they seldom note that the current defense budget accounts for just 3.5 percent of GDP [gross domestic product]. That's less than the U.S. spent on defense as a percentage of GDP at any time during the Cold War—and far less than the 30 to 40 percent spent during World War II. In fact, Ferguson notes, the cost of the U.S. military was 10 percent of GDP in the 1950s. One reason for this is the enormous size of the U.S. economy. Gerard Baker of the *Times of London* notes that the U.S. economy will be twice as big as Europe's by 2021, and that, compared to China, the U.S. is adding "twice as much in absolute terms to global output." Ferguson also notes that the U.S. share of global productivity "exceeds the highest share of global output ever achieved by Britain by a factor of more than two."

In short, with a much larger economy, much larger population, and much smaller global footprint, the America of today is no more "overstretched" than the America of 1950 or 1970 or 1990.

Nor is it weaker on the diplomatic front.

Consider the U.S.-led Proliferation Security Initiative, which was born just weeks after the fall of Baghdad. To date, some 60 nations have signed on to the PSI to strengthen their capacity to secure the seas and intercept weapons of mass destruction and their precursors while in transit.

Consider the U.S.-led Container Security Initiative, which deploys U.S. Customs agents to the world's largest, busiest ports to screen goods and containers coming into the United States. Today, 43 ports in dozens of nations participate in the program, creating a ring of security well beyond America's shores.

Consider Libya's preemptive surrender of its WMD [weapons of mass destruction] arsenal in late 2003, which happened without the firing of a shot and, tellingly, came after Saddam's overthrow and capture.

Consider North Korea, which has been a challenge of the highest order for nearly six decades. It is a challenge that the current administration, like the previous ten, has not been able to fully solve—an understatement underscored by Pyongyang's penchant for testing missiles and brandishing nukes. But if diplomacy is an end in itself, as so many critics of the current administration seem to believe, then North Korea represents an example of America's diplomatic power. Recall that U.S. diplomacy cajoled four other regional powers into talks, pressured North Korea into a multilateral setting (which it opposed) and then extracted Pyongyang's promise to give up its nuclear weapons. Whether the North Koreans end up keeping this promise is a subject for another essay. What is relevant here is that Washington pursued a major policy objective to persuade all of the regional powers of its importance to them and to secure a promise from North Korea. In the 1990s, that was hailed by many in the foreign-policy establishment as something to applaud. In the 2000s, it was dismissed as evidence of U.S. weakness.

With regard to "soft power," from McDonald's to Microsoft, American culture is in high demand. Whether or not we Americans like everything our culture produces, its attractiveness around the world is undeniable—and yet another expression of U.S. power. We see this in the global popularity of Google, which was created by a pair of Stanford students without any government help at all but so dominates the web that the European Union is pouring $294 million into birthing an answer; in the PC primacy of Dell and HP; in the 330 million (and counting) PCs running Microsoft Windows; in Apple iTunes, which has swept into 20 countries and displaced local powers such as Japan's own Sony. We see this, too, in the life and times of Yao Ming, who was recognized in 2005 as China's "vanguard worker"—an honor once awarded to citizens wholeheartedly embracing communism—yet is a Texas multimillionaire who plays for the Houston Rockets.

Indeed, America has a magnetic pull on peoples of every race, religion, and region. Thirty-two million of those who live in the U.S. were born somewhere else, notes Ferguson. When they arrive, these would-be Americans find a culture eager to graft in the new and the different—a nation where a refugee from Czechoslovakia [Madeleine Albright] could be entrusted to oversee U.S. foreign policy as secretary of state, where an Austrian bodybuilder [Arnold Schwarzenegger] could become governor of the most populous state, where an Afghan immigrant [Zalmay Khalilzad] could represent U.S. interests in Kabul and Baghdad, where a Polish immigrant [John Shalikashvili] would be asked to head the Joint Chiefs or restore what 9/11 maimed.

Land of Wonders

"Declinism performs a useful historical function," Huntington has observed. "It provides a warning and a goad to action in order to head off and reverse the decline that it says is taking place." At its best, then, it is an expression of the American tendency toward self-criticism and continual improvement. This is a restless nation. Its capacity for change, its desire for change, its willingness to reevaluate and reassess itself make it easy to extrapolate periodic corrections or momentary uncertainties into downward trends—declinism at its worst. Perhaps this is why its practitioners find themselves forced to revise and defer their predictions again and again.

Writing when America was still young, Tocqueville described this country as "a land of wonders, in which everything is in constant motion and every change seems an improvement." Closer to our times, Yale historian C. Vann Woodward called optimism "a national philosophy in America." America's openness to change grows out of its optimism, which explains why most Americans do not subscribe to declinism's pessimism.

Given the breadth and depth of history, it would be foolish to think that U.S. power might not some day recede like a setting sun. Still, given our history so far, it would be just as foolish to overlook the less than stellar record of the declinists and conclude that "some day" is now.

POSTSCRIPT

Is the United States a Declining Power?

At its most superficial level, the answer to the question of whether U.S. power is in decline is "yes." Few countries have even achieved hegemonic status, and all have eventually lost that status. There was almost no chance that the United States could/can maintain the kind of hegemonic moments that it briefly had in the late 1940s and early 1990s or even the clear superpower status it has enjoyed for more than 6 years. Even as he welcomed the unipolar moment, Krauthammer also had conceded its end, "No doubt . . . will come. . . . In perhaps another generation or so there will be great powers coequal with the United States."

What really divides the so-called "declinists" who seen U.S. power ebbing from those who see a more resilient future for the U.S. presence in the world is whether the country will become just one of many relatively equal power or even fall to a second rank behind an ascendant superpower. In this scenario, China is considered the most likely replacement superpower (see Issue 6).

One of the immediately looming tests of U.S. power relates to the willingness of Americans to carry the burdens of the war in Afghanistan (see Issue 15). For good or ill, a quick U.S. exit that allows the return of the Taliban and al-Qaeda will be a retreat from power. Another looming test is what the United States will do to repair its tattered economy, including reining in the budget deficit and reducing the current accounts deficit. Without a sound economic base, American power will surely falter.

Robert J. Lieber, "Falling Upwards: Declinism, The Box Set," *World Affairs* (Summer 2008), is available at http://www.worldaffairsjournal.org/articles/2008-Fall/indexFall2008.html. Also taking that view is Fareed Zakaria, "The Future of American Power: How American Can Survive the Rise of the Rest," *Foreign Affairs* (May/June 2008). A view from an economist that in the aftermath of the Great Recession the U.S decline is accelerating is Paul Krugman, "Losing America," *The New York Times* (February 9, 2010). A common analogy when discussing U.S. power is to compare the United States with ancient Rome. A skeptical view of that analogy can be found in Vaclav Smil, *Why America Is Not a New Rome* (MIT Press, 2010).

Questions for Critical Thinking and Reflection

1. Maintaining hegemonic, or even superpower, status requires a country to expend a great deal of its economic resources and to sometimes use its military power to maintain a favorable world order. If you are an American, are you willing to commit the "blood and treasure" necessary to be a hegemonic power?

2. How do you think the course of world events would change if the United States were to take a much more restrained role in foreign affairs? This might include, for example, no longer taking the lead in pressing Iran not to develop nuclear weapons, keeping Afghanistan out of the hands of the Taliban and al-Qaeda, or ensuring that no single country dominates the oil-rich Middle East.
3. What do you think the distribution of world power will look like in 2050? Will that make for a more peaceful and prosperous world or a more turbulent one?

ISSUE 5

Should the Jackson–Vanik Amendment Targeting Russia Be Repealed?

YES: Stephen Sestanovich, from Testimony during Joint Hearings on "A Relic of the Cold War: Is It Time to Repeal Jackson–Vanik for Russia?" before the Subcommittees on Europe and on Terrorism, Non-Proliferation, and Trade, Committee on Foreign Affairs, U.S. House of Representatives (April 27, 2010)

NO: David Satter, from Testimony during Joint Hearings on "A Relic of the Cold War: Is It Time to Repeal Jackson–Vanik for Russia?" before the Subcommittees on Europe and on Terrorism, Non-Proliferation, and Trade, Committee on Foreign Affairs, U.S. House of Representatives (April 27, 2010)

ISSUE SUMMARY

YES: Stephen Sestanovich, the Kathryn and Shelby Cullom Davis Professor at the School of International and Public Affairs at Columbia University, says that it is hard to think of another piece of legislation with such an honorable past that has sunk into a comparable state of purposelessness and confusion as the Jackson–Vanik amendment.

NO: David Satter, a senior fellow at the Hudson Institute and a fellow at the Foreign Policy Institute, Johns Hopkins University School of Advanced International Studies, contends that the Jackson–Vanik amendment is far from obsolete when applied to Russia today and should be left in force.

This debate occurs at two levels. One has to do with the Jackson–Vanik amendment itself, the other relates to the current nature of the Russian government.

During the early 1970s, a major debate in the United States revolved around relations with the Soviet Union. President Richard M. Nixon was among those who sought "détente" (eased relations) with the Union of the Soviet Socialist Republics (USSR). As part of that effort, Nixon signed an agreement with the USSR in 1972 that gave its exports most-favored-nation (MFN) status. This meant that U.S. tariffs on imports from the USSR would be no higher than the lowest rate applied to the nations most favored under U.S. trade law.

Those who opposed the goal of Nixon and others to move toward normalizing relations with the USSR (and China, as well), and viewed this goal as being soft on communism, sought ways to derail détente. One such measure was an amendment to the 1974 Trade Act by Senator Henry M. Jackson (D-WA) and Representative Charles Vanik (D-OH). The amendment, which passed both houses unanimously, blocked MFN status for the USSR and other communist countries as they violated human rights by limiting emigration. The focus on emigration was in response to the efforts by Moscow to stem an increasing "brain drain" caused by scientists and other highly educated Soviets (the *intelligencia*), especially Jews, seeking to leave the country for Israel, the United States, and elsewhere. In the immediate aftermath of the amendment's passage, the Soviet Union rejected the pressure as interference in its domestic affairs and clamped down even harder on emigration. Thus, the amendment served its anti-détente goal by dampening relations between Washington and Moscow, but the amendment failed in its effort to loosen restrictions on the emigration of Jews and others from the USSR.

Because Russia is considered the "successor" country to the USSR, which atomized in 1991 into 15 countries including Russia, the Jackson–Vanik amendment still technically applies to it, and MFN status for Russia requires an annual report to Congress from the president certifying that Russia is not restricting emigration. This certification has occurred each year since 1994.

In the first selection, Stephen Sestanovich approaches the Jackson–Vanik amendment as a relic of the cold war that should be repealed because there are no significant restrictions on emigration from Russia and because the amendment serves as an unnecessary irritant to U.S.–Russia relations. David Satter disagrees in the second selection. He argues from the different level about the amendment. For Satter, the important issue is the current state human rights within Russia. Satter warns against taking the amendment too literally and contends that it can serve as a useful way to pressure Russia in response to its deteriorating democracy and accompanying restrictions on the civil liberties of Russians. Satter also notes the increase of what he terms "anti-American propaganda" by the Russian government. As such, he is among those who oppose repealing the amendment in an atmosphere of what they depict as an increasingly hostile Russian foreign policy that is at odds with U.S. foreign policy at many points, seeks to diminish U.S. global influence, and aims to reassert Moscow's control over the countries that were once part of the USSR.

YES

Stephen Sestanovich

A Relic of the Cold War: Is It Time to Repeal Jackson–Vanik for Russia?

I appreciate the opportunity to join you in today's very timely discussion of the Jackson–Vanik amendment. It is hard to think of another piece of legislation with such an honorable past that has sunk into a comparable state of purposelessness and confusion.

No one has a monopoly on this confusion. I have encountered eminent journalists who are taken aback to learn that the amendment is still on the books; senior officials of the Executive Branch who believe that the president blocks the application of its terms to Russia by sending Congress an annual waiver (he does not); and knowledgeable businessmen, in both countries, who believe that it limits the growth of trade between Russia and the United States (it does not). In my experience, there are even members of Congress who are a little fuzzy about the exact legal status of the Jackson–Vanik amendment. And it is entirely possible that some of the witnesses assembled here today (I definitely include myself) will make their own mistakes in describing its origins, its current meaning, and how it should be handled in the future.

Confusion about the amendment's continuing value or relevance in no way detracts from its historic achievements. During the Cold War it gave concrete and much needed expression to American concerns over Soviet human rights violations, and eventually facilitated the free emigration of many hundreds of thousands of people. But all this was a long time ago. It has been almost sixteen years since Bill Clinton reported to Congress that Russia was in full compliance with the terms of Jackson–Vanik. (To put this span of time in perspective, the amendment actually restricted trade with the Soviet Union for only fifteen years, between the time when it first took effect in 1975 and President Bush's decision to waive its application in 1990.) Each subsequent administration has supported President Clinton's assessment.

Today this legislation remains in force for reasons that have nothing to do with free emigration—which Russia has allowed for years—and everything to do with trade. Russia's long negotiations to join the World Trade Organization seem to be drawing to an end. And some members of Congress believe—incorrectly, to my mind—that by keeping the amendment on the books they can assure better treatment of American products in the Russian market. The unhampered movement of human beings was your concern in the past. Now it is the unhampered movement of frozen chicken.

U.S. Senate, April 27, 2010.

For many who were associated with human rights struggles over the years, this is dispiriting. A great tool for the advancement of human rights has become, as Natan Sharansky complained two years ago, "a weapon of the U.S. agricultural lobby." Having done hard time in the gulag for his desire to emigrate to Israel, Sharansky is entitled to his criticism. But there is no avoiding the fact that the Jackson–Vanik amendment is now inextricably intertwined with disputes about meat and poultry. No proposal for how to deal with it will succeed unless it also takes commercial interests into account.

The most obvious—and certainly the easiest—way to address this historical anachronism is to do nothing until Russia's accession talks with the WTO are concluded. Once accession is done, and the concerns of every nation in that organization have been satisfied, members of Congress—perhaps of these very subcommittees—can then hold a final round of hearings on Jackson–Vanik. After that they will presumably bring a resolution to the floor that "graduates" Russia—that is, declares that the amendment no longer applies to it. In this way, Russia and the United States will finally establish "permanent normal trade relations" (PNTR) with each other.

Since the end of the Cold War, most administrations have eventually been led to this strategy, and chances are that the Obama administration will do so as well. Yet there are drawbacks to waiting for the WTO to finish the job. After all, while most administrations have settled on this approach, they have not yet made it succeed. For Congress, the principal drawback of waiting for the WTO is that it actually fails to make use of leverage available to this body. Members feel that they are exercising influence on the administration's negotiation position, but this is largely an illusion. No matter what the details are of Russia's accession to the WTO, when a resolution to "graduate" Russia is finally introduced in the Congress, there is no chance that it will fail. You may think that you are reserving for yourselves the last word on WTO accession by holding on to Jackson–Vanik. The reality is different. You will simply be rubber-stamping the result.

Waiting for the WTO to act has potential drawbacks for American business as well. Russia's accession has been an almost unimaginably long process, and the longer it takes the longer American exporters will be vulnerable to arbitrary restrictions imposed on them by the Russian bureaucracy. (To take just one example, I note the April 8, 2010, letter to President Obama from the National Pork Producers Council, which complained that Russian treatment of American pork exports is incompatible with the WTO's Sanitary and Phytosanitary Agreement. When Russia finally joins the WTO, our exporters will be able to have such practices struck down through the organization's dispute-resolution procedures.)

Finally, waiting for WTO accession to produce "graduation" dodges one of the most important tasks that the U.S. government will face after "graduation"—how to think, talk, and act to advance the original goals of the Jackson–Vanik amendment. In one way or another, Russia's domestic evolution remains a concern for all states that have relations with it. It has been a large part of American policy for many decades, but today this element of our policy is badly in need of modernization. We should be thinking about the problem now. Congress—which contributed long ago by passing the amendment—can play a role in creating a new policy.

It is completely understandable that Congress is reluctant to act on "graduation" at this time. The Russian government has done too much in the last year to undermine confidence in its handling of trade issues. From the continuing imposition of new protectionist measures against American agricultural products to Prime Minister [Vladimir] Putin's peculiar announcement last June that Russia would try to join the WTO jointly with the other members of its new customs union, Russia has given few reasons for other governments to meet it halfway in these negotiations. But this may be changing. Today a very senior delegation of Russian economic policymakers is in Washington to meet with American officials, and one of the reasons for its presence may be a recognition that Russian policies have been unsustainable and counter-productive. If the next few months bring signs of a new Russian approach to trade issues, Congress should be prepared to devise a new approach as well. Its goal should be to advance both American commercial interests as well as the original concerns of the Jackson–Vanik amendment. Here's how it might do so:

- A new approach would, of course, have as its basic ingredient a willingness to "graduate" Russia from the coverage of the law, just as Congress has done with other post-Soviet states. (I should note that, despite the title of today's hearing, such a vote would not "repeal" Jackson–Vanik.)
- Before voting, Congress might also require—perhaps in the form of side-letters from the president or secretary of state—a full explanation of the administration's view of remaining accession problems. Congress will naturally want firm and specific commitments about how the administration intends to address these problems.
- As a third ingredient of its approach, Congress should also require—before agreeing to vote on "graduation"—that the administration present in some detail its future strategy for addressing issues of human rights, democracy promotion and engagement with Russian civil society.
- Fourth, the resolution that "graduates" Russia from Jackson–Vanik should specify that PNTR will come into force between Russia and the United States only with Russia's full accession to the WTO.
- Fifth, Congress might give itself the option of a final vote on the matter by requiring a further report by the secretary of state when the terms of Russian WTO accession have been agreed. If Congress objected to these terms, it would have the right—within a specified period of time—to vote a resolution of disapproval of the secretary's report. If passed by both chambers, this resolution would restore a version of the status quo. That is, "normal trade relations"—what we have now between Russia and the U.S.—would be automatically renewed each year unless the President reported that Russia was no longer in compliance with the terms of the Jackson–Vanik amendment.

Compared to the current strategy of waiting for the WTO to complete the process of accession, this approach would serve American interests in three important respects. First is a possible economic payoff. Russian–American trade is already recovering from last year's sharp downturn, but the action by Congress that I have described might help regain lost ground more quickly. By confirming that PNTR would take effect automatically with WTO accession, it would add to Russian incentives to drop the neo-protectionist measures it adopted last year in the depths of the economic crisis. An early "graduation" vote by Congress at this time might have a second, political payoff as well. President [Dimitry] Medvedev [of Russia] has emphasized how much he looks for economic benefits from the so-called "reset" of Russian–American relations. The formula described above would make no unilateral concessions to Moscow, but it would set out a mechanism for removing Russia from the coverage of the Jackson–Vanik amendment, probably without any further Congressional votes. This would surely be viewed positively in Russia—at no real cost to the integrity of American policy. It would also highlight how little Russia has done, by comparison, to put aside the pre-occupations of the Cold War.

Third, this approach would focus the attention of both Congress and the administration on the key issue that led to the adoption of Jackson–Vanik amendment in the first place—the evolution of Russia's own political and legal system. Then, as now, how Russia evolves will determine not only its moral standing in the world (this is not the view simply of Russian human rights activists—President Medvedev himself has said the same thing), but its viability as an effective partner for the United States. Yet the fact that this issue remains an American concern thirty-five years after Jackson–Vanik became law does not mean that we can expect to advance our interests in the same way that we did in the 1970s. We need a modernized strategy—one that reflects both the dramatic changes that have taken place and those that have not. We need to make use of our increased access to Russian civil society while understanding our diminished diplomatic leverage. The administration has some interesting ideas in this regard, and some of them have already begun to be put into practice. It has initiated a promising line of policy innovations that Congress can help to consolidate and institutionalize, by making them part of the process of "graduation."

The Jackson–Vanik amendment no longer offers us a viable policy. It provides no shred of usable leverage. Our task—above all, the task of Congress—is to use "graduation" to develop a strategy that re-focuses on the importance of Russia's continuing democratic evolution.

David Satter  **NO**

A Relic of the Cold War: Is it Time to Repeal Jackson–Vanik for Russia?

The future of the Jackson–Vanik amendment has now become an important issue in U.S.–Russian relations. The reason is that the U.S., having announced a "reset" in U.S.–Russian relations, cancelled an anti-missile system in Eastern Europe, and ignored Russian human rights abuses, all with little positive result, is running out of ways to show its goodwill.

Those who support rescinding the amendment point out that Russia has been in compliance with its provisions for the last 16 years. They argue that it makes no sense to retain a measure that has accomplished its purpose and now only serves to embitter bilateral relations. Unfortunately, however, we are in danger of being too literal. It is true that Russia now allows free emigration. But the Jackson–Vanik amendment was never based on an unbreakable link between trade and emigration. Opponents of the amendment correctly argued at the time that trade has nothing to do with emigration. The purpose of the amendment was to use the economic power of the United States to compel the Soviet Union to respect human rights. In this respect, it is far from obsolete when applied to Russia today.

By any measure, Russia is more liberal and tolerant than [was] the Soviet Union. Russia, however, is almost totally lawless and the absence of secure rights is not an accident. It exists in order to assure the power of a kleptocratic [thieving] elite which puts its own interests ahead of those of the nation. This creates a parallel with what existed under the Soviet Union. Like the Soviet authorities, the present Russian leaders use a supposed foreign menace to divert the attention of the population from their rightless [without rights] situation. The target of choice is not Iran or North Korea, which could pose a threat to Russia, but rather the United States.

The Jackson–Vanik amendment, in and of itself, cannot have a decisive impact on U.S.–Russian relations. But in deciding whether to rescind the amendment, it is important to remember that "good relations" with Russia are not an end in themselves. The late Andrei Sakharov [leading Soviet dissident] pointed out that there was a direct connection between the Soviet Union's internal repression and its external expansionism. In Russia, massive corruption and lawlessness give rise to policies that frustrate U.S. objectives as a matter of proactive self-defense. The object of American policy should be to seek to change this fundamental relationship.

U.S. Senate, April 27, 2010.

The Jackson–Vanik amendment should not be eliminated to "bury the Cold War," or "reinvigorate the reset." It can be rescinded but this should be done only in response to examples of clear progress in democratic governance, capable of limiting the scope of arbitrary power in Russia and improving the lot of the population. The following are examples of areas in which improvements could legitimately be tied to the elimination of Jackson–Vanik.

The Legal System

The Russian legal system, in the opinion of Russian respondents to a survey is "prejudiced, inefficient, corrupt and ready to defend whoever can pay for it." At a meeting of a group of state-controlled NGOs [nongovernmental organizations, those whose members are private individuals, groups, and/or organizations] in the Kremlin in January, 2007, the former Supreme Court judge Tamara Morshchakova argued that judicial independence was non-existent in Russia, stating that, "Any official can dictate any decision in any case." The situation with the legal system is illustrated by the case of Mikhail Khodorkovsky, a [former President, now Prime Minister Vladimir] Putin opponent and once Russia's wealthiest individual. Khodorkovsky, in an echo of Stalin era practices, is on trial for a second time on clearly fabricated charges of stealing virtually the entire production of the Yukos Oil Company. If convicted—and most observers consider conviction a foregone conclusion—he could spend the rest of his life in prison. He was convicted in 2005 of failing to pay taxes on Yukos profits and sentenced to eight years in a labor camp despite the fact that Russian tax authorities and international auditors certified that the taxes had been paid. At that time, there was no indication that the oil on which taxes had allegedly not been paid was stolen. The real reason for the second trial may be to prevent Khodorkovsky from regaining his liberty when his first sentence, which he began serving after his arrest in 2003, ends next year.

Another sign of the state of the rule of law in Russia is that Russians file more complaints with the European Court than people from any of the 46 countries that make up the Council of Europe. Most of the thousands of complaints are never heard but almost all of the small number that have been have gone against Russia.

Selective Terror

Although there is no mass repression in Russia, journalists and human rights activists risk their lives if their reporting threatens powerful interests. At least 17 journalists have been murdered in Russia since 2000. In not a single case, has the person who ordered the killing been found. In cases such as those of Anna Politkovskaya and Paul Klebnikov where underlings have been charged (only to be acquitted under puzzling circumstances) the alleged participants appear to have a maze of links to the security services themselves. Natalya Estimirova, a single mother who was virtually the only source of information on torture, abduction and murders carried out by the security services in Chechnya, was herself abducted in Grozny and murdered last year after being implicitly threatened by Ramzan Kadyrov, the president of Chechnya and a close ally of Putin. Sergei Magnitsky, a lawyer for Hermitage Capital Management who exposed a $230 million tax fraud scheme carried out by Russian officials, was accused of corruption and jailed. He then died in a prison medical unit isolation ward after being denied medical care. On the basis of the way he was treated, Magnitsky told the prison staff that someone was trying to murder him. Subsequent events indicate that he accurately foretold his fate.

Anti-American Propaganda

Despite the "reset," the U.S. is depicted in the Russian media, which is largely state controlled, as Russia's principal enemy. After the 2004 Beslan school massacre [of over 3334 hostages, including 186 children by Ingush and Chechen rebel terrorists, then President] Putin indicated that it was the West, led by the U.S. that was responsible for the tragedy. In fact, the Russian authorities bear full responsibilities for ordering troops to open fire with flame throwers and grenade launchers on a gymnasium packed with hostages including hundreds of children. At the time of the August 2008 war in [the country of] Georgia, Russians were told that a direct conflict between the U.S. and Russia seemed imminent and there were allegations that the U.S. had encouraged Georgia to attack Russia although Russian leaders were aware that the opposite was true. The global financial crisis was blamed in the Russian media on the U.S. and Russian television is replete with "Eurasianist" commentators who interpret world events as a struggle of nations as diverse as China, India, Iran and Venezuela to limit the U.S., which is intent on establishing its hegemony.

The Russian regime reacts badly to U.S. efforts to support Russian democracy but we have an interest in the success of democratic processes in Russia. Democracy in Russia, the world's second nuclear power, means stability. At the same time, undemocratic Russia is unpredictable. In a crisis, it is too easy to mobilize a rightless population against the U.S.

The Jackson–Vanik amendment will eventually be rescinded with regard to Russia. But this should be done in response to improvements in Russia's internal situation. In the absence of such improvements, haste in scrapping Jackson–Vanik is simply not necessary.

POSTSCRIPT

Should the Jackson–Vanik Amendment Targeting Russia Be Repealed?

Despite the hearings held in April 2010, no legislation had been introduced in Congress through late November of that year. An effort could still come during the final days 111th Congress (2009–2010) to try to repeal the Jackson–Vanik amendment, but given the already crowded legislative calendar and the impending shift of control of the House from the Democrats to the Republicans following the November 2010 congressional elections, it would appear likely that any such move is unlikely before the 112th Congress convenes in 2011.

Additional information on the issue is available in Julie Ginsberg, "Reassessing the Jackson–Vanik Amendment," a backgrounder, Council on Foreign Relations (July 2, 2009), which is available online at http://www.cfr.org/publication/ 19734/reassessing_the_jacksonvanik_amendment.html#/. A video of a debate among several scholars on "The Jackson–Vanik Amendment and U.S.–Russian Relations" held under the auspices of the Woodrow Wilson International Center for Scholars (February 3, 2010) is also available online at http://www.wilsoncenter .org/index.cfm?topic_id=470582&fuseaction=topics.event_summary&event_id=590749. For the views of the Russian government on the amendment, read "Jackson–Vanik Amendment Obstructs Russia–US relations—Putin" (June 18, 2010), and watch the embedded video on the Voice of Russia Web site at http://english.ruvr .ru/2010/06/18/10104777.html. Yet another online source, and one that contains the views of a representative of the Jewish community, is "The Jackson–Vanik Amendment and U.S.–Russian Relations," a briefing given by Sam Kliger, the director of Russian Jewish Affairs of the American Jewish Committee (February 3, 2010), available at http://www.ajc.org/site/apps/nlnet/content2.aspx?c=ijITI2PHKoG&b= 2818295&content_id=%7B269A3DE4-7F1B-4244-8F57-4CA2B825903A%7D&notoc=1.

More information and a relatively dispassionate view on the overarching question of the future of Russia's foreign policy are in Olga Oliker, *Russian Foreign Policy: Sources and Implications* (Rand, 2009). A more alarmed vision of Russian foreign policy is presented by Edward Lucas in *The New Cold War: Putin's Russia and the Threat to the West* (Palgrave Macmillan, 2009).

Questions for Critical Thinking and Reflection

1. The introduction to Issue 2 noted that mercantilism or economic statecraft is an alternative to capitalism and free trade as an economic model. The Jackson–Vanik amendment is an example of economic statecraft in

that it tries to manipulate trade in order to try to accomplish a political goal—free emigration. Is this a good way to conduct a country's trade relations?

2. According to the Soviet Union in the 1970s, its restrictions on emigration were not aimed specifically at any ethnic/religious group, including Jews. Instead the restrictions were meant to limit the emigration of scientists, engineers, and others, many of whom happened to be Jewish. The Soviet Union argued that emigration was hurting the ecnomy and that the émigrés had been trained at great expense in Soviet schools. Was this an irrational and/or discriminatory policy that warranted U.S. intervention?

3. Although emigration and immigration are somewhat different issues, how would you react if one or more other countries imposed sanctions on the United States unless it treated its illegal immigrants better?

ISSUE 6

Will China Soon Become a Threatening Superpower?

YES: John J. Tkacik, Jr., from "A Chinese Military Superpower?" *Heritage Foundation Web Memo* #1389 (March 8, 2007)

NO: Samuel A. Bleicher, from "China: Superpower or Basket Case?" *Foreign Policy In Focus* (May 8, 2008)

ISSUE SUMMARY

YES: John J. Tkacik, Jr., a senior research fellow in China policy at the Asian Studies Center of the Heritage Foundation in Washington, DC, contends that the evidence suggests instead that China's intent is to challenge the United States as a military superpower.

NO: Samuel A. Bleicher, principal in his international consulting firm, The Strategic Path LLC, argues that while China has made some remarkable economic progress, the reality is that the Chinese "Communist" central government and Chinese economic, social, political, and legal institutions are quite weak.

China has a history as one of the oldest and at times most powerful countries (and empires) in the world. During the Yuan dynasty (1271–1368) and most of the Ming dynasty (1368–1644), China was also arguably the world's most powerful empire, dominating most of Asia.

However, China's power compared with Europe's began to ebb with the Industrial Revolution beginning in Europe in the mid-1700s playing a major role. By the 1800s, the European powers, joined by the United States in the last years of the century, came to increasingly dominate China. The Chinese consider these years a period of humiliation, emblemized by a park in a European enclave in Shanghai that bore the sign, "Dogs and Chinese Not Allowed."

China's road back began in 1911 when Nationalist forces under Sun Yatsen overthrew the last emperor. Internal struggles and the invasion by Japan (1931–1945) blocked much advance in China's economic and political power until the Communists under Mao Zedong defeated the Nationalists under Chiang Kai-shek who fled and set up the remnants of the Nationalist government on Formosa (Taiwan) as the Republic of China.

Gradually, Communist China (the People's Republic of China, PRC) built up its strength. Military power came first. China's military was saddled by obsolete weapons, but it was the world's largest military force, numbering as many as 4.2 million troops in the 1980s. China also sought to acquire nuclear weapons and delivery capability, and succeeded in that quest by the mid-1960s.

Fundamental changes in China's status began in the 1970s. In 1971, the United Nations changed the rightful owner of China's seat, including its position as a permanent member of the Security Council, from the Nationalist government on Taiwan to the PRC. The following year, the United States relaxed its hostility, and President Richard Nixon visited China. In 1979, President Jimmy Carter shifted U.S. diplomatic recognition of the "legitimate" government of China from the Taiwan government to the PRC government. Domestically, the two great leaders of the Communist Revolution and government, Premier Zhou Enlai and Communist Party Chairman Mao Zedong both died in 1976. This opened the way for a less ideological approach to improving China's economy.

Since then, China has changed rapidly. It retains a communist government, but it has adopted many of the trappings of a capitalist economy. Where once China rejected global trade and other international economic organizations, it has now embraced them.

Economically, it is possible to argue that China is still a poor country, one whose 2009 per capita gross domestic product (GDP) of about $3,678 was far below the U.S. per capita GDP of $46,381. But China has also become one of the largest economies in the world. China's 2009 GDP was $4.9 trillion. That makes it the third largest economy in the world, still far behind the United States ($14.3 trillion), and poised to supplant Japan ($5.1 trillion GDP) in 2010 as the second largest economy. China has also become the second largest global trader, with its $2.2 trillion in exports and imports ousting Germany ($2.0 trillion) from that spot and leaving China behind only the United States ($3.5 trillion). China is also the fastest growing large economy, expanding by an annual average of over 8 percent since 1975. Much of this is industrial growth, and China is the world's fourth largest producer of automobiles and commercial vehicles and third greatest steel manufacturer.

China's growing economy and industrialization have allowed it to upgrade its military technology. The country's 2009 official defense budget was only $78 billion dollars, but there is little doubt that actual spending is higher than that, with estimates ranging from $100 billion to $150 billion. Still the amount, whatever it is, falls far short of the 2009 U.S. official defense budget ($515 billion).

What all this portends is the issue here. In the first reading, John J. Tkacik, Jr. warns that it is time to take China's military expansion seriously. Samuel A. Bleicher takes a much more restrained view of China's power and intentions in the second reading, believing that China could easily suffer major economic and political reversals.

YES

John J. Tkacik, Jr.

A Chinese Military Superpower?

On March 4, [2007,] China's National People's Congress announced that it would increase the country's military budget 17.8 percent in 2007 to a total of $45 billion. Despite the fact that this was the biggest single annual increase in China's military spending, the Chinese government reassured the world that this spending hike was normal and need not worry anyone. "China is committed to taking a path of peaceful development and it pursues a defensive military posture," a spokesman said. But the evidence suggests instead that China's intent is to challenge the United States as a military superpower.

A closer look at China's military spending raises profound questions about China's geopolitical direction. In terms of purchasing power parity (PPP), China's effective military spending is far greater than $45 billion, or even the U.S. Department of Defense's $105 billion estimate. In fact, it is in the $450 billion range, putting it in the same league as the United States and far ahead of any other country, including Russia. This figure reflects the reality that a billion dollars can buy a lot more "bang" in China than in the United States.

Within a decade, perhaps much sooner, China will be America's only global competitor for military and strategic influence. [U.S.] Director of National Intelligence Michael McConnell told the [U.S.] Senate on February 27[, 2007,] that the Chinese are "building their military, in my view, to reach some state of parity with the United States," adding that "they're a threat today, they would become an increasing threat over time." Nor is this a revelation to Washington policy-makers. McConnell's predecessor John Negroponte testified to the Senate Intelligence Committee in February 2006 that "China is a rapidly rising power with steadily expanding global reach that may become a peer competitor to the United States at some point." In June 2005, Secretary of State Condoleezza Rice observed that the U.S. must help integrate China into the international, rules-based economy before it becomes a "military superpower." Rice, with a doctorate in Soviet studies and years of experience in the White House during the last days of the Cold War, would not use the term "superpower" lightly.

It remains to be seen whether China's now massive stake in the global economy will result in Beijing becoming a responsible stakeholder in global affairs, but Beijing seems poised for true global status as a "military superpower." The latest figures from the econometricians at the Central Intelligence Agency—whose data come from the World Bank—peg China's 2006 GDP, adjusted for purchasing power parity, at $10 trillion, with a nominal exchange-rate value of $2.5 trillion.

From *The Heritage Foundation Web Memo* #1389, March 8, 2007. Copyright © 2007 by Heritage Foundation. Reprinted by permission.

Despite the Chinese Communist Party leadership's espousal of China's "peaceful rise," the unprecedented peacetime expansion of China's military capabilities betrays a clear intent to challenge the United States in the Western Pacific and establish itself as the region's predominant military power. With China's massive GDP [gross domestic product] and military spending at an estimated 4.5 percent of GDP, the resources that Beijing now devotes to its armed forces surely make it a top global power. The exact methodology that U.S. intelligence agencies use to arrive at this estimate is classified, but it reportedly takes into account the fact that China's budget figures do not include foreign arms purchases, subsidies to military industries, any of China's space program (which is under the command of the Central Military Commission), or the costs of the 660,000 strong "People's Armed Police." It appears that some defense spending sectors that are not counted in the defense budget have increased much faster than the budget itself.

At a time when The Heritage Foundation is encouraging sustained U.S. defense spending of 4 percent of GDP in an initiative called "Four Percent for Freedom," China's military budget could be called "Four-and-a-Half Percent Against Freedom" due to its involvement in countries like Burma, Sudan, Zimbabwe, North Korea, Uzbekistan, and Iran, not to mention its actions against freedom in Taiwan and, of course, in China itself.

U.S. intelligence agencies can plainly see where the money is going. China is assembling a blue-water navy, with a submarine fleet of 29 modern boats, including 13 super-quiet Russian-made Kilo class subs and 14 Chinese-made Song and Yuan class diesel electric submarines that are reportedly improved versions of the Kilos. At least 10 more of these submarines are in China's shipyards, together with five new nuclear ballistic missile and attack boats. China's surface fleet is also undergoing a similar modernization.

China's power in the air and in space is also on the rise. The People's Liberation Army (PLA) Air Force has about 300 Russian-designed fourth-generation Sukhoi-27 Flankers and a number of Chinese-built Jian-11 planes and 76 Sukhoi-30 multi-role jets. With Russian and Israeli assistance, the PLA Air Force has acquired an additional 50 or so Jian-10 fighters based on U.S. F-16 technology and reportedly plans to build 250 more. China's rocket forces are also expanding at an unprecedented pace, with production and deployment of short-range ballistic missiles targeted at Taiwan increasing from 50 per year during the 1990s to between 100 and 150 per year today. Presumably, output from Chinese ICBM factories is expanding at a similar pace. Most recently, China's January 12 test of highly sophisticated direct-ascent "kinetic kill vehicle" (KKV) technology, coupled with attempts to blind or laser-illuminate a U.S. reconnaissance satellite in 2006, are convincing evidence of the PLA's intention to neutralize the United States' military assets in space in any conflict.

Indeed, China's 2006 "White Paper" on national defense describes a China that is moving onto the offensive:

> The Army aims at moving from regional defense to trans-regional mobility, and improving its capabilities in air-ground integrated operations, long-distance maneuvers, rapid assaults and special operations.

The Navy aims at gradual extension of the strategic depth for offshore defensive operations and enhancing its capabilities in integrated maritime operations and nuclear counterattacks. The Air Force aims at speeding up its transition from territorial air defense to both offensive and defensive operations, and increasing its capabilities in the areas of air strike, air and missile defense, early warning and reconnaissance, and strategic projection. The Second Artillery Force aims at progressively improving its force structure of having both nuclear and conventional missiles, and raising its capabilities in strategic deterrence and conventional strike under conditions of informationization.

The ultimate question must be whether Beijing's leaders have any purpose in assembling a military machine worthy of a superpower other than to have the strength to challenge the United States' strategic position in Asia. It is time to take China's military expansion seriously.

Samuel A. Bleicher

 **NO**

China: Superpower or Basket Case?

China as an "emerging superpower" makes for a compelling story line in the media. It is reinforced by the propaganda image that the current Chinese leadership would like us to accept. But the reality is quite different. Although recent events in Tibet and western China—and the central government's response—appear to be generating pro-government patriotic feelings, they dramatically display the practical limits of the government's power. Other sources of unhappiness with the regime, including income disparities and the inevitable collapse of unsustainable price controls on fuel and food, could breed both urban and rural discontent that has no ready outlet besides unlawful opposition to the government.

Meanwhile, the West, in its fixation on its own economic difficulties in comparison to the Chinese "juggernaut," is neglecting to prepare for equally likely "weak China" contingencies. Just as we failed to predict and prepare for the implosion of the Japanese economy and the collapse of the Soviet Union, we appear unready for a dramatic economic and political reversal in China that would be a defining event of the 21st Century.

China is in every sense a world under construction, with the physical, social, economic, legal, and institutional blueprints being drawn and revised daily as the construction proceeds. The depth and scale of the transformation taking place in every dimension of Chinese social, economic, and political life is difficult even for the most knowledgeable observers to comprehend. With luck, this great experiment can be one of the most successful developments in human history. If it fails, the consequences for China and for the rest of us could be tragic, and possibly catastrophic.

Wow/Not Wow

As the U.S. economy slips into recession, the American media are filled with impressive-sounding statistics about Chinese economic, social, and military progress. The implicit or explicit tag line is: "Wow!" For example:

Beijing has three million vehicles and is adding 1,000 cars a day to its already gridlocked streets—Wow! In fact, the Beijing metro area of 16,000 square kilometers, with a permanent population of almost 13 million (plus another 4 million "transient" residents), has about three million vehicles. The Los Angeles

From *Foreign Policy In Focus,* May 8, 2008. Copyright © 2008 by The Institute for Policy Studies. Reprinted by permission. www.fpif.org

metro area, with a similar population but one-quarter the area, has over seven million vehicles. Nationally, China has 22 vehicles per 1,000 people, while the United States has 764 vehicles per 1,000. The Beijing gridlock reflects the serious lack of transportation infrastructure, not a large number of vehicles, and the three new subway lines opening this summer will hardly make a dent in this deficiency.

China is the world's third-largest economy and has been growing consistently at 10% per year for more than a decade—Wow! In fact, China's Gross Domestic Product (GDP) of $3.8 trillion, for 1.5 billion people, is less than one-fourth the $13.2 trillion U.S. economy, for 300 million people. (The European Union has a GDP almost five times that of China's with one third the population.) Based on energy consumption and other indicators, China's longer-term growth rate is probably more like 6% per year, according to MIT economist Lester Thurow. Or, if environmental degradation is included in the calculations, China has essentially no net growth, according to World Bank Reports and statements [of] the senior officials in the Chinese Ministry of Environment. Even assuming that the claimed 10% rate could continue uninterrupted indefinitely from China's small economic base, China would just catch up with the United States in GDP in about 20 years—but not nearly approach the United States in GDP per capita. The gap between the average Western citizen and the average Chinese citizen will not close for the indefinite future.

China's consumption of oil is responsible for about one-third of the increase in demand in recent years (and it is also consuming enormous amounts of iron, aluminum, cement, etc.)—Wow! In fact, China consumes about 9% of total global oil consumption, which compares to U.S. consumption of about 25% of the global total and over 10 times the Chinese per-capita consumption. Unquestionably the increase in consumption of oil and other natural resources by China, India, and other developing countries is raising demand more rapidly than supply, and probably more than the planet can deliver for long (even with more dramatic price increases). But the world's growing resource consumption would hardly be sustainable even without China's growing demand.

Of course the American media coverage is not all pure "wow!" Longer articles often embed the dramatic statistics in discussions of China's fundamental problems, which are legion. The disparity in income distribution exceeds even that of the United States, the government provides virtually nothing in the way of a social safety net, and most people have minimal access to health care. Its cities are choking on air pollution, and water is in short supply and unsafe to drink. But even the "balanced" articles often leave the impression that these problems are merely social welfare matters that do not fundamentally impinge on China's "superpower" status.

More scholarly works have also endorsed the "emerging superpower" image—perhaps in the hope that a catchy title will attract the necessary public attention to sell books and ideas. A valuable book of mostly economic analysis and statistics produced jointly by the Center for Strategic and International Studies and the Institute for International Economics, China: The Balance Sheet, carries a cover line, "What the WORLD needs to know now about the emerging SUPERPOWER." An article by G. John Ikenberry in the January/February 2008 issue of *Foreign Affairs* describes China as "on the way to becoming a formidable global power." Even Sinologist Susan Shirk's generally very thoughtful book on China and American foreign policy, *China—Fragile Superpower,* assumes that the country is a superpower and must be dealt with accordingly.

Inherent Weakness

It may not make such interesting reading to say that China is slowly emerging out of feudalism and desperately hopes to use the fruits of Western technology to pull its people away from the edge of starvation, at least for a few decades. And it is extraordinarily difficult to quantify the real economic limitations imposed by China's environmental and natural resource deficiencies. But these concerns are rarely given serious consideration as real constraints on China's future development. Equally important, the international policy consequences of a faltering China are not being seriously discussed or explored.

The reality is that the Chinese "Communist" central government and Chinese economic, social, political, and legal institutions are quite weak. China is ineffectually governed. It will be struggling for decades to get and stay beyond subsistence. It has built an export-dependent economy ill-suited to meeting its domestic needs, and it will shortly face insurmountable environmental and natural resource obstacles to its rapid growth. The central government has succeeded in unleashing the entrepreneurial, profit-driven economic engine, but it is unable to apply any brakes—that is, to address effectively any of the adverse effects of the single-minded focus on profit. The leadership claims that it recognizes the corrosive economic and social consequences of the current situation and is taking remedial actions. Even if it were seriously committed to these policies as a high priority, the government lacks the mechanisms to rein in the runaway horse.

China has satisfactory national laws about minimum wages and hours, child labor, food and other product safety, worker safety, intellectual property, and air and water pollution. But the central government has not effectively empowered judges and prosecutors to enforce these laws, because they are controlled by provincial and local party leaders. These officials, who often benefit personally or professionally from the success of local profit-making enterprises, are rarely inclined toward enforcement.

China's urban transformation is creating a need for a new government-managed social welfare system that disburses retirement, disability, unemployment, and child welfare benefits—functions formerly handled by the now-diluted extended family. This traditional culture is rapidly collapsing in the newly mobile, urban society.

The supposedly all-powerful central government is unable even to end its substantial subsidies of gasoline, electricity, and water consumption—for the same reasons the U.S. government is unable to raise gasoline taxes or end the mortgage interest deduction. Both fear strong popular opposition. Meanwhile, the dramatic increase in wealth has created more opportunities and incentives for corruption. The high visibility of some of this corruption—poorly-compensated expropriations of private property to help developers, for example—is creating an increasing public backlash.

The current Tibet conflict does not threaten the government domestically. But it shows how quickly events can get out of control in a globally linked media world and when there are no opportunities in China for democratic participation to absorb the energy of the dissatisfied. More threatening to the regime in this situation is public unhappiness with internal economic decisions. Though less publicized internationally, recent events like the unauthorized rallies in Shanghai in opposition to a new rail line in a middle class residential neighborhood, organized through Internet and cell phone messaging, and the demand for public hearings about the PX chemical plant in Xiamen, show the risks of decision-making without mechanisms for public participation.

The popular "emerging superpower" picture in our media mostly takes at face value the central government's assertions about the success of its governance. The government claims primary credit for the "economic miracle" and the dramatic transformation of Beijing, Shanghai, and other major cities. It asserts that all of the country's environmental, social, and economic problems are manageable, and that it controls everything that happens in China. The government may indeed be able to lock up or kill off several thousand dissidents (a comparatively easy task logistically, though recent events in Tibet have shown that there is still a significant domestic and international cost). But that is a much easier task than designing and implementing necessary modern economic, regulatory, and social welfare institutions and programs in a society that has almost none. So far it has not demonstrated real success in those arenas.

China is big in almost every dimension, and its international influence has been increasing, as one would expect of a society comprising one-quarter of the world's people. But does that make it a "superpower"? Or even a "power"? What exactly is the "power" of 500 million near-subsistence farmers who mostly lack substantial electricity, safe drinking water, and indoor plumbing, and whose education consists largely of the ability to write and read a few prescribed texts? How much "power" is gained by adding in another 500 million educated city-dwellers with Western consumer aspirations who may well be living in economically and ecologically unsustainable Potemkin Villages? Balanced against its very real difficulties, China's capabilities are certainly not as great as they are often portrayed.

Military Ambitions?

China is expanding its military spending and technical capabilities, but it is hardly a global threat in any rational context. The Pentagon estimates 2006 Chinese military spending at less than $90 billion; most other estimates are lower. Compare that amount to the $440 billion FY 2007 appropriation for U.S. military spending, not counting $50 billion for Iraq and Afghanistan. The growth in the Chinese military budget more likely reflects the Communist

Party's need to buy the army's loyalty, rather than any imperialist military ambitions. Chinese civilian worker productivity is about 4% of American worker productivity, and a roughly similar productivity ratio probably applies to its military machine as well. Against the combined U.S., Japanese, and Taiwanese military forces, any military venture would be nothing less than a catastrophe for China.

This military balance against China severely limits any rational military ambitions. China's only active military focus grows out of its adamant opposition to Taiwan's independence, an issue that appears likely to recede as a result of this year's elections in Taiwan. China certainly wants enough military capability to make its threat of military action credible to Taiwan, the United States, and Japan. The Chinese tradition of military strategy is built around outwitting and outmaneuvering the enemy, not applying overwhelming brute force.

For that purpose the appearance of strength is important, but the actual use of force would reflect a strategic failure. Worse, any serious, long-term military engagement could easily create just the kind of domestic economic dislocations and shortages that, after the initial burst of patriotic enthusiasm, would feed social and political dissatisfaction, which the regime rightly fears most. The months-long adverse consequences of last winter's blizzard show the true vulnerability of China's economic structure.

Economic Power?

China's economic "power" is significantly less than the often-quoted statistics suggest. U.S. industrial imports from China amounted to less than 3% of the U.S. GDP in 2006 (up from less than 0.5% of GDP in 1993). The standard statistics on U.S.–China trade volume vastly overstate China's economic benefit. Only about one-third of the nominal value of China's exports reflects goods actually manufactured in China. China is still largely an assembler, and most of the components come from abroad. China's manufacturing is heavily dependent on imports of components, raw materials, energy supplies, intellectual property, and financial and other management skills, which all result in economic outflows.

Moreover, a significant part of China's current price competitiveness has grown out of its postponement of the costs of safe and sustainable management of its natural and human resources. Recent indications are that some of these postponed costs are coming due. The government is already spending billions of yuan (directly and by ordered closures) to dismantle environmentally unredeemable manufacturing facilities in time for the Olympics. More billions are being invested to divert water from agricultural uses to supply the growing cities of dry northern China.

Thus the much-discussed financial reserves China has accumulated are mostly offset by real-world social welfare and environmental debits to repair and maintain their human and natural resources. And the value of China's international reserves, mostly invested in declining U.S. dollar paper assets, depends almost entirely on the economic viability of the United States, the

EU, and Japan. China was apparently a significant loser in the U.S. subprime mortgage collapse, though the actual amounts have not been revealed. This dependency deprives China of the kind of independent economic power of Saudi Arabia or Russia, which control substantial physical resources.

International political power is largely derived from the world's perception of a nation's independent military and economic resources, and its willingness to invest them—and risk them—in order to change the behavior of other nations. Thus China's international political influence depends in significant part on what the Chinese government says, and what we believe, about its capabilities and intentions. Though it would like the West to believe otherwise, China cannot afford to risk significant military or economic resources in international political competition.

The Real Threat

In light of these realities, the West is overly focused on the Chinese "emerging superpower" threat and giving far too little attention to the real risks and foreign policy challenges that would flow from a serious breakdown in Chinese economic, political, or social structures. A crisis might be triggered by any number of factors. A dramatic slowdown in the Chinese or world economy could disrupt the lives of millions of factory workers. Serious rationing of water, food, or energy, whether by dramatic price increases or some other mechanism, could be unacceptably painful for a large part of the population. The loss of individual savings from a stock market or banking collapse could fuel popular discontent among the new urban elite. Even with continuing economic progress, widening income disparities could generate increasingly serious opposition in rural areas. A widespread farmers' strike might cut off food to the urban centers, leaving them in a state of chaos.

Systemic crisis could then lead to an open challenge to the regime. Here are two scenarios to consider. In one, students, factory workers, and peasants gather again in Tiananmen Square to protest economic conditions and perceived political non-responsiveness. When urban professionals start to join them, the central government calls in the army. It begins a brutal campaign of violently repressing demonstrators, arresting domestic and foreign media representatives, and purging uncooperative members of the Party and civilian government, entirely disregarding the legal system. The demonstrations do not stop, and various groups ask for outside help to protect foreign residents and foreign investment and to end the wholesale disregard of human rights. Overseas Chinese and major U.S. banks and corporations with investments and supply lines at stake argue that the situation is too dangerous to ignore.

In the second scenario, the central government's inability to control the economy or cure the country's problems becomes increasingly obvious. The educated, urbanized residents of Shanghai and the urbanized areas around Hong Kong increase control over their regional governing systems, perhaps through more democratized Party elections, and disregard Beijing's directives. Taiwan offers economic and technical assistance to these areas, with the aim of creating more of a "one China, many systems" environment. In response, the Chinese military threatens to impose military rule on Shanghai and Hong Kong, and to recapture Taiwan. The new local leaders ask for help from Taiwan and other nations to avoid the bloodbath, economic disruption, danger to U.S. and other foreign citizens, and destruction of foreign investment property that will inevitably result if no one comes to their aid.

Responding to Chinese Instability

Some American hardliners may believe that the United States should encourage crisis and regime collapse in China. However, nothing in Chinese history, or in the history of revolutions and coups almost anywhere, gives any reason to believe that a collapse or violent change in Chinese leadership would be followed by a more stable, more reliable, more democratic, or more cooperative international actor than the current central government. The tragedies of the French revolution, the Russian revolution, the post-World War II coups in Eastern Europe, and the Chinese cultural revolution are far better indicators of what might come next if faltering economic progress or other stresses of transformation become unmanageable.

In our globalized economic world, the West could not simply sit back and smile as China disintegrates. Chaos in China is far more threatening, economically, politically, and militarily, to the United States and the world than China's current "peaceful rise." Both for China's sake and our own, we must help the Chinese succeed in their transition to a 21st-century economy and society. Being better prepared for possible failures along the way is an essential component of planning for and realizing that goal. Western leadership needs to think now about how it would rank and balance various potentially conflicting objectives, including protecting diplomats and foreign citizens, salvaging Western investments, ensuring the stability of the global economy, protecting human rights, avoiding unpredictable military action and reaction, and maintaining civil relations with those who claim to be in power in Beijing.

The West needs to act immediately and more vigorously to help strengthen Chinese civil institutions, recognizing the continuing imperative of the Chinese government to show improvements in its domestic economic and social structures. The 2007 Party Congress was filled with rhetoric about "democracy." But real democracy—the broad diffusion of power beyond the Party and its attendant government bureaucracies, to independent legal institutions, media, and non-government organizations—will only be implemented if it is seen as a means of promoting social harmony and strengthening the authority of national laws over local corruption and opportunism. Arguments that China should expand individual human rights as an independent moral objective are unlikely to motivate the central government. Rather, the central government should be persuaded to decentralize power and create a diverse civil society to create the social resilience, adaptability, and sense of participation that will enable it to survive through the coming storms. The current Tibet controversy, because it is perceived by most Chinese as an ungrateful challenge to territorial integrity, is only a shadow of what may lie ahead.

Finally, we must also prepare for the worst. First, our foreign policy and military planners must develop and publicly discuss contingency plans for the consequences of a dramatic setback in Chinese economic growth and resulting breakdowns in domestic order. Second, we need stronger mechanisms to avoid miscommunication of military movements, lest we lurch into a World War I-like disaster as hardline propaganda and sensationalist media lock both China and other governments into inflexible postures. Third, if the physical entry of national or multilateral military forces into any part of China is unthinkable under all circumstances, we must identify other steps that might be taken to minimize and mitigate the destruction of life, property, social order, and global economic activity. What leverage, if any, can the outside world bring to bear on the central government or the military, without military intervention? Can the threat, or imposition, of economic sanctions, embargoes, blockades, or other tools have a significant impact in time to avoid disaster? Can the UN make any difference at all in this context? Timely, coordinated response by the outside world might make a difference; slow reactions and uncoordinated U.S., EU, and Japanese positions will almost certainly accomplish nothing.

The Chinese propaganda machine is doing its best to make us (and the Chinese people) believe the government has everything under control and on track. We must not take its claims of economic and military strength at face value. We need a more realistic understanding and perspective on the nature and scope of China's growing capacity and hidden weaknesses, learning more about its limits as well as its strengths. And we must think seriously about how the West might proceed to address the global interest in conditions in China if a real breakdown occurs.

POSTSCRIPT

Will China Soon Become a Threatening Superpower?

One of the reasons that Richard Nixon sought to begin the process of normalizing relations with China more than three decades ago was that he believed China was not only on the road to becoming a superpower but also that it might become the predominant country in the twenty-first century. While it remains unclear if Nixon was correct or not, there can be no doubt that China's power continues to develop. It still has the world's largest military (about 2.3 million troops), and its array of nuclear weapons and delivery systems, while still smaller than those of the United States and Russia, is substantial. Preliminary data for 2008 indicate that China's economy and its defense spending continue to grow rapidly.

How to react to the growth of China is one of the hottest topics in national security circles. To a degree, it is only natural for China to seek a military capability to protect itself and to promote its interests in Asia and perhaps globally. That is what the United States does and, to a lesser degree, other countries do as well. Certainly China has come a long way toward that goal, but the Chinese began from a very low military technology point and their weaponry remains far behind U.S. standards. Still, China's military technology has improved substantially, and it is most likely to use its military muscle in Asia, where it has a geographical advantage over the far distant United States. Moreover, China's forces are concentrated in Asia; those of the United States are dispersed globally.

For a view that the status of Taiwan is the point of greatest peril for relations between China and the United States, see Richard C. Bush, Michael E. O'Hanlon, *A War Like No Other: The Truth about China's Challenge to America* (Wiley, 2007).

One key to China's intentions will be not only how much weaponry it acquires but also the configuration of those weapons. Those "power projection" weapons systems, such as aircraft carriers or amphibious landing capabilities, which would allow China to apply military power far from its own territory, are the most likely to signal expansive Chinese diplomatic ambitions. A recent study of the advances in Chinese military capabilities is in David Shambaugh, "China's Military in Transition: Politics, Professionalism, Procurement and Power Projection," *China Quarterly* (2009). There are numerous sources to keep track of China's weapons and military policy. Since many have a point of view, it is better to consult more than one. Three such sites are the Project on Defense Alternatives' "Chinese Military Power" Web page at http://www.comw.org/cmp/, that of GlobalSecurity.org at http://www

.globalsecurity.org/military/world/china/index.html, and that of China Defense Today at http://www.sinodefence.com/.

Whatever China's long-term intentions and prospects to be a global superpower may be, there is no doubt that the country is becoming increasingly important on the world stage. One of many projections about China's intentions is Samuel S. Kim, "Whither Post-Mao Chinese Global Policy?" *International Organization* (2009). In the regional balance of power in Asia, a status explored by David Shambaugh is *Power Shift: China and Asia's New Dynamics* (University of California Press, 2006).

There are numerous articles and books that focus on the future of U.S.–China relations. Two of the most recent are Rosemary Foot and Andrew Walter, *China, the United States, and Global Order* (Cambridge University Press, 2010) and Robert G. Sutter, *U.S.–Chinese Relations: Perilous Past, Pragmatic Present* (Rowman & Littlefield Publishers, 2010). For China's view of itself and its relations with the United States, visit the Web site of China's embassy in Washington, DC, at http://www.china-embassy.org/eng/.

Questions for Critical Thinking and Reflection

1. Would it be wiser for the United States to follow policies that try to restrain China's power and/or build alliances, weapons systems, and other measure to counterbalance it or to try to accommodate China now to ensure good relations with a budding superpower?
2. Which is a more valid measure of China's economic power: China's overall GDP, which is the world's second largest, or China's per capita GDP, which ranks China 124th of 213 countries and territories measured by the World Bank and is one-thirteenth the size of the U.S. per capita GDP?
3. Assume China is on the road to becoming a superpower. Other than the unlikely scenario of a nuclear attack on the United States, how specifically would that status for China threaten the United States?

ISSUE 7

Would It Be an Error to Establish a Palestinian State?

YES: Patricia Berlyn, from "Twelve Bad Arguments for a State of Palestine," An Original Essay Written for This Volume (2006)

NO: Rosemary E. Shinko, from "Why a Palestinian State," An Original Essay Written for This Volume (October 2006)

ISSUE SUMMARY

YES: Patricia Berlyn, an author of studies on Israel, primarily its ancient history and culture, refutes 12 arguments supporting the creation of an independent state of Palestine, maintaining that such a state would not be wise, just, or desirable.

NO: Rosemary E. Shinko, who teaches in the department of political science at the University of Connecticut, contends that a lasting peace between Israelis and Palestinians must be founded on a secure and sovereign homeland for both nations.

T he history of Israel/Palestine dates back to biblical times when there were both Hebrew and Arab kingdoms in the area. In later centuries, the area was conquered by many others; from 640 to 1917 it was almost continually controlled by Muslim rulers. In 1917 the British captured the area, Palestine, from Turkey.

Concurrently, a Zionist movement for a Jewish homeland arose. In 1917 the Balfour Declaration promised increased Jewish immigration to Palestine. The Jewish population in the region began to increase slowly, then it expanded dramatically because of refugees from the Holocaust. Soon after World War II, the Jewish population in Palestine stood at 650,000; the Arab population was 1,350,000. Zionists increasingly agitated for an independent Jewish state. When the British withdrew in 1947, war immediately broke out between Jewish forces and the region's Arabs. The Jews won, establishing Israel in 1948 and doubling their territory. Most Palestinian Arabs fled (or were driven) from Israel to refugee camps in Gaza and the West Bank (of the Jordan River), two areas that had been part of Palestine but were captured in the war by Egypt and Jordan, respectively. As a result of the 1967 Six Day War between Israel and Egypt, Jordan, and Syria, the Israelis again expanded their territory by capturing several areas, including the Sinai Peninsula, Gaza, the Golan Heights, and the West Bank. Also in this period the Palestine Liberation Organization (PLO) became the major representative of Palestinian Arabs. True peace was not possible because the PLO and the Arab states would not recognize Israel's legitimacy and because Israel refused to give up some of the captured territory.

Since then, however, continuing violence, including another war in 1973, has persuaded many war-exhausted Arabs and Israelis that there has to be mutual compromise to achieve peace. Perhaps the most serious remaining sore point between the Arabs and Israelis is the fate of the Palestinians, who live primarily in the West Bank and Gaza.

In 1991 Israelis and Palestinians met in Spain and held public talks for the first time. Israeli elections brought Prime Minister Yitzhak Rabin's liberal coalition to power in 1992. This coalition was more willing to compromise with the Arabs than had been its more conservative predecessor. Secret peace talks occurred between the Israelis and Palestinians in Norway and led to the Oslo Agreement in 1993. Palestinians gained limited control over Gaza and parts of the West Bank and established a quasi-government, the Palestinian authority led by Yasser Arafat.

The peace process was halted in 1995 when Prime Minister Rabin was assassinated by a Jewish fanatic opposed to Rabin's policy of trying to compromise with the Palestinians. Soon thereafter, conservative Prime Minister Benjamin Netanyahu came to power. He dismissed any possibility of an independent Palestine, made tougher demands on the PLO, and moved to expand Jewish settlements in the West Bank. With some 200,000 Jews already in the West Bank and East Jerusalem, these actions compounded the difficult issue of the fate of those people in a potentially Palestinian-controlled area.

Pressure from a number of quarters, including the United States, has kept the government of Israel and the Palestinians talking, at least at times. President George W. Bush announced his support of a Palestinian state, declaring in 2003, "A two-state solution to the Israeli-Palestinian conflict will only be achieved through an end to violence and terrorism." At times there has been optimism in the region. Arafat died in late 2004 and was succeeded by a seeming moderate, Mahmoud Abbas. Then Israel withdrew the last of its troops from Gaza in 2005, leaving it under full Palestinian control. Just a few months later, though, much of the world was appalled when the Palestinians gave representatives of Hamas, a terrorist organization, control of the Palestinian parliament. Matters worsened in June 2006 when Palestinian gunmen entered Israel and seized an Israeli soldier. The Israelis responded with a sharp military attack on Gaza. The next month, members of the militant Muslim group Hezbolla based in south Lebanon captured two other Israeli soldiers in a cross-border raid. The incident set off a major Israeli military response, which pummeled Lebanon for weeks, destroying a good part of the country infrastructure. It is at this juncture that Patricia Berlyn wrote her essay arguing that creating an independent Palestinian state would be a grave error and Rosemary E. Shinko wrote her reply contending that there is no hope for peace without a Palestinian state.

YES

Patricia Berlyn

Twelve Bad Arguments for a State of Palestine

In 1991, during the administration of President George H. W. Bush, the government of the United States officially pledged to the government of Israel:

> In accordance with the United States' traditional policy, we do not support the creation of an independent Palestinian state. . . . Moreover, it is not the United States' aim to bring the PLO into the [peacemaking] process or to make Israel enter a dialogue or negotiations with the PLO.

A decade later, President George W. Bush announced his administration's "vision" of establishing an Arab State of Palestine west of the Jordan River. The vision was quickly ensconced in a U.N. Security Council Resolution.

This reversal of policy is based on the supposition that the pesky Israel-Palestine-Arab problem can be solved via a Two-State Solution (Israel and Palestine). Actually, it would be a Three-State Solution, because both Israel and Jordan are states within the bounds of Mandate Palestine (see Argument 3).

The necessity of an additional division of that very small area is promoted with twelve arguments that have become a kind of mantra.

1. Israel's Occupation of Palestinian Territory Is the Cause of an Islamic Jihad That Spreads Much Discomfiture Across Several Continents. Only the End of Occupation and the Proclamation of a State of Palestine Can Relieve the World of This Discomfiture

On the contrary There is no Israeli occupation and no Palestinian Territory. Rather, there is Israeli administration of a section of Mandate Palestine that still has no assigned sovereignty. The right to this land may be debated, but it should not be dictated with a foregone conclusion based on casual assumptions.

This sliver of land, viewed as an issue of prime and urgent global importance, is hard to find on a map of the world without a magnifying glass. Israel knows it by its biblical name of Judea-Samaria. Jordan dubbed it the West Bank. It is not the crux of the Palestine problem and its growing international repercussions, and transforming it into a State of Palestine will exacerbate not solve that problem.

An original essay written for this volume by P. J. Berlyn (2006). Copyright © 2006 by McGraw-Hill Companies.

A realistic view depends on understanding the Muslim belief that the world is divided into two sections: *Dar al-Islam* [House of Islam] and *Dar al-Harb* [House of War]. Any land once acquired by Dar al-Islam must remain within it forever and ever. If it is lost—as in Spain—it must one day be regained. Dar al-Harb will eventually be conquered by *jihad* [struggle for the faith], military or otherwise.

"Palestine" was once part of the Ottoman Turkish Caliphate, and thus Dar al-Islam. It must never be yielded to any infidel, least of all to Jews, those despised and downtrodden *dhimmis,* the "sons of apes and pigs." Thus, Israel's existence as a sovereign nation is permanently intolerable, and will be so wherever its borders are set. The goal, whether declared or disguised, is the total obliteration of Israel. [Note: *Dhimmis,* an Arabic word, are non-Muslims living in a country governed by the sharia, Muslim religious law.]

The current half-and-half approach to the Palestine problem is futile. It will not satisfy Israel's foes nor lead them toward genuine peace. Rather, it will dilute Israel's ability to defend itself against those foes and thereby encourage them to go to war. Policymakers who grasp the real issue have two options: (1) Facilitate the destruction of Israel, in hopes that it will mollify Dar al-Islam and postpone jihad against Dar al-Harb. (2) Strengthen, not weaken, Israel because it is the frontline of defense against jihad, and if the jihadis can overcome so staunch a nation they will be emboldened to move on to other prey.

2. The United States Will Benefit from Establishing a State of Palestine, and Win Arab Support for Its War on Terror

On the contrary   A Palestine-Arab State will be an enemy of the United States, not a friend or ally. The "vision" of a State of Palestine that is a democracy, has leaders untainted by terror, and wants to live peacefully side-by-side with Israel is not a vision but a mirage.

Under the Oslo Accords of 1993, Israel put much of Judea-Samaria under the control of the PA [Palestine Authority], and it quickly became a terrorist entity. In advance of Israel's withdrawal from Gaza in 2005, President Bush stated: "I can understand why people think this decision is one that will create a vacuum into which terrorism will flow. . . . I think this will create an opportunity for democracy to emerge. And democracies are peaceful." The Hamas/Fatah regime that was soon elected in Gaza quickly demonstrated that terrorism flows and democracy does not emerge.

The Palestine-Arabs for whom the U.S. administration evinces much sympathy are fiercely anti-American. They admire and side with every enemy of the United States: Nazi Germany, the Soviet Union, Saddam Hussein, Al-Qaeda. They rejoice at events that bring pain and loss to the American people, and celebrate them with cheering, singing, dancing, and distributing sweets. The official religious leaders of the Palestine Authority curse America and pray for its destruction.

Israel, in contrast, is strongly and sincerely pro-American, and shares its values, many of them rooted in a shared biblical heritage. The American people sense this affinity, and strongly oppose the notion of a State of Palestine imposed on the Land of Israel.

If the Administration compulsively pursues its vision, it will create a dysfunctional terrorist entity that is both hostile to the United States and a perpetual dependent of the American taxpayers who have already been made to waste billions of ill-spent dollars on the Palestinian experiment.

3. It Will Rectify an Historic Injustice to the Palestine-Arabs

On the contrary   Of all that Arabs have demanded for themselves since the end of World War I, they have been given 99.5 percent. They were given 22 states, with a combined area of 6,145,389 square miles. Israel has 8,000 square miles of sovereign territory and 2,000 square miles of disputed territory.

Judea was conquered by Rome 2000 years ago, and renamed "Palastina." It was not again a nation or sovereign state until 1948. In the interval, it was a province of one foreign empire or another; usually a backward, neglected, and misgoverned province. In recent centuries Western travelers to the Holy Land found the Land of Milk and Honey now desolate, barren, decayed, uncultivated, and almost empty of population.

From the late nineteenth century onward, Jewish pioneers came to restore the land of their fathers, bringing it back to life by clearing rocks, draining swamps, carrying water, planting crops, and building villages and towns.

After World War I and the collapse of the Ottoman Turkish Empire, Great Britain governed Palestine under a League of Nations Mandate that covered the area that is now Israel, Jordan, the West Bank, and Gaza. The terms of the Mandate repeated those proclaimed by Great Britain itself in the Balfour Declaration, issued by Foreign Secretary Arthur Balfour in 1917: Palestine was to be developed as a "Jewish National Home," open to "close Jewish settlement."

If Britain had honored these terms, there might never have been a Palestine problem. Instead, the British government violated them.

First, it detached all the land east of the Jordan River, more than three-quarters of Mandate Palestine, to provide a kingdom for a protégé Arab emir who had been expelled from Saudi Arabia. There was no historic name suitable for this kingdom so it was called after a river: Trans-Jordan and later Jordan.

In the remaining sector west of the Jordan River, Jewish immigration and settlement were progressively restricted and then banned. There was a rigid blockade against Jews trying to escape the hell-fires of Nazi Europe that consigned an incalculable number of them to death. At the same time, Britain allowed massive immigration of Arabs into Mandate Palestine, filling up the empty places meant for but denied to the Jews.

The offspring of these recent Arabs migrants and those who had preceded them by a few decades are today's "Palestinians" who claim the Land of Israel as their ancient ancestral heritage. Neither the name nor the claim predates the year 1967. Until then, Arab spokesmen and scholars insisted that there was not and never had been any such place as Palestine—only Southern Syria.

In 1948, the United Nations undertook a second partition of the Jewish National Home to create a second Arab state therein. Had the Arabs accepted the offer, they would have had 83 percent of Mandate Palestine. Instead, they went to war to get 100 percent of it. The series of wars that the Arab states launched were for the destruction of Israel and for their own aggrandizement. There was no interest in a state for the Palestine-Arabs.

The failure of the concerted Arab attack on Israel in the Six-Day-War of 1967, led to a revision in Arab rhetoric. The fight against Israel would continue, but it would win more sympathy if it were fought in the cause of "Falastin." This name is an Arabic mispronunciation of the Greco-Roman Palastina. The would-be-nation that claims to have held this land since the dawn of history has no name of its own. The ploy was so successful, that soon most of the world's governments, media, and academics adopted and disseminated with precipitate enthusiasm the fabrication of a Palestine unjustly stolen and unlawfully occupied by the Jews.

It is not unjust that the Arab world should have to make do with 22 states instead of 23. It is not unjust that there should be only one Arab state in Mandate Palestine instead of two. The injustice would be to deprive Israel of the heartland of its historic homeland, an erstwhile wilderness that it toiled to rebuild and restore.

4. It Will Satisfy the Demands of the Palestine-Arabs, Who Will Give Up Terrorism and War and Settle Down to Building a Society

On the contrary   The charters of Fatah, Hamas and Hezbollah define their goal as the destruction of Israel and they cling to that goal even when they fight each other for control of the areas that Israel gives up.

Hamas does not disguise its bloody intentions. Fatah's Mahmoud Abbas/ Abu Mazen, chairman of the PA, speaks literally in two tongues: In English he professes a willingness to recognize Israel and co-exist with it; in Arabic he says the opposite. He is a lifelong terrorist, former second-in-command to Yasser Arafat, but if he says the right word in at least one language, Western policymakers can embrace him without violating their own rule of not dealing with terrorists, and demand that Israel jeopardize its own most vital interests to strengthen him in the interests of the Peace Process.

A plurality of the Palestine-Arab population has demonstrated through both election polls and opinion polls that it prefers the Hamas line, approves of suicide bombings and murder of Israelis, and believes that a prospective State of Palestine should keep up such attacks until Israel disappears.

Where the Palestine Authority is in power, maps show Palestine as an all-Arab entity with Israel obliterated. In the year 2006 it is declared that the Israeli Occupation has been going on for 58 years—dating it back to Israel's Declaration of Independence in 1948, not the loss of territory in 1967. In schools and summer camps, children are taught to aspire to martyrdom by killing Jews. None of this suggests that Palestine-Arabs plan ever to co-exist with Israel on any terms.

The PLO (Palestine Liberation Organization) in 1974 formally adopted a plan to be carried out in two stages: (1) Take whatever territory Israel can be persuaded or forced to yield. (2) Use that territory as a base for the future war to take all of Israel. Stage 1 was achieved with the Oslo Accords and the empowerment of the PA. Yet one of its top ministers and spokesmen, Faisal al-Husseini, defined the forthcoming Stage 2 as: "Whatever we get now, cannot make us forget this supreme truth. If we agree to declare our state over . . . the West Bank and Gaza, our ultimate goal is the liberation of all historic Palestine from the River [Jordan] to the Sea [Mediterranean]."

This purpose and intent has never been changed.

5. It Will Bring Peace and Stability to the Middle East

On the contrary   It will establish a sovereign national base for violent jihad. This can be deduced from the evidence of experience.

Every area from which Israel withdrew its administration and security patrols is now a base for terrorism and/or preparation for military attack: In Ramallah and other PA enclaves, bombings are planned and perpetrators dispatched to their targets. In the border zone of Lebanon, the Iranian-sponsored Hezbollah installed missile bases and launchers, whence they have so far fired some 4,000 deadly Katyusha missiles into Israel and brought devastation to Lebanon. In Gaza, Fatah and Hamas steadily shoot Kassam rockets into Israeli towns. When Israel relinquishes control, it opens the way for massive imports of weapons and explosives, and infiltration by Al-Qaeda. These are consequences of withdrawal, and no measures to prevent or counter them have any effect.

There is no reason to suppose that a State of Palestine will deviate from this pattern. It will be a base for terror and jihad, in a location where it can imperil both Israel and Jordan. Secretary of State Condoleeza Rice has said, "There can be no peace without a Palestinian state." That forecast can be amended by cutting a mere three letters: "There can be no peace with(out) a Palestinian state."

6. A State of Palestine Will Be Demilitarized and Not a Danger to Israel

On the contrary   A State of Palestine cannot be kept demilitarized. If it signs an agreement or treaty to that effect it will be worthless because promises to infidels are not binding. Arafat compared the Oslo Accords to a treaty Muhammad made with an Arabian tribe that he then attacked and annihilated.

The PA was bound by signed agreement to have only a police force of no more than 8,000 with no heavy weapons. It acquired a military force of at least 50,000 with heavy weapons. Nothing was done about this violation because neither Israel nor any other nation demands that Arabs adhere to agreements. It is prudent to anticipate that a State of Palestine will not be subject to any effective restrictions on its doings. As in Gaza and the Lebanese border zone there will be a massive influx of heavy weapons and trained fighters.

The strategic danger to Israel of a Palestine-Arab state was analyzed by the U.S. Joint Chiefs of Staff, who reported that Israel must at the very least keep control of the highlands of Judean Hills and the Jordan valley. Without them, Israel at its narrowest point is only nine miles wide. "Palestine" holding the adjacent highlands can bombard much of Israel with missiles and rockets and shoot down civilian aircraft. Foreign troops can sweep in across the Jordan Valley without hindrance.

An administration that forces Israel out of these vitally strategic points rejects the counsel of its own highest-ranking military men. As though this were not ill-advised enough, it also demands that a State of Palestine must have "contiguity." That is: Judea-Samaria and Gaza must be linked together. It is geographically impossible to satisfy this demand without splitting Israel in half.

To render Israel so vulnerable is an invitation to massive military attack upon it.

7. If a State of Palestine Commits Aggression Against Israel, Then Israel Can Take Back the Land It Gave Away

On the contrary   The supporters of the Oslo Accords said. "If they [the PLO] do not keep their commitment to peace, we will just take the land back." No commitment was kept, and nothing was taken back.

Regaining the forfeited land would require a military campaign, difficult, perhaps long, and costly in casualties. It would be carried out against a background chorus of denunciations and demands to cease and desist. In the past, when the Israel Defense Force has gone into PA-held areas even briefly, to close down terrorist bases and weapons factories and depots, there were international howls for Israel to "get out of Palestinian territory immediately." Any such defensive move against a State of Palestine would be branded as aggression against a sovereign state, perhaps even with a threat of sanctions against Israel and/or intervention by foreign troops.

In the event of a full-scale military attack on Israel, it might be granted some right of self-defense, but even that would be limited. If Palestine were on the verge of crumbling, the United Nations would likely save it with an imposed ceasefire. If Israel were to regain any or all of its forfeited land, there would be international pressure for it to yield the land to the defeated aggressor, just as there has been with territories won in the Six-Day War.

8. If Israel Does Not Cut Away from Regions with Large Arab Populations, the Arabs Will Soon Become a Majority and Rule over the Jews

On the contrary   This argument, sometimes dubbed "The Demographic Time-Bomb," rests on erroneous statistics and unsound projections.

The calculations are based on a census by the Palestine Authority. An examination of the statistics and the methods of compiling them found that the number of Arabs was over-estimated by one million or more. Estimates of population growth depend on an inflated anticipated Arab birthrate.

More precise calculations yield both a smaller Arab population and an ongoing drop in the Arab birthrate. Furthermore, there is little if any immigration to PA areas, and indeed a high percentage of the residents say they would like to emigrate if they had the means. In Israel, in contrast, the birthrate is steady or rising, and there is ongoing immigration.

9. It Will Secure the Human Rights of the Palestinian Arabs and Solve the Arab Refugee Problem

On the contrary   The PA regime in areas of Judea-Samaria and with full sway in Gaza has nothing to its credit in human rights.

Wherever Fatah and/or Hamas rules, there are no human or civil rights or rule of law. Those under their rule are subject to oppression, extortion, and brutality. Those accused of offenses have no right of fair trial, and at times are lynched without trial. Christians are especially vulnerable to harassment and abuse, and desecration of their churches. Their communities, which long pre-date the Muslim incursion into the region, are shrinking and dwindling away. There would not be a live Jew anywhere in a State of Palestine.

To the Arab refugees, whose plight the United Nations has deliberately perpetuated for almost 60 years, a State of Palestine would bring no relief. The chieftains of Fatah and Hamas, along with the rulers of Saudi Arabia and other Arab states, insist on a Right of Return. That is: Israel itself must take in the massive population of the United Nations camps for Palestine refugees and their descendants, who are taught and trained to loathe it and dedicate them-selves to destroying it. This impossible demand is designed to evade solving a problem deliberately perpetuated for propaganda.

10. It Will Encourage Civic and Economic Development, Raise the Standard of Living and Bring Contentment to the People

On the contrary   In areas under PA control, the standard of living drops and hardship increases.

When the disputed territories were entirely under Israeli administration, there was economic growth, a rise in the standard of living, improved health care, and the establishment of the first universities. Since administration was turned over the PA, there has been a slide backwards. Economic develop-ment is strangled by graft and corruption, and revenues are squandered. The development of an economy and a civic infrastructure are not a priority.

The United States and the European Union have subsidized the PA so lavishly that the Palestine-Arabs have received per capita more donations than any other group in the world. The bulk of the money melted away, ended up in private foreign bank accounts, or was spent on buying weapons and train-ing terrorists. Some individuals have gotten very rich, but little benefit has seeped down to the working-class or the unemployed-class.

In civil society, schools are for the indoctrination of martyrs-to-be; radio and television stations are for propaganda, recruitment of terrorists, and curses upon Israel and America; streets are for gang-warfare. There is water and electricity only because Israel still provides it.

As the standard of living sinks, international agencies cry "Humanitarian Crisis!" and blame it on Israel—especially in Gaza, where there has been no Israeli presence or control since August 2005.

11. Israel Must Comply with United Nations Resolutions

On the contrary The United Nations is a world epicenter of corruption engaged in active hostility against Israel. It has made itself a foe and should be treated as such.

Israel has never been granted the rights and protections due to a member state. Since 1948, Arab states that are U.N. members have perpetrated every form of aggression against Israel, without interference or even rebuke. There is a built-in anti-Israel majority that churns out anti-Israel resolutions, while no resolution with even a shade of balance can pass.

The Secretariat that is the administrative branch of the United Nations celebrates an annual Day of Solidarity with the Palestinian People, and the Secretary-General poses in front of a map of Palestine from which Israel has been obliterated. Peacekeeping troops aid and abet Arab terrorists in the kidnapping and murder of Israelis. Demands for Israeli compliance focus on the obsolete Security Council Resolution 242, passed in the wake of the Six Day War of 1967. The Council did nothing to hinder the Arab states in their openly announced intent of launching a war to exterminate Israel. When they had lost the war and along with it control of Judea-Samaria [West Bank], East Jerusalem, Gaza, the Sinai Peninsula, and the Golan Heights, the Council presumed to dictate the terms of a future peace settlement: Israel should withdraw from unspecified "territories" to "agreed and secure borders." The United States and Great Britain, who wrote the resolution, gave official and unequivocal assurances that it did not mean Israel's return to the pre-war frontiers, which were merely the ceasefire lines of the War of Independence of 1948–1949. This Resolution is widely misquoted in a falsified version that requires Israel's full and unconditional withdrawal from all of the land the Arabs lost in 1967, and the establishment of a Palestinian state. This is not true.

The United States and Great Britain, the authors of Resolution 242, have since reneged on the words of their own past governments and call for Israel's full or near-full surrender of the disputed territories to a Palestine-Arab state-to-be. This flip-flop demonstrates that if Israel makes any sacrifice in deference to the United Nations there will be more demands for more severe sacrifices.

12. It Will Win the Respect of World Opinion for Israel

On the contrary Honest and informed opinion does not need to be bought. Dishonest and ignorant opinion is not worth buying.

Some holders and makers of opinion are fair-minded or even friendly toward Israel. Their views can include reasonable disagreements and criticisms made without malice.

Some are automatically hostile to Israel because of Judeophobia, or ideology, or financial interests in the Arab world, or a desire to curry favor with Israel's foes, or simply because it is a fad. They do not make their judgments according to anything Israel does or does not do, and Israel cannot affect them.

Some judge only by what they hear from teachers—many of whom fit into the "automatically hostile" category—and the popular news media, whose practitioners have slipped from slanting news against Israel to complicity in lies and hoaxes.

Israel can and should do more to bring accurate facts and explanations to public attention. It should never compromise its own best interests and jeopardize its own security to oblige distant opinion-makers.

Conclusion

Giving up Judea-Samaria would cut the Jewish People off from the heart of the land to which they have been bound for almost 4,000 years. Arabs would destroy ancient Jewish sites and relics, as they have already done in Jerusalem. There would be no chance for scholars and archeologists to make new discoveries, and much knowledge of the past would be lost. And all this loss would be on behalf of an ill-advised political experiment.

Even so, it may be said "It is useless to oppose a State of Palestine—it is inevitable." Such passive submission is moral indolence, a limp acceptance of a plan regardless of the harm it is bound to do.

For 2000 years, the Jewish people did not despair of restoration to their land. When the restoration has at last come, those who toss it away betray both their ancestors and their descendants.

Rosemary E. Shinko  **NO**

Why a Palestinian State

A Two State Solution

On July 8, 1937, the Palestine Royal Commission (Peel Commission) offered its recommendations to the British government regarding the disposition of the Palestinian question. The commission expressed serious reservations about the possibility of reconciliation between Arabs and Jews and thus concluded: "only the 'surgical operation of partition' offers a chance of ultimate peace." The commission proposed the establishment of two separate states—a sovereign Arab State and a sovereign Jewish State.

President, Bill Clinton reiterated these same sentiments in a speech he delivered on January 7, 2001. "I think there can be no genuine resolution to the conflict without a sovereign, viable, Palestinian state that accommodates Israel's security requirements and the demographic realities." Any settlement, he continued, must ultimately be "based on sovereign homelands, security, peace and dignity for both Israelis and Palestinians." In 2002 the UN Security Council adopted a US supported resolution supporting the establishment of an independent Palestinian state. The current Bush administration has also expressed support for statehood as part of its roadmap for peace in the Middle East.

Why is it then that Patricia Berlyn argues that the creation of a 23rd Arab state would be unwise, unjust and undesirable? Her arguments revolve around the following five main assertions: (1) there is no such thing as a 'Palestinian territory' (2) nor do the Arabs constitute a 'Palestinian people,' (3) if such a state were established the Arabs would be unable to fulfill the rights and duties associated with statehood, (4) it would not be in the self-interest of the State of Israel because its [the Palestinian state's] aim would be Israel's demise, and finally it would betray the sacrifices of the past and the promises of the future of the Jewish people.

Berlyn's arguments follow an all too familiar pattern, one which seeks to denigrate the 'other,' in this case the Palestinian other, at the expense of constituting an Israeli identity that encircles itself with all of the admirable qualities, distances itself from any responsibility for the plight of the Palestinians, and claims the moral high ground of victimization at the hands of an illegitimate, infidel other. For instance she equates all Palestinians with former and current enemies of the United States: the Nazis, Communists, Saddam Hussein and al-Qaeda. Jewish settlements in the late 19th century are characterized as making profitable and industrious use of land that was otherwise wasted, uncultivated, and barren. These characterizations bear a striking resemblance to [English philosopher John] Locke's arguments in his fifth chapter on property in the *Second Treatise of Government* [1689], which were a carefully crafted argument intended to justify European colonization and deny the consent of the wasteful, non-industrious indigenous inhabitants whose land was taken from them.

What is a 'state' and why does the possibility of the creation of a Palestinian state; in particular, provoke such a strong, emotional response from Berlyn? What does the term 'state' signify? According to [German philosopher Georg Wilhelm Friedrich Hegel (1770–1831)], "only those peoples that form states can come to our notice" because it is the state that provides the foundation for "national life, art, law, morality, religion, [and] science." The political identity of most peoples is inextricably bound up with the notion of statehood. According to an international relations text, *International Politics on the World Stage,* written by John Rourke and Mark Boyer, "States are territorially defined political units that exercise ultimate internal authority and that recognize no legitimate external authority over them." The political implications of legitimacy that would flow from the establishment and recognition of a Palestinian state are extremely significant in this particular instance.

As scholar Malcom Shaw notes in his 1999 Cambridge University Press book *International Law,* a state is recognized as having a 'legal personality,' which includes the capacity to possess and exercise certain rights and to perform specific duties. These rights and duties encompass the attributes of independence, legal equality, and peaceful coexistence. Thus a Palestinian State would claim the right to exercise jurisdiction over its population and territory, as well as the right to self-defense. Such a state would also have a concomitant duty not to intervene in the internal affairs of another state and a duty to respect the territorial integrity and sovereignty of other states.

The Palestinians have been denied anything that has even remotely resembled an independent sovereign existence that is not determined by and ultimately reliant upon Israeli dictates. Israeli settlements have served to cut the West Bank in half, isolating East Jerusalem, and carving the economic heart out of the Palestinian territories, according to Jeff Halper in the *Catholic New Times* on April 24, 2005. The patchwork of Palestinian designated areas currently resembles apartheid inspired Bantustans, which serve to further isolate and impoverish their residents. [Note: Bantustan was one of the segregated, theoretically autonomous enclaves in South Africa in which white South Africans once forced many of the country's blacks (who speak Bantu and other languages) to live.]

Legitimacy and Equality

The establishment and recognition of a Palestinian state would confirm the political legitimacy and legal equality of the Palestinian people. Historically they have been denied recognition as a people, and the legitimacy of their claims to the territory of Palestine has been dismissed. Berlyn's arguments are designed to foster the sense of Palestinian illegitimacy with her intimations that the Arabs have 'no roots and no history' in Palestine and that there is 'no such thing as a Palestinian territory'. To round out her argument, she employs the [traditional Hebrew] term 'Judea-Samaria' when referring to the territory that would constitute a Palestinian State in order to historically delegitmate and rupture Palestinian connections to their homeland, while attempting to privilege the historical primacy and unbroken continuity of Israeli claims. Only a state troubled by its own legitimacy would find it necessary to work so hard to represent their historical lineage in the form of an unbroken line from the dim mists of the past to the clarity of the present.

All states are man-made creations; all states are reflective of the political, legal, social, and economic conditions which led to their rise. All states, even the State of Israel, are current and ongoing political creations of contemporary men and women. But more importantly, she attempts to cover over the fact that states are not divinely sanctioned nor guaranteed by claims to lineage alone, but instead created out of hard fought political struggles, compromises, and bargains. Berlyn's arguments, which are framed to effect the dismissal of a Palestinian presence and history, are an extension of earlier Zionist attempts to portray Palestine as a 'land without people for a people without land'. Such a perception promotes the view that the territory of Palestine was 'empty' and that its only inhabitants were uncivilized, backward nomads.

Demographic realities, however, prove otherwise. "There were always real, live Palestinians there; there were census figures, land-holding records, newspaper and radio accounts, eyewitness reports and the sheer physical traces of Arab life in Palestine before and after 1948," according to Edward W. Said, and Christopher Hitchens in their 1988 study, *Blaming the Victims, Spurious Scholarship and the Palestinian Question*. In 1947 when the United Nations Committee on Palestine (UNSCOP) made its recommendation that Palestine be portioned into two separate states, there were 1.2 million Arabs as compared to 570,000 Jews living in the territory. Clearly the Arabs formed the majority of the population in Palestine. On what basis then can it be maintained that the Palestinians had no history, had no roots, and had no presence in Palestine? "The fact is that [when] the people of Israel . . . came home, the land was not all vacant," President Clinton commented in 2001. Statehood confirms presence, establishes legitimacy, confers recognition, and provides a focal point for a people's identity.

Recognition and Self-Determination

David Shipler in an October 15, 2000 article in the *New York Times* commented astutely that "Recognizing the authenticity of the other in that land comes hard in the midst of the conflict. Yet the conflict cannot end without that recognition." Ultimately legitimacy and recognition are the keys to the end of conflict and to the establishment of peace in the Middle East. Peace cannot occur without the recognition of the Palestinian people's right to self-determination and without their consent to a government that exercises authority within a territorial sovereign entity of their own. "The six wars with the Arabs created a situation in which 3 million Jews came to control territories that contained nearly 2 million Arabs," scholar John G. Stoessinger observed in his 2001 book, *Why Nations Go to War*. The United Nations General Assembly also concluded that without "full respect for and the realization of these inalienable rights of the Palestinian people," namely the right to self-determination and the right to national independence and sovereignty, there would be no resolution of the question of Palestine.

Statehood implies the capacity to maintain certain rights and the performance of specific duties. Berlyn maintains that even if the Palestinians were granted their own state they would not live up to the duties of a state because a Palestinian State would be committed to the destruction of Israel and would merely serve as a base for further acts of terror. In her estimation a Palestinian State would not respect the territorial integrity and sovereignty of the State of Israel. Furthermore, she even questions the ability of such a state to be able to fulfill the requirements of statehood, including civic and economic development and the promotion of human rights. Fundamentally such a negative assessment rests on conjecture and an underlying sense of distrust born of conflicting claims of legitimacy to the same parcel of land.

No one can claim to profess the future, and not even Berlyn can with any certainty predict the actions of a State of Palestine, much less characterize an entire people as terrorists. One thing does however appear to be foreseeable, and that is the continued agitation of the Palestinians for recognition, self-determination and legitimacy. As Professor Stoessinger concluded in *Why Nations Go to War*, "The shock inflicted on the Arab consciousness by the establishment of Israel and the resulting homelessness of a million native Palestinians grew more, rather than less, acute as Arab nationalism gathered momentum." The Arabs perceive Israel as the ever-expanding and ever-growing threat to their survival, thus a state is the only way to insure their continued existence as a people. Declaring that a Palestinian State would be unable to fulfill the requirements of statehood is merely a thinly veiled ethnocentric critique, which smacks of patronization and cultural superiority. What precisely do the Palestinians lack that would deem them ill suited to exercise self-rule and incapable of founding a government that rests on consent which would secure their rights to life, liberty and property? The Lockean assertion that the only legitimate form of government is that which rests on consent is as true for the Jews as the Arabs of Palestine.

Equivalence and Justice

Israel feels exposed and vulnerable as a direct result of the Palestinians' unrelenting quest for legitimacy and recognition. Israel's economic strength and military power dwarfs that of the Palestinians, yet despite all of the material aspects of power, the Israeli quest for security remains more elusive than ever. Berlyn's arguments reiterate the mantra that Israel will never be secure unless the Palestinians are erased via absorption into neighboring Arab states. The very existence of the Palestinians serves as a constant reminder of the ongoing exclusionary colonization practices carried out in furtherance of Israel's quest for ethnic and religious homogeneity. Thus a case can be made that Israel ultimately wishes to expunge the Palestinians and obliterate any traces of their existence.

However, Israel's self-interest may ultimately rest with the establishment of a separate Palestinian state in order to diffuse the longstanding animosities and hatreds that have arisen between the two peoples. Walid Khalidi, in a 1978 article in *Foreign Affairs*, forcefully argued that a sovereign Palestinian state would end their "anonymous ghost-like existence as a non-people" because their own state could serve as "a point of reference, a national anchorage, a center of hope and achievement." We have seen where the denial of legitimacy has taken us, and it has not nurtured the seeds of peace. In a spasm of frustration in January 2006 the Palestinians elected a Hamas-dominated leadership to the Palestinian Legislative Council. In a setting in which all of the really significant political decisions are made by Israel, moderation has no chance to prevail when desperation is the defining attribute of life itself within the occupied territories. Peace can only be established in the wake of the recognition of legitimacy and equality between the two peoples.

Berlyn offers us 12 justifications why a Palestinian state is a bad idea; however, the Palestinian case rests on only one singular point: that justice demands equivalence. In order to secure the national character and the cultural identity of the Israelis, the national character and the cultural identity of the Palestinian Arabs must likewise be secured. This can only occur with the establishment of a separate, sovereign Palestinian State.

POSTSCRIPT

Would It Be an Error to Establish a Palestinian State?

More about the history of the current conflict between Jews and Palestinian Arabs is in Bernard Wasserstein's *Israelis and Palestinians: Why Do They Fight? Can They Stop?* (Yale University Press, 2008). A somewhat critical view of Israel is former President Jimmy Carter's *Palestine: Peace Not Apartheid* (Simon & Schuster, 2006), a book that evoked a spirited response by Alan Dershowitz in *The Case Against Israel's Enemies: Exposing Jimmy Carter and Others Who Stand in the Way of Peace* (Wiley, 2008).

Complicating matters for Israel is its division between relatively secular Jews, who tend to be moderate in their attitudes toward the Palestinians, and Orthodox Jews, who regard the areas in dispute as land given by God to the Jewish nation and who regard giving up the West Bank and, especially, any part of Jerusalem as sacrilege. Furthermore, more than 400,000 Israelis live in the West Bank, and removing them would be traumatic for Israel. The issue is also a matter of grave security concern. The Jews have suffered mightily throughout history; repeated Arab terrorism represents the latest of their travails. It is arguable that the Jews can be secure only in their own country and that the West Bank (which cuts Israel almost in two) is crucial to Israeli security. If an independent Palestine centered in the West Bank is created, Israel will face a defense nightmare, especially if new hostilities with the Palestinians occur. Additional material on a prospective Palestinian state is available in Virginia Tilley, *The One-State Solution: A Breakthrough for Peace in the Israeli–Palestinian Deadlock* (University of Michigan Press, 2010).

Thus, for the Israelis the "land for peace" choice is a difficult one. Some Israelis are unwilling to cede any of what they consider the land of ancient Israel. Other Israelis would be willing to swap land for peace, but they doubt that the Palestinians would be assuaged. Still other Israelis think that the risk is worth the potential prize: peace.

Palestinians do not march in political lockstep any more than do Israelis. Indeed, there has been serious tension and even fighting between Fatah, the more moderate Palestinian faction led by Palestinian National Authority Mahmoud Abbas, and the more militant group Hamas, which the United States considers a terrorist organization. Further complicating matters, Israel's government has been somewhat unstable in recent years. In 2010, nine political parties have seats in the Knesset, with no party holding more than 23 percent of the seats. The United States has tried to encourage peace in the area, but failed to achieve it. An inside look at that process by former U.S. ambassador to Israel Martin Indyk is his *Innocent Abroad: An Intimate Account of American*

Peace Diplomacy in the Middle East (Simon & Schuster, 2009). As President Bush did, President Obama favors a separate Palestinian state.

During recent years, there had been no movement of note on the issue until at the urging of the United States, Israel and the Palestinians agreed in early September 2010 to resume direct negotiations for the first time in two years. "This moment of opportunity may not soon come again," Obama said heralding the talks, and Palestinian President Mahmoud Abbas and Israeli Prime Minister Benjamin Netanyahu expressed cautious optimism. Yet the same obstacles remain and such hopeful statements have been common in the past, only to prove to be false prophets.

Questions for Critical Thinking and Reflection

1. Under what terms other than a Palestinian state is there any chance of establishing a stable peace?
2. Is it possible to have a truly stable Palestinian state if, as it is true now, about 17 percent of its population is made up of Jewish "settlers" living in enclaves within West Bank that are not subject to the authority of the Palestinian government?
3. Given the history of violence against Israel and the continuing strength of Hamas among the Palestinians, how would it be possible to make Israel feel secure enough to allow a Palestinian state to come into existence?

ISSUE 8

Is Patient Diplomacy the Best Approach to Iran's Nuclear Program?

YES: Christopher Hemmer, from "Responding to a Nuclear Iran," *Parameters* (Autumn 2007)

NO: Norman Podhoretz, from "Stopping Iran: Why the Case for Military Action Still Stands," *Commentary* (February 2008)

ISSUE SUMMARY

YES: Christopher Hemmer, an associate professor in the Department of International Security Studies at the Air War College, Maxwell Air Force Base, Montgomery, Alabama, writes that while a nuclear-armed Iran will pose challenges for the United States, they can be met through an active policy of deterrence, containment, engagement, and the reassurance of America's allies in the region.

NO: Norman Podhoretz, editor-at-large of the opinion journal *Commentary,* argues that the consequences of Iran acquiring nuclear weapons will be disastrous and that there is far less risk using whatever measures are necessary, including military force, to prevent that than there is in dealing with a nuclear-armed Iran.

The global effort to control the spread of nuclear weapons centers around the Nuclear Non-Proliferation Treaty (NPT) of 1968. Under it, 85 percent of the world's countries that adhere to the NPT pledge not to transfer nuclear weapons or assist a nonnuclear state to make or otherwise acquire nuclear weapons. Nonnuclear countries also agree not to build or accept nuclear weapons and to allow the UN's International Atomic Energy Agency (IAEA) to monitor their nuclear facilities to ensure their exclusive use for peaceful purposes.

The NPT has not been a complete success. India and Pakistan both tested nuclear weapons in 1998. Israel's possession of nuclear weapons is an open secret. None of them agreed to the treaty. Currently, there are tensions over two countries that have agreed to the NPT. One of those countries is North Korea, which adhered to the NPT in 1970, then violated the treaty in the early

1990s by moving toward building nuclear weapons. Diplomacy failed to halt the development program, and North Korea tested a nuclear weapon in 2006.

Iran, like North Korea, agreed to the NPT in 1970. At that time, Iran was ruled by a pro-Western monarch, Shah Mohammad Reza Pahlavi, who was overthrown in 1979. After the Shah fled, the Ayatollah Ruhollah Khomeini returned from exile and founded a theocratic political system that condemned Western values and influence.

During the 1980s, Iran fought a horrendous eight-year war with Iraq, one in which Iraq used chemical weapons. Partly because of that war and the assumption that Iraq had nuclear weapons ambitions, Iran moved not only to generate enriched uranium and take other steps necessary to generate nuclear fuel for energy, but also to build nuclear weapons. This program also reflected a combination of Iran's desire to become a regional power and its fear of the United States. Among other concerns, President George W. Bush had said Iran was one of the "axis of evil" countries promoting terrorism and had ordered the U.S. invasion of two neighboring Muslim countries, Afghanistan in 2001 and Iraq in 2003. The United States by 2003 was urging international pressure to force Iran to give up its program. Three European Union countries—France, Germany, and Great Britain (the EU-3)—took the lead trying to persuade Iran to end its dual-use efforts. Iran negotiated, but also claimed that its intentions were peaceful and that it had the sovereign right to develop nuclear power. With no progress being made, the council of the International Atomic Energy Agency (IAEA) voted overwhelmingly in February 2006 to refer the matter to the UN Security Council. Since then, the EU-3 have become increasingly critical of Iran, and indications that the country intends to acquire nuclear weapons have grown, but there has been little progress toward persuading Iran to abandon that effort. Christopher Hemmer writes in the first article that moving militarily to disarm Iran would probably damage America's interests in the region so much that the likely costs would far outweigh the benefits. Norman Podhoretz disagrees in the second reading, saying that allowing Iran to acquire nuclear weapons will set the stage for the outbreak of a nuclear war that will become as inescapable then as it is avoidable now.

YES

Christopher Hemmer

Responding to a Nuclear Iran

What should American foreign policy be if current efforts to discourage Iran from developing nuclear weapons fail? Despite the recent resumption of high-level contacts between Iran and the International Atomic Energy Agency, and the potential for stronger action by the United Nations Security Council, an Iranian nuclear weapon remains a distinct possibility. The current debate regarding US policy toward Iran revolves around the relative merits of a preventive military strike, including the possibility of seeking regime change in Tehran, versus a policy that focuses on diplomacy and economic sanctions to dissuade Iran from pursuing a nuclear bomb. This debate, however, risks prematurely foreclosing discussions regarding a wide-range of foreign policy options should diplomacy and sanctions fail to persuade Tehran to limit its nuclear ambitions.

The choices America would face if Iran developed nuclear weapons are not simply between preventive military action and doing nothing. The calculations America would face are not between the costs of action versus the costs of inaction. A nuclear-armed Iran will certainly pose a number of challenges for the United States. Those challenges, however, can be met through an active policy of deterrence, containment, engagement, and the reassurance of America's allies in the region.

American Interests

The United States has three strategic interests in the Persian Gulf: maintaining the flow of oil onto world markets, preventing any hostile state from dominating the region, and minimizing any terrorist threat. Given these interests, the challenges posed by a nuclear-armed Iran need to be addressed by a policy that minimizes the threat to key oil production and transportation infrastructure and negates any Iranian bid for regional hegemony. Additionally, any action taken toward Iran has to be weighed against the potential impact it may have with regard to the global war on terrorism and ongoing US initiatives related to nation-building in Iraq and Afghanistan. Moreover, such a policy needs to be executed in a manner that avoids any nuclear threat to the United States or its allies.

The end-state the United States should be working toward, as a result of these strategic interests, is an Iran that is an integral part of the global economy, at peace with its neighbors, and not supportive of terrorist organizations. While

From *Parameters*, by Christopher Hemmer (37:3), Autumn 2007, pp. 42–43. Published by the U.S. Army War College. Reprinted by permission.

America's strategic interests do not include the proliferation of democracy, any acceptable end-state will likely require some measure of democratic reform. Given the fact that anti-Americanism and anti-Zionism are an integral part of the Islamic Republic's identity, some measure of regime evolution will be required in an effort to advance America's long-term interests.

The Perils of a Preventive Strike

Any attempt to disarm Iran through the use of military options would in all likelihood damage America's interests in the region. While a military option might inflict significant damage on Iran's infrastructure by damaging or destroying its nuclear weapons program, disrupting its regional ambitions, and possibly serving as a deterrent to future proliferators, the likely costs would far outweigh the benefits.

First, any military action against Iran would send seismic shocks through global energy markets at a time when the price of oil is already at record highs. Since Iran relies heavily on the income derived from oil exports, it is unlikely that it would withhold petroleum from global markets. Iran may, however, threaten to disrupt the flow of traffic through the Strait of Hormuz or sponsor attacks on key oil infrastructure on the territory of America's Gulf allies. Such actions could hurt the US economy and potentially bolster Iranian revenue by raising the price of oil. While it is true that the world market would eventually adjust to such actions, as James Fallows has noted, that is a bit like saying eventually the US stock market adjusted to the Great Depression.

Any direct military action against Iran could also have a significant impact on America's war on terrorism. Such action would only serve to confirm many of Osama bin Laden's statements that the United States is at war with the world of Islam. This charge would be difficult to counter, given the fact that the United States has looked the other way for years with regard to Israel's nuclear program, accepted India as a legitimate nuclear-state, and is negotiating with North Korea regarding its nuclear ambitions.

Any military action against Iran would also undermine America's nation-building efforts in Iraq and Afghanistan, due to possible Iranian retaliation in both countries. While Iranian efforts toward stabilizing these two states have been sporadic at best, and purposively obstructive at worst, there is little reason to doubt that Iran could make achieving US objectives in Iraq and Afghanistan far more difficult. Although mostly bluster, there is some truth to former Iranian President Ali Rafsanjani's argument that as long as American troops maintain a formidable presence on Iran's borders, "it is the United States that is besieged by Iran." The same holds true regarding Iran's ties to Hezbollah and its presence in Lebanon. By targeting Iran's nuclear program the United States would unwisely encourage Iranian escalation in a number of these arenas.

Military strikes against Tehran would also undermine Washington's long-term goal of seeing reform movements succeed in Iran. If the history of military incursions and the Iranian nation teach us anything it is the fact that intervention is likely to solidify support for the current regime. The idea that the

Iranian people would react to a military strike by advocating the overthrow of the existing regime is delusional. Instead the likely outcome of any direct military incursion would be the bolstering of the current regime.

Moreover, any preventive attack, no matter how effective, is only a temporary fix. First, such a campaign will eliminate only that portion of Iran's nuclear program known to intelligence agencies. Even after the extensive bombing campaign of the 1990–1991 Gulf War, subsequent inspections discovered large parts of Iraq's unconventional weapons programs that were previously unknown. More importantly, even if such an attack succeeded in eliminating significant facets of Iran's nuclear program, it would do little toward discouraging Iran from rebuilding those assets. Thus, even after a fully successful denial campaign, the United States, in a number of years, would likely face the prospect of having to do it all over again.

The Problem with Regime Change

Given the limits of any preventive strike, perhaps the United States should not restrict its goal in Iran to simply nuclear disarmament, but opt instead for the broader objective of regime change. If successful, regime change in Iran could provide for a number of benefits. It may eliminate the Iranian threat of interrupting the flow of oil from the region; it would also send a strong message to potential proliferators about the costs of similar actions; it might diminish Iran's support for terrorism; even possibly eliminate the threat of official Iranian meddling in Iraq and Afghanistan; and could potentially curtail Iran's nuclear ambitions.

The reason a policy advocating regime change is a bad idea, given its potential benefits, is the fact that such a policy is beyond America's means. While the United States certainly possesses the capability to eliminate the regime in Tehran, as the invasion of Iraq has shown, eliminating the present leadership is the easy part of regime change. The more difficult and costly challenge is installing a new government. With America's resources already overly committed in Afghanistan and Iraq, taking on a new nation-building mission in a country far larger and in some ways far more nationalistic than Iraq would be the epitome of strategic overreach.

Additionally, one of the few scenarios where Iran might use its nuclear capability would be if Tehran believed that the United States intended to exercise forcible regime change. A nuclear strike against any American presence in the region might be seen by the leadership in Tehran as its last hope for survival. It goes without saying that once any government has crossed the nuclear threshold, forcible regime change by an external actor is no longer a viable option. The threat of nuclear retaliation would simply be too great. Indeed, this is probably the most important reason why states such as Iran and North Korea desire nuclear weapons. Does this mean that the United States should therefore seek regime change before Iran develops its nuclear capability? No; even without nuclear weapons, forcible regime change in Iran and the ensuing occupation would entail too great a commitment of resources on the part of the United States. Pursuing regime change in Iran as a response to its nuclear program would be akin to treating a brain tumor with a guillotine. The proposed cure is worse than the disease.

A Better Policy: Deter, Contain, and Engage

Fortunately, US policy options for dealing with a nuclear Iran are not limited to preventive military strikes, regime change, or doing nothing. A more promising option would have four key components. First, deter Iran from ever using its nuclear weapons. Second, prevent Iran from using its nuclear status to increase its influence in the region. Third, engage Iran in a meaningful way that encourages the creation of a government friendly to the United States and its regional allies, one that does not sponsor terrorism. Finally, such a policy should reassure US allies in the region that America's commitment to their security is steadfast. This four-pronged strategy would do a better job of protecting American interests in the region than any military strike or forcible regime change.

Deter

America's overriding concern regarding Iran's nuclear weapons program is that these weapons are never used against the United States or its allies. Fortunately, the strategy of nuclear deterrence can go a long way in resolving this problem. The threat of annihilation as the result of an American retaliatory strike can be a powerful deterrent. As the United States and the Soviet Union discovered during the Cold War and as India and Pakistan have recently learned, the threat of nuclear retaliation makes the use of such weapons problematic.

The central question in any debate over America's policies toward a nuclear Iran is whether or not the regime in Tehran is deterrable. If in fact it is, then deterrence is a less costly and risky strategy than prevention. Proponents of the preventive use of military force argue, as did the alarmists in the late 1940s with regard to the Soviet Union and in the early 1960s about China, that Iran is a revolutionary state seeking to export its destabilizing ideology. For these analysts Iran is often depicted as a regime of religious zealots that cannot be deterred because they are willing to accept an apocalyptic end to any conflict.

While Iran's track record with regard to its foreign policy does indicate a regime that is hostile to America, nothing would indicate that Iran is beyond the realm of nuclear deterrence. The bulk of the revolutionary fervor demonstrated by the Islamic Republic during its infancy died during the long war with Iraq. Moreover, the power of nuclear deterrence lies in the fact that precise calculations and cost and benefit analyses are not needed given the overwhelming costs associated with any nuclear exchange. Iranian leaders are rational enough to understand that any use of nuclear weapons against the United States or its allies would result in an overwhelming and unacceptable response.

What about President Mahmoud Ahmadinejad talking of wiping Israel off the map or the former President Rafsanjani declaring that while Israel could not survive a nuclear war, the Islamic world could survive a nuclear exchange? Fears related to such rhetoric need to be viewed in a historical context. Similar arguments were made about the Soviets and Chinese as they developed their nuclear arsenals. The fear of many Cold War hawks was that the Kremlin was run by ideologues. Wasn't it a fact that they did not shirk while watching 25 million of their own killed in World War II; nor did they flinch while millions more were murdered in internal purges? This demonstrated, many argued, that the Soviet leadership would be impervious to the logic of mutually assured destruction. Indeed, at times Mao Tse-Tung offered strikingly similar rhetoric to that coming out of Tehran today. He also boasted about how China could afford to lose millions in a nuclear exchange and still emerge victorious. Such worries turned out to be baseless with regard to the Soviets and the Chinese, and such rhetoric proved to be just that, rhetoric. While the bizarre views and hostile statements coming from Iran's current President are cause for concern, one must also be cognizant of the fact that the President of Iran is not the commander-in-chief of the armed forces and, in reality, has little influence over the nuclear program. The Supreme Leader does, however, and Ayatollah Ali Khameni has distanced himself from the most bellicose of Ahmadinejad's rhetoric.

To counter these ominous tirades one could look to more reassuring statements, such as Supreme Leader Khameni's argument that nuclear weapons are un-Islamic. More enlightening, however, than comparing dueling quotes, is an examination of what Iran has done in terms of its foreign policy. Iran has shown itself to be pragmatic in its actions to protect national interests, foregoing the activities one associates with a religiously driven revolutionary state.

Following the collapse of the Soviet Union, contrary to expectations, Iran did not seek to export its revolution to parts of the former Soviet Union, understanding that their national interest lay in forging a solid and profitable relationship with Russia. Iran even went so far as to dismiss the war in Chechnya as an internal Russian matter. Similar calculations of national interests led Iran to support Christian Armenia over Muslim Azerbaijan. Following the 1991 Gulf War, Iran did not push for a Shia revolution in Iraq, fearing that the outcome would probably be too dangerous and destabilizing. Following its isolation during the Iran–Iraq War Iran worked vigorously to improve relations with its Gulf neighbors.

But does Tehran's antipathy toward the United States and Israel outweigh its long-term national interests? No; indeed, during the Iran–Iraq War Tehran was willing to engage in arms shipments with the United States and Israel in an effort to further its war against Iraq. Given the difficulties the Iranians had with the Taliban, Tehran has also been fairly supportive of the American intervention in Afghanistan, to include offering the United States the use of its airfields and ports. While Tehran was less supportive of America's subsequent intervention in Iraq, the leadership was astute enough to recognize the benefits associated with the destruction of Saddam Hussein's regime. The point of these examples is not to discount any policy differences that Washington has with Tehran, but to stress that Iran is not run by ideologues, rather by a group of pragmatists devoted to protecting Iranian interests. Leaders who are rational enough to understand that the use of nuclear weapons against America would not be in their national interests.

There has also been a good deal of international media reports related to the fear that Iran might provide nuclear weapons to terrorist organizations. Ironically, the very use by Iran of surrogate terrorist organizations, rather than more overt attacks, is evidence that Tehran is sensitive to the calculations associated with the strategy of deterrence. It is also an affirmation that the Iranian leadership is attempting to minimize the risks to its foreign policy objectives. Such acts argue strongly against any possibility that Iran might provide terrorist organizations with nuclear weapons. Any move of this nature carries with it a great amount of risk; Iranians would lose control over the employment of the weapons while still having to worry that they might be blamed and targeted for response.

Contain

The second pillar of US strategy toward a nuclear Iran should be a policy of containment, to be certain that Iran does not succeed in exercising its nuclear capability as a tool of coercive diplomacy against US or allied interests in the region. Given Iran's perception of itself as the historically preeminent power in the region, Tehran can be expected to continue its policy attempting to increase its regional influence at the expense of the United States.

How would the possession of a deliverable nuclear weapon impact Tehran's foreign policy agenda? One possibility is that a nuclear Iran might be more, rather than less, restrained in its regional agenda. If any of Iran's actions are driven by a sense of insecurity with regard to America's intentions (or the threat created by a nuclear Pakistan or Israel, even the possibility of a resurgent Iraq), the security that Tehran would gain from having its own nuclear deterrent could make the nation's leadership less worried about the regional balance of power. Moreover, possession of a nuclear weapon would certainly increase the attention other world-powers paid Iran. The leadership in Tehran would have to continually worry that if any crisis developed involving another nuclear power the potential foe might opt for a preemptive attack on Iranian nuclear facilities. The fear that even a limited conflict might escalate into a nuclear exchange could make Tehran more cautious across the entire spectrum of conflict.

While such pressures may play a limited role in Iran's decision-making, it would be unwise for the United States to put too much faith in such possibilities. First, Iran's regional behavior is only partially driven by security fears. Even if Iran believed there was no threat from the United States, its status as a potential regional hegemon gives it incentive to increase its role in regional affairs. Second, while a limited amount of learning related to nuclear crisis management did take place during the Cold War, it took the United States and the Soviets a number of crises to fully appreciate these lessons.

Although the existence of this Cold War record might enable Iran to learn such lessons more quickly, the limits of vicarious learning offer ample reasons to doubt that Iran will internalize these dictums without experiencing similar crises.

The result is that Iran can probably be expected to continue furthering its regional agenda in an attempt to increase its stature and diminish that of the United States. At least initially, any increased nuclear capability will likely embolden rather than induce caution on the part of Iran's leadership. Having gone to great lengths and paid significant costs to develop its nuclear capabilities, Iran is likely to continue testing the regional and international waters. Such efforts are bound to create challenges for the United States and its allies. The good news is that nuclear weapons have proven to be poor tools for coercive diplomacy, especially against states that already possess nuclear weapons or who may be allied with a nuclear power. Nuclear weapons have proven to be extraordinarily effective at two tasks: deterring the use of such weapons against other nuclear powers or their allies, and deterring states from directly challenging the vital interests of a nuclear power. Beyond these two critical tasks, however, nuclear weapons have not proven particularly useful as diplomatic tools of intimidation. For the United States and its allies, a policy of containment against Iranian attempts to expand its influence in the region is the correct foreign policy strategy. Certainly, such a strategy far outweighs any policy based on preventive war.

Engage

To advance America's long-range goal of an Iran that is part of the global economy, at peace with its neighbors, and not supporting terrorism, Washington would be better served by engaging Iran rather than attempting to isolate it. A policy of engagement could take two forms: the establishment of direct diplomatic relations and the encouragement of Iran's involvement in the global economy.

The United States broke diplomatic ties with Iran in April 1980, during the hostage crisis. The establishment of direct diplomatic ties between the United States and Iran, however, should not be seen as any form of a reward to Iran or as approval of Iranian policies. Nor should the reestablishment of formal relations be seen as the final stage in some sort of grand bargain. Instead, diplomatic relations should be viewed as part of the normal business of conducting America's foreign policy. There is little reason to doubt that Iran would portray any US initiative to reestablish diplomatic relations as a victory, as Tehran did with the recent moves by the Bush Administration to engage in direct talks related to the situation in Iraq. America should not let fear of such a reaction stand in the way of any initiative that would advance America's long-term security interests.

Over the years the United States has found that it needs diplomatic relations with hostile states as well as with allies. Such relationships were maintained throughout the Cold War with the Soviet Union, despite numerous crises and conflicts. In the case of Iran the absence of direct governmental links makes it more difficult to deter and contain Iran. Obviously, Iran would have to concur in the reestablishment of any form of diplomatic relations.

Given the number of domestic challenges the Islamic Republic is facing, most notably a tremendous growth in its youthful population, combined with the incompetence and corruption that has marked its stewardship of the Iranian economy, it is hard to imagine that this regime can continue to avoid collapse without significant reform. At the same time, there is little reason to expect that a democratic revolution is imminent. The reform movements that seemed so promising in the late 1990s have largely been defeated. The best strategy for revitalizing these movements is to encourage Tehran's involvement in the world economy, as opposed to further attempts at isolation. Increasing the Iranian people's exposure to the world economy is much more likely to increase motivation and expand the resources available to any future reform movement. Iran's eventual inclusion in the World Trade Organization is one of the carrots currently being held out to Iran as part of ongoing negotiations regarding its nuclear program. Such incentives may advance America's long-term foreign policy goals in the region even if those efforts fail to negate Iran's development of a nuclear weapon.

Potential economic sanctions against Iran related to its nuclear program need to be carefully addressed. Iran's stagnant economy, as well as its reliance on the international energy market, make it acutely vulnerable to economic sanctions. While the threat of sanctions may be useful in dissuading the development of nuclear weapons, it is less clear that the actual imposition of sanctions would advance US foreign policy interests. While economic sanctions might extract a high toll on the Iranian economy, the reality is that the political effect that accompanies such sanctions often strengthens, rather than undermines, a regime. Sanctions tend to increase a government's control over the country's economic activity, thereby starving potential opponents of resources. Sanctions can also create a "rally round the flag" effect that permits a regime to blame international hostility for the state's internal weaknesses.

In the case of a nuclear Iran, sanctions are only likely to be useful under a fairly stringent set of circumstances. To significantly impact Iran's economy, any sanctions regime would have to be multilateral and include at a minimum the United States, European Union, Russia, and China. Sanctions would also have to be properly targeted against the leadership of the current regime and not structured in such a manner as to inflict indiscriminate damage to Iran's economy. Finally, penalties inflicted by the sanctions need be directly attributable to the regime's development of nuclear weapons.

Creating sanctions that meet these requirements would not be easy. The importance of Iran as a market for Russia and an energy supplier to China makes any sanctions regime a tough sell in Moscow and Beijing. The complicated and often opaque nature of Iranian domestic politics also presents a challenge to the development of "smart sanctions." Finally, given the distrust that exists in Iran regarding the history of external interventions, it is doubtful that any sanctions regime would be interpreted as anything except another attempt to interfere in internal politics. In all likelihood, the United States would be better off by not making sanctions the focal point for its policies regarding a nuclear Iran. Engagement has often proven to be a surer path to regime evolution than economic isolation.

Reassure Iran's Neighbors

The final portion of a US strategy toward a nuclear-armed Iran should focus on convincing Iran's neighbors that the American commitment to their security remains strong. If the United States wants regional powers to resist Iranian attempts at expanding its influence, then Washington needs to bolster security ties in the region. Improving security cooperation with Iran's neighbors could advance a number of American interests beyond simple containment. Such efforts could also help increase the security of the oil infrastructure in the region, as well as expand intelligence cooperation related to international terrorism.

A more definite US security commitment to Iran's neighbors may also decrease the chance that the development of a nuclear weapon would increase the threat of nuclear proliferation in the region. Egypt, Turkey, and Saudi Arabia have been cited as states likely to respond to any Iranian nuclear capability with increased nuclear programs. Egypt, however, has been able to tolerate a nuclear Israel for more than 30 years, as well as accommodate Libya's weapons programs. Given that historical precedent, it is unlikely that an Iranian bomb would dramatically change Cairo's calculations. Similarly, Turkey's membership in the North Atlantic Treaty Organization and its desire to join the European Union are likely to dissuade Ankara from attempting to join the nuclear fraternity. Saudi Arabia and the other members of the Gulf Cooperation Council, however, would more than likely attempt to strengthen security ties with the United States in an effort to bolster their position against a nuclear Iran.

Part of America's strategy regarding regional allies needs to focus on assuring individual states that as long as Iran is contained, the United States will not take any preventive military action. While the Gulf States certainly would prefer that Iran not develop nuclear weapons, it is also important to recognize that they fear any US-Iranian conflict more than they fear the prospect of a nuclear Iran. America's most promising strategy toward a nuclear-armed Iran should be the development of a security architecture based on deterrence and containment.

Conclusion

The United States should be under no illusions regarding the problems that a nuclear-armed Iran would present. The challenges that development would pose for American interests in the region would be monumental and lasting. The strategy of deterrence, containment, engagement, and reassurance provides the framework for achieving America's long-term regional objectives. Such a strategy would minimize disruptions to the international flow of oil, blunt Iran's attempts at regional hegemony, stabilize US efforts in Afghanistan and Iraq, and aid in countering the global war on terrorism. Ultimately, it will provide the time that reformers in Iran need to recast the Iranian government from within. It is this reformation of Iran's government that will offer the best guarantee for preserving America's interests in the region.

When U.S. diplomat George Kennan proposed the doctrine of containment against the Soviet Union at the outset of the Cold War, he argued that Soviet diplomacy was:

> At once easier and more difficult to deal with than the diplomacy of aggressive leaders like Napoleon and Hitler. On the one hand it is more sensitive to contrary force, more ready to yield on individual sectors of the diplomatic front when that force was felt to be too strong, and thus more rational in the logic and rhetoric of power. On the other hand it cannot be easily defeated or discouraged by a single victory on the part of its opponents.... [I]t can be effectively countered not by sporadic acts which represent the momentary whims of democratic opinion, but only by intelligent long-range policies.

Admittedly, the Iran of today is quite different than the Soviet Union of the 1940s. It represents what is at best a regional rather than a global challenge, and its distinctive Persian and Shia ideologies are likely to have limited appeal abroad. These differences aside, Kennan's insight still applies. Iranian nuclear ambitions can best be deterred by means of an intelligent long-range foreign policy, not the threat of military intervention.

Norman Podhoretz

Stopping Iran: Why the Case for Military Action Still Stands

Up until a fairly short time ago, scarcely anyone dissented from the assessment offered with "high confidence" by the National Intelligence Estimate [NIE] of 2005 that Iran was "determined to develop nuclear weapons." Correlatively, no one believed the protestations of the mullahs ruling Iran that their nuclear program was designed strictly for peaceful uses.

The reason for this near-universal consensus was that Iran, with its vast reserves of oil and natural gas, had no need for nuclear energy, and that in any case, the very nature of its program contradicted the protestations.

Here is how *Time* magazine put it as early as March 2003—long before, be it noted, the radical Mahmoud Ahmadinejad had replaced the putatively moderate Mohamed Khatami as president:

> On a visit last month to Tehran, International Atomic Energy Agency [IAEA] director Mohamed ElBaradei announced he had discovered that Iran was constructing a facility to enrich uranium—a key component of advanced nuclear weapons—near Natanz. But diplomatic sources tell *Time* the plant is much further along than previously revealed. The sources say work on the plant is "extremely advanced" and involves "hundreds" of gas centrifuges ready to produce enriched uranium and "the parts for a thousand others ready to be assembled."

So, too, the Federation of American Scientists about a year later:

> It is generally believed that Iran's efforts are focused on uranium enrichment, though there are some indications of work on a parallel plutonium effort. Iran claims it is trying to establish a complete nuclear-fuel cycle to support a civilian energy program, but this same fuel cycle would be applicable to a nuclear-weapons development program. Iran appears to have spread their nuclear activities around a number of sites to reduce the risk of detection or attack.

And just as everyone agreed with the American intelligence community that Iran was "determined to develop nuclear weapons," everyone also agreed with President George W. Bush that it must not be permitted to succeed. Here, the reasons were many and various.

To begin with, Iran was (as certified even by the doves of the State Department) the leading sponsor of terrorism in the world, and it was therefore reasonable to fear that it would transfer nuclear technology to terrorists who would be only too happy to use it against us. Moreover, since Iran evidently aspired to become the hegemon of the Middle East, its drive for a nuclear capability could result (as, according to the *New York Times,* no fewer than 21 governments in and around the region were warning) in "a grave and destructive nuclear-arms race." This meant a nightmarish increase in the chances of a nuclear war. An even greater increase in those chances would result from the power that nuclear weapons—and the missiles capable of delivering them, which Iran was also developing and/or buying—would give the mullahs to realize their evil dream of (in the words of Ahmadinejad) "wiping Israel off the map."

Nor, as almost everyone also agreed, were the dangers of a nuclear Iran confined to the Middle East. Dedicated as the mullahs clearly were to furthering the transformation of Europe into a continent where Muslim law and practice would more and more prevail, they were bound to use nuclear intimidation and blackmail in pursuit of this goal as well. Beyond that, nuclear weapons would even serve the purposes of a far more ambitious aim: the creation of what Ahmadinejad called "a world without America." Although, to be sure, no one imagined that Iran would acquire the capability to destroy the United States, it was easy to imagine that the United States would be deterred from standing in Iran's way by the fear of triggering a nuclear war.

Running alongside the near-universal consensus on Iran's nuclear intentions was a commensurately broad agreement that the regime could be stopped from realizing those intentions by a judicious combination of carrots and sticks. The carrots, offered through diplomacy, consisted of promises that if Iran were (in the words of the Security Council) to "suspend all enrichment-related and reprocessing activities, including research and development, to be verified by the IAEA," it would find itself on the receiving end of many benefits. If, however, Iran remained obdurate in refusing to comply with these demands, sticks would come into play in the form of sanctions.

And indeed, in response to continued Iranian defiance, a round of sanctions was approved by the Security Council in December 2006. When these (watered down to buy the support of the Russians and the Chinese) predictably failed to bite, a tougher round was unanimously authorized three months later, in March 2007. When these in turn failed, the United States, realizing that the Russians and the Chinese would veto stronger medicine, unilaterally imposed a new series of economic sanctions—which fared no better than the multilateral measures that had preceded them.

What then to do? President Bush kept declaring that Iran must not be permitted to get the bomb, and he kept warning that the "military option"— by which he meant air strikes, not an invasion on the ground—was still on the table as a last resort. On this issue our Western European allies were divided. To the surprise of many who had ceased thinking of France as an ally because of [President] Jacques Chirac's relentless opposition to the policies of the Bush administration, Nicholas Sarkozy, Chirac's successor as president, echoed Bush's warning in equally unequivocal terms. If, Sarkozy announced, the Iranians pressed on with their nuclear program, the world would be left with a choice between "an Iranian bomb and bombing Iran"—and he left no doubt as to where his own choice would fall. On the other hand, Gordon Brown, who had followed Tony Blair as prime minister of the UK, seemed less willing than Sarkozy to contemplate military action against Iran's nuclear installations, even as a last resort. Like the new chancellor of Germany, Angela Merkel, Brown remained—or professed to remain—persuaded that more diplomacy and tougher sanctions would eventually work.

This left a great question hanging in the air: when, if ever, would Bush (and/or Sarkozy) conclude that the time had come to resort to the last resort?

Obviously the answer to that question depended on how long it would take for Iran itself to reach the point of no return. According to the NIE of 2005, it was "unlikely . . . that Iran would be able to make a nuclear weapon . . . before early-to-mid next decade"—that is, between 2010 and 2015. If that assessment, offered with "moderate confidence," was correct, Bush would be off the hook, since he would be out of office for two years at the very least by the time the decision on whether or not to order air strikes would have to be made. That being the case, for the remainder of his term he could continue along the carrot-and-stick path, while striving to ratchet up the pressure on Iran with stronger and stronger measures that he could hope against hope might finally do the trick. If he could get these through the Security Council, so much the better; if not, the United States could try to assemble a coalition outside the UN that would be willing to impose really tough sanctions.

Under these circumstances, there would also be enough time to add another arrow to this nonmilitary quiver: a serious program of covert aid to dissident Iranians who dreamed of overthrowing the mullocracy [rule by mullahs, Muslim clerics] and replacing it with a democratic regime. Those who had been urging Bush to launch such a program, and who were confident that it would succeed, pointed to polls showing great dissatisfaction with the mullocracy among the Iranian young, and to the demonstrations against it that kept breaking out all over the country. They also contended that even if a new democratic regime were to be as intent as the old one on developing nuclear weapons, neither it nor they would pose anything like the same kind of threat.

All well and good. The trouble was this: only by relying on the accuracy of the 2005 NIE would Bush be able in all good conscience to pass on to his successor the decision of whether or when to bomb the Iranian nuclear facilities. But that estimate, as he could hardly help knowing from the CIA's not exactly brilliant track record, might easily be too optimistic.

To start with the most spectacular recent instance, the CIA had failed to anticipate 9/11. It then turned out to be wrong in 2002 about Saddam Hussein's possession of weapons of mass destruction, very likely because it was bending over backward to compensate for having been wrong in exactly the opposite direction in 1991, when at the end of the first Gulf war the IAEA discovered that the Iraqi nuclear program was far more advanced than the CIA had estimated. Regarding that by now notorious lapse, Jeffrey T. Richelson, a leading (and devoutly nonpartisan) authority on the American intelligence community, writes in *Spying on the Bomb*:

> The extent that the United States and its allies underestimated and misunderstood the Iraqi program [before 1991] constituted a "colossal international intelligence failure," according to one Israeli expert. [IAEA's chief weapons inspector] Hans Blix acknowledged "that there was suspicion certainly," but "to see the enormity of it is a shock."

And these were only the most recent cases. Gabriel Schoenfeld, a close student of the intelligence community, offers a partial list of earlier mistakes and failures:

> The CIA was established in 1947 in large measure to avoid another surprise attack like the one the U.S. had suffered on December 7, 1941 at Pearl Harbor. But only three years after its founding, the fledgling agency missed the outbreak of the Korean war. It then failed to understand that the Chinese would come to the aid of the North Koreans if American forces crossed the Yalu river. It missed the outbreak of the Suez war in 1956. In September 1962, the CIA issued an NIE which stated that the "Soviets would not introduce offensive missiles in Cuba"; in short order, the USSR did precisely that. In 1968 it failed to foresee the Warsaw Pact invasion of Czechoslovakia. . . . It did not inform Jimmy Carter that the Soviet Union would invade Afghanistan in 1979.

Richelson adds a few more examples of hotly debated issues during the cold war that were wrongly resolved, including "the existence of a missile gap, the capabilities of the Soviet SS-9 intercontinental ballistic missile, [and] Soviet compliance with the test-ban and antiballistic missile treaties." This is not to mention perhaps the most notorious case of all: the fiasco, known as the Bay of Pigs, produced by the CIA's wildly misplaced confidence that an invasion of Cuba by the army of exiles it had assembled and trained would set off a popular uprising against the Castro regime.

On Bush's part, then, deep skepticism was warranted concerning the CIA's estimate of how much time we had before Iran reached the point of no return. As we have seen, Mohamed ElBaradei, the head of the IAEA, had "discovered" in 2003 that the Iranians were constructing facilities to enrich uranium. Still, as late as April 2007 the same ElBaradei was pooh-poohing the claims made by Ahmadinejad that Iran already had 3,000 centrifuges in operation. A month later, we learn from Richelson, ElBaradei changed his mind after a few spot inspections. "We believe," ElBaradei now said, that the Iranians "pretty much have the knowledge about how to enrich. From now on, it is simply a question of perfecting that knowledge."

We also learn from Richelson that another expert, Matthew Bunn of Harvard's Center for Science and International Affairs, interpreted the new information the IAEA came up with in April 2007 as meaning that "whether they're six months or a year away, one can debate. But it's not ten years." This chilling estimate of how little time we had to prevent Iran from getting the bomb was similar to the conclusion reached by several Israeli experts (though the official Israeli estimate put the point of no return in 2009).

Then in a trice, everything changed. Even as Bush must surely have been wrestling with the question of whether it would be on his watch that the decision on bombing the Iranian nuclear facilities would have to be made, the world was hit with a different kind of bomb. This took the form of an unclassified summary of a new NIE, published early last December. Entitled "Iran: Nuclear Intentions and Capabilities," this new document was obviously designed to blow up the near-universal consensus that had flowed from the conclusions reached by the intelligence community in its 2005 NIE. In brief, whereas the NIE of 2005 had assessed "with high confidence that Iran currently is determined to develop nuclear weapons," the new NIE of 2007 did "not know whether [Iran] currently intends to develop nuclear weapons."

This startling 180-degree turn was arrived at from new intelligence, offered by the new NIE with "high confidence": namely, that "in fall 2003 Tehran halted its nuclear-weapons program." The new NIE was also confident—though only moderately so—that "Tehran had not restarted its nuclear-weapons program as of mid-2007." And in the most sweeping of its new conclusions, it was even "moderately confident" that "the halt to those activities represents a halt to Iran's entire nuclear-weapons program."

Whatever else one might say about the new NIE, one point can be made with "high confidence": that by leading with the sensational news that Iran had suspended its nuclear-weapons program in 2003, its authors ensured that their entire document would be interpreted as meaning that there was no longer anything to worry about. Of course, being experienced bureaucrats, they took care to protect themselves from this very accusation. For example, after dropping their own bomb on the fear that Iran was hell-bent on getting the bomb, they immediately added "with moderate-to-high confidence that Tehran at a minimum is keeping open the option to develop nuclear weapons." But as they must have expected, scarcely anyone paid attention to this caveat. And as they must also have expected, even less attention was paid to another self-protective caveat, which—making doubly sure it would pass unnoticed—they relegated to a footnote appended to the lead sentence about the halt:

> For the purposes of this Estimate, by "nuclear-weapons program" we mean Iran's nuclear-weapon design and weaponization work and covert uranium conversion-related and uranium enrichment-related work; we do not mean Iran's declared civil work related to uranium conversion and enrichment.

Since only an expert could grasp the significance of this cunning little masterpiece of incomprehensible jargon, the damage had been done by the time its dishonesty was exposed.

The first such exposure came from John Bolton, who before becoming our ambassador to the UN had served as Under Secretary of State for Arms Control and International Security, with a special responsibility for preventing the proliferation of weapons of mass destruction. Donning this hat once again, Bolton charged that the dishonesty of the footnote lay most egregiously in the sharp distinction it drew between military and civilian programs. For, he said,

> the enrichment of uranium, which all agree Iran is continuing, is critical to civilian *and* military uses [emphasis added]. Indeed, it has always been Iran's "civilian" program that posed the main risk of a nuclear "breakout."

Two other experts, Valerie Lincy, the editor of Iranwatch.org, writing in collaboration with Gary Milhollin, the director of the Wisconsin Project on Nuclear Arms Control, followed up with an explanation of why the halt of 2003 was much less significant than a layman would inevitably be led to think:

> [T]he new report defines "nuclear-weapons program" in a ludicrously narrow way: it confines it to enriching uranium at secret sites or working on a nuclear-weapon design. But the halting of its secret enrichment and weapon-design efforts in 2003 proves only that Iran made a tactical move. It suspended work that, if discovered, would unambiguously reveal intent to build a weapon. It has continued other work, crucial to the ability to make a bomb, that it can pass off as having civilian applications.

Thus, as Lincy and Milhollin went on to write, the main point obfuscated by the footnote was that once Iran accumulated a stockpile of the kind of uranium fit for civilian use, it would "in a matter of months" be able "to convert that uranium . . . , to weapons grade."

Yet, in spite of these efforts to demonstrate that the new NIE did not prove that Iran had given up its pursuit of nuclear weapons, just about everyone in the world immediately concluded otherwise, and further concluded that this meant the military option was off the table. George Bush may or may not have been planning to order air strikes before leaving office, but now that the justification for doing so had been discredited by his own intelligence agencies, it would be politically impossible for him to go on threatening military action, let alone to take it.

But what about sanctions? In the weeks and months before the new NIE was made public, Bush had been working very hard to get a third and tougher round of sanctions approved by the Security Council. In trying to persuade the Russians and the Chinese to sign on, Bush argued that the failure to enact such sanctions would leave war as the only alternative. Yet if war was now out of the question, and if in any case Iran had for all practical purposes given up its pursuit of nuclear weapons for the foreseeable future, what need was there of sanctions?

Anticipating that this objection would be raised, the White House desperately set out to interpret the new NIE as, precisely, offering "grounds for hope that the problem can be solved diplomatically—without the use of force." These words by Stephen Hadley, Bush's National Security Adviser, represented the very first comment on the new NIE to emanate from the White

House, and some version of them would be endlessly repeated in the days to come. Joining this campaign of damage control, Sarkozy and Brown issued similar statements, and even Merkel (who had been very reluctant to go along with Bush's push for another round of sanctions) now declared that it was:

> dangerous and still grounds for great concern that Iran, in the face of the UN Security Council's resolutions, continues to refuse to suspend uranium enrichment. . . . The Iranian president's intolerable agitation against Israel also speaks volumes. . . . It remains a vital interest of the whole world community to prevent a nuclear-armed Iran.

As it happened, Hadley was right about the new NIE, which executed another 180-degree turn—this one, away from the judgment of the 2005 NIE concerning the ineffectiveness of international pressure. Flatly contradicting its "high confidence" in 2005 that Iran was forging ahead "despite its international obligations and international pressure," the new NIE concluded that the nuclear-weapons program had been halted in 2003 "primarily in response to international pressure." This indicated that "Tehran's decisions are guided by a cost-benefit approach rather than a rush to a weapon irrespective of the political, economic, and military costs."

Never mind that no international pressure to speak of was being exerted on Iran in 2003, and that at that point the mullahs were more likely acting out of fear that the Americans, having just invaded Iraq, might come after them next. Never mind, too, that religious and/or ideological passions, which the new NIE pointedly neglected to mention, have over and over again throughout history proved themselves a more powerful driving force than any "cost-benefit approach." Blithely sweeping aside such considerations, the new NIE was confident that just as the carrot-and-stick approach had allegedly sufficed in the past, so it would suffice in the future to "prompt Tehran to extend the current halt to its nuclear-weapons program."

The worldview implicit here has been described by Richelson (mainly with North Korea in mind) as the idea that "moral suasion and sustained bargaining are the proven mechanisms of nuclear restraint." Such a worldview "may be ill-equipped," he observes delicately:

> to accept the idea that certain regimes are incorrigible and negotiate only as a stalling tactic until they have attained a nuclear capability against the United States and other nations that might act against their nuclear programs.

True, the new NIE did at least acknowledge that it would not be easy to induce Iran to extend the halt, "given the linkage many within the leadership probably see between nuclear-weapons development and Iran's key national-security and foreign-policy objectives." But it still put its money on a:

> combination of threats of intensified international scrutiny and pressures, along with opportunities for Iran to achieve its security, prestige, and goals for regional influence in other ways.

It was this pronouncement, and a few others like it, that gave Stephen Hadley "grounds for hope that the problem can be solved diplomatically." But that it was a false hope was demonstrated by the NIE itself. For if Iran was pursuing nuclear weapons in order to achieve its "key national-security and foreign-policy objectives," and if those objectives explicitly included (for a start) hegemony in the Middle East and the destruction of the state of Israel, what possible "opportunities" could Tehran be offered to achieve them "in other ways"?

So much for the carrot. As for the stick, it was no longer big enough to matter, what with the threat of military action ruled out, and what with the case for a third round of sanctions undermined by the impression stemming from the NIE's main finding that there was nothing left to worry about. Why worry when it was four years since Iran had done any work toward developing the bomb, when the moratorium remained in effect, and when there was no reason to believe that the program would be resumed in the near future?

What is more, in continuing to insist that the Iranians must be stopped from developing the bomb and that this could be done by nonmilitary means, the Bush administration and its European allies were lagging behind a new consensus within the American foreign-policy establishment that had already been forming even before the publication of the new NIE. Whereas the old consensus was based on the proposition that (in Senator John McCain's pungent formulation) "the only thing worse than bombing Iran was letting Iran get the bomb," the emerging new consensus held the opposite—that the only thing worse than letting Iran get the bomb was bombing Iran.

What led to this reversal was a gradual loss of faith in the carrot-and-stick approach. As one who had long since rejected this faith and who had been excoriated for my apostasy by more than one member of the foreign-policy elites, I never thought I would live to see the day when these very elites would come to admit that diplomacy and sanctions had been given a fair chance and that they had accomplished nothing but to buy Iran more time. The lesson drawn from this new revelation was, however, a different matter.

It was in the course of a public debate with one of the younger members of the foreign-policy establishment that I first chanced upon the change in view. Knowing that he never deviated by so much as an inch from the conventional wisdom of the moment within places like the Council on Foreign Relations and the Brookings Institution, I had expected him to defend the carrot-and-stick approach and to attack me as a warmonger for contending that bombing was the only way to stop the mullahs from getting the bomb. Instead, to my great surprise, he took the position that there was really no need to stop them in the first place, since even if they had the bomb they could be deterred from using it, just as effectively as the Soviets and the Chinese had been deterred during the cold war.

Without saying so in so many words, then, my opponent was acknowledging that diplomacy and sanctions had proved to be a failure, and that there was no point in pursuing them any further. But so as to avoid drawing the logical conclusion—namely, that military action had now become necessary—he simply abandoned the old establishment assumption that Iran must at all costs be prevented from developing nuclear weapons, adopting in its place the complacent idea that we could learn to live with an Iranian bomb.

In response, I argued that deterrence could not be relied upon with a regime ruled by Islamofascist revolutionaries who not only were ready to die for their beliefs but cared less about protecting their people than about the spread of their ideology and their power. If the mullahs got the bomb, I said, it was not they who would be deterred, but we.

So little did any of this shake my opponent that I came away from our debate with the grim realization that the President's continued insistence on the dangers posed by an Iranian bomb would more and more fall on deaf ears—ears that would soon be made even deafer by the new NIE's assurance that Iran was no longer hell-bent on acquiring nuclear weapons after all. There might be two different ideas competing here—one, that we could live with an Iranian bomb; the other, that there would be no Iranian bomb to live with— but the widespread acceptance of either would not only preclude the military option but would sooner or later put an end even to the effort to stop the mullahs by nonmilitary means.

And yet there remained something else, or rather someone else, to factor into the equation: the perennially "misunderestimated" George W. Bush, a man who knew evil when he saw it and who had the courage and the determination to do battle against it. This was also a man who, far more than most politicians, said what he meant and meant what he said. And what he had said at least twice before was that if we permitted Iran to build a nuclear arsenal, people fifty years from now would look back and wonder how we of this generation could have allowed such a thing to happen, and they would rightly judge us as harshly as we today judge the British and the French for what they did at Munich in 1938. It was because I had found it hard to understand why Bush would put himself so squarely in the dock of history on this issue if he were resigned to an Iran in possession of nuclear weapons, or even of the ability to build them, that I predicted in these pages, and went on predicting elsewhere, that he would not retire from office before resorting to the military option.

But then came the new NIE. To me it seemed obvious that it represented another ambush by an intelligence community that had consistently tried to sabotage Bush's policies through a series of damaging leaks and was now trying to prevent him from ever taking military action against Iran. To others, however, it seemed equally obvious that Bush, far from being ambushed, had welcomed the new NIE precisely because it provided him with a perfect opportunity to begin distancing himself from the military option.

But I could not for the life of me believe that Bush intended to fly in the face of the solemn promise he had made in his 2002 State of the Union address:

> We'll be deliberate, yet time is not on our side. I will not wait on events, while dangers gather. I will not stand by, as peril draws closer and closer. The United States of America will not permit the world's most dangerous regimes to threaten us with the world's most destructive weapons.

To which he had added shortly afterward in a speech at West Point: "If we wait for threats to fully materialize, we will have waited too long."

How, I wondered, could Bush not know that in the case of Iran he was running a very great risk of waiting too long? And if he was truly ready to run that risk, why, in a press conference the day after the new NIE came out, did he put himself in the historical dock yet again by repeating what he had said several times before about the judgment that would be passed on this generation in the future if Iran were to acquire a nuclear weapon?

> If Iran shows up with a nuclear weapon at some point in time, the world is going to say, what happened to them in 2007? How come they couldn't see the impending danger? What caused them not to understand that a country that once had a weapons program could reconstitute the weapons program? How come they couldn't see that the important first step in developing a weapon is the capacity to be able to enrich uranium? How come they didn't know that with that capacity, that knowledge could be passed on to a covert program? What blinded them to the realities of the world? And it's not going to happen on my watch.

"It's not going to happen on my watch." What else could this mean if not that Bush was preparing to meet "the impending danger" in what he must by now have concluded was the only way it could be averted?

The only alternative that seemed even remotely plausible to me was that he might be fixing to outsource the job to the Israelis. After all, even if, by now, it might have become politically impossible for us to take military action, the Israelis could not afford to sit by while a regime pledged to wipe them off the map was equipping itself with nuclear weapons and the missiles to deliver them. For unless Iran could be stopped before acquiring a nuclear capability, the Israelis would be faced with only two choices: either strike first, or pray that the fear of retaliation would deter the Iranians from beating them to the punch. Yet a former president of Iran, Hashemi Rafsanjani, had served notice that his country would not be deterred by the fear of retaliation:

> If a day comes when the world of Islam is duly equipped with the arms Israel has in its possession, . . . application of an atomic bomb would not leave anything in Israel, but the same thing would just produce damages in the Muslim world.

If this was the view of even a supposed moderate like Rafsanjani, how could the Israelis depend upon the mullahs to refrain from launching a first strike? The answer was that they could not. Bernard Lewis, the leading contemporary authority on the culture of the Islamic world, has explained why:

> MAD, mutual assured destruction, [was effective] right through the cold war. Both sides had nuclear weapons. Neither side used them, because both sides knew the other would retaliate in kind. This will not work with a religious fanatic [like Ahmadinejad]. For him, mutual assured destruction is not a deterrent, it is an inducement. We know already that [the mullahs ruling Iran] do not give a damn about killing their own people in great numbers. We have seen it again and again. In the final scenario, and this applies all the more strongly if they kill

large numbers of their own people, they are doing them a favor. They are giving them a quick free pass to heaven and all its delights.

Under the aegis of such an attitude, even in the less extreme variant that may have been held by some of Ahmadinejad's colleagues among the regime's rulers, mutual assured destruction would turn into a very weak reed. Understanding that, the Israelis would be presented with an irresistible incentive to preempt—and so, too, would the Iranians. Either way, a nuclear exchange would become inevitable.

What would happen then? In a recently released study, Anthony Cordesman of the Center for Strategic and International Studies argues that Rafsanjani had it wrong. In the grisly scenario Cordesman draws, tens of millions would indeed die, but Israel—despite the decimation of its civilian population and the destruction of its major cities—would survive, even if just barely, as a functioning society. Not so Iran, and not its "key Arab neighbors," particularly Egypt and Syria, which Cordesman thinks Israel would also have to target in order "to ensure that no other power can capitalize on an Iranian strike." Furthermore, Israel might be driven in desperation to go after the oil wells, refineries, and ports in the Gulf.

"Being contained within the region," writes Martin Walker of UPI in his summary of Cordesman's study, "such a nuclear exchange might not be Armageddon for the human race." To me it seems doubtful that it could be confined to the Middle East. But even if it were, the resulting horrors would still be far greater than even the direst consequences that might follow from bombing Iran before it reaches the point of no return.

In the worst case of this latter scenario, Iran would retaliate by increasing the trouble it is already making for us in Iraq and by attacking Israel with missiles armed with non-nuclear warheads but possibly containing biological and/or chemical weapons. There would also be a vast increase in the price of oil, with catastrophic consequences for every economy in the world, very much including our own. And there would be a deafening outcry from one end of the earth to the other against the inescapable civilian casualties. Yet, bad as all this would be, it does not begin to compare with the gruesome consequences of a nuclear exchange between Israel and Iran, even if those consequences were to be far less extensive than Cordesman anticipates.

Which is to say that, as between bombing Iran to prevent it from getting the bomb and letting Iran get the bomb, there is simply no contest.

But this still does not answer the question of who should do the bombing. Tempting as it must be for George Bush to sit back and let the Israelis do the job, there are considerations that should give him pause. One is that no matter what he would say, the whole world would regard the Israelis as a surrogate for the United States, and we would become as much the target of the ensuing recriminations both at home and abroad as we would if we had done the job ourselves.

To make matters worse, the indications are that it would be very hard for the Israeli air force, superb though it is, to pull the mission off. Thus, an analysis by two members of the Security Studies Program at MIT concluded that while "the Israeli air force now possesses the capability to destroy even well-hardened targets in Iran with some degree of confidence," the problem is that for the mission to succeed, all of the many contingencies involved would have to go right. Hence an Israeli attempt could end with the worst of all possible outcomes: retaliatory measures by the Iranians even as their nuclear program remained unscathed. We, on the other hand, would have a much bigger margin of error and a much better chance of setting their program back by a minimum of five or ten years and at best wiping it out altogether.

The upshot is that if Iran is to be prevented from becoming a nuclear power, it is the United States that will have to do the preventing, to do it by means of a bombing campaign, and (because "If we wait for threats to fully materialize, we will have waited too long") to do it soon.

When I first predicted a year or so ago that Bush would bomb Iran's nuclear facilities once he had played out the futile diplomatic string, the obstacles that stood in his way were great but they did not strike me as insurmountable. Now, thanks in large part to the new NIE, they have grown so formidable that I can only stick by my prediction with what the NIE itself would describe as "low-to-moderate confidence." For Bush is right about the resemblance between 2008 and 1938. In 1938, as Winston Churchill later said, Hitler could still have been stopped at a relatively low price and many millions of lives could have been saved if England and France had not deceived themselves about the realities of their situation. Mutatis mutandis, it is the same in 2008, when Iran can still be stopped from getting the bomb and even more millions of lives can be saved—but only provided that we summon up the courage to see what is staring us in the face and then act on what we see.

Unless we do, the forces that are blindly working to ensure that Iran will get the bomb are likely to prevail even against the clear-sighted determination of George W. Bush, just as the forces of appeasement did against Churchill in 1938. In which case, we had all better pray that there will be enough time for the next President to discharge the responsibility that Bush will have been forced to pass on, and that this successor will also have the clarity and the courage to discharge it. If not—God help us all—the stage will have been set for the outbreak of a nuclear war that will become as inescapable then as it is avoidable now.

POSTSCRIPT

Is Patient Diplomacy the Best Approach to Iran's Nuclear Program?

Since the hearings, there has been much ado about Iran's alleged nuclear program, but little has actually changed. Led by the diplomats from the European Union and urged on by the United States, the West has continued to put pressure on Iran to halt all activities that could lead to acquiring nuclear weapons. Iran, for its part, continues to deny a nuclear weapons program or ambitions and to play a cat-and-mouse game with the IAEA by allowing it to inspect some things sometimes, but also being uncooperative at other times in a pattern reminiscent of the on-again-off-again approach of Iraq under Saddam Hussein to IAEA inspectors. The UN Security Council has responded to Iran's lack of full cooperation with the IAEA with rounds of sanctions, including a complete embargo in 2010 on the sale of weapons to Iran. However, these sanctions have not been strong enough to change Iran's path, in part because the UN prohibitions have been widely ignored. Tough sanctions favored by the United States have not been passed because of, among other reasons, the resistance of Russia and China, each of which has a veto in the Security Council. In the meantime, Iran has built new nuclear facilities, and according to the IAEA has already enriched enough uranium to build two nuclear weapons. Iran insists its enrichment program is for peaceful purposes, and to date the IAEA has not been willing to declare that Iran has a nuclear weapons program under way.

Given the virtual stalemate, there appears to be growing possibility that with at least tacit U.S. backing, Israel might launch an attack on Iran's nuclear sites. Israelis are understandably alarmed, given President Ahmadinejad's statement that Israel is a "disgraceful stain on the Islamic world" that should be "wiped away." Israel's concerns have been heightened even further by intelligence that Iran is reconfiguring its Shahab-3 missile to enable it to carry a nuclear warhead. According to Iran, the missile has a range of 1,250 miles, putting Israel well within range. Indeed, former general and Israeli army chief Moshe Ya'alon has called war with Iran "inevitable."

President Barack Obama began his tenure by showing a greater willingness to negotiate with Iran than President Bush had demonstrated, but he has also called a nuclear-armed Iran a direct threat to the United States and declared that he would not "take any options off the table, including military, to prevent [Iran] from obtaining a nuclear weapon." In a separate interview on the program, John McCain said that if it's a provable direct threat that Iran had weapons, then "it's obvious that we would have to prevent what we're absolutely certain is a direct threat to the lives of the American people."

To understand Iran better, read Ervand Abrahamian, *A History of Modern Iran* (Cambridge University Press, 2008). For a periodically updated background article on this nuclear issue, go to the Council on Foreign Relations' "backgrounder," *Iran's Nuclear Program* at http://www.cfr.org/publication/16811/. The very latest news accounts and an opportunity to join the debate are at the site of Iran Nuclear Watch at http://www.irannuclearwatch.blogspot.com/. An effort to understand Iran's diplomatic strategy is Balkan Devlen, "Dealing or Dueling with the United States? Explaining and Predicting Iranian Behavior During the Nuclear Crisis," *International Studies Review* (2010). A recent overview is contained in Dana Allin and Steven Simon, *The Sixth Crisis: Iran, Israel, America, and the Rumors of War* (Oxford University Press, 2010).

Questions for Critical Thinking and Reflection

1. Why would a nuclear-armed Iran be a particular threat to the United States?
2. If it comes down to letting Iran build nuclear weapons or sending in U.S. troops to topple Iran's government and destroy its nuclear weapons and its ability to produce more, which option do you favor?
3. Iran claims that it has a sovereign right to build nuclear facilities and enrich uranium, just as numerous nonnuclear weapon countries, like Japan and Germany, do. What are Iran's rights as a country?

ISSUE 9

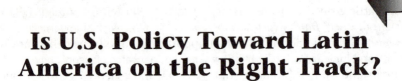

Is U.S. Policy Toward Latin America on the Right Track?

YES: Arturo A. Valenzuela, from Testimony during Hearings on "U.S. Policy Toward the Americas in 2010 and Beyond" before the Subcommittee on the Western Hemisphere, Committee on Foreign Affairs, U.S. House of Representatives (March 10, 2010)

NO: Otto J. Reich, from Testimony during Hearings on "U.S. Policy Toward the Americas in 2010 and Beyond" before the Subcommittee on the Western Hemisphere, Committee on Foreign Affairs, U.S. House of Representatives (March 10, 2010)

ISSUE SUMMARY

YES: Arturo A. Valenzuela, the U.S. assistant secretary of state for Western Hemisphere affairs, describes the views and policies of the Obama administration regarding the Western Hemisphere, as focused on three priorities critical to everyone in the region: promoting social and economic opportunity, ensuring safety, and strengthening effective institutions of democratic governance.

NO: Otto J. Reich, the U.S. assistant secretary of state for Western Hemisphere affairs during the administration of President George H. W. Bush, tells Congress that he believes the U.S. government today is underestimating the security threats in the Western Hemisphere.

For most of U.S. history, policy toward Latin America and the Caribbean has been marked by conquest and domination. In 1819, the United States first acquired territory in what was arguably Latin America when threats forced Spain to surrender Florida and parts of what are now Alabama and Mississippi. Less directly, the United States acquired a huge tract of formerly Mexican territory after American settlers had seized the territory, briefly created the Republic of Texas, and then agreed to annexation by the United States (1845). The Mexican–American War (1846–1848) broke out the following year, and the U.S. victory diminished Mexico's remaining territory by about 50% and increased U.S. territory by about one-third.

During these early years, Washington had also declared that much of the Western Hemisphere was, in essence, a U.S. sphere of influence. The (President

James) Monroe Doctrine (1823) proclaimed that the United States would view any move by a country outside the Western Hemisphere to colonize land or interfere with countries in the Americas as acts of aggression requiring U.S. intervention. This unilateral U.S. move gave some protection to the newly independent countries in Latin America and the Caribbean, but it also included the U.S. presumption that it had special authority over the hemisphere. In 1904 the (President Theodore) Roosevelt Corollary (to the Monroe Doctrine), by which the United States granted itself the authority to intervene in the domestic affairs of all countries to the south in cases of "flagrant . . . wrongdoing" by them, was declared. During the decades that followed, the corollary was used to justify repeated interventions, including military occupations of Cuba (1898–1992), the Dominican Republic (1916–1924), Haiti (1915–1934), Honduras (1924–1925), Mexico (1914–1917), and Nicaragua (1912–1913).

The Roosevelt Corollary came at a time of distinct U.S. imperialism. The Spanish–American war had led to the U.S. acquisition of Puerto Rico and the temporary control of Cuba. Elsewhere, the war and other events led to such U.S. colonial possessions as the Philippines, Guam, and Hawaii. Roosevelt's maneuvering was critical in creating the new country of Panama, which then dutifully agreed to U.S. control over the Panama Canal Zone.

Efforts to establish a more benevolent, partner-like U.S. policy began when President Franklin Roosevelt declared the "Good Neighbor Policy" in 1933 pledging to avoid the heavy-handed excesses of the past. Washington was also instrumental in creating the Organization of American States (OAS), which was created in 1948. Although originally meant primarily as a cold war alliance, the OAS did advance the ideal of equality and cooperation among the countries of the Western Hemisphere. Also spurred by cold war worries about the spread of communism, President John F. Kennedy launched the Alliance for Progress to increase U.S. economic aid to the hemisphere. Since then, new U.S. presidents have routinely pledged friendship toward and respect for the region's other countries. It is also the case that on average U.S. policy has been less assertive and more cooperative than it was. Still, American actions have not fully matched the rhetoric. Instead, the U.S. sphere-of-influence approach to hemispheric relations has continued in many ways. There have been occasional military interventions (Dominican Republic, 1965; Grenada, 1983; Panama, 1988; and Haiti, 1994) and a number of other instances where a government in a country to the south was brought to power, kept in power, or toppled from power because of less direct actions by Washington.

Currently, U.S.–Latin American relations are being roiled by a number of issues. The most prominent of these is the coming to power of government leaders who are populists and critical of the United States. President Hugo Chávez of Venezuela and President Evo Morales of Bolivia are prime examples. In the following debate, two individuals who have been the top U.S. diplomat for Latin America represent different streams of U.S. approach to the region. Arturo Valenzuela, who is Chilean American, argues from the Obama administration's somewhat more cooperative approach. Cuban American Otto Reich favors the more assertive approach that marked the previous Bush administration.

YES

Arturo A. Valenzuela

U.S. Policy Toward the Americas in 2010 and Beyond

Thank you for the opportunity to talk about U.S. policy in the Americas. I am just back from a six-nation trip to Latin America with Secretary [of State Hillary] Clinton, where we had the chance to meet with over a dozen heads of state, and many leaders in civil society and the private sector, and talk about our highest priorities and responsibilities. We were particularly moved by the eloquent words of President-elect [José] Mujica who in his inaugural address outlined a bold vision of progress for Uruguay and a powerful defense of democratic values and institutions, including the respect for opposition parties and the value of dialogue and compromise in public affairs. So this is a particularly welcome opportunity to take stock of where we are and, more importantly, where we want to go in our relations with the countries of the Americas. It is very important, at the outset, to recognize how much our growing interdependence makes the success of our neighbors a compelling U.S. national security interest. Advancing that interest is a fundamental goal of our engagement in the Americas.

In 1961 the Alliance for Progress captured the imagination of the Americas with a bold shared vision. We live in a very different world at the beginning of the 21st century. With few exceptions, the countries of the region are much more inclusive, prosperous, and democratic. But, today, much of what we must help accomplish in this hemisphere also hinges on the power of a shared vision: a vision of an Inter-American community with shared values, shared challenges, a shared history and, most importantly, shared responsibility. Advancing that vision will require sustained, informed, creative, and competent engagement. That engagement must be sophisticated and variegated. We speak, accurately, of a "region," and of big unifying agendas, but we know at the same time that our community comprises profoundly diverse nations and sub-regions. To be successful, our approach must be able to disaggregate when necessary.

Our challenge is to carefully use our diplomatic and development tools, and our limited resources, to optimal effect. We need to help catalyze networks of practical partnerships, among all capable stakeholders in the Americas, focused on three priorities critical to people in every country of this region: promoting social and economic opportunity for everyone; ensuring the safety of all of our citizens; and strengthening effective institutions of democratic governance, respect for human rights, and accountability. Across all of these

U.S. House of Representatives, March 10, 2010.

142

priorities, I want to emphasize, we are also working on practical initiatives to advance us toward a secure, clean energy future.

There is a strong element of community in the Americas today, and it will only get stronger with time. That feeling was nowhere more evident than in the extraordinary outpouring of support and assistance to the people of Haiti following the devastating earthquake there. Or in the region's unanimous feelings of solidarity with Chile after it, too, was hit by one of the biggest earthquakes the world has ever experienced.

Haiti is a special case. Shortly after taking office, well before the earthquake, President [Barack] Obama and Secretary Clinton emphasized their personal commitment to helping Haiti break the cycles of poverty and poor government that have crippled its development. We have reaffirmed our commitment in the aftermath of the earthquake. You know the extent of the damage, the loss of life, and the urgent need. The Government of Haiti faces daunting tasks. Meeting them will require a sustained and substantial commitment from the international community, in support of the Government and people of Haiti as they define what their future should look like. On March 4, the United States and United Nations announced that in cooperation with the Government of Haiti, and with the support of Brazil, Canada, the European Union, France, and Spain, they will co-host a ministerial—the *International Donors' Conference Toward a New Future for Haiti*—at the United Nations in New York on March 31, 2010. The goal of the conference is to mobilize international support for Haiti's development needs and to begin to lay the foundation for Haiti's long-term recovery.

We in the Americas are joined together by many intersecting and overlapping interests, needs, and affinities. We share the common, though sometimes contentious, history of the Americas, developing from diverse European colonization, displacement of indigenous peoples, forced African immigration, assimilation of later immigrant groups, and the gradual coalescence of adaptable new societies. The populations of our countries reflect a particularly rich and largely harmonious racial and cultural diversity that differentiates this hemisphere from large parts of Europe, Asia, and Africa.

We share a common history of independence movements inspired by the human ideals of the enlightenment, followed by the long and difficult processes by which our peoples have struggled to build the just, free, inclusive, and successful societies envisioned by our founding fathers. Many of our nations have followed policies in the past that have hindered this process, as when the United States put Cold War priorities ahead of democratization in the region.

Today, however, fundamental values of democracy, respect for human rights, accountability, tolerance, and pluralism are increasingly ingraining themselves into practice throughout the Americas. So many of the Americas' leading democracies have recently gone through, or are preparing for, peaceful electoral transfers of power. Alternation in power, increasingly effective institutions, responsible fiscal policies, open trade policies, and greater accountability—exemplified by such countries as Brazil, Chile, Colombia, Costa Rica, Peru, Uruguay, and El Salvador—embody the hemispheric reality. The significance of this trend cannot be overstated.

Our common legacy, our shared values, and the nature of today's global challenges must underpin a new and converging agenda for cooperation that helps unite diverse peoples and governments around a shared task: building stable, safe, inclusive societies that are supported by effective and legitimate institutions of governance. This agenda should also protect our diversity through tolerance and pluralism as a key factor in our region's success and competitiveness in a globalized economy. Energy security and global climate change are crucial issues for our partners and us and offer opportunities for deeper collaboration. Our broad common agenda, not individual differences or outliers, should define our interaction in the Americas. I know some governments in the region will not embrace this approach, will do so only very selectively, or will seek to undermine this common cause. Working together with others, we need to be clear-eyed and proactive in countering efforts to undermine our common agenda. These can include attempts to expand authoritarian or populist rule at the expense of effective democratic governance based on the rule of law and representative government. They can also include the ill-conceived embrace of dangerous or problematic external actors.

We are concerned about the persistent erosion of democratic institutions and fundamental freedoms in several countries, particularly freedom of the press. These freedoms reflect the regional consensus and are enshrined in fundamental instruments of the Inter-American system. The recent Inter-American Human Rights Commission report on Venezuela was a complete and dispassionate review of the current state of affairs, and it represents an opportunity for Venezuela's government to begin a dialogue internally and with the hemispheric community. In Cuba, we want to promote respect for human rights and fundamental freedoms. We have taken measures to increase contact between separated families and to promote the free flow of information to, from, and within Cuba. We have engaged the Cuban government on key bilateral matters like migration and direct mail service and will continue to engage Cuba to advance U.S. national interests, as in our effort to respond to the humanitarian crisis in Haiti. We remain deeply concerned by the poor human rights situation in Cuba, which contributed to the recent death of prisoner of conscience Orlando Zapata as a result of a hunger strike. We are also focused on securing the release of the U.S. citizen jailed in Cuba in December; a matter of great importance to the United States.

Our response to the coup d'état in Honduras [the January 2009 overthrow of somewhat-to-the-left President Manuel Zelaya by the military] shows that our interests are served by leveraging multilateral mechanisms, in concert with our partners, to support the implementation of principled policies. In Honduras we helped to strengthen the "collective defense of democracy" as a cornerstone of the Inter-American System. Today, Honduras is governed by elected leaders who are moving quickly to promote national reconciliation and their country's return to the fold of hemispheric democracies. [After a long crisis, new presidential election was held in November 2009 and won by somewhat rightist candidate Porfirio Lobo.] As Honduras moves forward, we will continue to maintain a vigilant eye on the human rights situation there in light of serious concerns that have been raised.

To help advance our national interests, as reflected in the broad common agenda I outlined, the President has submitted an FY 2011 [fiscal year 2011; the U.S. fiscal year runs from October 1, 2011, to September 30, 2012] request for foreign assistance in the region that reflects a continuing shift toward greater economic and development assistance, over traditional security assistance. Specifically, of the total FY 2011 request, 62 percent is economic and development assistance, versus only 50 percent in the FY 2009 and FY 2010 enacted levels.

This does not mean we face a diminished threat to our national security from transnational crime and other menaces. These include the global drug trade, the largest criminal industry in the world, involving every country in the region. Nor does it mean we are shying away from doing our utmost to safeguard the security of our citizens and citizens throughout the region. Instead, our request recognizes the critical importance of strong institutions, broad economic opportunity, and social inclusion in building resilient societies that can protect people from threats to their safety. For example, the request includes specific funding for innovative regional initiatives reflecting our commitment to shared prosperity and a sustainable future—such as the Inter-American Social Protection Network and the Energy and Climate Partnership of the Americas.

Our request also reflects our continued commitment to key hemispheric citizen safety initiatives including the Merida Initiative, our programs in Colombia, the Caribbean Basin Security Initiative, and the Central America Regional Security Initiative. [The Merida Initiative is a U.S. program that the State Department characterizes as helping "Mexico, the nations of Central America, the Dominican Republic, and Haiti to confront criminal organizations whose illicit actions undermine public safety, erode the rule of law, and threaten the national security of the United States."] The security challenges in the region are profoundly interconnected. Our initiatives are grounded in a common strategic vision and coordinated internally and with the interagency to ensure comprehensive and coherent planning and implementation. While these initiatives are mutually reinforcing, sharing broad objectives and some key activities, they vary considerably in size, level of U.S. support, complexity, and level of development. The combination of a common strategic approach and distinct, but interlocking, regional initiatives provides the necessary unity of effort as well as the flexibility necessary to help address unique circumstances that vary by country or sub-region.

The evolving mix of our assistance is also a function of successful partnerships—such as those with Colombia and Mexico—that have enabled others to assume an increasing share of responsibility for their own citizens' safety. It is also a function of the leadership of many members of this committee, and the administration's clear understanding of the connection between major security challenges and a combination of weak institutions, social exclusion, and lack of economic opportunity that plague many societies.

Earlier I referred to three priorities critical to people throughout the Americas. They are mutually reinforcing, and they inform and influence our diplomatic and development policy throughout the Americas, so I would like to expand upon them in that context.

Opportunity

Through social and economic partnerships with governments, civil society, and the private sector we can leverage investments in people and infrastructure to make societies more competitive in the world and inclusive at home. Our public diplomacy initiatives—scholarships, exchange programs, in-country language programs, other activities through our bi-national centers—advance these goals, bringing huge return on our investment. We are now exploring the potential to significantly expand such programs. The inclusion into the economic mainstream of traditionally marginalized groups is crucial to economic growth.

The Pathways to Prosperity initiative, which we have re-cast as a strategic platform for promoting sustainable development, trade capacity building and regional competitiveness, is also key to promoting more equitable economic growth. The initiative, which includes those countries in the hemisphere that are committed to trade and market economies, comprises a number of programs to help ensure that the benefits of trade and economic growth are equitably shared among all sectors of society. Despite its macroeconomic growth, poverty and income inequality remain key challenges in this hemisphere. Pathways countries share a commitment to promote a more inclusive prosperity and responsive democratic institutions.

Countries throughout the Americas have experience, creativity, and talent to address these challenges and through Pathways we are working with partners to help exchange information and share best practices to benefit all. Secretary Clinton participated in the Pathways ministerial last week and cited a number of areas that we have identified for cooperation under Pathways. These include the creation of small business development centers; support for women entrepreneurs; modernizing customs procedures; expanded opportunities for English and Spanish language instruction; helping small- and medium-sized enterprises decrease their carbon footprint; and promoting the use of secured transaction to help small businesses better access capital.

We are also working with partners in the Western Hemisphere to fight poverty through the Inter-American Social Protection Network, which our leaders committed to support at the Summit of the Americas in Trinidad and Tobago last April. The launch of the Network in New York City in September 2009 was important—demonstrating the commitment of governments and citizens throughout the Americas to helping each other achieves social justice in creative and innovative ways. Examples of innovative social protection strategies include Conditional Cash Transfers (CCTs)—a simple idea linking responsibility with opportunity.

We will continue to work closely with partner nations such as Canada in promoting greater opportunity in the region. Canada's major development commitment to Haiti—both before and after the earthquake—as well as their programs in the Caribbean, Bolivia, Honduras, and Peru are effective multipliers to our own efforts.

We are also in serious discussion with other nations, such as Spain, and the EU, who provide substantial development assistance in the Americas.

In particular, we see important opportunities to more effectively coordinate our programs in Central America, bilaterally and through SICA [Sistema de Integración Centroamericana]. When I met in Madrid with my Spanish counterparts last month we agreed to move quickly to assess and take advantage of these opportunities. It is very important to address too our pending free trade agreements with Colombia and Panama. These accords are important components of economic engagement with the Americas. As the President has made clear, we remain committed to working with both Panama and Colombia to address outstanding issues, including concerns voiced by members of Congress and other critical stakeholders. We are confident that together we can advance our interests and values through these agreements and our deep and diverse relationships with both Panama and Colombia.

Sustaining the opportunity generated by economic growth requires vastly enhanced cooperation on energy and climate change. The Energy and Climate Partnership of the Americas helps achieve this. The State Department is working together with the Department of Energy to lead U.S. efforts under the Partnership, and we and other governments in the region (Brazil, Chile, Colombia, Costa Rica, Mexico, and Peru) have developed initiatives focused on energy efficiency, renewable energy, infrastructure, energy poverty, and cleaner fossil fuels. Secretary of Energy Steven Chu will host an ECPA [Energy and Climate Partnership of the Americas] Ministerial April 15–16 in Washington, with Secretary Clinton's participation. There, we will further existing ECPA initiative and identifying new ones. We are excited about the countless opportunities for cooperation under ECPA.

Scientific partnerships in our Hemisphere also hold the promise of opportunity. Economic growth, promoting security, and unleashing the potential of developing countries are inextricable from the sustainable development of our common resources and building our capacity for innovation. The number of researchers in the workforce, doctoral degrees awarded, and research and development expenditures in Latin America are well below that of OECD [Organization of Economic Cooperation and Development] countries. Even so, scientific publications and patent applications have increased steadily in the region particularly in Argentina, Brazil, Chile, Mexico, and Uruguay. It is vital that we encourage this continued growth and use international scientific cooperation as the way to build further capacity. Increased cooperation in science addresses key development goals for the countries in the region, but also directly benefits the U.S. economy. The countries of Latin America and the Caribbean not only look to the United States for leadership in S&T [science and technology] activities, but we are their largest trading partners, their largest source of foreign direct investment, and our universities are the destination of many of the best and brightest Latin American students. Investing in S&T cooperation with Latin America today will strengthen our U.S. universities and research institutions, but as we look past the immediate financial crisis, will help position American companies in the innovative industries of the future, ranging from clean energy to biotechnology. Bringing prosperity and economic growth to some of our strongest trading partners will also have a positive impact for traditional U.S. exporters.

Citizen Safety

Citizen Safety encompasses a similarly multi-dimensional set of partnerships that broker cooperation and institution building to fight transnational crime and assure a secure daily existence for individuals throughout the Inter-American community. To get sustained buy-in, it is vital that our security partnerships be understood by publics as *responsive* to the very local insecurity they face (crime, human trafficking, drug addiction, and poor environment, lack of reliable energy, or clean water), and not simply a means of securing the United States regardless of the cost to others.

Strong public diplomacy has a vital tactical role in building wider awareness of the ways these jointly developed partnerships, for example, with Colombia, Peru, Mexico, Central America, and the Caribbean address shared concerns, strengthen institutions, and help build resilient communities in which people can thrive. Our diplomacy must also emphasize to publics all we do domestically to live up to our responsibility to address some of the key factors of transnational crime, including demand for drugs, and illicit traffic in firearms and bulk cash.

A variety of security partnerships in the region, the Merida Initiative, the Central American Regional Security Initiative (CARSI), and the Caribbean Basin Security Initiative (CBSI), seek to strengthen partners' ability to fight transnational crime, protect citizens, and prevent the spread of illicit goods and violence to the United States. In the process these partnerships are transforming relationships, brokering growing cooperation and trust between those countries and the United States, and between the partner nations themselves.

The United States and Mexico have forged a strong partnership to enhance citizen safety and fight organized crime and drug trafficking organizations. In 2009, the United States and Mexico agreed to new goals to broaden and deepen the cooperation between the two countries. These include expanding the border focus beyond interdiction of contraband to include facilitating legitimate trade and travel; cooperating to build strong communities resilient to the corrupting influence of organized crime; disrupting organized crime; and institutionalizing reforms to sustain the rule of law and respect for human rights. The Caribbean Basin Security Initiative (CBSI) seeks to substantially reduce illicit trafficking, increase safety for our people, and promote social justice. More than a series of programs, this partnership will be an ongoing collaboration that draws upon, and helps develop, the capacity of all to better address common and inter-related challenges. Partnership activities will be designed in a manner that maximizes synergies with other regional efforts (e.g. Merida). Under CBSI we will jointly seek the greatest possible support from extra-regional partners in pursuit of key objectives.

The Central American Regional Security Initiative (CARSI), in coordination with Merida Initiative and CBSI, strengthens and integrates security efforts from the U.S. Southwest border to Panama, including the littoral waters of the Caribbean. The desired end-state is a safer and more secure hemisphere—in which the U.S., too, is protected from spread of illicit drugs, violence, and transnational threats. CARSI recognizes a sequenced approach to resolving the challenges, consisting of: the immediate need to address the rapidly deteriorating security environment; the medium-term requirement to augment civilian law enforcement and security entities; the capabilities to reestablish control and exert the rule of law; and the long-term necessity to strengthen the justice sector and other state institutions.

In the Andes, it remains in our national interest to help the Colombian people achieve the lasting and just peace they want, making irreversible the gains they have sacrificed so hard to achieve. Colombia has made major progress reducing violence and kidnappings, improving human rights, expanding the rule of law, and advancing the country's social and economic development. Important challenges remain including in the area of human rights. We will continue to work closely with the Colombian government to promote respect for human rights, ensure access to justice, and end impunity. We will also continue to collaborate with Colombia to prevent and respond to the disturbingly high rates of internal displacement. The Colombia Strategic Development Initiative (CSDI) is our plan to support the government of Colombia's "National Consolidation Plan." CSDI is a whole-of-government approach that integrates civilian institution–building, rule of law, and alternative development programs with security and counternarcotics efforts.

In Colombia, Mexico, and elsewhere in the region the Secretary has emphasized that we understand that effective and collaborative counterdrug policies must be based holistically on four key goals: demand reduction, eradication and interdiction, just implementation of the law, and public health. To be sustainable, any gains will require economic and social opportunity sufficiently strong to provide compelling alternatives to involvement in illicit drug production and trafficking.

We tend to speak of U.S. security initiatives in the region, but in reality these are overwhelmingly joint in their development increasingly plurilateral [a few more than two countries or other partners] in their implementation, and multi-faceted in their impact. As countries strengthen their internal capacity to address security challenges they are forming their own partnerships with neighbors in ways that multiply the effectiveness of programs. Canada is an increasingly important and committed security partner with regional countries; Mexico and Colombia are sharing vital capacity and experience; countries such as Uruguay, Chile, and Brazil are showing notable leadership in international security initiatives such as MINUSTAH [La Mission des Nations Unies pour la Stabilisation en Haïti, the UN peacekeeping force] in Haiti.

Effective Democratic Governance

Capable and legitimate institutions, including a vibrant civil society, are vital to successful societies that meet their citizens' needs. Our strong support for democracy and human rights is rooted in this fundamental fact. The capacity and integrity of democratic institutions [are] uneven in the Americas. All our nations have a broad co-responsibility to help strengthen both. Many are, in fact, reaching beyond their national success to share experience and technical capacity in the region and beyond.

U.S. democracy programs focus on broadening citizen participation, supporting free elections and justice sector reform, developing anti-corruption initiatives and governmental transparency, supporting human rights and fostering social justice through stronger rule of law. Strong and effective multilateral institutions in the Americas can play a vital role in strengthening effective democratic institutions. The Organization of American States (OAS), at the center of the inter-American system, has a mandate from its membership to do so.

We must work through the OAS to strengthen democratic institutions at a time in which these institutions are being seriously challenged in some countries in the region. As part of this effort, we should apply the valuable lessons of the success of the independent Inter-American Commission on Human Rights, as an impartial arbiter on human rights issues, to address critical governance issues affecting our region. We must also build the political will necessary among OAS member states to fulfill the promise of the Inter-American Democratic Charter as an effective tool in the collective defense of democracy.

Recent experience should demonstrate to us that both the Secretary General [SYG] and the Permanent Council should be less hesitant to use their existing authorities under the OAS Charter and the Inter-American Democratic Charter to take preventive action in situations that may affect the viability of democratic institutions in a member state. Such actions must be undertaken with the consent of the member state involved, of course.

As an organization, the OAS can do a better job of defending and promoting democracy and human rights, consistent with our shared commitment to implement and apply the Inter-American Democratic Charter. We need more effective mechanisms for foreseeing and counteracting emerging threats to democracy before they reach the crisis stage. The SYG's 2007 Report to the Permanent Council contained some useful recommendations in this regard that warrant further examination. The 2007 Report stressed the need for a "graduated response" to brewing political crises, and called for a more comprehensive linkage of the existing mechanisms of the OAS—particularly our peer review processes—into a coordinated response mechanism in support of member states' democratic institutions. We would welcome a serious discussion on the operationalization of these recommendations. We need to view the Democratic Charter more as resource states can call on when they need it and less as a punitive instrument to be feared and avoided. After all, the Democratic Charter was initially envisioned to function as a preventive toolbox in support of our region's democratic institutions. New regional or subregional institutions may also be able to promote democratic integration and effective governance. The extent to which they do so may ultimately determine their usefulness, staying power, or even legitimacy in their members' eyes. We are willing partners with new collectives that are capable instruments of this common cause.

We already work closely and successfully with many multilateral groupings of which we are not part, such as SICA and CARICOM [Caribbean Community: an international organization with 15 members and 4 associate members]. This engagement is about much more than just aid—it is about co-responsibility, a point Secretary Clinton highlighted during her recent trip to South and Central America. In a time of budgetary challenge in the United States, it is difficult to ask our Congress for assistance resources for countries unable to invest in social programs because they fail to collect taxes from those in their own country who should be contributing to their societies. In many countries in the region tax collection represents less than 15 percent, sometimes less than 10 percent, of GDP.

Mr. Chairman, I cannot close without reiterating here something that I have had occasion to say privately to you and some of the members on the sub-committee. Last April in Trinidad and Tobago President Obama asked his elected counterparts from throughout the Americas to look forward, together, toward the great tasks before us. He signaled clearly that partnership would be the leitmotif of the United States' engagement in the Americas.

That partnership is not just something we seek externally. It is something to which I commit, with you, and the other members of the sub-committee, as we work together to sustain smart policies that advance our national interests, and advance critical agendas we share with people all over the hemisphere. . . . I look forward to continuing this dialogue, and working with Congress to advance our positive agenda with the Americas.

Otto J. Reich  **NO**

U.S. Policy Toward the Americas in 2010 and Beyond

Thank you . . . for this opportunity to address the topic of US policy toward Latin America. The overriding objective of US policy—in Latin America and elsewhere—should be to advance US national interests, not to win international popularity contests. If we can be liked while advancing our interests, so much the better. But let's be realistic: when we try to befriend undemocratic leaders and ignore their belligerence, we are *neither* liked *nor* do we advance our interests. Some of the despots in this hemisphere to whom the [President Barack] Obama Administration extended an open hand only to encounter a clenched fist include the rulers of Cuba, Venezuela, Bolivia, Nicaragua, Ecuador, and Honduras' former President [Manuel] Zelaya. Foremost among our national interests is security. Without security we cannot promote other goals such as democracy, human rights and socio-economic growth. I believe the US government today is underestimating the security threats in the Western Hemisphere. Rather, we seem to be fighting the ghosts of dictatorships past and trying too hard to be liked.

The main threat to the peace, freedom, prosperity and security of the US and the hemisphere does not come from military coups, but from a form of creeping totalitarianism self-described as 21st-Century socialism and allied with some of the most virulent forms of tyranny and anti-Western ideology in the world.

Today in Latin America, democracy is being undermined by a new gang of autocrats who, counseled by the oldest dictator in history, gain power through elections and then dismantle democracy from within. Following Fidel Castro's direction, that has already happened in Venezuela and Bolivia; is happening in Nicaragua and Ecuador; almost happened in Honduras; and could happen in any other nation that falls into the grasp of something called ALBA [Alternativa Bolivariana para las Américas], or the Bolivarian Alternative for the Americas.

ALBA's ruling pattern is clear: after gaining power democratically, they use force to intimidate political adversaries and the media; politicize the police and the military and place them at the orders of the ruling party; pack the judiciary with compliant judges; rewrite electoral laws to eliminate opposition candidates and parties; seize private property or force businesses to close using

U.S. House of Representatives, March 10, 2010.

bogus charges; incite mob violence to force potential opponents into silence or exile; and attack the churches, civic associations, the press, labor unions and any other civil institution that dares to challenge the government. Their stated model is Cuba, and the result will be an Orwellian dictatorship, a pauperized prison-nation whose citizens risk everything to flee.

ALBA was conceived in Havana and is financed by Venezuela's petro-dollars. It is actually the revival of Fidel Castro's half-century goal of uniting international radical and terrorist movements of the developing world under his leadership, a movement that in the 1960s he financed and called "The Tricontinental."

The first foreign country Fidel Castro visited after the overthrow of the [President Fulgencio] Batista dictatorship, in 1959, was Venezuela. While there, he secretly asked Venezuelan President Romulo Betancourt for $300 million (about $3 billion in today's dollars) to "undermine the Yankees (the US) . . ." in Latin America. Betancourt, a center-left leader but a committed democrat, flatly turned Castro down. Three years later Castro was supporting guerrilla warfare in Venezuela and sending an armed expedition of Cuban soldiers to join Marxist rebels in an attempt to destroy Venezuelan democracy and acquire its oil wealth. Today thanks to [Venezuela's President] Hugo Chavez, Castro has finally achieved his goal. Castro also targeted Bolivia in the 1960s, because of its strategic location and enormous mineral wealth. Bolivia has land borders with Argentina, Brazil, Paraguay, Peru and Chile—more than two thirds of South America. In 1967 Castro's lieutenant Ernesto (Che) Guevara selected Bolivia as the site to begin his communist takeover of the continent. Guevara failed miserably, but today a Castro disciple, [President] Evo Morales, is turning Bolivia into one of those 21st-Century dictatorships.

US policy cannot be solely focused on the ALBA Axis, but neither can we ignore it, because the Havana-Caracas-La Paz Axis is undermining the peace and prosperity of the rest of the hemisphere.

I cannot mention in our limited time all the bilateral relationships we have in the hemisphere. But the most sensitive dealings for the US remain those with Mexico, Brazil and Colombia. I contend that these nations and those of the rest of the hemisphere are confused by the signals sent by the Obama Administration in its first year. These three countries are following free market economic policies, providing greater opportunities for their population within a framework of civil liberties, and therefore making steady socio-economic progress. Yet, with the exception of Colombia, their foreign policy seems oddly antagonistic and even self-defeating.

We see Brazil, for example, distancing itself from the US and from Europe on critical matters such as Iran sanctions. Mexico, the Latin American country closest to the US in geography and economy, last month hosted a summit of Latin American leaders that included two military rulers, General Raul Castro of Cuba and Lieutenant Colonel Hugo Chavez of Venezuela, both of whom still wear their rank and uniform at home, but excluded the freely elected civilian leader of Honduras, Pepe [Porfirio] Lobo. This is bizarre, unless they are trying to send a message that they do not share our values or else are misreading the signals sent from Washington. I believe it is the latter.

Some observers explain Brazil's behavior as diplomatic "muscleflexing" by an economically emergent nation, or in the case of Mexico as a return to the traditional nationalistic foreign policy of decades past. Under the undemocratic 70-year rule of the PRI party [*Partido Revolucionario Institucional*], Mexico steered its foreign policy to the left, so as to distract its domestic radicals and keep them from interfering with the management of the more important domestic security and financial policies. These explanations are plausible, but US national interests are nevertheless damaged by the behavior of these friends. And while Mexico and Brazil are still friends, the ALBA nations are not, and are openly and actively undermining US interests.

For example, Venezuela has played an active destabilizing role in Ecuador, Peru, Nicaragua, and above all Colombia, where Hugo Chavez maintains explicit strategic and political alliances with the narco-terrorist Revolutionary Armed Forces of Colombia (FARC). (By the way, the term narco-terrorist is not mine, it is applied to the FARC by various agencies of the US and European governments.) Just last week the Spanish government accused Chavez of supporting with the Spanish Basque terrorist group ETA [Euskadi Ta Askatasuna/ Basque Homeland and Freedom] as well as the FARC. Not satisfied with merely supporting the FARC and allowing guerilla leaders and fighters to hide, train and recuperate inside Venezuelan territory, Chavez has repeatedly closed the commercial border and threatened war against Colombia. The impact on the Colombian economy has been devastating. But Chavez is not just involved in armed intervention against Colombia.

The US, Colombia, and other governments in the region have abundant evidence of massive flows of FARC-controlled cocaine through Venezuela. Senior Chavez regime officials have been designated by the US DEA [Drug Enforcement Agency] as drug kingpins and active collaborators of FARC drug trafficking. These kingpins include the current head of Venezuela's military intelligence services, General Hugo Carvajal, former Interior and Justice Minister Ramon Rodriguez Chacin, and former political police [intelligence service] chief Henry Rangel Silva. Weapons are smuggled to the FARC through Venezuela with the active collusion of senior Chavez regime officials including Army General Cliver Alcala Cordones. This is public record.

Last year, Peruvian intelligence services found evidence that Hugo Chavez actively supported the indigenous groups responsible for violent protests in that country. Former Bolivian Presidents Jorge Quiroga and Gonzalo Sanchez de Lozada have charged that the Chavez regime clandestinely financed and supported riots in that country as far back as 2002, which toppled two governments in quick succession and led to the election of Evo Morales. Chavez also actively supports radical groups in Ecuador, which under President Rafael Correa became a command, control, operations and training base for the Colombian FARC.

In Central America, Chavez actively supports the regime of Nicaraguan President Daniel Ortega. Chavez financed and encouraged Manuel Zelaya's efforts to violate the constitution and laws of Honduras. The disruption to the economy of Central America of the six-month-long Honduran political crisis is said to have cost hundreds of millions of dollars to those impoverished economies. Chavez used Venezuela's oil resources to strengthen El Salvador's

Marxist FMLN [Frente Farabundo Martí para la Liberación Nacional] party, and poured millions of dollars into both El Salvador and Panama's presidential elections. He succeeded in one and failed in the other. Mexico's intelligence services have found links between the Chavez regime and radical groups in that country.

Venezuela's oil wealth has been used to influence Caribbean states through the PetroCaribe program [Venezuelan program that allows favored nations in the region to buy oil at low prices]. PetroCaribe, however, merely postpones the payment for oil purchased today. A few forward thinking Caribbean leaders, in Trinidad-Tobago and Barbados for example, have warned that the PetroCaribe program is saddling the Caribbean's poor island nations with a debt burden they will never be able to repay. But cheap oil today is politically appealing to elected leaders who wish to continue winning elections even at the expense of future generations.

What PetroCaribe has done is to allow Chavez to manipulate the OAS, as evidenced before and during the Honduras crisis. This past week Chavez named Honduras' ousted would-be dictator Manuel Zelaya as the head of PetroCaribe's "Political Council"—a body that does not yet exist, obviously a position created to give Zelaya a salary with which to travel the Americas doing Chavez's bidding.

There is another country, Argentina, that although not a member of ALBA bears watching because of authoritarian tendencies by its ruling presidential couple and close ties to Cuba and Venezuela, lack of official transparency, massive corruption, harassment of private enterprise, and interference with the free market and with the institutions of democracy.

It is no secret that President Cristina Kirchner received millions of dollars from Hugo Chavez for her election campaign, money that was taken illegally from the Venezuelan state, introduced illegally into Argentina, and given to the Kirchner campaign in violation of Argentine law. We know much about the transfer of that money because of a Federal trial that took place in Miami, Florida, and because of an accidental search of a suitcase by an Argentine customs officer who was doing her job. It is well known that similar transfers have taken place in at least a half dozen countries in this region, but that have not yet been publicized.

Like Castro's before him, Chavez's ambitions are global, and the principal goal of his international activities is to weaken, undermine or cripple US strategic interests in the world, not just in the Americas. Chavez is very open about his determination to bring down what he calls the US Empire.

To this end, Chavez has forged strong bonds with undemocratic states such as Russia, Belarus and Iran. Chavez has signed numerous economic and military agreements with all three countries. He has purchased over $4 billion in Russian military equipment. He invited the Russian Navy to maneuver in the Caribbean, which it did, for the first time since the end of the Cold War. Russia's hard-line Prime Minister Vladimir Putin is going to Venezuela soon, reportedly to sign a nuclear energy deal with Chavez.

Chavez has visited Teheran [Iran] numerous times, has signed many commercial, financial and other agreements with Iran, hosted Iranian leader

[President Mahmoud] Ahmadinejad in Caracas and sponsored Ahmadinejad's travel to Bolivia and Nicaragua. He has supported Iran's efforts to acquire nuclear weapons capable of striking targets in Europe and throughout the Middle East. He is a vociferous enemy of Israel and a supporter of regimes dedicated to the destruction of Israel and the US, and the sponsorship of terrorism, such as Iran and Syria.

During Chavez's 11 years in power, Hamas and Hezbollah [Middle East-based terrorist groups] have established a presence in Venezuela. Israeli military intelligence recently disclosed that a shipment of arms seized last November by Israeli commandos departed from a Venezuelan port and docked in an Iranian port before sailing through the Suez Canal bound for Lebanon. The weapons, including missiles, reportedly were to be delivered to Hezbollah.

Chavez also has turned Venezuela over to the Castro regime. Today there are between 40,000 and 50,000 Cubans in Venezuela on official missions, by the Chavez regime's own admission. Since 2005 Venezuela's armed forces have been obliged to embrace Cuba's national security doctrine, which considers the US the greatest external threat to the survival of the 21st-Century socialist revolutionary regime in Caracas.

In spite of its alliances with Russia, China, Belarus, Iran, Syria, FARC, Hezbollah and other criminal, terrorist or rogue governments and non-state actors, there are still policymakers in Washington, D.C., who maintain that the Castro-Chavez-Morales alliance is no more than a nuisance to US interests.

It is time to care less about what others think of us and focus more on what they do to us.

POSTSCRIPT

Is U.S. Policy Toward Latin America on the Right Track?

The ongoing tensions between the older sphere-of-influence U.S. approach to Latin America and the Caribbean and the more recent good neighbor approach are evident in events that unfolded in Honduras beginning in 2009. That year, an attempt by left-leaning President Manuel Zelaya to hold an assembly to change the Constitution sparked a crisis that led the Honduran military to arrest Zelaya and send him into exile. Most countries condemned the coup and refused to recognize the new government. Additionally, the OAS suspended Honduras' membership for violating the democratic process. After some months, a new election was held, and right-leaning Porfirio Lobo was elected president. The duality of U.S. thinking is evident in Washington's reactions. At first, the Obama administration took a clear good neighbor approach by condemning Zelaya's overthrow, refusing to recognize the interim government, and supporting the suspension of Honduras by the OAS. Critics charge, however, that once the new elections were held, the sphere-of-influence approach reemerged in U.S. policy, with Washington too willing to accept the new, rightist president, when, arguably, what should have occurred was to restore the deposed leftist president to power. One flash point is at the OAS, where, as of 2010, the United States has been working to restore Honduras' membership but has been blocked by a number of countries such as Argentina, Brazil, and Mexico that still do not recognize the Lobo government.

A good place to begin for study is with a broad overview of U.S. policy in the region such as Brian Loveman, *No Higher Law: American Foreign Policy and the Western Hemisphere Since 1776* (University of North Carolina Press, 2010). An overview with an emphasis on current relations is Lester D. Langley, *America and the Americas: The United States in the Western Hemisphere* (University of Georgia Press, 2010). A call for the Obama administration to pay close attention to Latin America and generally follow a good neighbor policy is Abraham F. Lowenthal, Theodore J. Piccone, and Laurence Whitehead (eds.), *The Obama Administration and the Americas: Agenda for Change* (Brookings Institution Press, 2009).

Questions for Critical Thinking and Reflection

1. Imagine that you are the U.S. secretary of state and that a Latin American country has democratically elected a very left-wing president. The new president is strongly critical of the United States and its policies in the region, pledges to give financial support to left-wing movements throughout the hemisphere, and otherwise makes every

effort to thwart U.S. foreign policy goals. A secret emissary from dissidents in the other country comes to you and says that pro-U.S. groups, including the army, are ready to overthrow the antagonistic president if the United States signals that after a decent interval it will recognize the new government and resume economic and military aid. What would your response be and why?

2. Throughout history it has been common for major powers to control a sphere of influence in regions near their border. Is it appropriate for the United States to operate under the assumption that Latin America and the Caribbean are its sphere of influence?

3. In the second reading, Otto Reich argues, "It is time to care less about what others think of us [the United States/Americans] and focus more on what they do to us." Is this a sound foundation for a successful foreign policy?

Internet References . . .

IPE Net

The International Political Economy Network hosted by Indiana University and sponsored by the IPE section of the International Studies Association is a good starting point to study the intersection of politics and economics globally.

http://www.indiana.edu/~ipe/ipesection/

United Nations Development Programme (UNDP)

This United Nations Development Programme (UNDP) site offers publications and current information on world poverty, the UNDP's mission statement, information on the UN Development Fund for Women, and more.

http://www.undp.org

Office of the U.S. Trade Representative

The Office of the U.S. Trade Representative (USTR) is responsible for developing and coordinating U.S. international trade, commodity, and direct investment policy and leading or directing negotiations with other countries on such matters. The U.S. trade representative is a cabinet member who acts as the principal trade adviser, negotiator, and spokesperson for the president on trade and related investment matters.

http://www.ustr.gov

The U.S. Agency for International Development (USAID)

This is the home page of the U.S. Agency for International Development (USAID), which is the independent government agency that provides economic development and humanitarian assistance to advance U.S. economic and political interests overseas.

http://www.usaid.gov/

World Trade Organization (WTO)

The World Trade Organization (WTO) is the only international organization dealing with the global rules of trade between nations. Its main function is to ensure that trade fl ows as smoothly, predictably, and freely as possible. This site provides extensive information about the organization and international trade today.

http://www.wto.org

Third World Network

The Third World Network (TWN) is an independent, nonprofit international network of organizations and individuals involved in economic, social, and environmental issues relating to development, the developing countries of the world, and the North-South divide. At the network's Web site you will find recent news, TWN position papers, action alerts, and other resources on a variety of topics, including economics, trade, and health.

http://www.twnside.org.sg

Economic Issues

International economic and trade issues have an immediate and personal effect on individuals in ways that few other international issues do. They influence the jobs we hold and the prices of the products we buy—in short, our lifestyles. In the worldwide competition for resources and markets, tensions arise between allies and adversaries alike. This section examines some of the prevailing economic tensions.

- Does China's Currency Manipulation Warrant International and National Action?
- Is Immigration an Economic Benefit to the Host Country?
- Should Export Controls on High Technology Be Eased Substantially?

ISSUE 10

Does China's Currency Manipulation Warrant International and National Action?

YES: C. Fred Bergsten, from "Correcting the Chinese Exchange Rate: An Action Plan," Testimony during Hearings on "China's Exchange Rate Policy" before the Committee on Ways and Means, U.S. House of Representatives (March 24, 2010)

NO: Pieter Bottelier and Uri Dadush, from "The RMB: Myths and Tougher-To-Deal-With Realities," Testimony during Hearings on "China's Exchange Rate Policy" before the Committee on Ways and Means, U.S. House of Representatives (March 24, 2010)

ISSUE SUMMARY

YES: C. Fred Bergsten, the director of the Peterson Institute for International Economics and former (1977–1981) assistant secretary of the treasury for international affairs, argues that China is manipulating the value of its currency in a way that is harming the U.S. international economic position and that it is time to use international and, if necessary, national pressure to remedy the situation.

NO: Pieter Bottelier, the senior adjunct professor of China studies at the School of Advanced International Studies at Johns Hopkins University and the former chief of the World Bank's resident mission in Beijing, and Uri Dadush, the director of the International Economics Program at the Carnegie Endowment for International Peace and former (2002–2008) World Bank's director of international trade, contend that dangerous myths about China's currency may unwisely touch off a strong U.S. reaction while more effective solutions will be overlooked.

T o follow this debate, it is essential to understand three facts about money. First, money has no inherent value. Domestically, the value of the U.S. dollar and every other currency decreases during inflation or, more rarely, increases during deflation. Internationally, the "exchange rate" between two countries' currencies normally varies based on supply of and demand for each currency.

Comparing the dollar to China's *renminbi* (RMB, people's currency, also yuan), one dollar could be exchanged for 8.28 RMB in 2000. In mid-2010, you would only get 6.78 RMB for a dollar.

The second key point is that the comparative values of two currencies have major impact on the flow of trade and investment between those countries and, therefore, on each country's economy. If, as occurred in our example, the dollar loses value (weakens) versus the RMB, then it should be easier (cheaper) for China to buy products imported from the United States and harder (costlier) for Americans to buy products exported by China.

Third, fair trade and global economic rules require that countries generally allow their currencies to "float" against one another, that is, to have their value determined by market forces rather than by government intervention. This third point is the core of this debate.

During the 1980s, as the cold war eased and trade between China and the West grew, China moved to artificially lower the value of its currency in order to promote exports. Among other things, from 1997 through 2004, China "pegged" the exchange rate at 8.62 RMB = $1 by making any other rate of exchange in China illegal. Virtually all experts agreed the RMB was far overvalued, with some putting the disparity as much as 50%. Partly as a result of the artificial exchange rate, Chinese exports to the United States boomed, while U.S. exports to China lagged. In 1995, China sold $46 billion in goods to the United States but bought only $12 billion in U.S. products. Thus, China's exports to the United States exceeded its imports 3.8 times (3.8:1) over, or by $34 billion. By 2005, China was selling $244 billion in goods to the United States but buying only $42 billion in U.S. products. Thus, the U.S. trade deficit with China worsened between 1995 and 2005 both in terms of the ratio (from 3.8:1 to 5.8:1) and the amount (from $34 billion to $202 billion).

As the U.S. deficit grew amid charges of unfair practices on China's part, pressure to retaliate mounted. Among other things, legislation was introduced to impose a 27.5% increase in the U.S. tariff on goods from China unless it devalued its currency. Perhaps in response, in July 2005, China "unpegged" its currency from the dollar in July 2005. However, China continued to use other methods to keep the RMB from changing too fast against the dollar, and in mid-2008 amid global economic turmoil, Beijing once again pegged the RMB to the dollar.

Overall since 2005, China has let the RMB weaken some, with the exchange rate per dollar dropping from an average of 8.19 RMB in 2005 to 6.79 in mid-2010, or about 17% for the period. This drop has had a positive impact on the trade deficit, with the ratio declining from 5.8:1 in 2005 to 4.7:1 in 2008 and 3.9:1 in 2009. While this is better, the gaping U.S. trade deficit with China ($266 billion in 2009) and the view of such respected analysts as Fred Bergsten in the first reading show that the fair RMB–dollar ratio would be about 5 RMB = $1. He tells Congress that it is time to intensify the pressure on China to let the RMB truly float and find a fair exchange rate. Pieter Bottelier and Uri Dadush take a very different view, arguing, among other things, that China is not artificially manipulating the value of the RMB and that weakening the RMB versus the dollar will not help the U.S. economy overall.

YES

C. Fred Bergsten

Correcting the Chinese Exchange Rate: An Action Plan

The Problem

The Chinese renminbi (RMB) [China's basic currency unit, like the dollar for the United States] is undervalued by about 25 percent on a trade-weighted average basis [compared to other currencies based on each country's share of world trade] and by about 40 percent against the dollar. The Chinese authorities [use their foreign reserves—supply of foreign currencies—to] buy about $1 billion [in RMB] daily in the exchange markets to keep their currency from rising and thus to maintain an artificially strong competitive position. Several neighboring Asian countries of considerable economic significance—Hong Kong, Malaysia, Singapore and Taiwan—maintain currency undervaluations of roughly the same magnitude in order to avoid losing competitive position to China. [Note: Hong Kong is not a country, but an autonomous special administrative region of China. Whether Taiwan is a country or not is highly debatable.]

This competitive undervaluation of the RMB is a blatant form of protectionism. It subsidizes all Chinese exports by the amount of the misalignment, about 25–40 percent. It equates to a tariff of like magnitude on all Chinese imports, sharply discouraging purchases from other countries. It would thus be incorrect to characterize as "protectionist" a policy response to the Chinese actions by the United States or other countries; such actions should more properly be viewed as anti-protectionist.

Largely as a result of this competitive undervaluation, China's global current account surplus [all money going abroad compared to all money coming into the country] soared to almost $400 billion and exceeded 11 percent of its GDP in 2007, an unprecedented imbalance for the world's largest exporting country and second largest economy. China's global surplus declined sharply during the [worldwide] great recession [beginning in 2008], as its foreign markets weakened, but it remained above 5 percent of China's GDP (almost $275 billion) even in 2009. The International Monetary Fund [IMF] estimates that the surplus is rising again and, at current exchange rates, will exceed the global deficit of the United States by 2014. In a world where high unemployment and below-par growth are likely to remain widespread for some time, including in the United States, China is thus exporting very large doses of unemployment to the rest of the world—including the United States but also

U.S. House of Representatives, March 24, 2010.

to Europe and to many emerging market economies including Brazil, India, Mexico and South Africa.

China's exchange rate policy violates all relevant international norms. Article IV, Section 1 of the Articles of Agreement of the International Monetary Fund commits member countries to "avoid manipulating exchange rates or the international monetary system in order to prevent effective balance-of-payment adjustment or to gain unfair competitive advantage over other member countries." Moreover, the principles and procedures for implementing the Fund's obligation (in Article IV, Section 3) "to exercise firm surveillance over the exchange rate policies of members" call for discussion with a country that practices "protracted large-scale intervention in one direction in exchange markets"—a succinct description of China's currency policy over the past seven years. Article XV(4) of the General Agreement on Tariffs and Trade (GATT), which is now an integral part of the World Trade Organization [WTO], similarly indicates that "Contracting parties shall not, by exchange action, frustrate the intent of the provisions of this Agreement."

Huge current account imbalances, including the US deficit and the Chinese surplus, of course reflect a number of economic factors (national saving and investment rates, the underlying competitiveness of firms and workers, etc.) other than exchange rates. Successful international adjustment of course requires corrective action by the United States, particularly with respect to its budget deficit and low national saving rate, and other countries as well as by China. But it is impossible for deficit countries to reduce their imbalances unless surplus countries reduce theirs. And restoration of equilibrium exchanges rates is an essential element of an effective global "rebalancing strategy" as agreed by the G-20 over the past year. [The G-20, Group of 20 consists of the leading high-income countries and several of the leading middle- and low-income countries and is meant to promote economic discussions and cooperation among them.]

The competitive undervaluation of the Chinese RMB and several neighboring Asian countries has a very substantial impact on the United States. As noted, an appreciation of 25–40 percent is needed to cut China's global surplus even to 3–4 percent of its GDP. This realignment would produce a reduction of $100–150 billion in the annual US current account deficit.

Every $1 billion of exports supports about 6,000–8,000 (mainly high-paying manufacturing) jobs in the US economy. Hence such a trade correction would generate an additional 600,000–1,200,000 US jobs. Correction of the Chinese/Asian currency misalignment is by far the most important component of the President's new National Export Initiative. As its budget cost is zero, it is also by far the most cost-effective step that can be taken to reduce the unemployment rate in the United States.

China did let its exchange rate appreciate gradually from July 2005 until the middle of 2008 (and rode the dollar up for a while after it re-pegged in the fall of 2008). During that time, the maximum increase in its trade-weighted and dollar values was 20–25 percent (which represented good progress although it still left an undervaluation of roughly a like amount at that time). It has since depreciated again significantly, riding the dollar down, so that its net rise over the past five years is only about 15 percent. Moreover, despite China's declared adoption of a "market-oriented" exchange rate policy in 2005, its intervention to block any further strengthening of the RMB against the dollar is about twice as great today ($30–40 billion per month) as it was then ($15–20 billion per month); on that metric, China's currency policy is now about half as market-oriented as it was prior to adoption of the "new policy."

The present time is highly opportune for China to begin the process of restoring an equilibrium exchange rate. The Chinese economy is booming, indeed leading the world recovery from the Great Recession (and China deserves great credit for its effective crisis response strategies). Inflation is now rising and the Chinese authorities have begun to take monetary and other measures to avoid renewed overheating; currency appreciation would be an effective and powerful tool to this end by lowering the price of imports and dampening demand for exports. Appreciation of the RMB at this time would in fact serve both the internal and external policy objectives of the Chinese authorities, as part of their long-stated intention and international commitment to rebalance the country's economic growth away from exports and toward domestic (especially consumer) demand.

An Action Plan

The case for a substantial increase in the value of the RMB is thus clear and overwhelming. Some observers believe that China is in fact preparing to shortly renew the gradual appreciation of mid-2005 to mid-2008 (5–7 percent per year) or even to announce a modest (5–10 percent) one-shot revaluation (with or without resuming the upward crawl in addition). On the other hand, Premier Wen Jiabao recently denied that the RMB was undervalued at all and accused other countries (!) of seeking to expand exports and create jobs by unfairly depreciating their exchange rates.

Unfortunately, the two preferred strategies for promoting Chinese action—sweet reason and implementation of the multilateral rules, especially in the IMF—have to date had limited success. Both efforts should continue, however, and it is particularly important that any stepped-up initiatives toward China be multilateral in nature. The Chinese are much more likely to respond positively to a multilateral coalition rather than bilateral pressure from the United States, especially if that coalition contains a number of emerging market and developing economies whose causes the Chinese frequently claim to champion. Moreover, the multilateral efforts have been halfhearted at best and it is especially important for the United States to exhaust that route before contemplating more severe unilateral steps.

Much of the blame for this failure of policy to date falls on the US Government, which has been unwilling to label China the currency manipulator that it has been so clearly for a number of years. The unwillingness of the United States to implement the plain language of the Trade Act of 1988 has substantially undermined its credibility in seeking multilateral action against China in the IMF, the WTO, the G-20 or anywhere else. A sensible and effective strategy must begin by reversing that feckless position.

Hence I would recommend that the Administration adopt a new three-part strategy to promote early and substantial appreciation of the exchange rate of the RMB:

1. Label China as a "currency manipulator" in its next foreign exchange report to the Congress on April 15 and, as required by law, then enter into negotiations with China to resolve the currency problem.
2. Hopefully with the support of the European countries, and as many emerging market and developing economies as possible, seek a decision by the IMF (by a 51 percent majority of the weighted votes of member countries) to launch a "special" or "ad hoc" consultation to pursue Chinese agreement to remedy the situation promptly. If the consultation fails to produce results, the United States should ask the Executive Board to decide (by a 70% majority of the weighted votes) to publish a report criticizing China's exchange rate policy.
3. Hopefully with a similarly broad coalition, the United States should exercise its right to ask the World Trade Organization to constitute a dispute settlement panel to determine whether China has violated its obligations under Article XV ("frustration of the intent of the agreement by exchange action") of the WTO charter and to recommend remedial action that other member countries could take in response. The WTO under its rules would ask the IMF whether the RMB is undervalued, another reason why it is essential to engage the IMF centrally in the new initiative from the outset.

A three-pronged initiative of this type would focus global attention on the China misalignment and its unwillingness to initiate corrective action to date. The effort would have maximum impact if it could be undertaken by the United States in concert with countries that constituted a substantial share of the world economy, including emerging market and developing economies as well as the Europeans and other high-income nations. Asian countries, such as Japan and India, will be skittish in confronting China in this way but are hit hard by the Chinese undervaluation and should be increasingly willing to join the coalition as its size grows.

The objective of the exercise is of course to persuade, or "name and shame," China into corrective action. Unfortunately, the IMF has no sanctions that it can use against recalcitrant surplus countries. Hence the WTO, which can authorize trade sanctions against violations of its charter, needs to be brought into the picture from the outset. Unfortunately, there are technical and legal problems with the WTO rules too (like the IMF rules) so they may also need to be amended for future purposes. The United States could of course intensify its initiative by taking unilateral trade actions against China. For example, the [US] administration could decide that the undervaluation of the RMB constitutes an export subsidy in determining whether to apply countervailing duties against imports from China. Congress could amend the current countervailing duty legislation to make clear that such a determination is legal. In either case, China could appeal to the WTO and the United States would have to defend its actions under the Subsidy Code.

Countervailing duties and other product-specific or sector-specific steps, such as the Section 421 case on tires last year or traditional Section 201 safeguard cases, are basically undesirable, however, because they distort and disguise the across-the-board nature of the Chinese currency misalignment. These measures are intended to address problems that are unique to a particular product or sector rather than affecting trade and the economy as a whole. As noted above, China's competitive undervaluation represents a subsidy to all exports and a tariff on all imports. Hence it requires a comprehensive response via the exchange rate itself since there is no good alternative. A US effort that encompasses unilateral, IMF and WTO dimensions to that end is likely to be the most effective strategy we can undertake at this time.

**Pieter Bottelier and
Uri Dadush**

 **NO**

The RMB: Myths and Tougher-
To-Deal-With Realities

China fever will again grip Washington as the U.S. Treasury nears its mid-April deadline for pronouncing whether China manipulates its currency. Dangerous myths about the RMB will again be propagated, feeding China bashers and protectionist lobbies. Meanwhile, more important and politically tougher reforms in both the United States and China will be conveniently overlooked.

Most economists would agree that the RMB is undervalued and that it is in China's interest to allow appreciation. By pegging its exchange rate to the dollar, China abdicates a large measure of control over its monetary policy. In addition, an undervalued currency increases prices for Chinese consumers and contributes to inflationary pressures and excessive accumulation of low-yielding reserves.

However, the benefits of RMB appreciation for the United States are mixed at best and—whether net positive or negative—are certainly exaggerated. U.S. policy makers should prioritize maintaining a collaborative relationship with China, now the world's largest trading nation, over staging another fruitless debate on the RMB.

The Myths
China's Growth Has Depended Primarily on Exports

While integration into world markets has been vital for China's development, domestic demand has always been the country's primary growth driver. During the decade before the crisis, net-exports accounted for only about 1 percentage point of China's 9.5 percent average annual growth, as imports grew almost as fast as exports.

China Did Not Contribute Enough
to Global Demand during the Crisis

Chinese demand was integral to Asia's early emergence from the recession, and the rest of the world benefited as well. In 2008, China accounted for over 50 percent of world growth; last year, China expanded rapidly while the world economy contracted.

Domestic demand in China expanded 12.3 percent in 2009, while domestic demand in the United States and industrialized countries contracted 2.6 percent and 2.7 percent, respectively. China's output was able to grow nearly 9 percent even as exports plummeted 16 percent. Imports held up much better than exports, and China's current account surplus declined from 9.6 percent of GDP in 2008 to 5.8 percent in 2009. Data till February this year suggests that the surplus is still shrinking.

Furthermore, during the most acute phase of the crisis—the fourth quarter of 2008 to the first quarter of 2009, when the dollar appreciated against nearly all currencies—China maintained the RMB's peg to the dollar. This helped other countries weather the demand collapse.

China's Consumption Is Not Growing Fast Enough

Private consumption in China grew by an average of about 7.5 percent over the ten years prior to the crisis, faster than in any other large economy. In the United States, private consumption grew at an annual rate of 3.6 percent over the same period. Nonetheless, consumption's share of China's national income fell over that period as investment grew even faster. In 2009, however, consumption's share rose, another hopeful sign that the economy may be rebalancing toward domestic demand at the expense of exports.

The United States Depends on China to Buy Its Government Debt

At the end of 2009, China held only about 7 percent of U.S. federal government debt outstanding. Sold at a high price (low yield), U.S. government debt is a popular security. At the same time, the United States is benefiting China: China has few good alternatives to hold its reserves and U.S. firms are large investors and employers in China. In the investment arena, as in others, the United States and China are mutually dependent.

China Has Been Manipulating Its Currency to Get an Unfair Advantage in Trade for Years

About 60 countries peg their exchange rates to the dollar today, and they are not all currency manipulators. The real question is whether a country systematically pegs its currency at an artificially low rate in order to gain competitive advantage—a violation of IMF [International Monetary Fund] and WTO [World Trade Organization] rules.

The evidence against the RMB is mixed at best. China pegged the RMB to the dollar at the end of 1997, in the midst of the Asian crisis. At that time, the United States and other countries applauded the peg as a generous act that promoted stability in the region. Serious complaints did not emerge until 2003, when China's trade surplus and America's trade deficit (with the world and with China) began to rise sharply.

However, the RMB/dollar rate, which had not changed, was not the primary reason for the growing imbalance. Rather, in the United States, the fiscal surpluses of the final Clinton years had shifted to large deficits and the Greenspan Fed [the US Federal Reserve Board under the chairmanship Alan Greenspan from 1987 to 2006] was pursuing very loose monetary policies while the financial sector generated additional liquidity as a result of inadequate oversight and regulation. In China, aggressive domestic reforms had prompted exceptional productivity growth in manufacturing, while the government promoted both exports and import substitution.

Recognizing these shifts, China adopted a policy of gradual RMB appreciation in July 2005. Three years later, the RMB had risen 21 percent against the dollar. Because of the sharp, crisis-induced drop in export orders, however, China suspended the policy. China's central bank governor recently confirmed that the suspension is a special, crisis-related measure, implying that gradual appreciation will resume as the crisis abates.

Revaluation of the RMB Will Help the U.S. Economy

The immediate effect of RMB appreciation would be to raise prices for U.S. consumers. A 25 percent revaluation of the RMB, which some economists have said is needed, would—if not offset by a reduction in China's prices—add $75 billion to the U.S. import bill. Since the United States imports three times as much from China as it exports there, higher U.S. exports to China would not nearly offset the welfare loss to U.S. consumers from higher Chinese prices.

It would take years for adjustment to a higher RMB to occur, but in the end, though some U.S. firms would gain and some export jobs would be created, the U.S. consumer would be the loser, and the net welfare effect on U.S. workers would probably be negative.

Revaluation of the RMB Is Critical for Reducing Global Trade Imbalances

A revaluation of the RMB by itself would do little to redress global imbalances, and could, as mentioned, initially lead to a wider U.S.–China trade deficit. Most likely, unless U.S. domestic demand falls for other reasons, the overall U.S. trade deficit would hardly budge in the end as the United States would simply import more from other countries that would resist following China's lead in allowing currency appreciation.

The (Tougher-To-Deal-With) Realities

China's Policies Artificially Promote Investment, Exports, and Import Substitution at the Expense of Consumption

Many leaders in China acknowledge the need to address the country's pervasive export and import-substitution policies, as well as the suppressed interest rates, which lower the cost of capital for Chinese firms. However, tough internal policy battles lie ahead as powerful vested interests resist change. International pressure on these issues would strengthen the hand of reformers.

China Needs to Improve Its Safety Nets

Although budget outlays for health and education have increased significantly in recent years, much more needs to be done. Further improvements would probably prompt households to reduce savings and increase consumption. However, the impact on China's trade balance would depend on how the safety nets were financed. If social security contributions to the de-facto pay-as-you-go system were simply raised, national savings would change little. If, on the other hand, these outlays increased government deficits and borrowing, national savings and China's trade surplus might decline.

Overwhelmingly, U.S. External Deficits Are Determined by U.S. Policies

All fair-minded economists recognize that measures to reduce the U.S. fiscal deficit and encourage household savings will do infinitely more to correct U.S. current account deficits than any conceivable policy change in China. Though the needed measures are well known, and include raising consumption and energy taxes, increasing competition and efficiency in healthcare, and establishing a needs-tested social security system, these changes are politically complicated to say the least.

Conclusion

China's economy has become so large and globally integrated that its exchange rate policy is a matter of international concern. But, more than an international issue, it is crucial for China. Given the realities outlined above, it makes little sense for the United States to point to China's exchange rate as a major bilateral issue. Designating China a currency "manipulator" will only impair a crucial relationship. In addition, the debate diverts attention from the politically difficult, but much more significant, domestic reforms that are needed in both the United States and China.

POSTSCRIPT

Does China's Currency Manipulation Warrant International and National Action?

In June 2010, about 3 months after the congressional hearings from which the two readings in this debate were held, China announced that it would once again unpeg its currency from the dollar. During the following month, the dollar weakened against the RMB by just one-half of 1 percent, so it remains unclear how quickly or how far Beijing will be willing to let the RMB float against the dollar and other currencies. It is also uncertain what impact these changes will have on the U.S. trade deficit with China. As of late July, the 2010 deficit appears likely to be about $230 billion. That would be a welcome 14% decrease from 2009, but would still be far out of balance. One measure is that the trade deficit with China would constitute approximately half of the overall projected U.S. trade deficit of about $500 billion.

Although the two readings focus on the economic consequences of confronting China on its currency, it is important to remember that issues between countries are often not treated in isolation. The two countries have a complex strategic relationship, and the United States needs China's help in many areas. For example, China is one of the few countries with any influence in North Korea, and Chinese participation is important to the effort to resolve the ongoing confrontation with North Korea over its nuclear weapons program. China also has a veto in the UN Security Council and could block U.S. efforts there on such matters as getting sanctions or even military action authorized against Iran in response to its nuclear program (see Issue 8). At the least, strong U.S. pressure on China would hurt short-term political relations and could even promote long-term animosity (see Issue 6). Therefore, the costs of a trade war with China cannot be calculated only in dollars and cents. None of this means, however, that the United States should do nothing.

A book by a U.S. senator advocating strong corrective measures is Byron L. Dorgan (D-ND), *Take This Job and Ship It* (Thomas Dunne Books, 2006). For the less combative official U.S. position, go to the Web site of the U.S. Trade Representative at http://www.ustreas.gov/ and keyboard in "China and currency" in the search window. For background, read the Congressional Research Service report, "China's Currency: A Summary of the Economic Issues" (December 7, 2009). It is available on many Web sites including http://opencrs.com/document/RS21625/. An interesting view that sees China and the Untied State as cocreators of an international economic condition that cannot persist without great damage is Niall Ferguson and Mortiz Schularick, "The End of Chimerica" (November 9, 2009), Harvard Business

School BGIE Unit Working Paper No. 10-037, available at SSRN: http://ssrn
.com/abstract=1502756. An article by two Chinese American scholars that
emphasizes the mutual entwinement of the United States and China and the
resulting policy challenges is Quansheng Zhao and Guoli Liu, "Managing the
Challenges of Complex Interdependence: China and the United States in the
Era of Globalization," *Asian Politics & Policy* (January 2010).

Questions for Critical Thinking and Reflection

1. What should be the single most important goal of U.S. relations with
   China?
2. Trade sanctions on China would mean higher prices for some goods
   and also retaliatory sanctions by China that would limit some U.S.
   exports and therefore also harm the U.S. economy. Are the costs to
   Americans worth the fight?
3. Should the United States pressure China solely through multilateral
   avenues as the World Trade Organization or should Washington also
   pressure unilateral action by such means as imposing trade sanctions
   on Beijing?

ISSUE 11

Is Immigration an Economic Benefit to the Host Country?

YES: Dan Siciliano, from Testimony during Hearings on "Immigration: Economic Impact," before the Committee on the Judiciary, U.S. Senate (April 24, 2006)

NO: Barry R. Chiswick, from Testimony during Hearings on "Immigration: Economic Impact," before the Committee on the Judiciary, U.S. Senate (April 24, 2006)

ISSUE SUMMARY

YES: Dan Siciliano, executive director, Program in Law, Business, and Economics, and research fellow with the Immigration Policy Center at the American Immigration Law Foundation, Stanford Law School, contends that immigration provides many economic benefits for the United States.

NO: Barry R. Chiswick, UIC Distinguished Professor, and program director, Migration Studies IZA—Institute for the Study of Labor, Bonn, Germany, takes the position that legal immigration has a negative impact on the U.S. economy and that illegal immigration increases the problems.

P art of the saga of human history is the migration of people ranging from individuals to entire populations from their homes to new ones in search of a better life. Indeed, the development of some countries, such as the United States, is substantially based on the inflow of immigrants. Sometimes such influxes have gone fairly smoothly. At other times they have met significant opposition within the country of destination. Such is the case currently, with the global tide of refugees and immigrants, both legal and illegal, facing increasing resistance. A poll that asked people in 44 countries whether immigrants were having a good or bad impact found that a plurality in 28 countries said bad, with a plurality answering good in just 13 countries, and 3 countries evenly divided. Moreover, a lopsided 72 percent of the respondents favored stricter controls on immigration. Support for this position averaged 76 percent in the wealthiest countries such as the United States, Canada, and Western Europe. But opposition was even slightly higher in Latin America (77 percent) and sub-Saharan Africa (79 percent) and also strong among East Europeans (67 percent), Asians (61 percent), and Middle Easterners (66 percent).

Opposition to immigration comes from several sources. One is prejudice based on race, ethnicity, religion, or some other characteristic. More legitimate in the view of many is worry that immigrants are diluting the host country's language and other aspects of its national culture. Security concerns are a third source of opposition to immigration. Some critics of immigration argue that crime is higher among immigrant populations, and in recent years the possibility of immigrants being terrorists has increased this worry for some. Economic concerns are a fourth source of opposition to immigrants. One economic argument is that immigrants work for low wages, thereby undercutting the wages of native-born workers. Another charge is that immigrants are an economic burden, requiring far more in terms of welfare, medical care, education, and other services than the migrants return to the economy in terms of productivity and taxes. These charges are met by counterarguments that depict immigrants as providing needed workers and otherwise giving a boost to their new country's economy.

Immigration into the United States has changed markedly in recent decades. One difference is that it has increased significantly, with legal immigration growing almost 300 percent from a yearly average of 330,000 in the 1960s to an annual average of 978,000 in the 1990s and just over 1 million during 2000–2007. A second difference is that immigrants are more likely to be people of color from Africa, Asia, and Latin America. European-heritage whites made up more than 70 percent of all immigrants as late as the 1950s. Now, because of changes in U.S. immigration law, only 14 percent are from such countries, while 48 percent of legal immigrants are from Latin America and the Caribbean, 34 percent are from Asia, and 4 percent are from Africa. Adding to both the overall number of immigrants and the percentage who are not from Europe, Canada, and other European-heritage countries is an estimated 400,000 to 500,000 illegal (undocumented, unauthorized) immigrants who arrive in the United States yearly. Perhaps 11 million such immigrants are currently in the United States, with approximately 80 percent of them from Central America, especially Mexico.

The presence of so many undocumented immigrants has become a major political issue in the United States. At one level, it is a question unto itself. It also relates to the general concerns about immigration that many Americans have regarding culture and security. Certainly, American attitudes are different for legal and illegal immigrants, but there is also an overlap, illustrated by the fact that polls find that most Americans favor decreasing immigration overall. When Americans are asked what bothers them about illegal immigration, they express concern about the impact of unauthorized immigrants on wages, job availability, and the cost of social and educational services. Taking up this concern, Dan Siciliano examines the economic impact of both documented and undocumented immigrants on the United States in the first reading and finds that the country benefits. Barry Chiswick disagrees in the second reading, finding economic damage from legal and illegal immigration alike.

YES

Dan Siciliano

Immigration: The Positive Impact

Today's hearing on U.S. immigration policy and its impact on the American economy comes at a critical time. Efforts are underway in the House and in the Senate to repair a system that is generally acknowledged to be broken. I suggest that any reform to immigration policy should be evaluated by considering how immigrants directly, and as the evidence now seems to indicate, positively impact our nation's economic prosperity.

Much of the public debate over immigration in the United States has focused on the rapid growth of the undocumented population over the past decade and a half. However, undocumented immigration is just one symptom of the larger disconnect between U.S. immigration policy and the reality of our economy's fundamental reliance on a diverse and, hopefully, growing pool of available labor. The U.S. economy has become increasingly reliant on immigrant workers to fill the growing number of less-skilled jobs for which a shrinking number of native-born workers are available. Yet current immigration policies offer very few legal avenues for workers in less-skilled occupations to enter the country. Undocumented immigration has been the predictable result of the U.S. immigration system's failure to respond effectively to actual labor demand.

Many critics of immigration point to economic arguments that the presence of immigrants, particularly undocumented immigrants, has broad negative consequences for the native-born workforce. Some claim that immigration reduces employment levels and wages among native-born workers. This is generally not true. These arguments are largely the result of an over-simplified economic model used to measure the impact of immigration on the workforce, while ignoring the role that immigrants play in expanding the economy and stimulating labor demand through their consumer purchases and investments. Moreover, the empirical evidence indicates that businesses expand through the investment of more capital when the labor supply is not artificially constrained. Careful analysis and more recent studies add a dynamic component to the economic analysis of immigration by treating immigrants (both documented and undocumented) as real economic agents: earning, spending, and investing in the economy. Businesses, in turn, are considered dynamic as well: adjusting to the available resources and expanding accordingly. Or, if this issue should be mishandled, rediverting resources and shrinking accordingly.

Few argue with the notion that immigration provides many benefits to the United States. As a nation of immigrants, our culture, customs, and

U.S. Senate, April 24, 2006.

traditions reflect the diverse backgrounds of the millions of individuals who have made their way to America over time. But more than cultural benefits, recent economic analysis, including work by Giovanni Peri of the University of California, shows that the United States sees real economic benefits from immigration. Native-born wages increased between 2.0 and 2.5 percent during the 1990s in response to the inflow of immigrant workers. Overall annual growth in the Gross Domestic Product is 0.1 percentage point higher as a result of immigration—a misleadingly small number that represents billions of dollars in economic output and, when compounded across a generation, represents a significant improvement in the standard of living of our children and grandchildren.

The positive impact of immigration results in part from the fact that immigrants help to fill growing gaps in our labor force. These gaps develop as aging native-born workers, in larger numbers than ever before, succeed in attaining higher levels of education and subsequently pursue higher-skill, higher-wage jobs. If the United States were to reform the immigration system to better address the demand for foreign-born labor, largely through ensuring that such workers were a part of the transparent and competitive "above ground" economy, the economic benefits of immigration could be even greater than what we have already experienced. Immigrants and their employers would likely benefit from a more predictable workforce environment and less time and resources would be spent addressing the dysfunction that is a result of a strong demand for a labor force that our laws do not accommodate.

Undocumented immigration is largely the result of two opposing forces: an immigration policy that significantly restricts the flow of labor and the economic reality of a changing native-born U.S. population. The extent to which the U.S. economy has become dependent on immigrant workers is evident in the labor force projections of the Bureau of Labor Statistics (BLS). According to BLS estimates, immigrants will account for about a quarter of labor force growth between 2002 and 2012. Given that roughly half of immigrants now arriving in the United States are undocumented, this means that 1 in 8 workers joining the U.S. labor force over the coming decade will be undocumented immigrants. Many of the jobs that would be harder to fill without this labor supply are already associated with immigrant labor: construction, agriculture, meatpacking, and hospitality. A growing number of immigrants, however, are also filling jobs in fields that are vitally important to serving America's aging population, such as home healthcare. This indicates that while policymakers debate the relative merits of various immigration reform proposals, immigration beyond current legal limits has already become an integral component of U.S. economic growth and will likely remain so for the foreseeable future.

The Impact of Immigrants on Native-Born Wages

Despite the critical role that immigration plays in preventing labor shortages that might impede economic growth, many critics of immigration argue that foreign-born workers reduce the wages of native-born workers with whom they compete for jobs. However, this argument relies on an overly simplistic understanding of labor supply and demand that fails to capture the true value that immigrants bring to the economy. If you are to gauge accurately the economic impact of immigration, the role that immigrants play in creating jobs is just as important as the role they play in filling jobs.

To analyze the impact of immigration on the U.S. economy as a whole, particularly in the studies relied upon in this debate, economists typically use one of two models: "static" or "dynamic." The static model is the simplest and most frequently used by critics of immigration, yet it is the least realistic because it fails to account for the multi-dimensional role that immigrants play as workers, consumers, and entrepreneurs. The dynamic model, on the other hand, offers a more nuanced portrait of immigrants as economic actors. The net economic benefits of immigration are apparent in both models, but are larger in the dynamic model.

Under the static model, economists assume that immigrant workers serve only to increase the labor supply, which results in slightly lower wages and thus higher profits for the owners of capital. In other words, if there are more workers competing for a job, an employer might pay a lower wage for that job and pocket the difference. For instance, under a popular version of the analysis that utilizes the static model, the 125 million native-born workers in the United States in 1997 would have earned an average of $13 per hour if not for the presence of immigrants. However, the 15 million immigrant workers who were actually in the country increased the labor force to 140 million and, under the static scenario, thereby lowered average wages by 3 percent to $12.60 per hour. Nonetheless, the net benefit to the U.S. economy of this decline in wages would have amounted to about $8 billion in added national income in 1997.

Despite the seeming simplicity of this logic (more workers competing for jobs results in lower wages for workers and higher profits for businesses), the assumptions underlying the static model bear little resemblance to economic reality. Recent evidence supports the contention that the impact of immigration on wages is not as simple, or negative, as the static model would suggest. A 2004 study found that, despite the large influx of immigrants without a high-school diploma from 1980 to 2000, the wages of U.S.-born workers without a diploma relative to the wages of U.S.-born workers with a diploma "remained nearly constant." More importantly, [research shows] . . . that the dynamic response of small and medium sized businesses to this phenomena means that nearly all U.S.-born workers, especially those with a high school education or better, have benefited from higher wages due to the presence of this low skilled, often undocumented, immigrant labor.

The inability of the static model to explain this finding rests in part on the fact that the model incorrectly assumes immigrant and U.S.-born workers are perfectly interchangeable; that is, that they substitute for each other rather than complement each other in the labor force. Common sense alone suggests that this is not always the case. For example, less-skilled foreign-born construction laborers enhance the productivity of U.S.-born carpenters, plumbers, and electricians, but do not necessarily substitute for them. More broadly, the different educational and age profiles of foreign-born and native-born workers indicate that they often fill different niches in the labor market.

More importantly, the static model fails to account for the fact that immigrants spend money or invest capital, both of which create jobs and thus exert upward pressure on wages by increasing the demand for labor. This amounts to more than a minor omission given the scale of immigrant purchasing power and entrepreneurship. For instance, in 2004, consumer purchasing power totaled $686 billion among Latinos and $363 billion among Asians. Given that roughly 44 percent of Latinos and 69 percent of Asians were foreign-born in that year, the buying power of immigrants reached into the hundreds of billions of dollars.

The dynamic model accounts for many of these additional economic contributions by immigrants. In the dynamic scenario, immigrant workers spend some of their wages on housing and consumer goods, which in turn increases the demand for labor by creating new jobs. Rising labor demand then increases wages relative to what would have existed if immigrant workers had not been present in the labor market. Businesses in turn invest more capital, expand, and hire more workers across the spectrum of skill levels. The result is a larger economy with higher employment.

The Impact of Immigrants on Native-Born Employment Levels

An IPC research report released in November of 2005 provides strong demographic evidence that the impact of immigrants on native-born employment levels is extremely limited or, in some cases, positive. The report examines the significant differences between the native-born workforce and the immigrant workforce and finds that immigrants are largely complementary to the native-born in education, age and skill profile. The complementary nature of immigrant labor makes it unlikely that immigrants are replacing a significant number of native-born workers, but are instead moving into positions that allow native-born workers to be more productive.

As the number of less-skilled jobs continues to grow, it will become increasingly difficult for employers to find native-born workers, especially younger workers, with the education levels that best correspond to those jobs. In this sense, immigrant workers are a vital complement to a native-born labor force that is growing older and better educated. On average, foreign-born workers tend to be younger than their native-born counterparts and a larger proportion have less formal education. In addition, immigrants participate in the labor force at a higher rate. As a result, immigrants provide a needed source of labor for the large and growing number of jobs that do not require as much formal education.

Immigrant Workers Are More Likely to Have Less Formal Education

Immigrants comprise a disproportionate share of those workers who are willing to take less-skilled jobs with few or no educational requirements. In 2004, 53.3 percent of the foreign-born labor force age 25 and older had a high-school diploma or less education, compared to 37.8 percent of the native-born labor force. Immigrant workers were more than four times as likely as native workers to lack a high-school diploma. In contrast, immigrant workers were nearly as likely to have a four-year college degree or more education, amounting to more than 30 percent of both the native-born and foreign-born labor force.

In general, foreign-born workers are more likely to be found at either end of the educational spectrum, while most native-born workers fall somewhere in the middle. Roughly three-fifths of the native-born labor force in 2004 had either a high-school diploma or some college education short of a four-year degree, whereas three-fifths of the foreign-born labor force either did not have a high-school diploma or had at least a four-year college degree. Given their different educational backgrounds, most native-born workers are therefore not competing directly with foreign-born workers for the same types of jobs.

Immigrant Workers Tend to Be Younger

Immigrants also include a large number of younger workers, particularly in the less-skilled workforce. In 2004, 67 percent of the foreign-born labor force with a high-school diploma or less education was between 25 and 45 years old, as opposed to 52 percent of the native-born labor force with no more than a high-school diploma. While relative youth is not a requirement for many jobs, it is an asset in those less-skilled jobs that are physically demanding or dangerous.

Given the different age and educational profiles of foreign-born and native-born workers, it is not surprising that immigrants comprise a disproportionately large share of younger workers with little education. In 2004, immigrants made up more than a quarter of all workers 25–34 years old with a high-school diploma or less, and more than half of workers 25–34 years old without a high-school diploma. Employers searching for younger workers in less-skilled positions therefore often find that a large portion of prospective hires is foreign-born.

The Fiscal Costs of Immigration

Critics of immigration often focus on the fiscal costs of immigration instead of the economic benefits. These costs are often exacerbated by the undocumented status of many immigrants. An immigration policy that acknowledged the economic need for and benefits of immigration would significantly reduce these costs. To support the contention that immigrants are a net fiscal drain, critics cite studies indicating that immigrants contribute less per capita in tax revenue than they receive in benefits. However, these studies fail to acknowledge that this has more to do with low-wage employment than with native-born status. Native-born workers in low-wage jobs similarly receive benefits in excess of the level of taxes paid. However, net tax revenue is not the same as net economic benefit. Generally accepted analysis reveals that the net economic benefit compensates for and exceeds any negative fiscal impact. The "fiscal only" analysis ignores the fact that in the absence of sufficient immigrant labor, unfilled low-wage jobs, regardless of the relative tax implications, hurt the economy.

Conclusion

Immigration is a net positive for the U.S. economy and the presence of immigrants does not generally harm the native-born workforce. Studies that purport to demonstrate a negative impact on native-born wages and employment levels rely on an overly simplistic economic model of immigration and the economy. The most recent demographic analysis in conjunction with more sophisticated economic analysis reveals that most immigrants, including undocumented immigrants, do not compete directly with native-born workers for jobs. Instead, these immigrants provide a critical element of our nation's economic success and continued resiliency: a relatively young, willing, and dynamic supply of essential workers in areas such as healthcare, construction, retail, and agriculture. These are jobs that, once filled, enable our economy to continue the cycle of growth and job creation.

Indeed, this makes clear that the implication of the government's own BLS data cannot be ignored. To prosper, our economy desperately needs workers at both ends of the spectrum: young and less skilled as well as more educated and highly skilled. As a nation, we are in the midst of a slow-motion demographic cataclysm unlike any we have previously experienced. Immigration is not the only tool for seeing our way clear of the coming storm—but it is one without which we will not prosper. Without a continued and normalized flow of immigrant labor our workforce will fall well short of the numbers needed to meet the emerging demand for labor. The result will be an erosion of both the growth and increased standard of living that our citizenry has come to expect and to which future generations are entitled. Until the United States adopts a more articulated and thoughtful immigration policy that accommodates these economic realities, the insufficiency of current immigration and the problematic nature of undocumented immigration, in particular, will continue to hobble the economy.

Barry R. Chiswick

Immigration:
The Negative Economic Impact

When I am asked the question "What is THE economic impact of immigration?" where the tone indicates the emphasis on the word "the," I respond that this is not the best way to couch the question. There are two fundamental questions. One is: "What is the optimal size of the immigrant population?" The other is: "What are the different impacts of immigrants that differ in their productivity-related characteristics?"

Impacts on Relative Wages

Let us begin with a discussion of the second question. Conceptually, it is best to think in terms of two types of immigrants, which for simplicity we will call high-skilled and low-skilled, with the same two skill groups represented in the native-born population. High-skilled immigrants will have some characteristics in common, without regard for their country of origin. They tend to have high levels of schooling, which means they tend to have a high degree of literacy, perhaps also numeracy, critical thinking or decision-making skills. Many, but not all, will have a high degree of scientific or technical knowledge, and in the modern era a high comfort level with computer technology. Many, but certainly not all, will either have a degree of proficiency in the destination language (in this case, English) or the ability to acquire proficiency in that language shortly after arrival. These are all characteristics that have been shown to improve the earnings of immigrants and to facilitate their economic adjustment in the host country.

Although particular individuals may differ, low-skilled immigrants generally have little formal schooling, limited literacy proficiency in their mother tongue (the language of their origin country), and limited scientific and technical knowledge. These are characteristics associated with low earnings in the destination.

High-skilled and low-skilled immigrants will, in general, have different impacts on the host economy and labor market. Labor markets behave in a manner similar to other markets, in that a greater supply of a given type of labor tends to depress the market wage of workers with similar characteristics. An increase in the supply of a given type of worker also increases the productivity of the complementary factors of production with which it

U.S. Senate, April 24, 2006.

works, including other types of labor and capital. To give a simple example, an increase in the supply of low-skilled restaurant kitchen help will result in more competition for this type of job and lower wages for ordinary kitchen workers. Yet this will increase the productivity (and hence wages) of the master chefs because with more help for the menial kitchen chores they can spend their time on the highly specialized tasks for which they have trained. By the same token, an increase in the supply of high-skilled chefs would raise the productivity of low-skilled restaurant kitchen workers since they would have more master chefs for whom to work.

The result of high-skilled immigration tends to be an increase in the wages of all low-skilled workers (and reduce their use of public income transfers) and a decrease in the wages of high-skilled natives. This reduces income inequality, which we generally view as a good development. Like high-skilled natives, the taxes paid by high-skilled immigrants tend to be greater than the costs they impose on the public treasury through the income transfers they receive, the schooling received by their children, and the publicly subsidized medical care that they receive. High-skilled immigrants are also more likely to bring with them the scientific, technical and innovative skills that expand the production capabilities of the economy. As a result, the population as a whole tends to benefit from high-skilled immigration, although with some benefiting more than others.

Now consider the impacts of low-skilled immigration. While these immigrants tend to raise the earnings of high-skilled workers, their presence in the labor market increases competition for low-skilled jobs, reducing the earnings of low-skilled native-born workers. This not only increases income inequality, which is rightly considered to be undesirable, it also increases the need among low-skilled natives for public assistance and transfer benefits. Because of their low earnings, low-skilled immigrants also tend to pay less in taxes than they receive in public benefits, such as income transfers (e.g., the earned income tax credit, food stamps), public schooling for their children, and publicly provided medical services. Thus while the presence of low-skilled immigrant workers may raise the profits of their employers, they tend to have a negative effect on the well-being of the low-skilled native-born population, and on the native economy as a whole. These points are not purely theoretical arguments. In the past two decades the real wages of low-skilled workers have remained stagnant even as the real earnings of high-skilled workers have risen. As a result, income inequality has increased. Several factors have been responsible for this development, but one of them has been the very large increase in low-skilled immigration.

The "Need" for Low-Skilled Immigrants

"But," I am often asked, "don't we need low-skilled immigrant workers to do the jobs that native workers are unwilling to do?" I respond: "At what wage will native workers decline to take these jobs?" Consider the following thought experiment: What would happen to lettuce picking or the mowing of suburban lawns if there were fewer low-skilled workers? Earlier this month on ABC's Nightline program a winter lettuce grower in Arizona provided the answer. He acknowledged that he would pay higher wages to attract native-born workers and he would speed up the mechanization of lettuce harvesting. The technology is there, but with low wages for lettuce pickers there is no economic incentive for the growers to mechanize or invest in other types of new technology. If the supply of low-skilled immigrant workers decreased substantially, mechanical harvesting would replace many of them with capital (machines) and more highly paid native workers. How would suburban lawns get mowed if there were fewer low-skilled immigrant workers? Wages for lawn care workers would surely rise. The result would be that more teenagers and other low-skilled native workers would find it worth their while to make themselves available for this work.

In addition to this substitution of one type of labor (youthful and low-skilled natives) for another (low-skilled immigrants), there would be other adjustments to the higher cost of lawn mowing. One would be letting the grass grow longer between mows—say, every ten days instead of weekly. Another would be the substitution of grass that grows more slowly, or the substitution of ground cover or paving stones for grass, etc. The point is that there would be many ways for consumers and employers/producers to respond to the higher wages of low-skilled workers to mitigate the adverse effects of having fewer low-skilled immigrants.

A Century Ago

At this point in the conversation, someone usually points to the period of mass immigration of unskilled workers from the 1880s to the 1920s: If these arguments are valid now, wouldn't they have applied at that time as well?—and we know that immigration was a tremendous net benefit to the United States at that time. The answer is both yes and no. The economy and economic institutions of 100 years ago were quite different from those of today in ways that are both important and relevant to our discussion. Then, rapid industrialization of the American economy generated a very large demand for unskilled workers in mines and in factories producing everything from steel to shirts. This is no longer the case. Technological change, the increased cost of even low-skilled labor (wages plus fringe benefits and employment taxes), the falling cost of capital equipment, and globalization/international trade have sharply reduced the demand for low-skilled workers in U.S. manufacturing, mining, agriculture, and even service occupations and industries. Moreover, 100 years ago income inequality and income distribution issues were not a matter of public policy concern. If there were poor people in the United States—so be it. If private individuals and charities helped the poor—fine, but there was nothing like the tax-funded income transfer system in place today.

Yet in some ways the mass immigration from Europe 100 years ago had a similar impact as the one we are facing today. By holding down the wages of low-skilled workers in the industrializing centers of the economy, especially in the Northern states, rural-urban and South-North migration was slowed. Rural and Southern poverty persisted longer than they might have otherwise, and it was only after war (WWI) and immigration restrictions (in the 1920s) had effectively stopped the European migration that these poverty-reducing internal migrations resumed. While there is no question that there were long-term benefits from the massive wave of immigrants for the country as a whole, it is also true that the low-skilled native-born workers of that time paid a price.

Fallacies in Estimating Immigrant Impacts

In the course of these hearings on the economic impact of immigration, you may receive testimony regarding a body of literature that attempts to estimate this impact. In this literature a statistical technique, regression analysis, is used to show how the wages of native workers (or low-skilled natives in particular) in a state or metropolitan area are affected by the extent to which there are immigrants (or low-skilled immigrants) in the same area. These studies tend to find no relation, or sometimes a very small relation, between the presence of immigrants and wage levels.

There is nothing wrong with regression analysis per se as a statistical technique, but its application in this case is flawed. This application of regression analysis requires us to assume that each state or metropolitan area is a self-contained economy, with little or no in-and-out movement of workers, of capital, or even of goods and services. We know, however, that this is not the case. Labor, capital and goods are highly mobile across state boundaries and metropolitan areas. What we learn from these studies is not that immigrants have no effect on wages, but that these wage effects—whatever they may be—have spread throughout the country. Although it does provide evidence that markets in the United States function quite efficiently, the impacts of immigration cannot be detected by this statistical technique.

At the aggregate level, many analyses consider immigrants as an undifferentiated whole without distinguishing between high-skilled and low-skilled workers. These also provide misleading implications, often to the effect that immigrant impacts on wages and income distribution are small. When the positive economic benefits of high-skilled immigration are lumped together with the more negative consequences of low-skilled immigration, they appear to cancel each other out because there are both gains and losses. In the real world, however, the penalty paid by low-skilled natives because of high levels of low-skilled immigration is not so easily cancelled out by the positive impacts of high-skilled immigration.

Does Country of Origin Matter?

To this point I have not said anything about country of origin. That is because country of origin per se is not really relevant for an analysis of economic impacts. What is most relevant is the skills that immigrants bring with them.

Immigration Law and Low-Skilled Immigrants

I have also not said anything yet about legal status. For various reasons, most individuals working in the United States in violation of immigration law are low-skilled workers. But most low-skilled workers are not "undocumented" aliens. Most low-skilled workers were born in the United States and hence are citizens by birth.

Current U.S. immigration law, however, encourages the legal immigration of low-skilled workers. This encouragement comes through the kinship preferences for various relatives built into our legal immigration system and to the smaller diversity visa program. Our immigration law permits a "snowball effect" where even immigrants granted a visa for the skills they bring to the U.S. labor market can sponsor low-skilled relatives who will then legally work in the U.S.

Of the 946,014 people who received Permanent Resident Alien visas in 2004, 65.6 percent entered under one of the several kinship categories, 8.8 percent entered as refugees or asylees, 5.3 percent entered under "diversity" visas, and 3.5 percent had a cancellation of deportation order. The 155,330 employment-based visas represented only 16.4 percent of the total. However, only about half of those who received an employment-based visa were themselves skill-tested (less than 73,000), while the remainder of these visas were received by their spouses and children. Thus, only about 7.6 percent of the nearly one million visa recipients were asked a question about their skills. . . .

The 1986 Immigration Reform and Control Act (IRCA) was sold to the American public as having two major features—amnesty which was to "wipe the slate clean" of undocumented workers, and employer sanctions which was to "keep the slate clean"—along with some increased border enforcement of the immigration law. Employer sanctions were intended to cut off the "jobs magnet" that attracted undocumented workers to the United States. Half of the political bargain was fulfilled. Under its two major amnesty provisions legal status was granted to nearly 3 million undocumented individuals, nearly all of whom were low-skilled workers, and millions more have subsequently been able to immigrate as their relatives. It is noteworthy that while in 1986 the word "amnesty" was used outright, in the current political debate the "A" word is anathema to the proponents of what is euphemistically called "earned legalization." This by itself is testimony to public perception of the failures of the 1986 Act.

Border and Interior Enforcement

Border enforcement, both at land borders and at airports, is a necessary element in the enforcement of immigration law. Border enforcement by itself has not, cannot, and will not work in controlling illegal entry of undocumented immigrants. If a potential immigrant is unsuccessful in penetrating the border on the first try, success may be had on the second or third try. This may be done by "entry without inspection" (i.e., sneaking across the border) or by using "fraudulent documents" at a border crossing point. Alternatively, a "visa abuser" enters into illegal status by violating a condition of a legally obtained visa—by working while on a tourist visa, for example, or by overstaying the time limit permitted on a temporary visa.

Thus, border enforcement must be complemented with "interior enforcement." The 1986 Act focused on "employer sanctions," penalties for employers who knowingly hire people who do not have the legal right to work in this country. There has, however, been no serious effort over the past two decades to enforce employer sanctions. Modern technology makes it easier to create fraudulent documents, but it also makes it easier to develop more stringent identity checks. There are two major failings in the current system. Employers are not given a "foolproof" mechanism to readily identify those with a legal right to work, and the Federal authorities show no interest in enforcing the law, except for an occasional "show raid."

It is not obvious that new enforcement legislation (e.g., to criminalize an illegal status) is called for. What is obvious is that illegal immigration cannot be controlled without a political will to enforce current immigration law. This includes providing employers with a simple and "foolproof" mechanism for identifying workers with a legal right to work in the U.S. along with more stringent enforcement of employer sanctions.

The Current Immigration System

The current legal immigration system is not serving the best economic interests of the United States. Only a small percentage of the immigrants who enter the U.S. legally in any year (less than 8 percent) are screened for their likely economic contribution to this economy. The vast majority enter under a nepotism system (the kinship preferences), with a smaller group entering under a lottery (diversity visas). To enhance the competitiveness of the U.S. economy in this increasingly globalized world, where efficient competitors are emerging across the world, the U.S. needs to change the basic question from "To whom are you related?" to "What can you contribute to the U.S. economy?"

Other highly-developed democratic countries—Canada, Australia, New Zealand—introduced "skills-based" immigration policies several decades ago. More recently, some countries in Western Europe have done the same. Some, like Canada and Australia, use a "points system" in which points are awarded based on characteristics that research has shown to enhance the earnings of immigrants such as age, schooling, technical training, and proficiency in the host country's language. Those with more than the threshold number of points receive a visa for themselves, their spouse and their minor accompanying children. This shift in emphasis in the rationing of visas would increase the skill level of immigrants and provide greater economic benefits to the U.S. economy than the current system.

A points system has many advantages over the current targeted employment-based visas. Under the current system a complex and very expensive bureaucratic process is required for employers to demonstrate to the U.S. Department of Labor not only that the visa applicant is qualified for a specific job but also that there is no qualified person with a legal right to work in the

U.S. who will take the job at "prevailing wages." Even then, the worker who obtains a visa through this process is not obliged to remain on that job or with that employer.

Other proposals would use market mechanisms to "close the gap" between the large demand for visas and the much smaller supply that the U.S. is willing to make available. One possibility would involve auctioning visas; another involves charging a large market-clearing "visa fee." Among other advantages of these market mechanisms is that people in the U.S. can express their preferences for bringing relatives and friends by contributing to the price of their visa. Nor does there need to be only one mechanism—a skill-based system and a market-based system could both be used.

How Many Immigrants?

This returns us to a question posed early in this testimony: "What is the optimal size of the immigration flow?" The optimal immigration policy is neither a completely open door nor a completely closed one. There is no magic number or proportion of the population. Currently, legal immigration is running at approximately one million immigrants per year. This is on a par with the peak period of immigration from 1905 to 1914, when immigration also averaged one million per year. Yet, relative to the size of the U.S. population, current legal immigration is about one-fourth of the ratio in this earlier period. There is no clear evidence that the U.S. has exceeded—or even reached—its absorptive capacity for immigration. The U.S. economy and society exhibits a remarkable adaptability to immigrants, and thus far immigrants continue to show considerable adaptability to the U.S. economy and society. This adaptability means that the U.S. economy can absorb a continuous stream of immigrants without fracturing the system.

The demand for visas to enter the U.S. is very strong and, if anything, it seems to be increasing. This is a credit to the U.S. economy, society, and political system. The number of visas the U.S. political process is willing to supply is not immutable. The greater the economic benefits of immigration, the larger the optimal number of visas and the greater the willingness of the American public to provide them.

A comprehensive immigration policy reform would reduce undocumented migration by more stringent enforcement of existing law. It should also include the adoption of a skill-based points system and/or market mechanisms to ration visas, while limiting kinship migration to the immediate relatives of U.S. citizens (spouse, minor children, aged parents). These policies would increase the benefits of immigration for the American public, providing economic incentives to increase the supply of visas and hence the annual total number of immigrants entering the country legally.

POSTSCRIPT

Is Immigration an Economic Benefit to the Host Country?

Whatever reality may be, most Americans think that immigrants cause economic problems. A CNN poll in 2010 that asked about immigrants, not just unauthorized immigrants, found 69% of Americans saying immigrants are a "burden on American taxpayers" and 59% believing that immigrants "take jobs away from Americans." Some people argue that such views are rooted in racism, but the same survey revealed 73% of the respondents expressing the view that the immigrants "are basically good, honest people" and 85% describing the immigrants as "hardworking." It is also worth noting that when asked about the number of immigrants in the country, 65% wanted the number of immigrants to remain the same and 23% favored an increase, while only 11% wanted to decrease the number of immigrants in the country or expel them altogether. Americans are even fairly forgiving about illegal immigrants. When asked in another 2010 poll, "Do you favor or oppose giving illegal immigrants who pay taxes and obey the law a second chance and allow them to stay in the United States?" 68% said yes and only 27% said no, with 5% undecided.

The debate in the United States is very similar to that going on in many countries. Whatever public opinion may be, one certainty is people will abandon their homelands and seek new ones as long as widespread poverty and violence exist in many countries. Border barriers can impede, but not stop, the flow of those desperately seeking physical and economic security. Therefore, it might be wise to address the cause of immigration and also to avoid annual spending of huge amounts on immigration control to help Mexico, Central America, and other developing countries achieve greater prosperity so that the people in those countries would no longer be willing to experience the dislocation and danger that leaving home and slipping into the United States or some other developed country entails.

An overview of the history of U.S. immigration and policy is found in Aristide R. Zolberg, *A Nation by Design: Immigration Policy in the Fashioning of America* (Harvard University Press, 2008). A group that favors fewer immigrant is the Center for Immigration Studies at http://www.cis.org/. Taking a positive view of immigration and immigrants is the National Immigration Forum at http://www.immigrationforum.org/. To read opposing points of view, go to Mark Krikorian, *The New Case Against Immigration: Both Legal and Illegal* (Sentinel, 2008), and Jason L. Riley, *Let Them In: The Case for Open Borders* (Gotham, 2008). For the impact of immigration beyond the United States, read Craig A. Parsons and Timothy M. Smeeding (eds.), *Immigration and the Transformation of Europe* (Cambridge University Press, 2006).

Questions for Critical Thinking and Reflection

1. Some countries decide who can enter as an immigrant based on such factors as degree of education, specific skills, and achievements. Would you favor using such criteria to govern U.S. immigration?
2. Do immigrants do low-wage, arduous jobs like working in crop fields and meatpacking plants that Americans disdain or do they "underbid" unemployed Americans for those jobs?
3. Is there a difference in economic impact between legal and illegal immigrants?

ISSUE 12

Should Export Controls on High Technology Be Eased Substantially?

YES: John L. Hennessy, from Testimony during Hearings on "The Impact of U.S. Export Controls on National Security, Science and Technological Leadership" before the Committee on Foreign Affairs, U.S. House of Representatives (January 15, 2010)

NO: William C. Potter, from Testimony during Hearings on "The Impact of U.S. Export Controls on National Security, Science and Technological Leadership" before the Committee on Foreign Affairs, U.S. House of Representatives (January 15, 2010)

ISSUE SUMMARY

YES: John L. Hennessy, the president of Stanford University, focuses on export control that involves sharing knowledge and says that it is negatively impacting Americans' ability to conduct fundamental research that can benefit the United States economically and militarily.

NO: William C. Potter, the founding director of the James Martin Center for Nonproliferation Studies at the Monterey Institute of International Studies, urges caution when deciding what export control to loosen or abolish.

Technology has historically been a key component of national power and security. As the Iron Age eclipsed the Bronze Age some two-and-a-half millennia ago, those kingdoms that successfully developed and employed iron swords and other weapons had a military advantage over those kingdoms that continued to use more brittle bronze weapons. In 1945, the United States made a technological breakthrough when it developed the atomic bomb. Its possession and use allowed the United States to obliterate Japan's last resistance to surrender. Moreover, U.S. sole possession of atomic weapons put the United States in a position of arguably unchallengeable military superiority from July 16, 1945, the date of the first U.S. test at Alamogordo, New Mexico, through August 29, 1949, when the Soviet Union tested its first atomic bomb at Semipalatinsk.

The years since 1800 and, even more since 1900, have speeded up the technological factor in national power. The pace of innovation has increased. According to one estimate, only about 10 percent of all scientific and technological innovation in world history occurred before 1800, while the 1800s saw about 40 percent of the innovation, and half or more of all breakthroughs have occurred since 1900. Over thousands of years, military technology had only advanced to the point in 1800 where countries fought with wooden ships, roundball cannons, muskets, and saber-wielding cavalry charges. In the little more than two centuries since then, military technology advances have hyperaccelerated to add supersonic, radar-invisible (stealth) warplanes; guided "smart bombs"; thermonuclear weapons; intercontinental ballistic missiles; nuclear submarines; and a host of other "star wars" weapons capabilities to the world's arsenals. This increasing speed of innovation has been accompanied by an increasing speed at which new technologies become widely available to others, including competitors, and/or are made less critical or even obsolete by yet newer technological and scientific innovation.

Technology can be spread in several ways. Once the basic principles behind it are known, others can sometimes move quickly to duplicate it. Intelligence needed to duplicate technology can also be gained through espionage or by having it given or sold to you. Yet another path for de facto technology transfer is sharing its intricacies through joint research projects with engineers, scientists, and other researchers in foreign countries.

If export controls just applied to clearly military technology, there would still be issues about what is sensitive and what is not. But those questions pale when compared to the difficulty in agreeing about the so-called "dual-use" items and information. These involve anything that has both a peaceful, commercial application and a military application. An extreme example is the technology to create enriched uranium. One application for enriched uranium is as the explosive core of nuclear weapons. The other application is to fuel civilian nuclear power plants. For this purpose, facilities to enrich uranium are operating in such nonnuclear weapons countries as Argentina, Brazil, Germany, Japan, and the Netherlands.

Perhaps the most important source of pressure to ease export controls has been the business community, which argues that controls are so tight that they even sometimes forbid U.S. firms to sell technology that is readily available from European, Japanese, and other sources. According to the National Association of Manufacturers (NAM), the controls are a major contributor to an employment decline of 26 percent in U.S. high-tech industries between 2001 and 2010. NAM also argues that easing controls could increase U.S. exports by $60 billion and add 350,000 new jobs to the U.S. economy.

Elements of the U.S. academic community are a second group urging less restrictive export controls. Representing this view in the first reading, John Hennessy argues that current export controls are damaging the ability to do fundamental research that can benefit the United States economically and militarily. William C. Potter acknowledges in the second reading that in an increasingly globalized world, it is important to be wary of restrictions on the flow of information, technology, and scientists in the name of national security, but he adds that it would be equally unwise to abandon prudent export controls on dual-use technologies and material directly relevant to nuclear, chemical, and biological weapons.

YES

John L. Hennessy

The Case for Easing Export Controls on Sensitive Technology

In January 2009, the National Academies [composed of the National Academy of Sciences, the National Academy of Engineering, the Institute of Medicine, and the National Research Council] released a . . . report, *Beyond "Fortress America": National Security Controls on Science and Technology in a Globalized World* [authored by Committee on Science, Security and Prosperity, which Hennessy co-chaired]. Although I will reference the committee's findings in my remarks, today I speak on behalf of higher education and the scientific research community, rather than as a representative of the committee or the Academy.

It has become a broadly accepted principle that the United States' leadership in science and technology is crucial both to our national security and our country's economic prosperity. Last April, in a speech at the National Academy of Sciences, President [Barack] Obama called science "more essential for our prosperity, our security, our health and our environment than it has ever been."

The American Recovery and Reinvestment Act of 2009 approved by Congress included $17 billion for scientific research, research infrastructure and education, mostly through the National Science Foundation and the National Institutes of Health. This followed on the promise of the America COMPETES Act. [First passed in 2007, the act annually allocates about $11 billion to a range of science and technology research and education projects.]

What is less well understood, however, is how the conduct of science and technology has changed—over the past two decades in particular—as a function of both the end of the Cold War and the globalization of science and technology. In this new century, the conduct of science takes place in a highly collaborative and geographically distributed research community, with the Internet enabling exchanges of information at an unprecedented pace. Much of it—particularly the breakthrough advances and innovations—involves many players from wide-ranging backgrounds and areas of expertise. Thus today, excellent science happens not only in the United States and Europe but also in countries such as India and China.

Thirty years ago, the United States dominated in many fields of science and technology. Today the United States is still the overall leader, but in many fields we are one of the leaders rather than the sole leader, and in a few fields

U.S. House of Representatives, January 15, 2010.

the United States is clearly not at the top. As noted in a quote cited in *Beyond "Fortress America"*:

> Japan leads in a number of key technologies such as flat screens, Korea has become a world leader in semiconductor memory, Europe leads in some aspects of telecommunications and embedded systems, and China is increasingly a center for high-technology manufacturing.

Or if we look at the attached graph showing the papers published over the past 25 years by the American Physics Society in *Physical Review* and *Physical Review Letters*, the trend is clear: The rate of publication among physicists outside of the United States and western Europe has increased at an astonishing rate.

In the coming decades, remaining a leader requires that we fully participate in the international research community. To do so requires that unclassified information be able to flow among researchers and industry leaders in the various fields, and it requires the United States to continue to attract the best and brightest minds from around the world to work in our laboratories. As the Center for Strategic and International Studies' (CSIS) Commission on Scientific Communication and National Security noted, "In a world of globalized science and technology, security comes from windows not walls." I would add that those windows onto global science are equally vital for scientific leadership and for economic competitiveness.

There is no question that the U.S. needs export controls to maintain military advantage on the battlefield and to sustain the homeland. However, as advances in science and technology have transformed our world and our ways of conducting research, many of the export controls regulations that served the United States well 40 years ago no longer meet the country's needs. The current system actually impedes our national security and thwarts our ability to compete. As the committee noted in its report, our success depends on our ability to "Run Faster." A more agile and responsive system of controls would allow us to focus our energies on serious challenges, make informed decisions and make them more quickly.

I would like to look specifically at the impact of export controls on higher education in the U.S. and the implications for innovation.

Last week President Obama expanded the "Educate to Innovate" campaign, a K-12 initiative to inspire American students to excel in science, technology, engineering and mathematics, often referred to as the STEM fields. He was unequivocal about their importance, saying, "Make no mistake: Our future is on the line. The nation that out-educates us today is going to out-compete us tomorrow."

A strong educational foundation is key to the innovation that occurs later in universities and industry. Other countries realize this, as evidenced by the flow of international students to U.S. universities seeking degrees in the STEM fields.

So what is required to lead today and tomorrow? We must continue to attract and retain the best scholars and researchers worldwide and nurture their work by providing an environment that encourages innovation.

We have a long and rich tradition of doing so: The United States' 20th-century dominance in science and technology owes much to immigrants such as Albert Einstein, Edward Teller, Enrico Fermi and An Wang. Indeed, Intel, Google, Yahoo! and Sun Microsystems—as well as an estimated 52 percent of Silicon Valley startups—have one or more founders who were born outside of the United States. Today, we continue to attract brilliant young minds from around the world, and it is important that we continue to attract and to retain them.

At Stanford, we attract leading researchers and faculty from around the world, and 32 percent of our graduate students are from countries other than the U.S., with the percentage of international Ph.D. students exceeding 50 percent in engineering and the physical sciences. As a matter of policy, we do not engage in classified research that would limit participation of any of our students or faculty on the basis of citizenship. Our focus is on fundamental research, which both by its nature and by National Security Decision Directive 189 is intended to be open to all and freely communicated. Nonetheless, current export controls and related security measures have caused us difficulties. Let me give you three brief examples from Stanford.

Gravity Probe-B

Gravity Probe-B is an experiment being undertaken to test Einstein's general theory of relativity. A satellite orbiting above the Earth houses an instrument that includes four spherical gyroscopes and a telescope, designed by Stanford researchers. The instrument's design and fabrication were basic research; for example, it required making the world's most perfect sphere, which is at the core of the instrument. The technical details—blueprints and schematics—are openly published. It does not have a strategic use, but it happens to be on a satellite. Because the International Traffic and Arms Regulations (ITAR) consider satellites to be munitions, Stanford researchers are prohibited from providing "technical assistance" to foreign national students and scholars abroad by discussing the published performance characteristics of the materials and hardware used in the development of the probe. U.S. universities consider their ability to share the details of published research results to be a crucial element of scientific inquiry and a requirement for evaluating the instrument and its measurements of the basic physics of our universe. ITAR, however, considers the activity to be a "defense service" requiring an export license. With deemed export regulations, there are even limitations in sharing information with some international students here on our campus.

Synapse Microchip

A U.S.-based Fortune 100 high-technology company has been given a DARPA contract to develop a microchip that will attempt to simulate the human brain based on what we know of the electrical properties of neurons and synapses. While this work is quite basic, the potential future applications from treating brain disorders to building autonomous systems are both widespread and of high impact. [DARPA is the Defense Advanced Research Projects Agency, part of the U.S. Department of Defense.]

This is the kind of research we excel in at Stanford, and the technology company has asked us to participate on the project. Our team is headed by a faculty member who is a leader in his field and includes half a dozen Stanford graduate students. The faculty member is a U.S. citizen, some of the students on the team were born outside of the U.S., and two are Chinese nationals. Soon after the project began, we learned that the use of export-controlled technology was central to the work. For the Stanford team to participate, our Chinese students would have to be excluded. Stanford does not, and will not, discriminate between its students or disadvantage them on the basis of citizenship: All of our students and faculty must be able to participate and contribute to the intellectually significant portions of research. Since the export-controlled technology is central to the project, the Stanford research team's involvement and the benefit of their potential contributions to the project have been greatly reduced. This has impeded the progress of the collaboration and Stanford's ability to contribute its full wealth of intellectual capital.

Vaccine Creation

A closely related problem has occurred in the area of biosecurity. Professor Stanley Falkow, one the world's most distinguished researchers in the area of microbial pathogenesis, had been working with a non-pathogenic version of plague, a version actually used in the creation of a vaccine. After the USA PATRIOT Act [passed in 2001 soon after the 9/11 attacks], this organism was designated as a Select Agent, requiring greatly enhanced security and background checks on lab personnel. Falkow viewed this as incompatible with his research approach, destroyed the organism and stopped working in the area. The result was clearly a net loss for our country.

In these examples, our nation can lose multiple times. First we lose the benefit of input from great scientists, both students and faculty, and the advantages of their research contributions. Second, recognizing that many of the young researchers are likely to remain and contribute to the advancement of our country's knowledge in science and technology, we lose when we deprive them of opportunities to innovate. And the impact on students—who might have become loyal and contributing citizens and residents of our country—can be devastating. As these examples illustrate, the negative impacts of control regulations can lead to a loss of scientific leadership and a reduction in our nation's security.

Our goal should be to design national security controls without negatively impacting our ability to conduct fundamental research that can benefit the United States economically and militarily. The growing trend to label fundamental research as "Sensitive But Unclassified" is a deep concern, since it would further blur the lines between controlled and uncontrolled research in an unpredictable fashion.

There are policies in place that can serve as a straightforward and rational interpretation of export controls. Through National Security Decision Directive

189 (NSDD-189, also known as the National Policy on the Transfer of Scientific, Technical and Engineering Information), for example, government agencies with concerns about work could specify restrictions when they issue the contract, including, when appropriate and necessary, classifying the work. Maintaining the openness of basic research as clearly intended in NSDD-189 is crucially important for the long-term health of U.S. academic research. [NSDDs are a type of executive order issued by the U.S. president.] Export controls are challenging and complex, and I am very pleased that this committee has undertaken this important task of examining them and considering the need for reform.

William C. Potter

 **NO**

The Case Against Easing Export Controls on Sensitive Technology

I. Introduction

The subject of the hearing is very timely and important, and I applaud the committee . . . for undertaking this initiative.

By way of introduction and as a caveat, I wish to emphasize that while the center I direct covers the entire range of weapons of mass destruction and their delivery systems, my own expertise lies primarily in the nuclear sector and issues associated with illicit nuclear trafficking and the dangers posed by non-state actors and nuclear terrorism. As such, my prepared remarks will emphasize these areas.

A number of recent studies, including the important National Research Council report on *Beyond "Fortress America,"* co-chaired by Stanford President John Hennessy and General Brent Scowcroft, have correctly observed that many U.S. export controls developed during the Cold War were designed for a world that no longer exists and are ill-suited to meet today's national security challenges. It is also the case that in an increasingly globalized world, one must be very cautious about imposing restrictions on the flow of information, technology, and scientists in the name of national security without carefully weighing the costs and benefits of such action. It would be equally shortsighted, however, for the United States to abandon prudent export controls on dual-use technologies and material directly relevant to nuclear, chemical, and biological weapons in the name of economic competitiveness on the grounds that some other states have failed to adopt stringent export controls. Similarly, it would be most unfortunate from the standpoint of weapons of mass destruction (WMD) proliferation were the United States to signal its diminished support for adherence to the export guidelines of existing international nonproliferation regimes, based on the premise that some states already disregard inconvenient nonproliferation export control norms and principles. Unfortunately, one can point to recent examples of both outmoded U.S. and international approaches to export controls and changes to export policy that have been detrimental to U.S. national security.

Illustrative of the problem of outmoded U.S. export controls are current nonimmigrant visa regulations that make it difficult for credentialed academic researchers to work with U.S.-based colleagues and for international students

U.S. House of Representatives, January 15, 2010.

with advanced degrees in the science and engineering sectors to extend their stays in the United States for employment purposes. I fully endorse the National Research Council's recommendations with respect to remedies in this sphere, but I also would note the need for more nonproliferation education and training in U.S. industry and academe. Greater self-awareness and self-regulation regarding the security and export of WMD-related material, technology, and know-how may be the best antidote to more intrusive government controls.

Regrettably, it is also the case that U.S. national security was impaired when, in the name of economic competitiveness and in pursuit of a new strategic partnership with India, the United States gutted important components of its own domestic export control laws and led the charge to exempt one country from the export guidelines of the Nuclear Suppliers Group. A similarly ill-considered congressional initiative in 2005 to make it easier to export highly enriched uranium (HEU) to U.S. allies—promoted in the name of economics and medical necessity—directly undermined U.S. efforts to persuade other countries to combat nuclear terrorism by minimizing the use of HEU in the civilian nuclear sector.

My point is not to contest the desirability of reviewing and, where appropriate, revising export control policies to reflect new realities. I fully endorse such a general approach. It is essential, however, to guard against changes in those U.S. export controls that have served us well in curbing the spread of WMD and whose abandonment might inadvertently contribute to the proliferation of nuclear, chemical, or biological weapons. Therefore, in thinking about where possible reform of export control regulations should be pursued, it may make sense to distinguish between export controls targeting WMD-relevant items (especially those in the nuclear sector where technological change has been less dynamic) and those directed at the much larger body of dual-use strategic goods unrelated to WMD. Moreover, it is important to recognize that to the extent that the United States wishes other states to attach greater priority to the development and implementation of domestic nonproliferation export controls, as required by United Nations Security Council Resolution 1540, it must lead by example.

I will leave it to leaders from industry and science to depict the shortcomings of the current U.S. export control system as they pertain to economic competitiveness and the unfettered exchange of ideas and information. What I would like to highlight in my prepared remarks this morning are several new nonproliferation realities and how associated WMD proliferation risks are compounded by gaps and weaknesses in the U.S. export control system and the associated international regimes. I will then conclude with a few specific recommendations about what might be done to improve the situation.

II. The Evolving Proliferation Challenge

The world has changed in many ways since the end of the Cold War. Although the new international strategic environment has reduced the risks of a superpower nuclear exchange, it also has contributed to the growth of new challenges involving the spread and potential use of weapons of mass destruction.

These challenges include the tendency on the part of many states to subordinate nonproliferation considerations to economic and political interests, the development of a global black market in sensitive dual-use technology and material useful for the production and delivery of WMD, and the rise of non-state actors as nuclear suppliers, middlemen, and end users. Elsewhere I have analyzed how the first two developments have been affected by technological advances, as well as by changes in the international political and economic environment. In the interests of time, I will restrict my oral testimony to a few new nuclear dangers posed by non-state actors.

Although discussions of nuclear terrorism typically focus on the potential use by non-state actors of nuclear explosives, it is important to recognize the proliferation risks posed by non-state actors as suppliers of nuclear material, technology, know-how, weapons designs and, conceivably, the weapons themselves. The extensive nuclear supplier network masterminded by Pakistani scientist A.Q. Khan [head of Pakistan's nuclear weapons program] is illustrative of this proliferation challenge. An analytically distinct but related variant of this threat, also illustrated in part by the Khan network, is the operation of non-state actors as middlemen, connecting nuclear suppliers—both state and non-state entities—with end users, which also may be either state or non-state actors.

Most available information indicates that Dr. Khan was the entrepreneur behind the emergence of what former IAEA [International Atomic Energy Agency] Director General Mohamed ElBaradei has called a "nuclear weapons Wal-Mart." Nevertheless, one should take care not to equate the international network with one individual or to assume that his enforced retirement has put illicit non-state nuclear suppliers out of business. Indeed, the so-called "Khan network" was relatively nonhierarchical and involved an international leadership that was widely dispersed around the globe, including locations in Europe, Dubai, South Africa, and Malaysia. Few of its members were ever prosecuted and even fewer were convicted and served prison terms.

Fortunately for nonproliferation, a large gulf usually has separated most individuals with ready access to nuclear material, technology, and know-how from those pariah states or terrorist organizations that covet nuclear weapons. In the former Soviet Union, for example, many of the documented attempts at nuclear trafficking were foiled when amateur thieves incautiously sought to find customers for their contraband. In stark contrast to would-be Russian nuclear entrepreneurs, the Khan network was distinguished by the direct and ready access of its leadership to both Pakistan's own civilian and military nuclear programs and that of prospective nuclear weapons aspirants. Although it is unlikely that future non-state actors will rival the Khan network in terms of its access to a wide array of sensitive nuclear commodities and practical experience in covert procurement for a dedicated nuclear weapons program, criminal and terrorist organizations will almost certainly attempt to link those with access to sensitive nuclear goods and services to state and non-state actors that covet such commodities.

It is to be expected that middlemen already engaged or seeking business in brokering illicit nuclear trade will gravitate toward bases of operations in states with weak or non-existent export control regulations and underdeveloped enforcement mechanisms. Unfortunately, these undesirable characteristics are not limited to the developing world. Indeed, one is hard-pressed to find examples of successful prosecutions of illicit nuclear trafficking in which the accused received more than a slap on the wrist, leading some to conclude that there are greater penalties for driving under the influence than for driving with illicit nuclear goods! This phenomenon is not confined to the developing world, as evidenced by the difficulty officials from Australia, the European Union, and Japan, among other states, have experienced in prosecuting and convicting many of those implicated in various nuclear and chemical weapons-related trafficking incidents. The United States may have been more successful than most other states in prosecuting nonproliferation export control violations, because it now has a team of specialized prosecutors and a national coordinator, but it continues to be frustrated by divergent foreign laws and practices. To the extent that the United States is the pacesetter regarding export control enforcement, it is important that penalties for export violations be commensurate with the violation in order to serve a useful deterrent purpose.

III. Gaps in the Current U.S. System and Practice of Export Controls

The NRC study, among other reports, catalogues a long list of shortcomings in the current U.S. system of dual-use exports. Many of these deficiencies pertain primarily to controls outside of the narrow area of WMD-related commodities. With respect to WMD controls in particular, I would call attention to the need to:

- *Reorganize the U.S. government bureaucracy for enforcing export controls.* When the U.S. Customs Service was incorporated into the Department of Homeland Security in November 2002, it was split into two separate agencies, Immigration and Customs Enforcement (ICE) and Customs and Border Protection (CBP). Both agencies have other high-profile missions (immigration control and border protection), which constrain their ability to enforce nonproliferation export controls effectively. As a result, many experienced customs inspectors and investigators have been demoralized by the reorganization and left the Federal service, while others are waiting to retire. One solution to this problem would be to reunite the two halves of the former U.S. Customs Service into a specialized agency that is separate from the immigration and border protection missions of DHS.
- *Improve U.S. cooperation with foreign customs services.* The United States cannot prevent WMD proliferation on its own but must cooperate with other like-minded states to control WMD-relevant commodities and equipment. The more countries are aware of illicit trafficking and have effective laws in place to counter it, including criminal sanctions and extradition treaties, the better the odds of success.
- *Devise effective controls in WMD proliferation-relevant areas where new technologies are emerging.* The logic of adjusting export controls to changing

conditions should not mean simply relaxing or reducing controls. In some instances, it may be necessary to introduce more sophisticated and tailored approaches. One of the greatest challenges is to devise *effective* (as well as more *efficient*) controls in WMD proliferation-relevant areas where new technologies are emerging, sometimes at a rapid pace.

IV. International Export Control Regime Deficiencies

To be sure, one can identify significant shortcomings in both the design and performance of the major international export control regimes: the Nuclear Suppliers Group (NSG), the Missile Technology Control Regime (MTCR), the Australia Group, and the Wassenaar Arrangement. These deficiencies include nonmembership of some key exporting countries, inconsistent implementation of "catch-all" and "no-undercut" provisions, inadequate reporting and intelligence sharing practices among member states, and lack of familiarity by industry in member states of the provisions governing exports. These problems, however, should not obscure the very useful contribution to WMD nonproliferation made by the NSG, MTCR, and the Australia Group.

It also should be noted that these nonproliferation regimes were not driven primarily by Cold War considerations or attempts to stymie the Soviet Union's quest for WMD. Indeed, in the nuclear sector during much of the Cold War the United States and the Soviet Union pursued remarkably similar nuclear export control and nonproliferation policies, and Washington often found it easier to cooperate closely with Moscow on nuclear nonproliferation and export control issues than it did with some of its close allies. As such, it does not follow logically that these export control arrangements should be scrapped or substantially modified simply because the Cold War has ended.

Despite progress in expanding international support for prudent nonproliferation export control measures designed to address the growing threat posed by non-state actors, many countries today still regard WMD terrorism as someone else's problem. As my CNS colleague Dr. Jonathan Tucker has demonstrated in the realm of chemical weapons precursors, states either may "not share U.S. concerns about the need to prevent the diversion of dual-use materials and equipment to WMD programs or lack the resources to perform this task effectively." A tendency to discount nonproliferation considerations is reinforced by "just-in-time" inventory practices and free-trade zones, which depend on and are designed to expedite and/or avoid export controls. Indeed, many exporters prefer to use ports and transit hubs where customs enforcement is minimal or lax, making them easier and faster to transit—but also facilitating illicit trade in WMD-related items. As Tucker observes, "[i]n addition to economic pressures, the lack of a global consensus on 'best practices' for customs inspections has hampered the development of international standards." Yet another challenge is that throughout the Asia-Pacific region, information on cargo manifests is considered proprietary and few details must be declared.

The difficulty of prosecuting export control violations—in the United States and abroad—further undermines the deterrent value of export controls.

Many countries, including our closest allies do not recognize the U.S. legal concept of extraterritorial jurisdiction and do not permit the extradition of their citizens. As one contemplates reforms for the U.S. export control system, one must be aware of the liabilities that result from divergent international practices and priorities, as well as the shortcomings of existing international export control regimes. It is also the case, however, that many states do follow the U.S. lead on nonproliferation export policy and that, by and large, nonproliferation export control norms and practices have become more prudent and widespread over time. This positive trend in strengthening domestic export controls is perhaps most obvious with respect to China's national trade control system, although further improvements in enforcement are still needed. Although the 2008 NSG exemption granted to India marked a major step backward in the international nuclear export control arena, it is all the more imperative today to strengthen the NSG and the other international mechanisms that focus on WMD proliferation.

V. Corrective Measures

A sound U.S. approach to nonproliferation export controls requires a two-pronged approach: (1) recognition and retention of those aspects of the system that have performed well, and (2) introduction of new features that will enhance economic competitiveness and information and technology flow without weakening the international nonproliferation regime. Let me conclude my prepared remarks by suggesting how these dual objectives may be pursued in tandem.

Retain the "Catch-All Rule"

Whatever the United States does, it must be very careful not to make matters worse. Among other things this dictum cautions against acceptance of the advice of those who would like to dilute or restrict further the "catch-all" provision in Part 744 of the Export Administration Regulations. This provision holds that that dual-use items or technologies that are not on the Commerce Control List may still require an export license if the exporter has reason to believe that the item is intended for the development, production, or delivery of nuclear, biological, or chemical weapons. In fact, an increasing number of companies today have made strides in incorporating the "catch-all" philosophy into their internal compliance programs, and greater efforts should be made to encourage the adoption of WMD nonproliferation objectives as a component of corporate social responsibility goals.

Work with Other Countries to Reform
Their National Laws and Practices

A major step forward in promoting WMD-related export controls internationally was taken in April 2004 when the United Nations Security Council adopted Resolution (UNSCR) 1540. This measure, among other things, requires all UN member states to adopt and enforce effective laws that prohibit non-state actors from acquiring WMD, their delivery systems, and the materials needed to produce them. Although few states directly challenge this mandate, its implementation has been undermined in many countries due to lack of resources, competing demands, and poor understanding of the relevance of the measure for their own national security interests. If UNSCR 1540 is to be effective as an export control initiative, it will be necessary for the United States to increase its support for regional and national 1540 training programs. To comply fully with UNSCR 1540, it also would be desirable for states to amend their extradition treaties to cover WMD-related export violations.

Increase Funding for Export Control Enforcement

Effective export control enforcement continues to be hampered by the lack of sufficient personnel to undertake proper end-use checks and aggressively pursue investigations of suspected violations. It does little good, for example, to identify new cases that merit investigation if one is unable to assign trained personnel to conduct investigations at home and abroad.

Explore New Remedies for Export Control Violations

The demanding legal standard for proving criminal violations of the Export Administration Regulations suggests that new types of remedies are needed in an age of economic globalization. One promising approach is to impose financial sanctions against companies and persons involved in WMD-related trafficking, such as those mandated by the Iran Nonproliferation Act of 2000 and Executive Order 13382 of June 2005. Other possible sanctions against companies and persons involved in the trafficking of WMD-related materials and equipment include the denial of export rights to the United States or restrictions on individual travel.

Invest More in Nonproliferation Education and Training

It is necessary but not sufficient to adopt new rules and regulations internationally with respect to WMD-related exports. Equally important is the need to build a global nonproliferation and security culture in which government and industry officials, scientists, and graduate students who work with dual-use WMD-related technology and materials in the nuclear, biological, and chemical fields learn to appreciate the potential dangers posed by these items and become familiar with the domestic and international regulations governing their use.

I will conclude my remarks by touching on the issue of nonproliferation export controls as it pertains to the university environment. At a time when the great majority of U.S. government officials and politicians of different political persuasions agree on the dangers posed by WMD proliferation, it is surprising how limited the opportunities are for students at all levels of education to acquire formal training in the field. In a very small way, the Monterey Institute of International Studies is trying to address this knowledge gap by offering a new Masters degree program in Nonproliferation and Terrorism

Studies—the first of its kind in the world. But many more universities will need to follow suit if we are to train the next generation of nonproliferation specialists or even introduce our future leaders in government, science, and industry to the subject.

One practical step to remedy the problem, at least in the United States, would be to pass a National Nonproliferation Education Act, perhaps modeled after the National Defense Education Act or the National Security Education Act. Such legislation, ideally funded by a one-time appropriation of around $50 million, would provide up to 50 fellowships per year to graduate students to pursue advanced multidisciplinary training in nonproliferation studies at the universities of their choice. An act of this sort would have the dual positive benefit of attracting top-notch young talent to the field and encouraging more universities to offer courses on nonproliferation issues (including export controls) in order to attract tuition-paying students. While not a short-term solution to our current predicament, this approach would help to create the next generation of experts on whom the United States will rely to tackle increasingly complex task of preventing the proliferation of nuclear, biological, and chemical weapons of mass destruction.

POSTSCRIPT

Should Export Controls on High Technology Be Eased Substantially?

While President George W. Bush was unsympathetic to calls to substantially revise the U.S. export control system, President Barack Obama has been more responsive. In August 2010, the outlines of his response began to emerge in a speech he gave at the Department of Commerce and in an op-ed piece by National Security Adviser General James Jones in the *Wall Street Journal*. As suggested by the sites of the speech and article, the remarks focused on easing export controls as an economic benefit. There were, of course, assurances that the changes would not endanger national security. As evident in the readings, the debate over export controls seldom touches on specific items and instead centers on procedures such as streamlining the approval system and moving many dual-use components found in weapons systems from the highly restrictive U.S. Munitions List (USML) to the less sensitive Commerce Control List (CCL). In the end, though, the point of changing (or preserving) the approval process is to ease (or maintain) the current level of export controls.

While easing export controls will almost certainly help the U.S. trade balance and employment picture at least a bit, it is also true that it will also benefit other countries. That is why China, India, and other countries have been pressing the United States, as well as the European Union, to ease the barriers. In 2010, for example, Vice Premier Wang Qishan of China met with Treasury Secretary Timothy Geithner and other top Obama administration officials in the "hope," as Wang put it, of hearing "from the U.S. side in detail its timetable and roadmap for gradually removing barriers to high-tech exports to China." What changes the Obama administration will propose remain to be seen. The president has some unilateral ability to change export—by using executive orders, but other changes would require congressional action as well and are likely to meet with staunch resistance on the Hill.

As for the impact on research and the work of foreign graduate students in some fields, there can be no doubt the controls over the export of sensitive information create issues. Nevertheless, some analysts worry about the growing share of foreign students among graduate students in U.S. universities doing work in many areas in science and engineering. In 2006, for instance, the percentages of Ph.D. degrees in the following fields received by foreign students were aeronautical/astronautical engineering (49 percent), chemistry (40 percent), computer science (55 percent), electrical engineering (69 percent), mathematics (50 percent), materials/metallurgical engineering (56 percent), and physics (52 percent). These percentages create concerns among some about how relatively few Americans are getting advanced training in these areas and also the degree to which the United States is exporting training and knowledge that will help other countries compete with the United States economically and perhaps even militarily.

An overview of this topic is provided by Dennis A. Lloyd, *U.S. Export Control: Background and Issues* (Nova Science, 2010). Two key U.S. agencies are the Bureau of Industry and Security of the U.S. Department of Commerce at http://www.bis.doc.gov/index.htm and the U.S. State Department's Directorate of Defense Trade Controls at http://www.pmddtc.state.gov/. More on the impact on university research and graduate students can be found in Nelson G. Dong, *U.S. Export Controls and Research Universities: What Deans Should Know* (Council of Graduate Schools, December 5, 2007).

Questions for Critical Thinking and Reflection

1. Should the United States refuse to allow the export of a sensitive technology even if another country already has it and also is willing to export it?

2. How do you relate this debate to the issues raised in Issue 8 about Iran's claimed right to acquire the technology to enrich uranium?

3. Currently, there are U.S. export controls on the most sophisticated night-vision goggles. As a dual-use technology, are these controls appropriate? For background, go to the Web site of American Technologies Network Corporation at http://www.atncorp.com/exportinformation.

Internet References . . .

Disarmament Diplomacy

This site, maintained by the Acronym Institute for Disarmament Diplomacy, provides up-to-date news and analysis of disarmament activity, with a particular focus on weapons of mass destruction.

http://www.acronym.org.uk

The Center for Security Policy

The Web site of this Washington, DC–centered "think tank" provides a wide range of links to sites dealing with national and international security issues.

http://www.centerforsecuritypolicy.org

National Defense University

This leading center for joint professional military education is under the direction of the Chairman of the U.S. Joint Chiefs of Staff. Its Web site is valuable for general military thinking and for material on terrorism.

http://www.ndu.edu/

Office of the Coordinator for Counterterrorism

This worthwhile site explores the range of terrorist threats and activities, albeit from the U.S. point of view, and is maintained by the U.S. State Department's Counterterrorism Office.

http://www.state.gov/s/ct/

Centre for the Study of Terrorism and Political Violence

The primary aims of the Centre for the Study of Terrorism and Political Violence are to investigate the roots of political violence; to develop a body of theory spanning the various and disparate elements of terrorism; and to recommend policy and organizational initiatives that governments and private sectors might adopt to better predict, detect, and respond to terrorism and terrorist threats.

http://www.st-ANDREWS.ac.uk/academic/intrel/research/cstpv/

Armament and Violence Issues

*W*hatever we may wish, war, terrorism, and other forms of physical coercion are still important elements of international politics. Countries calculate both how to use the instruments of force and how to implement national security. There can be little doubt, however, that significant changes are under way in this realm as part of the changing world system. Strong pressures exist to expand the mission and strengthen the security capabilities of international organizations and to gauge the threat of terrorism. This section examines how countries in the international system are addressing these issues.

- Is U.S. Strategic Nuclear Weapons Policy Ill-Conceived?

- Should U.S. Forces Continue to Fight in Afghanistan?

- Does Using Drones to Attack Terrorists Globally Violate International Law?

ISSUE 13

Is U.S. Strategic Nuclear Weapons Policy Ill-Conceived?

YES: **Ariel Cohen**, from "Dangerous Trajectories: Obama's Approach to Arms Control Misreads Russian Nuclear Strategy," Backgrounder on Arms Control and Non-Proliferation, Nuclear Arms Race and Russia and Eurasia, The Heritage Foundation (November 9, 2009)

NO: **Robert Farley**, from "The Nuclear Posture Attack," *Right Web* (June 2, 2010)

ISSUE SUMMARY

YES: Ariel Cohen, a senior research fellow in Russian and Eurasian studies at the Heritage Foundation, charges that President Obama's arms control strategy is overambitious and based too much on unilateral concessions that will not prevent a new arms race.

NO: Robert Farley, faculty member of the University of Kentucky's Patterson School of Diplomacy and International Commerce, defends the Obama administration's nuclear weapons policy and characterizes the arguments from groups like the Heritage Foundation as outdated, nostalgic concepts from the heyday of the cold warriors.

Since U.S. atomic bombs leveled Hiroshima and Nagasaki in 1945, and even more since the possibility of a two-sided nuclear war emerged in 1949 when the Soviet Union also acquired atomic bombs, the world has struggled with how to deal with the apocalyptic potential of the nuclear age. One aspect of the politics of nuclear weapons has been to restrain them. In part restraint involves keeping more countries from acquiring nuclear weapons. A key part of that effort has been the nuclear Non-Proliferation Treaty (NPT, 1970, which was made permanent in 1995), by which countries without nuclear weapons pledge not to acquire them and countries with nuclear weapons pledge not to help any other country acquire them. The NPT has not been absolutely successful, but only four countries (Israel, India, Pakistan, and North Korea) have acquired since 1970, with a fifth, Iran, possibly on the verge of doing so.

Another way to restrain nuclear weapons focuses on the countries that already have them and capping or reducing the number, types of these weapons, and delivery vehicles (missiles and bombers). This effort has primarily involved the two countries, the United States and the Soviet Union (now Russia), with huge nuclear arsenals, and has included numerous agreements including two strategic arms limitation treaties (SALT I, 1972, and SALT II, 1979), two strategic arms reduction treaties (START I, 1991, and START II, 1993, but never ratified), and the Moscow Treaty (2002). These treaties reduced the combined American and Russian arsenal of nuclear warheads and bombs from nearly 60,000 in 1970 to about 7,000 deployed and 12,000 nondeployed weapons today. Limits on testing such as by the Limited Test Ban Treaty (1963) have added to the restraints by making it difficult to develop reliable new nuclear weapons. There were 140 tests during 1962 alone; only two (both by North Korea) have occurred since 1998. The last Soviet test was in 1990 and the last U.S. test was in 1992.

In addition to restraining the spread and number of nuclear weapons, another policy issue has been setting doctrines about how to structure nuclear forces and how to, if necessary, use them. An important issue has been how to deter a nuclear attack, and in significant part that has rested on the idea of building a nuclear arsenal that will have enough power, even after an attack, to utterly destroy the attacker, thereby making it totally illogical to attack in the first place. If both the United States and Russia have this capability, the peace is ensured by their mutual assured destruction (MAD) capabilities.

A third policy consideration is whether to try to build a defense system against nuclear attack. Mostly because neither country could do it anyway, the United States and Soviet Union agreed in the Antiballistic Missile (ABM) Treaty (1972) not to try to construct a ballistic missile defense (BMD) system. However, President Ronald Reagan revived the idea in the 1980s, and in 2002 President George W. Bush ordered the U.S. withdrawal from the ABM treaty. Proponents argue that it can provide at least some protection from an attack by countries such as North Korea and potentially a much broader defense system. Opponents charge U.S. BMD efforts are too unreliable to justify their huge cost and that a BMD system undermines deterrence by making mutual destruction no longer assured.

The arrival of the Democrats in the White House in the form of Barack Obama brought with it, for good or ill, the possibility of significant revisions to the country's nuclear weapons policies during eight years of Republican George W. Bush White House. The two presidents differ in a number of ways. Obama decreased support for BMD by cutting $1.2 billion from the programs and by scrapping an agreement made by Bush with Poland and the Czech Republic that would have put elements of a U.S. BMD system in those countries. In the first reading, Ariel Cohen, warns that Obama's negotiating position on nuclear arms talks with the Russian includes concessions that are counterproductive and self-defeating because they may result in a worse endgame position for the United States. By contrast, Robert Farley charges that much of the opposition to Obama's policies is based on "rejectionism" rather than rational thought and that serious debate has been marginalized because there are fewer new voices on the right arguing for a responsible nuclear weapons policy.

YES

Ariel Cohen

Dangerous Trajectories: Obama's Approach to Arms Control Misreads Russian Nuclear Strategy

As the Obama Administration negotiates a range of arms control initiatives with Russia, U.S. policymakers need to critically examine Russia's views on nuclear weapons and doctrine. While successive U.S. Administrations have announced that Russia is no longer the enemy, Russia still considers the United States its "principal adversary," despite President Barack Obama's attempts to "reset" bilateral relations. U.S. national leadership and arms control negotiators need to understand Russia's nuclear doctrine and negotiating style as they are, not as the U.S. wants them to be.

U.S. nuclear policymakers need to protect the United States from nuclear threats; reduce the risk of nuclear conflict; and negotiate transparent, verifiable, and workable arms control agreements with Russia and other nuclear powers. It is in U.S. interests to convince Russia to adopt a similar agenda and to pursue arms control and nonproliferation in areas where U.S. and Russian national interests coincide. A win-win strategy may conflict with 800 years of Russian history in which it fought regional and global powers, but the alternative—a new arms race reminiscent of the Cold War—is economically and politically unpalatable to both nations.

The Obama Administration's approach of unilateral concessions will not prevent a new arms race. Nor should the Administration pursue an overambitious arms control strategy. Instead, it should negotiate a verification and transparency protocol to the [2002] Strategic Offensive Reductions Treaty (SORT or Moscow Treaty). Meanwhile, the U.S. should not accept a Russian strategic posture designed to threaten the U.S. and its allies or the further reduction of Russia's threshold for using nuclear weapons. Rather, the U.S. should pursue a "protect and defend" strategic posture, which includes a defensive nuclear posture, missile defense, and nuclear modernization. Finally, the U.S. should propose a realistic, detailed, transparent, verifiable, and enforceable arms control and nonproliferation agenda with the Russian Federation.

Only by understanding the evolution and current state of Russia's nuclear doctrine and its approach to negotiations can U.S. decision makers develop a coherent policy toward Russia.

From *The Heritage Foundation Backgrounder,* November 9, 2009. Copyright © 2009 by The Heritage Foundation. Reprinted by permission.

Looking Back to Look Forward

Russia's approach to arms control is a product of Soviet and subsequent Russian nuclear strategy. Russia integrates its nuclear strategy with arms control, missile defense, a lower threshold for the first use of nuclear weapons, nonproliferation, nuclear modernization, and development of next-generation weapons into a strategic posture that maximizes deterrence and warfighting capability at a minimal cost.

The Obama Administration has been preoccupied with pushing Russia to sign a successor to the Strategic Arms Reduction Treaty (START) before the December 2009 deadline. The proposed treaty, which is opposed by a number of Members of Congress, would limit both countries to 1,500–1,675 warheads and 500–1,100 delivery platforms (land-based missiles, submarine-launched missiles, and strategic bombers). The Moscow Treaty, signed by President George W. Bush and President Vladimir Putin in 2002, limits both sides to 2,200 warheads and 1,600 delivery vehicles until 2012, but its verification procedures are flawed.

The Obama Administration's arms control strategy to date has been deeply flawed. The Administration cancelled deployment of 10 ground-based missile interceptors in Eastern Europe and publicly embraced the "road to zero" (full nuclear disarmament), which is unrealistic in today's unstable and proliferating world. This approach based on outdated 1970s arms control strategy and 1960s idealism and naïveté will not work because it does not account for Russian nuclear strategy, which is based on approximate parity between the two sides, Mutual Assured Destruction (MAD), denial of missile defenses to the U.S., and nuclear warfighting capability.

The Burden of History

Twenty years after the collapse of the Soviet Union, communist ideology is almost dead in Russia, but Russian great power ideology has replaced it. Russian national leaders, generals, and experts are still captives of the czarist and Soviet geopolitical thinking and military traditions. Theirs is a deeply suspicious and xenophobic worldview shaped by incessant wars against regional and global powers—from the Tatars to the Germans.

In the 20th century, the USSR could compete with the United States only in the military arena. By the late 1960s, Russia had almost caught up with the United States in the size and sophistication of its nuclear deterrent. In all else the socialist camp lagged hopelessly behind the West, including consumer goods, popular culture, health care, and standard of living.

Ostensibly, the purpose of the Soviet-era arms control was to lock the U.S. and the USSR into nuclear parity, reducing the chances of either side launching a first strike. Meanwhile, the USSR pursued illegal defense options and obtained a first-strike capability. At the same time, the Soviet Union pursued strategic challenges to the U.S. through Third World expansion, Finlandization of Europe, and intelligence-based influence operations ("active measures"). ["Finlandization" means following a foreign policy like Finland during the cold war of not doing anything to antagonize the Soviet Union.]

Arms control agreements, such as the Strategic Arms Limitation Treaty (SALT) and the Anti-Ballistic Missile (ABM) Treaty, limited both offensive and defensive weapons. SALT I limited strategic nuclear forces on both sides and froze deployment of anti-ballistic missile defenses, but not research and development. The USSR had already deployed a missile defense system around Moscow, and the U.S. decided not to deploy one. Yet SALT I failed to stop the arms race. By 1981, Russia had almost quadrupled its arsenal to more than 8,000 warheads, while the U.S. had more than doubled its stockpile to more than 10,000 warheads.

The follow-on Strategic Arms Reduction Treaty (START), signed by President George H. W. Bush and President Mikhail Gorbachev on July 31, 1991, drastically cut the number of warheads to reflect the end of the Cold War. On May 24, 2002, President George W. Bush and President Putin signed the Moscow Treaty, the shortest and least detailed arms control agreement of the post-Cold War era.

The Moscow Treaty called for each side to reduce the number of nuclear warheads from the 6,000 under START to 1,700–2,200 operationally deployed warheads, but it did not limit the number of tactical nuclear weapons (TNW). Russia reportedly has several thousand TNWs. SORT abandoned qualitative and quantitative parity in offensive strategic nuclear capabilities and relied on less explicit verification and implementation arrangements, although the START verification provisions that applied to warheads and delivery vehicles remained in place. SORT allowed Russia to pursue nuclear modernization, eliminate obsolete or costly weapons systems, and design and produce more cost-effective and modern missiles.

Today, Russia is pursuing an arms control regime that would allow it to accomplish these goals while keeping U.S. programs, such as global missile defense, in check or even discrediting them. It also designed to maintain Russia's prestige and the semblance of strategic parity with the United States.

Restoring Russia's Power

Under Putin's leadership, Russia is reviving its great power status by rebuilding its military, especially its nuclear component, and capitalizing on its massive energy resources. Russia's geopolitical clout is benefiting from Europe's dependence on Russian energy exports.

After the Soviet collapse, many in the upper echelons of the Russian elite retained the vision of global grandeur. As early as 1999, retired General Makhmout Gareyev, a leading Soviet and Russian military thinker and former deputy chief of the Soviet general staff, stated:

> One of the most important unifying factors is the idea of Russia's rebirth as a great power, not a regional power . . . but a truly great power on a global scale. This is determined not by someone's desire, not just by possession of nuclear weapons or by size of territory, but by the historic traditions and objectives met in the development of the Russian society and state.

Today's Russia is continuing the strategic stance and policies that characterized the Soviet military, including MAD targeting plans, strategic bomber flights over the Atlantic and the Pacific Oceans near U.S. and allied airspace, navy and air force visits to Venezuela and Cuba, and military base construction in the Arab world. The increasing militarization of Russian foreign policy has also brought a buildup of nuclear weapons.

Nuclear Weapons as a Policy Tool

The Russian elites view nuclear weapons as a warfighting tool and an instrument of foreign and security policy. In 2006, President Putin emphasized the importance of the nuclear arsenal:

> When looking at today's international situation and the prospects for its development, Russia is compelled to realize that nuclear deterrence is a key element in guaranteeing the country's security. . . . The Russian nuclear weapons complex constitutes the material basis for this nuclear deterrence policy. . . . Keeping the necessary minimum of nuclear deterrence remains one of the main priorities of Russian Federation policy in this arena.

During the Cold War, the USSR pursued the "struggle for peace." The Soviet intelligence services recruited "useful idiots" and fellow travelers to mouth the disarmament propaganda for consumption by the West. Even today, the Russian leadership makes peaceful statements for dissemination abroad, which are often clearly contradicted by "true confessions" at home. For example, in 2003, Defense Minister Sergei Ivanov said:

> What we say is one thing. That sounds cynical, but everything that we plan does not necessarily have to be made public. We believe that from the foreign-policy viewpoint it is better to say that. But what we actually do is an entirely different matter if we're talking about nuclear weapons. They are the chief components of our security, and there can be no doubt that attention toward them cannot be relaxed.

This statement reflects the old Soviet approach in which speeches for external consumption were understood as just propaganda. The USSR launched and operated dozens of front organizations to support the disarmament of the West, all of them ultimately run and/or supervised by the KGB [the *Komitet Gosudarstvennoy Bezopasnosti* or Committee for State Security— the Soviet Union's spy and secret police organization]. At the same time, the Soviet intelligence apparatus was busy stealing Western technology to develop a superior nuclear arsenal.

Ex-Soviet intelligence officers, such as Putin and Ivanov, cannot easily forget their Soviet-era conditioning. Under their leadership, Russia's attempts to rebuild its regional and global power are founded on modernizing its nuclear weapons, updating its nuclear doctrine, and clinging to the nexus between missile defenses and offensive weapons in the arms control negotiations.

The Russian Strategic Objective: Parity with the United States

Since the Soviet victory in World War II and the occupation of Eastern Europe, Soviet leaders and later Russian leaders believed that the United States should treat their country as an equal, especially in the military realm. The constant barrage of demands for honor, recognition, and status has continued since the end of World War II, freezing the adversarial U.S.–Russia relationship in a posture of mutual deterrence. If the sides looked at each other without the prism of nuclear deterrence, the comparatively small size of Russia's economy (approximately one-ninth of the U.S. economy) would be visible to all. The American "adversary" is a projection of Russia's chronically insecure rulers. It is also a standing justification for Russia's bloated military, intelligence, and secret services budgets and a useful means of consolidating domestic support for the regime.

However, additional threats have appeared on Russia's security horizon. In 1969, Soviet troops clashed with Chinese infantry in the Russian Far East. Today, China is numerically and economically superior to Russia, and it possesses long-range and intermediate-range nuclear-armed ballistic missiles. Furthermore, with Soviet and Russian assistance, North Korea and Iran have acquired intermediate-range ballistic missiles and are busy developing nuclear weapons, despite international pressure. Russia may eventually need to address these developing threats.

At the same time, qualitatively new weapon systems in Western military arsenals—including missile defenses, conventionally armed intercontinental ballistic missiles (ICBMs), stealth technology, space systems, and unmanned aerial vehicles (UAVs)—highlight the Russian military's conventional inferiority. More than ever before, Russia relies on nuclear weapons, and the United States and NATO remain its proclaimed principal security concerns.

Dark Vision: The Kremlin's Threat Perception

When President Boris Yeltsin led an independent Russian Federation out of the ruins of the USSR in January 1992, official security doctrine proclaimed that Russia had no enemies. Yet that attitude was undermined by those, such as spy chief and later Foreign Minister and Prime Minister Yevgeny M. Primakov, who yearned for a multipolar world in which U.S. power would be diluted by Russia, China, India, and the Islamic world. The Russian military leadership articulated an anti-American strategy due to a combination of belief and pragmatism. It would also justify multi-billion dollar budgets for weapons modernization and much-needed reform.

After the confrontation with NATO in Kosovo in spring 1999, two rounds of NATO expansion, and the Iraq war, Russia's anti-American rhetoric escalated. Statements by Russian leaders from Putin on down demonstrated that the Russian national leadership still viewed the United States as Russia's *glavny protivnik* (principal adversary). For example, after the horrific 2004 terrorist attack [on a school] in Beslan [by Chechen and Ingush rebels that killed 334 hostages, including 186 children], Putin stated:

> Some want to cut off a juicy morsel from us while others are helping them. They are helping because they believe that, as one of the world's major nuclear powers, Russia is still posing a threat to someone, and therefore this threat must be removed. And terrorism is, of course, only a tool for achieving these goals.

Putin and his surrogates clarified that he blamed the West led by the U.S., despite the total lack of evidence that the West was involved in the barbaric hostage taking. Vladislav Surkov, Putin's chief of ideology, announced in the daily *Komsomolskaya Pravda* that Russia was being confronted by "[a]ctors that still live by Cold-War phobias" and that "[t]heir goal is destroying Russia and filling its immense space with multiple weak quasi-states." He warned, "The enemy is at the gate. The front line crosses every city, every street, every house."

Putin also addressed the trauma caused by the breakup of the USSR, terming it "the greatest geopolitical catastrophe of the 20th century." This trauma is at the root of the inferiority complex of today's post-Soviet Russian ruling elite, which demands symbolic compensation: oil, territory, nuclear weapons, restoration of a Russian sphere of influence throughout the former Soviet Union and in areas of former Soviet influence, such as in the Middle East.

Russian Nuclear Weapons: Defense on the Cheap

Russia views its nuclear deterrent as the most cost-effective way to preserve its security. Its formidable strategic triad consists of silo-based and mobile missiles of the Strategic Nuclear Forces, submarine-launched ballistic missiles (SLBMs), and strategic bombers. These are regulated by extant arms control agreements. In addition, Russia has thousands of TNWs, which are not regulated by such treaties. Russia sees these weapons as "nuclear equalizers," compensating for Russia's conventional inferiority vis-à-vis the U.S., NATO, and China.

In November 2008, President Dmitry Medvedev threatened Poland with short-range Iskander missiles, while Chief of the General Staff Nikolai Makarov publicly proclaimed that Russia would retain its tactical nuclear weapons as a guarantee of Russian security as long as Europe is "packed with armaments." Prime Minister Putin has repeatedly promised to boost military allocations, including funding for nuclear modernization.

Nuclear Modernization and Military Reform

Putin has repeatedly reaffirmed that, despite the economic crisis, Russia will maintain a robust weapons procurement budget to purchase advanced military equipment, including nuclear weapons and space systems. Russia's defense procurement budget is $37 billion for 2009 and will total $114 billion over three years (2009–2011).

Nevertheless, Russia is experiencing difficulties deploying the Bulava SLBM [submarine-launched ballistic missile]. Reportedly one *Borey*-class ballistic missile nuclear submarine is not armed with any missiles. Production of Topol-M mobile ICBMs [intercontinental ballistic missiles] is insufficient to maintain the numbers permitted by the START follow-on agreement and the number of deployed nuclear warheads may fall below 1,000. Another bottleneck of nuclear modernization is the age and the depletion of Russia's technical and scientific personnel.

As a part of its military reforms, Russia is drastically cutting the number of serving generals and officers. A senior policy adviser to the Minister of Defense told this author that the deep cuts in the officer corps and "paper" divisions are connected to the need to restructure the military away from its Soviet-era legacy toward the ability to deter foreign states and protect the long Russian borders, especially in the south and east. With its considerably smaller conventional forces, challenges in modernizing the military, and difficulties in deploying and integrating information technology and sufficient numbers of high-tech weapons, Russia will rely on a lower threshold for using nuclear weapons, including first strike.

Nuclear Use Threshold

Current Russian military doctrine provides for:

> . . . nuclear forces capable of delivering required damage to any aggressor state or a coalition thereof under any circumstances. The Russian Federation retains the right to use nuclear weapons in response to use against it and/or its allies, of nuclear and other weapons of mass destruction, as well as in response to wide scale aggression which uses regular weapons in a situation critical to the national security of the Russian Federation.

The 2003 document "The Priority Tasks of the Development of the Armed Forces of the Russian Federation" clarifies that the nuclear forces of the Russian Federation, in addition to the strategic nuclear forces (land-based missiles, submarines, and strategic bombers), include non-strategic nuclear forces, such as tactical nuclear weapons.

Russian experts do not fully exclude the possibility of the U.S. using force against their state, especially after the wars in Yugoslavia and Iraq. Russian conventional forces clearly could not contain such a threat, so the "attention to nuclear weapons is a logical solution to the situation." Russian leaders assume that the U.S. will not risk the use of force as long as Russia has a credible nuclear deterrent. Furthermore, Russia might use nuclear weapons in a "wide-scale" war or in a regional conflict that escalated from a local war. However, the Russian leadership has since lowered the nuclear first-use threshold even more.

Nuclear weapons could be used in the Far Eastern, southern, or western theaters of operations. Russian generals explain the lowered nuclear threshold as an answer to both conventional inferiority and as a de-escalation tool. In other words, they believe that limited use of nuclear weapons early in a conflict could force the other side to cease hostilities.

General Nikolay Patrushev is Secretary of the Russian National Security Council, the body in charge of military doctrine. He is also a Putin confidante and has served as the head of the FSB secret police, a KGB successor agency. Patrushev recently made an unprecedented statement in an interview with *Izvestiya*. He declared that Russia not only may use nuclear weapons preemptively in local conflicts, such as Georgia or Chechnya, but may deliver a nuclear blow "against the aggressor in a critical situation . . . based on [intelligence] evaluation of his intentions." The second half of the comment was removed from the newspaper's Web site the following day without explanations. Alexander Golts, a leading Russian military analyst, views this statement as further lowering the nuclear threshold, allowing Russia to launch a first strike based on the Russian intelligence evaluation of a potential adversary. While some ascribed this declaration to bravado, Russia views the U.S. as its principal adversary.

Missile Defense and Weapons in Space

In the 1960s, the USSR developed and deployed a missile defense around Moscow. The United States pleaded with the Soviets to limit competition in missile defenses and concluded the 1972 ABM Treaty. The strategic stability paradigm based on MAD was thus locked in place. Today, Russia opposes the U.S. withdrawal from the ABM treaty in 2002, claiming that offensive and defensive strategic weapons are linked as they were in the 1970–1980s. Russia views the incremental deployment of U.S. missile defenses as detrimental to Russia's long-term ability to counter a U.S. first strike against Russian strategic weapons. Russia vociferously opposed the third missile defense site in central Europe and is equally opposed to any militarization of space with offensive (nuclear) or missile defense systems beyond current communications, command, control, and intelligence systems. Russia regularly works with China and other states at the United Nations Disarmament Commission to impose an international ban on deployment of weapons in space.

Tomorrow's Nuclear Weapons

Russian research into new categories of nuclear weapons is highly classified. However, publications indicate that the Russian military–industrial complex is developing precision low-yield nuclear weapons that are programmable to deliver yields less than the equivalent of 100 tons of TNT. According to former Atomic Energy Minister Victor Mikhaylov, Russia has also worked on developing penetrating nuclear weapons. Vladimir Belous, a retired general and nuclear expert, disclosed the development of fusion weapons that he characterized as mini neutron bombs [that kill by intense neutron radiation but have little blast or heat effect]. Other experts have emphasized that Russia has electromagnetic pulse (EMP) weapons capable of disabling all electronic systems in vast areas and that EMP research and development is continuing. According to Mikhaylov, Russia has emphasized development of high-precision and deep-penetration nuclear weapons, outstripping the U.S. in these areas.

Russian Violations of Arms Control

The U.S. Congress has been informed of numerous accusations of Russian violations of arms control agreements. For example, in 1991–1992, the U.S. and the USSR/Russia committed in the Presidential Nuclear Initiatives (PNIs) to dramatically reduce the number of deployed tactical nuclear weapons. In 2009, the Strategic Posture Commission stated, "Russia is no longer in compliance with its PNI commitments." Estimates of Russia's TNW arsenal are classified, but observers place the number as high as 3,800—several times larger than the U.S. stockpile.

The U.S. and Russia have also undertaken an informal moratorium on nuclear weapons tests. However, "the Russian nuclear labs continue an active underground test program at Novaya Zemlya [islands in the Artic Ocean] which includes release of low levels of nuclear energy." The U.S. interpretation of the testing moratorium involves a zero-yield standard; therefore, Russia is in violation of the arrangement.

A 2005 State Department report noted multiple Russian violations of START verification provisions. Specifically, the State Department asserted that Russia was testing multiple warheads on SS-27 ICBMs, which is forbidden under START. These provisions are at the heart of the START follow-on treaty that the Obama Administration is currently negotiating.

The U.S. intelligence community has accused Russia of violating nonproliferation agreements and arrangements by providing ballistic missile technology to Iran and North Korea. Kathleen Turner, Director of Legislative Affairs at the Office of the Director of National Intelligence, stated that "individual Russian entities continue to provide assistance to Iran's ballistic missile programs. We judge that the Russian-entity assistance . . . has helped Iran move toward self-sufficiency in production of ballistic missiles."

While negotiating with the Kremlin, the U.S. team should keep in mind more than just these violations and deceptions. Fifty years of nuclear talks indicate that the USSR/Russia customarily opens talks with maximalist negotiating positions, threatens to use nuclear weapons against neighbors and launches demagogic public "peaceful initiatives" for external consumption. It then adopts a more pragmatic posture behind closed doors. Moscow would be highly suspicious of anything different from Washington. In this light, the Obama Administration's early concessions are counterproductive and self-defeating because they may result in a worse endgame position for the United States.

What Congress and the Administration Should Do

As the deadline for START follow-on treaty negotiations approaches, U.S. policymakers and Congress need to focus on the long-term objectives rather than the short-term goal of simply concluding arms control agreements at any price. Specifically, the U.S. should:

- *Negotiate a transparent, verifiable, and enforceable protocol.* Members of Congress and weapons experts have raised concerns about the expedited negotiations and the advisability of concluding the START II treaty on an unrealistic breakneck timetable. The U.S. and Russia should negotiate a verification and transparency protocol to the Moscow Treaty, which expires in 2012 and lacks detailed verification procedures. The START verification protocol, which some have proposed using in the interim, does not fit the Moscow Treaty. Thus, a new verification protocol that includes measures to monitor reductions in the number of operationally deployed strategic nuclear warheads is needed. A transparent, adequately verifiable and enforceable protocol should be ratified by the U.S. Congress as a treaty document.

- *Pursue a "protect and defend" strategic posture.* The U.S. should pursue a "protect and defend" strategic posture that shifts away from retaliation-based configurations and toward a defensive posture adapted to the emerging international environment. Such a shift is particularly necessary in view of Russia lowering its threshold for using nuclear weapons. If Russia and the U.S. subscribe to a "protect and defend" posture, they would not target the population centers or economic infrastructure of each other's countries. However, with the escalating Iranian nuclear threat and China's nuclear buildup, the U.S. should not derail deployment of robust missile defenses in Europe and elsewhere. Finally, the Administration should follow the Strategic Posture Review recommendations to modernize U.S. strategic weapons systems selectively to address emerging nuclear threats.

- *Fight anti-Americanism with more effective public diplomacy.* The Russian state-controlled media and some in Moscow's expert community are propagating a negative image of the U.S., repeatedly alleging that America wants to undermine Russian security. This often plays into the hands of those who seek to justify increased military budgets. Through the State Department and independent research institutions, the U.S. should promote a robust debate on U.S.–Russian relations, encouraging those who seek improvement. U.S. security experts should engage their Russian counterparts and the media in in-depth discussions of common security threats, such as Afghanistan and radical Islamist terrorism. Through international broadcasters, Internet communities, joint conferences, and visits of American security experts to Russia, the U.S. should engage Russian opinion leaders in debating nuclear weapons, arms control, and other defense-related subjects. The U.S. should communicate to the Russian people the truth that America is not entertaining plans to attack Russia.

- *Propose a realistic, detailed, transparent, enforceable, and verifiable joint arms control and nonproliferation agenda.* The U.S. and Russia need to act jointly to prevent a renewed arms race and military confrontation. Instead, the U.S. should offer Russia an arms control and nonproliferation agenda that includes: (1) a bilateral transition to the "protect and defend" posture; (2) a Strategic Offensive Reduction Treaty (SORT II), which would encourage nuclear forces that hold at risk the means of strategic attack; and (3) a strategic defense cooperation treaty, including coordinated ballistic missile defense and programs for common defenses against chemical and biological weapons, cruise missiles, and aircraft delivering weapons of mass destruction. Russia and the United States should also encourage third countries, especially China, to join an Intermediate Nuclear Forces Treaty. Finally, the U.S. and Russia should continue to spearhead the multilateral cooperative effort to address the threat of nuclear-armed terrorism.

Conclusion

Nuclear weapons have been center stage in U.S.–Russian relations since the 1950s. The confrontation stemming from the arms race and the threat of nuclear destruction defined the Soviet and then Russian view of the United States as the "principal adversary." Today, both countries can avert a new Cold War and move beyond the MAD paradigm of the 20th century. [MAD, or mutual assured destruction was an approach to deterrence that relied on both sides in a possible nuclear exchange having enough retaliatory weapons to utterly destroy the other side even if it launched its weapons first.]

New threats have arisen that concern both countries. These threats can be countered together without the extremes of a new arms race or a utopian (and potentially dangerous) approach toward total nuclear disarmament. With a commitment to robust national defenses, prudent, transparent, and verifiable arms control and political–military cooperation, both countries can ensure security in the 21st century.

Robert Farley  **NO**

The Nuclear Posture Attack

In a May 11 [2010] *Washington Times* editorial, Frank Gaffney, Ed Meese, Clifford May, and four additional coauthors—all of whom represent institutions that form part of the hawkish extreme of the Republican Party establishment—called for a "renewed adherence to the national security philosophy of President Ronald Reagan: 'Peace Through Strength.'"

The authors argued that "freedom," "America's exceptional role," and even the country's very existence are at stake as a result of an astounding array of purported threats—which the Obama administration, they implied, was doing little to confront—including missile attacks, Sharia [Islamic religious] law, electromagnetic pulse weapons, Islamic terrorism, unlawful enemy combatants, illegal aliens, and a weak military. Echoing a message that was honed by neoconservative groups like the Project for the New American Century during the Clinton presidency, the authors championed the notion that U.S. global leadership was essential to guarantee the country's security.

This rhetorical broadside represents one facet of a larger assault on the administration's national security policy, with other facets including criticism about the size of the defense budget, Middle East policy, and terrorist detention policy. Arguably the most significant attacks, however, have developed around questions about strategic policies, in particular President Obama's efforts to restructure U.S. nuclear doctrine by restraining the country's nuclear retaliation policy and renegotiating the START [Strategic Arms Reduction Treaty] Treaty with Russia. The *Washington Times* op-ed went so far as to call for the resumption of nuclear testing, in contravention of the Comprehensive Test Ban Treaty and a two-decade testing moratorium.

In recent weeks, multiple lines of attack against the nuclear policy of the Obama administration have emerged from several bastions of U.S. right-wing politics, including the *National Review,* the *Weekly Standard,* the Center for Security Policy, and the Heritage Foundation. The angles of these attacks have varied, but they have centered on the claim that the Obama administration, in pursuit of international acclaim, has insufficiently provided for the security of the U.S. nuclear arsenal.

These right-wing attacks reveal the continued entrenchment of elements of the hawkish extreme in the Republican Party's foreign policy establishment, despite the significant setbacks they have suffered since helping drive the country into war with Iraq. Also, the arguments currently emanating from groups like the Heritage [Foundation] and the William Kristol-led Foreign Policy Initiative (FPI) show the degree to which the right has grasped onto outdated, nostalgic concepts from the heyday of the Cold Warriors. Discussions about "throw weight" and "rail mobile launchers" echo intra-conservative debates that took place during the Reagan era. However, conservatives who had advocated responsible arms control measures during that time have now been left behind. Voices that argued for engagement with the Soviet Union—such as [former Secretaries of State] George Schultz and James Baker—now stand outside the laboratories developing Republican foreign policy.

Attacking No First Use

Following its release early this year, the Obama administration's Nuclear Posture Review (NPR), which defines U.S. nuclear weapons policy and strategy, became the subject of a concerted right-wing attack. The NPR modified U.S. deterrence posture by declaring that the country would not respond to a chemical or biological attack as long as the attacker was a member in good standing of the Nuclear Non-Proliferation Treaty. This "no-first-use" policy, however, did not entail any change in the U.S. stance toward North Korea and Iran, as the former left the NPR in the 1990s and the United States has questioned the adherence of the latter.

In an effort to win conservative "buy in," the Obama administration made several major concessions. In addition to the caveats that significantly limit the impact of the "no-first-use" policy, the NPR includes significant appropriations for the modernization and maintenance of the existing nuclear stockpile. The NPR also revives "prompt global strike," a system designed to place conventional warheads on nuclear-like delivery systems. Perhaps most disappointing to progressives, the NPR reserves a key role for missile defense in U.S. security strategy.

Nevertheless, the NPR shifted the United States, however marginally, from a policy of ambiguity regarding nuclear retaliation to a no-first-use policy. This shift has spurred a series of bitter attacks from conservative foreign policy figures and organizations, who claim that it displays weakness in the face of the enemy. For example, John Noonan of the Foreign Policy Initiative and Stuart Koehl, an analyst for the defense contractor ARDAK Corporation and a fellow at Johns Hopkins University's School of Advanced International Studies (SAIS), argued in the *National Review* that the reduction of ambiguity in the NPR undercut U.S. deterrence and invited foreign aggression. "This has the potential to create a false impression in the minds of potential aggressors that such weapons can be used without fear of an equivalent reprisal, because the U.S. and its allies have eliminated their chemical and biological stockpiles."

This claim ignores the fact that the United States has stark, overwhelming conventional dominance over any foe or possible combination of foes, and that this conventional advantage provides its own deterrent. Noonan and Koehl neither explain this discrepancy, nor call for a reduction of U.S. conventional forces.

New START?

A similar line of attack has developed against the new START Treaty signed by the United States and Russia in April [2010]. The treaty reaffirms the limits on warheads and delivery devices developed at the end of the Cold War, and renews and further develops Washington and Moscow's commitments to reduce their nuclear arsenals. Again, the administration tried to win conservative support by negotiating very mild, non-restrictive language with the Russians on missile defense. These concessions may have won the president some room on the right, especially among moderately conservative senators like Richard Lugar and Joseph Lieberman, but generated considerable consternation on the hawkish extreme.

In an emblematic critique of the new START published in the *National Review*, two defense officials who served during the George W. Bush administration—Robert Joseph, senior scholar at the National Institute for Public Policy, and Eric Edelman, visiting scholar at Johns Hopkins SAIS—argued that the treaty could limit missile defense, diminish the ability to field prompt global strike weapons, and potentially result in the expansion of Russian and U.S. nuclear arsenals through exploitation of treaty loopholes regulating bombers and missiles launched from railcars. Remarkably, however, Joseph and Edelman do not call on the Senate to reject the treaty, but rather to simply examine it in detail.

Pavel Podvig, a researcher at the Center for International Security and Cooperation at Stanford University and a specialist on Russian weapon systems, responded to this line of argument with the refrain, "All this, of course, is just plain crazy." He noted that the new START placed no limitations on missile defense, no meaningful limitations on prompt global strike (a system likely a decade away from service), but *did* put limitations on rail-mounted ICBMs.

However, GOP elected officials such as Sen. Jim DeMint (R-SC) and think tanks such as the Heritage Foundation continue to echo, and occasionally elaborate upon, claims like those made by Joseph and Edelman. A report from Heritage's "New START Working Group," for example, reiterated the railcar assertion and made a series of additional arguments claiming that the new treaty does not place enough limits upon the use of MIRV (missiles with multiple independently targetable reentry vehicles) and tactical nuclear weapons, and places too many limitations upon some forms of missile defense.

Marginalizing the Moderates

Ironically, the attacks launched by the conservative foreign policy establishment against the Obama administration could also have been used against Ronald Reagan's administration. The defense and nuclear policy of the Reagan administration is often understood as the zenith of hawkish, anti-Soviet sentiment. While this largely applies to Reagan's first term in office, in the second term Reagan pursued far more conciliatory policies toward the Soviet Union and arms control. Reagan himself, as demonstrated by several historians, held almost radical views about the eventual abolition of nuclear weapons. In one famous case, Reagan's advisers had to restrain him from coming to an overarching deal with Soviet premier, Mikhail Gorbachev, that would have substantially reduced global nuclear weapon stockpiles.

As Max Bergman, Deputy Policy Director at the National Security Network, has argued, a divide has emerged between the "realist" wing of the Republican foreign policy establishment and its more radical right-wing counterpart. The debate over nuclear policy has demonstrated that the latter now essentially dominates the institutional apparatus of right-wing foreign policy thinking. Ideas and arguments that were welcome in the Reagan administration can now find no purchase at Heritage, or the *Weekly Standard,* or anywhere else on the right.

Many of the moderate Republicans who favored arms control and engagement with the Soviet Union are still around, but they have minimal influence on the institutional right. Henry Kissinger, James Baker, Brent Scowcroft, Colin Powell, and George Schultz have all played key roles in developing foreign policy for multiple Republican administrations. However, none have developed an extensive base within the institutional right wing, the constellation of independent organizations and foundations (including the Heritage Foundation and the American Enterprise Institute) that have emerged as key players in internal Republican Party debates. This faction has, by and large, concluded that the greatest threat posed by Russian nuclear weapons is loss, theft, or accidental launch, rather than preemptive attack.

In contrast, the signatories to the *Washington Times* op-ed mentioned above all represent organizations that are part of the institutional machinery of movement conservatism.

In addition, prominent political figures have been able to promote the studies and reports produced by these groups, including for instance Sarah Palin, who despite her clear lack of knowledge on the subject tried to use that hard-line rhetoric in attacking Obama's arms control initiatives.

The influence of the radical right over its realist counterpart has become clear in the behavior of many congressional Republicans. While some Republicans remain committed to arms control, others have adopted the rejectionism of the institutional right. For example, in a speech to the Heritage Foundation in early May, House Minority Whip Rep. Eric Cantor (R-VA) called on the Senate to reject the new START Treaty.

"Cognitive Closure"

Over the past month, the question of "cognitive closure" on the right has been discussed extensively in the blogosphere. Cognitive closure refers to the concept that the Republican political establishment and major conservative pundits review information from within a very limited circle of sources. The nuclear critique mounted by the right wing represents an example of conservative "cognitive closure," with the ironic outcome that those most eager to wave the banner of the Reagan administration's foreign policy are offering arguments that Reagan himself would have rejected.

Of course, President Obama also faces other domestic and international obstacles to his nuclear agenda. The major nuclear weapons labs favor developing new nuclear weapons, and they represent powerful economic interests in important states. Elements of the national security bureaucracy also oppose parts of the president's agenda, including officials in the Pentagon as well as at the State Department and the Energy Department. The ratification of START and the successful implementation of the goals outlined in the NPR will depend on more than just the outcome of internecine conflicts in the conservative movement. Indeed, as with health care, the success of extreme elements within the right to hijack the debate in the Republican Party may mean the functional exclusion of other conservative voices from key policy decisions.

At this point, the degree to which these attacks will find purchase with the American public is unclear. Nuclear issues appear to have relatively low salience among the public, although general charges of weakness on foreign affairs may have more influence. The general accommodation of these attacks within the context of a "peace through strength" political argument may make them more understandable to that part of the electorate responsive to GOP political arguments. However, the Republican Party may find it difficult to make the conceptual connection between a fear of underwear bombers and reloadable rail-launched ICBMs [intercontinental ballistic missiles]. The real constituency for the pro-nuclear message lies not with the GOP base, but rather within the right-wing institutions themselves—with the theorists and policymakers who have been fighting the nuclear fight since the 1980s.

The nature of these attacks against the Obama administration's nuclear policy [is] not so much evidence of a battle within conservative foreign policy circles as they are a sign of the ascendancy of one particular faction. One key to achieving this dominant position in the discourse on the right has been the establishment and nurturing of institutions for developing and promoting their views. The wing of the GOP foreign policy establishment once regarded as "realist" failed to construct an institutional structure to develop and promulgate its ideas. Consequently, the major organs of conservative foreign policy-making now follow one line, serious debate is marginalized, and there are fewer new voices on the right arguing for responsible nuclear weapons policy.

POSTSCRIPT

Is U.S. Strategic Nuclear Weapons Policy Ill-Conceived?

As is often true in many policy areas, President Obama's evolving nuclear weapons policy is a product of views that he held prior to becoming president tempered by the realities of holding that job. This moderation was evident in the *Nuclear Posture Review* (NPR) that the White House released in April 2010 outlining U.S. nuclear doctrine. By most reports, the NPR was the product of a pitched bureaucratic struggle between some Obama advisers who wanted major changes and opponents to a marked shift led by carryover Secretary of Defense Robert Gates and the military. Perhaps the most significant change from doctrine under George W. Bush was to pledge not to use nuclear weapons against a nonnuclear weapons state as long as it was in compliance with the Non-Proliferation Treaty. This left the door open to target Iran, helping to assuage the military, but it alarmed critics by giving up the option of nuclear retaliation for (and arguably deterrence against) a chemical, biological, or radiological attack. But liberals were also disappointed that the NPR did not forswear the first use of nuclear weapons under any circumstance, even the imminent threat of attack by a nuclear weapons power. In a second area, the NPR signaled an increase in the Obama administration's support to BMD, by calling it a central aspect of U.S. defense policy. This was accompanied by a 6 percent increase to $9.4 billion in the 2011 defense budget. Compromise was also evident regarding nuclear weapons laboratories. The 2010 NPR declared, "The United States will not develop new nuclear warheads." This differed from the interest Bush administration had in developing such new warheads as low-yield "bunker busters." However, the administration continued supporting the facilities that not only test the reliability of existing warheads but also potentially design new ones, and asked for a 10 percent increase in their budgets to 7.1 billion for 2011. There are other aspects of the NPR that illustrate the compromises that shaped it, but the point is that the NPR reflected a shift, but not a radical change, from existing doctrine. Fortunately, the 2010 NPR is the first to be entirely declassified and available to the public. This and a variety of other doctrine statements can be found at http://www.defense.gov/npr/. One review of the NPR is Morton H. Halperin, "A New Nuclear Posture," *Arms Control Today* (May 2010).

Almost simultaneously with the publication of the NPR in April 2010, President Obama and his Russian counterpart, Dmitry Medvedev, signed a new strategic arms limitation treaty called the New START Treaty rather than START III. Under this, the two countries will reduce their nuclear warheads and bombs to 1,550 (down from 2,200 by 2012 under the Moscow Treaty of 2002) and their strategic (long-range) delivery systems (bombers and missiles) to 700 (1,600 under the Moscow Treaty). The limits must be reached within 7 years after the treaty goes into force by being ratified by the U.S. Senate and Russia's Duma. Hearings began in the Senate Committee on Foreign Relations, with the administration hoping for ratification by September 1. However, the committee delayed voting, indicating that troublesome opposition exists in the Senate. The eight sessions of the hearings that held from May through July can be accessed at http://foreign.senate.gov/hearings/. For background on this debate, read Michael Quinlan, *Thinking About Nuclear Weapons: Principles, Problems, Prospects* (Oxford University Press, 2009).

Questions for Critical Thinking and Reflection

1. What do you think of the argument that nuclear weapons may actually be a force for peace by making war between two countries with nuclear weapons, such as the United States and Soviet Union during the cold war, too terrible to fight?
2. Do you prefer the Obama doctrine of only using nuclear weapons to deter nuclear attack or the Bush doctrine of also using nuclear weapons to deter attack by all forms of weapons of mass destruction?
3. Like many debates, this one is not truly two sided. Do you think Obama's NPR went too far, is a reasonable mid-level change, or did not go far enough in reducing the presence and role of nuclear weapons in U.S. defense policy?

ISSUE 14

Should U.S. Forces Continue to Fight in Afghanistan?

YES: Barack Obama, from "The Way Forward in Afghanistan and Pakistan," an address to the nation, delivered at the United States Military Academy at West Point (December 12, 2009)

NO: Dennis Kucinich, from "Removal of United States Armed Forces from Afghanistan," Debate on House Concurrent Resolution 248, *Congressional Record* (March 10, 2010).

ISSUE SUMMARY

YES: Barack Obama, the 44th president of the United States, tells the cadets at West Point and, beyond them, the American people that the United States did not ask for a war in Afghanistan but must successfully wage it.

NO: Dennis Kucinich, a member of the U.S. House of Representatives from Ohio's 10th Congressional District, explains to members of the House why he sponsored a resolution demanding the president to withdraw U.S. military forces from Afghanistan by December 31, 2010, and urges the members to pass the legislation.

With the rubble still smoldering at the site of the World Trade Center in New York City and the Pentagon outside of Washington, DC, in the aftermath of the 9/11 terrorist attacks, angry President George W. Bush told Vice President Richard Cheney, "We're at war, Dick. We're going to find out who did this and kick their ass." Americans overwhelmingly agreed with that sentiment. After the al Qaeda terrorist group and its supporter, the Taliban government of Afghanistan, were identified as the culprits, 82 percent of Americans favored military action to destroy al Qaeda and topple the Taliban. This level of support made the war in Afghanistan the second most popular in the U.S. history, trailing only support (97 percent) of the declaration of war against Japan following its attack on Pearl Harbor, Hawaii, on December 7, 1941.

Soon, U.S. troops aided by a much smaller number of allied, mostly British, troops ousted the Taliban from power and put them and al Qaeda to flight. Then began the much more difficult task of fully securing rural areas from continuing Taliban control, of creating a functioning government, and of uniting a historically fractious population. This daunting task was made even more challenging when the war with and occupation of Iraq that began in March 2003 diverted U.S. troops, funds, and attention away from Afghanistan. This persisted for about 5 years until the following two changes occurred 2008. One was that the U.S. combat role in Iraq began to wind down. In 2007, 914 American troops died in Iraq; only 314 perished in 2008. Second, part of Barack Obama's presidential campaign attack on the Bush administration and the Republicans was to charge that the ill-conceived Iraq war had diverted attention from the justified, antiterrorism war in Afghanistan. As Obama put it during a campaign speech, "What President Bush and Senator [John] McCain don't understand is that the central front in the war on terror is not in Iraq, and it never was—the central front is in Afghanistan . . . where the terrorists who hit us on 9/11 are still plotting attacks seven years later."

Two other factors also promoted the shift in American's attention to Afghanistan once Obama was in the White House. During his first year in office, Obama nearly doubled the number of U.S. troops in Afghanistan to about 68,000. Also in 2009, the number of American deaths in Afghanistan (317) exceeded those in Iraq (149). These rising human and budgetary costs accompanied by an unpromising military and political situation in Afghanistan undermined Americans' support of the war. The share of Americans thinking that the war was worth fighting dropped from 56 percent in February 2009 to 52 percent that December. As 2010 dawned, President Obama was faced with a situation in Afghanistan much like President Bush had faced in 2007 in Iraq. Bush responded by sending a "surge" of more than 20,000 troops into Iraq. Taking the same route, Obama announced in November 2009 that he would send more than 30,000 additional U.S. troops to Afghanistan. Americans supported Obama's move, but only be a tepid 51 percent. By then the war was in its ninth year, the second longest in U.S. history after Vietnam. As part of explaining to the country why the troop surge was necessary and why staying engaged in Afghanistan was important, President Obama gave a speech at West Point that forms the second reading. Representative Dennis Kucinich is among the Americans who were not persuaded. He introduced legislation in the House of Representatives to try to force the administration to soon begin withdrawing troops from Afghanistan, a move he explains in the first reading.

YES

Barack Obama

The Way Forward in Afghanistan and Pakistan

I want to speak to you tonight about our effort in Afghanistan—the nature of our commitment there, the scope of our interests, and the strategy that my administration will pursue to bring this war to a successful conclusion. It's an extraordinary honor for me to do so here at West Point—where so many men and women have prepared to stand up for our security, and to represent what is finest about our country.

To address these important issues, it's important to recall why America and our allies were compelled to fight a war in Afghanistan in the first place. We did not ask for this fight. On September 11, 2001, 19 men hijacked four airplanes and used them to murder nearly 3,000 people. They struck at our military and economic nerve centers. They took the lives of innocent men, women, and children without regard to their faith or race or station. Were it not for the heroic actions of passengers onboard one of those flights, they could have also struck at one of the great symbols of our democracy in Washington, and killed many more.

As we know, these men belonged to al Qaeda—a group of extremists who have distorted and defiled Islam, one of the world's great religions, to justify the slaughter of innocents. Al Qaeda's base of operations was in Afghanistan, where they were harbored by the Taliban—a ruthless, repressive, and radical movement that seized control of that country after it was ravaged by years of Soviet occupation and civil war, and after the attention of America and our friends had turned elsewhere.

Just days after 9/11, Congress authorized the use of force against al Qaeda and those who harbored them—an authorization that continues to this day. The vote in the Senate was 98 to nothing. The vote in the House was 420 to 1. For the first time in its history, the North Atlantic Treaty Organization invoked Article 5—the commitment that says an attack on one member nation is an attack on all. And the United Nations Security Council endorsed the use of all necessary steps to respond to the 9/11 attacks. America, our allies and the world were acting as one to destroy al Qaeda's terrorist network and to protect our common security.

Under the banner of this domestic unity and international legitimacy—and only after the Taliban refused to turn over Osama bin Laden—we sent our troops into Afghanistan. Within a matter of months, al Qaeda was scattered

From U.S. Congressional Record.

and many of its operatives were killed. The Taliban was driven from power and pushed back on its heels. A place that had known decades of fear now had reason to hope. At a conference convened by the U.N., a provisional government was established under President Hamid Karzai. And an International Security Assistance Force was established to help bring a lasting peace to a war-torn country.

Then, in early 2003, the decision was made to wage a second war, in Iraq. The wrenching debate over the Iraq war is well known and need not be repeated here. It's enough to say that for the next six years, the Iraq war drew the dominant share of our troops, our resources, our diplomacy, and our national attention—and that the decision to go into Iraq caused substantial rifts between America and much of the world.

Today, after extraordinary costs, we are bringing the Iraq war to a responsible end. We will remove our combat brigades from Iraq by the end of next summer, and all of our troops by the end of 2011. That we are doing so is a testament to the character of the men and women in uniform. Thanks to their courage, grit, and perseverance, we have given Iraqis a chance to shape their future, and we are successfully leaving Iraq to its people.

But while we've achieved hard-earned milestones in Iraq, the situation in Afghanistan has deteriorated. After escaping across the border into Pakistan in 2001 and 2002, al Qaeda's leadership established a safe haven there. Although a legitimate government was elected by the Afghan people, it's been hampered by corruption, the drug trade, an underdeveloped economy, and insufficient security forces.

Over the last several years, the Taliban has maintained common cause with al Qaeda, as they both seek an overthrow of the Afghan government. Gradually, the Taliban has begun to control additional swaths of territory in Afghanistan, while engaging in increasingly brazen and devastating attacks of terrorism against the Pakistani people.

Now, throughout this period, our troop levels in Afghanistan remained a fraction of what they were in Iraq. When I took office, we had just over 32,000 Americans serving in Afghanistan, compared to 160,000 in Iraq at the peak of the war. Commanders in Afghanistan repeatedly asked for support to deal with the reemergence of the Taliban, but these reinforcements did not arrive. And that's why, shortly after taking office, I approved a long-standing request for more troops. After consultations with our allies, I then announced a strategy recognizing the fundamental connection between our war effort in Afghanistan and the extremist safe havens in Pakistan. I set a goal that was narrowly defined as disrupting, dismantling, and defeating al Qaeda and its extremist allies, and pledged to better coordinate our military and civilian efforts.

Since then, we've made progress on some important objectives. High-ranking al Qaeda and Taliban leaders have been killed, and we've stepped up the pressure on al Qaeda worldwide. In Pakistan, that nation's army has gone on its largest offensive in years. In Afghanistan, we and our allies prevented the Taliban from stopping a presidential election, and—although it was marred by fraud—that election produced a government that is consistent with Afghanistan's laws and constitution.

Yet huge challenges remain. Afghanistan is not lost, but for several years it has moved backwards. There's no imminent threat of the government being overthrown, but the Taliban has gained momentum. Al Qaeda has not reemerged in Afghanistan in the same numbers as before 9/11, but they retain their safe havens along the border. And our forces lack the full support they need to effectively train and partner with Afghan security forces and better secure the population. Our new commander in Afghanistan—General [Stanley] McChrystal—has reported that the security situation is more serious than he anticipated. In short: The status quo is not sustainable.

As cadets, you volunteered for service during this time of danger. Some of you fought in Afghanistan. Some of you will deploy there. As your commander-in-chief, I owe you a mission that is clearly defined, and worthy of your service. And that's why, after the Afghan voting was completed, I insisted on a thorough review of our strategy. Now, let me be clear: There has never been an option before me that called for troop deployments before 2010, so there has been no delay or denial of resources necessary for the conduct of the war during this review period. Instead, the review has allowed me to ask the hard questions, and to explore all the different options, along with my national security team, our military and civilian leadership in Afghanistan, and our key partners. And given the stakes involved, I owed the American people—and our troops—no less.

This review is now complete. And as commander-in-chief, I have determined that it is in our vital national interest to send an additional 30,000 U.S. troops to Afghanistan. After 18 months, our troops will begin to come home. These are the resources that we need to seize the initiative, while building the Afghan capacity that can allow for a responsible transition of our forces out of Afghanistan.

I do not make this decision lightly. I opposed the war in Iraq precisely because I believe that we must exercise restraint in the use of military force, and always consider the long-term consequences of our actions. We have been at war now for eight years, at enormous cost in lives and resources. Years of debate over Iraq and terrorism have left our unity on national security issues in tatters, and created a highly polarized and partisan backdrop for this effort. And having just experienced the worst economic crisis since the Great Depression, the American people are understandably focused on rebuilding our economy and putting people to work here at home.

Most of all, I know that this decision asks even more of you—a military that, along with your families, has already borne the heaviest of all burdens. As president, I have signed a letter of condolence to the family of each American who gives their life in these wars. I have read the letters from the parents and spouses of those who deployed. I visited our courageous wounded warriors at Walter Reed. I've traveled to Dover to meet the flag-draped caskets of 18 Americans returning home to their final resting place. I see firsthand the terrible wages of war. If I did not think that the security of the United States and the safety of the American people were at stake in Afghanistan, I would gladly order every single one of our troops home tomorrow.

So, no, I do not make this decision lightly. I make this decision because I am convinced that our security is at stake in Afghanistan and Pakistan. This is the epicenter of violent extremism practiced by al Qaeda. It is from here that we were attacked on 9/11, and it is from here that new attacks are being plotted as I speak. This is no idle danger; no hypothetical threat. In the last few months alone, we have apprehended extremists within our borders who were sent here from the border region of Afghanistan and Pakistan to commit new acts of terror. And this danger will only grow if the region slides backwards, and al Qaeda can operate with impunity. We must keep the pressure on al Qaeda, and to do that, we must increase the stability and capacity of our partners in the region.

Of course, this burden is not ours alone to bear. This is not just America's war. Since 9/11, al Qaeda's safe havens have been the source of attacks against London and Amman and Bali. The people and governments of both Afghanistan and Pakistan are endangered. And the stakes are even higher within a nuclear-armed Pakistan, because we know that al Qaeda and other extremists seek nuclear weapons, and we have every reason to believe that they would use them.

These facts compel us to act along with our friends and allies. Our overarching goal remains the same: to disrupt, dismantle, and defeat al Qaeda in Afghanistan and Pakistan, and to prevent its capacity to threaten America and our allies in the future.

To meet that goal, we will pursue the following objectives within Afghanistan. We must deny al Qaeda a safe haven. We must reverse the Taliban's momentum and deny it the ability to overthrow the government. And we must strengthen the capacity of Afghanistan's security forces and government so that they can take lead responsibility for Afghanistan's future.

We will meet these objectives in three ways. First, we will pursue a military strategy that will break the Taliban's momentum and increase Afghanistan's capacity over the next 18 months.

The 30,000 additional troops that I'm announcing tonight will deploy in the first part of 2010—the fastest possible pace—so that they can target the insurgency and secure key population centers. They'll increase our ability to train competent Afghan security forces, and to partner with them so that more Afghans can get into the fight. And they will help create the conditions for the United States to transfer responsibility to the Afghans.

Because this is an international effort, I've asked that our commitment be joined by contributions from our allies. Some have already provided additional troops, and we're confident that there will be further contributions in the days and weeks ahead. Our friends have fought and bled and died alongside us in Afghanistan. And now, we must come together to end this war successfully. For what's at stake is not simply a test of NATO's credibility—what's at stake is the security of our allies, and the common security of the world.

But taken together, these additional American and international troops will allow us to accelerate handing over responsibility to Afghan forces, and allow us to begin the transfer of our forces out of Afghanistan in July of 2011. Just as we have done in Iraq, we will execute this transition responsibly, taking into account conditions on the ground. We'll continue to advise and assist Afghanistan's security forces to ensure that they can succeed over the long haul. But it will be clear to the Afghan government—and, more importantly, to the Afghan people—that they will ultimately be responsible for their own country.

Second, we will work with our partners, the United Nations, and the Afghan people to pursue a more effective civilian strategy, so that the government can take advantage of improved security.

This effort must be based on performance. The days of providing a blank check are over. President Karzai's inauguration speech sent the right message about moving in a new direction. And going forward, we will be clear about what we expect from those who receive our assistance. We'll support Afghan ministries, governors, and local leaders that combat corruption and deliver for the people. We expect those who are ineffective or corrupt to be held accountable. And we will also focus our assistance in areas—such as agriculture—that can make an immediate impact in the lives of the Afghan people.

The people of Afghanistan have endured violence for decades. They've been confronted with occupation—by the Soviet Union, and then by foreign al Qaeda fighters who used Afghan land for their own purposes. So tonight, I want the Afghan people to understand—America seeks an end to this era of war and suffering. We have no interest in occupying your country. We will support efforts by the Afghan government to open the door to those Taliban who abandon violence and respect the human rights of their fellow citizens. And we will seek a partnership with Afghanistan grounded in mutual respect—to isolate those who destroy; to strengthen those who build; to hasten the day when our troops will leave; and to forge a lasting friendship in which America is your partner, and never your patron.

Third, we will act with the full recognition that our success in Afghanistan is inextricably linked to our partnership with Pakistan.

We're in Afghanistan to prevent a cancer from once again spreading through that country. But this same cancer has also taken root in the border region of Pakistan. That's why we need a strategy that works on both sides of the border.

In the past, there have been those in Pakistan who've argued that the struggle against extremism is not their fight, and that Pakistan is better off doing little or seeking accommodation with those who use violence. But in recent years, as innocents have been killed from Karachi to Islamabad, it has become clear that it is the Pakistani people who are the most endangered by extremism. Public opinion has turned. The Pakistani army has waged an offensive in Swat and South Waziristan [regions in Pakistan along its border with Afghanistan]. And there is no doubt that the United States and Pakistan share a common enemy.

In the past, we too often defined our relationship with Pakistan narrowly. Those days are over. Moving forward, we are committed to a partnership with Pakistan that is built on a foundation of mutual interest, mutual respect, and mutual trust. We will strengthen Pakistan's capacity to target those groups that threaten our countries, and have made it clear that we cannot tolerate a safe haven for terrorists whose location is known and whose intentions are clear. America is also providing substantial resources to support Pakistan's democracy and development. We are the largest international supporter for those Pakistanis displaced by the fighting. And going forward, the Pakistan people must know America will remain a strong supporter of Pakistan's security and prosperity long after the guns have fallen silent, so that the great potential of its people can be unleashed.

These are the three core elements of our strategy: a military effort to create the conditions for a transition; a civilian surge that reinforces positive action; and an effective partnership with Pakistan.

I recognize there are a range of concerns about our approach. So let me briefly address a few of the more prominent arguments that I've heard, and which I take very seriously.

First, there are those who suggest that Afghanistan is another Vietnam. They argue that it cannot be stabilized, and we're better off cutting our losses and rapidly withdrawing. I believe this argument depends on a false reading of history. Unlike Vietnam, we are joined by a broad coalition of 43 nations that recognizes the legitimacy of our action. Unlike Vietnam, we are not facing a broad-based popular insurgency. And most importantly, unlike Vietnam, the American people were viciously attacked from Afghanistan, and remain a target for those same extremists who are plotting along its border. To abandon this area now—and to rely only on efforts against al Qaeda from a distance—would significantly hamper our ability to keep the pressure on al Qaeda, and create an unacceptable risk of additional attacks on our homeland and our allies.

Second, there are those who acknowledge that we can't leave Afghanistan in its current state, but suggest that we go forward with the troops that we already have. But this would simply maintain a status quo in which we muddle through, and permit a slow deterioration of conditions there. It would ultimately prove more costly and prolong our stay in Afghanistan, because we would never be able to generate the conditions needed to train Afghan security forces and give them the space to take over.

Finally, there are those who oppose identifying a time frame for our transition to Afghan responsibility. Indeed, some call for a more dramatic and open-ended escalation of our war effort—one that would commit us to a nation-building project of up to a decade. I reject this course because it sets goals that are beyond what can be achieved at a reasonable cost, and what we need to achieve to secure our interests. Furthermore, the absence of a time frame for transition would deny us any sense of urgency in working with the Afghan government. It must be clear that Afghans will have to take responsibility for their security, and that America has no interest in fighting an endless war in Afghanistan.

As president, I refuse to set goals that go beyond our responsibility, our means, or our interests. And I must weigh all of the challenges that our nation faces. I don't have the luxury of committing to just one. Indeed, I'm mindful of the words of President [Dwight D.] Eisenhower, who—in discussing our national security—said, "Each proposal must be weighed in the light of a broader consideration: the need to maintain balance in and among national programs."

Over the past several years, we have lost that balance. We've failed to appreciate the connection between our national security and our economy. In the wake of an economic crisis, too many of our neighbors and friends are out of work and struggle to pay the bills. Too many Americans are worried about the future facing our children. Meanwhile, competition within the global economy has grown more fierce. So we can't simply afford to ignore the price of these wars.

All told, by the time I took office the cost of the wars in Iraq and Afghanistan approached a trillion dollars. Going forward, I am committed to addressing these costs openly and honestly. Our new approach in Afghanistan is likely to cost us roughly $30 billion for the military this year, and I'll work closely with Congress to address these costs as we work to bring down our deficit.

But as we end the war in Iraq and transition to Afghan responsibility, we must rebuild our strength here at home. Our prosperity provides a foundation for our power. It pays for our military. It underwrites our diplomacy. It taps the potential of our people, and allows investment in new industry. And it will allow us to compete in this century as successfully as we did in the last. That's why our troop commitment in Afghanistan cannot be open-ended—because the nation that I'm most interested in building is our own.

Now, let me be clear: None of this will be easy. The struggle against violent extremism will not be finished quickly, and it extends well beyond Afghanistan and Pakistan. It will be an enduring test of our free society, and our leadership in the world. And unlike the great power conflicts and clear lines of division that defined the 20th century, our effort will involve disorderly regions, failed states, [and] diffuse enemies.

So as a result, America will have to show our strength in the way that we end wars and prevent conflict—not just how we wage wars. We'll have to be nimble and precise in our use of military power. Where al Qaeda and its allies attempt to establish a foothold—whether in Somalia or Yemen or elsewhere—they must be confronted by growing pressure and strong partnerships.

And we can't count on military might alone. We have to invest in our homeland security, because we can't capture or kill every violent extremist abroad. We have to improve and better coordinate our intelligence, so that we stay one step ahead of shadowy networks.

We will have to take away the tools of mass destruction. And that's why I've made it a central pillar of my foreign policy to secure loose nuclear materials from terrorists, to stop the spread of nuclear weapons, and to pursue the goal of a world without them—because every nation must understand that true security will never come from an endless race for ever more destructive weapons; true security will come for those who reject them.

We'll have to use diplomacy, because no one nation can meet the challenges of an interconnected world acting alone. I've spent this year renewing our alliances and forging new partnerships. And we have forged a new beginning between America and the Muslim world—one that recognizes our mutual interest in breaking a cycle of conflict, and that promises a future in which those who kill innocents are isolated by those who stand up for peace and prosperity and human dignity.

And finally, we must draw on the strength of our values—for the challenges that we face may have changed, but the things that we believe in must not. That's why we must promote our values by living them at home—which is why I have prohibited torture and will close the prison at Guantanamo Bay. And we must make it clear to every man, woman, and child around the world who lives under the dark cloud of tyranny that America will speak out on behalf of their human rights, and tend to the light of freedom and justice and opportunity and respect for the dignity of all peoples. That is who we are. That is the source, the moral source, of America's authority.

Since the days of Franklin Roosevelt, and the service and sacrifice of our grandparents and great-grandparents, our country has borne a special burden in global affairs. We have spilled American blood in many countries on multiple continents. We have spent our revenue to help others rebuild from rubble and develop their own economies. We have joined with others to develop an architecture of institutions—from the United Nations to NATO to the World Bank—that provide for the common security and prosperity of human beings.

We have not always been thanked for these efforts, and we have at times made mistakes. But more than any other nation, the United States of America has underwritten global security for over six decades—a time that, for all its problems, has seen walls come down, and markets open, and billions lifted from poverty, unparalleled scientific progress and advancing frontiers of human liberty.

For unlike the great powers of old, we have not sought world domination. Our union was founded in resistance to oppression. We do not seek to occupy other nations. We will not claim another nation's resources or target other peoples because their faith or ethnicity is different from ours. What we have fought for—what we continue to fight for—is a better future for our children and grandchildren. And we believe that their lives will be better if other peoples' children and grandchildren can live in freedom and access opportunity. (Applause.)

As a country, we're not as young—and perhaps not as innocent—as we were when Roosevelt was president. Yet we are still heirs to a noble struggle for freedom. And now we must summon all of our might and moral suasion to meet the challenges of a new age.

In the end, our security and leadership does not come solely from the strength of our arms. It derives from our people—from the workers and businesses who will rebuild our economy; from the entrepreneurs and researchers who will pioneer new industries; from the teachers that will educate our children, and the service of those who work in our communities at home; from the diplomats and Peace Corps volunteers who spread hope abroad; and from the men and women in uniform who are part of an unbroken line of sacrifice that has made government of the people, by the people, and for the people a reality on this Earth. (Applause.)

This vast and diverse citizenry will not always agree on every issue—nor should we. But I also know that we, as a country, cannot sustain our leadership, nor navigate the momentous challenges of our time, if we allow ourselves to be split asunder by the same rancor and cynicism and partisanship that ha[ve] in recent times poisoned our national discourse.

It's easy to forget that when this war began, we were united—bound together by the fresh memory of a horrific attack, and by the determination to defend our homeland and the values we hold dear. I refuse to accept the notion that we cannot summon that unity again. (Applause.) I believe with every fiber of my being that we—as Americans—can still come together behind a common purpose. For our values are not simply words written into parchment—they are a creed that calls us together, and that has carried us through the darkest of storms as one nation, as one people.

America—we are passing through a time of great trial. And the message that we send in the midst of these storms must be clear: that our cause is just, our resolve unwavering. We will go forward with the confidence that right makes might, and with the commitment to forge an America that is safer, a world that is more secure, and a future that represents not the deepest of fears but the highest of hopes.

Removal of United States Armed Forces from Afghanistan

In 2001 I joined the House [of Representatives] in voting for the Authorization for Use of Military Force [in Afghanistan and elsewhere to combat terrorism]. In the past 8½ years, it has become clear that the Authorization for Use of Military Force is being interpreted as carte blanche for circumventing Congress' role as a coequal branch of government.

My legislation [House Concurrent Resolution 248] invokes the War Powers Resolution of 1973. If enacted, it would require the president to withdraw U.S. Armed Forces from Afghanistan by December 31, 2010.

The debate today will be the first opportunity we have had to revisit the 2001 Authorization for Use of Military Force, which the House supported following the worst terrorist attack in our country's history. Regardless of your support or opposition to the war in Afghanistan, this is going to be the first opportunity to evaluate critically where the Authorization for Use of Military Force has taken us in the last eight and a half years.

This 2001 resolution allowed military action "to prevent any future acts of international terrorism against the United States." Those of us who support the withdrawal from Afghanistan may or may not agree on a timeline for troop withdrawal, but I think we agree that this debate is timely.

The rest of the world is beginning to see the folly of trying to occupy Afghanistan: The Dutch Government recently came to a halt over the commitment of more troops from their country. In Britain public outcry over the war is growing. A recent BBC poll indicated that 63 percent of the British public is demanding that their troops come home by Christmas. In Germany opposition to the war has risen to 69 percent. Russia lost billions of dollars in the 9 years [December 1979–February 1989] it spent attempting to control Afghanistan.

Our supposed nation-building in Afghanistan has come at the destruction of our own. The military escalation cements the path of the United States down the road of previous occupiers that earned Afghanistan its nickname as the "graveyard of empires."

One year ago last month, a report by the Carnegie Endowment concluded "the only meaningful way to halt the insurgency's momentum is to start withdrawing troops. The presence of foreign troops is the most important element driving the resurgence of the Taliban."

From U.S. Congressional Record, March 10, 2010.

So with this debate today, we will have a chance for the first time to reflect on our responsibility for troop casualties that are now reaching 1,000; to look at our responsibility for the costs of the war, which approaches $250 billion; our responsibility for the civilian casualties and the human costs of the war; our responsibility for challenging the corruption that takes place in Afghanistan; our responsibility for having a real understanding of the role of the pipeline in this war; our responsibility for debating the role of counter-insurgency strategies, as opposed to counterterrorism; our responsibility for being able to make a case for the logistics of withdrawal.

After eight and a half years, it is time that we have this debate. One of the things that really doesn't often get discussion here on this floor with respect to a war is the specifics about how it affects people back home. And because I come from Cleveland, I just want to share with you some things just about my community.

Cleveland, as some of you may know, was the epicenter of the subprime mortgage meltdown. Predatory lenders descended on neighbors in our community and were able to take people into contracts that eventually led them into foreclosure and losing their homes.

Now, I don't think that even the most powerful camera would be able to pick up the sea of red dots across our metropolitan area that represents foreclosures, but you get an idea that we have a desperate need not only in Cleveland but across the country for helping to keep people in their homes. And yet more and more, our priorities are to spend money not just on these wars but to increase the Pentagon budget. I would like to point out that just with respect to the amount of money that is being spent, allocated by congressional districts—this is the National Priorities Project that I am quoting which includes the fiscal 2010 budget. They point out that taxpayers in the 10th Congressional District that I represent will pay $591.9 million for total Afghanistan war spending, counting all the spending since 2001.

And they go on to say, here's what that money could have been spent for instead. It could have been used to provide 209,812 people with health care for 1 year. Or it could have been used to provide 13,404 public safety officers for 1 year, or 9,063 music and arts teachers for 1 year, or 68,299 scholarships for university students for 1 year. Or it could have been spent for 106,658 students receiving Pell grants of $5,550. Or it could have been spent to provide for 5,521 affordable housing units. It could be have been spent for providing 355,972 children with health care for 1 year, or 92,161 Head Start places for children for 1 year, or 9,433 elementary school teachers for 1 year, or 662,950 homes with renewable electricity for 1 year.

When we spend money on wars and we spend money expanding the budget for military spending, we may say we are making things safer at home, but there is plenty of evidence to suggest that the shift in allocation of funds and the shift for spending towards wars, which were off-budget for quite a while, have put our country in a position where we are not really able to meet our needs.

When you look at this, this is from the Friends Committee on National Legislation, they say for each dollar of federal income tax we paid in 2009, the government spent about 33 cents for Pentagon spending for current and past wars; 27 cents supporting the economy, which is the recovery and the bailouts; 17 cents for health care; 11 cents responding to poverty; 9 cents for general government, and of that 7 cents goes for interest on the public debt; 2 cents for energy, science and environment; and a penny of the Federal dollar for diplomacy, development, and war prevention.

We are setting our priorities here constantly. When we remain silent about war spending, we actually have put ourselves in a position where we go headlong. And the headlong momentum that occurs from being silent about a war just carries us into all these reshaped priorities, whether we realize it or not. That is why I have asked this resolution to be brought forth, so we could talk about this.

I just would like to talk for a minute about the mission in the context of what is going on with the government in Kabul [capital of Afghanistan]. *The Washington Post* did a story on February 25 [2010] which talks about how "Officials puzzle over millions of dollars leaving Afghanistan by plane for Dubai." Previous to that, *The Post* did a story entitled "In Afghanistan, Signs of Crony Capitalism," about money funneled through a Kabul bank and companies owned by the bank's founder to individual friends, family, and business connections of Hamid Karzai. When you consider the amount of corruption that is going on in Afghanistan, it can only be called, charitably, "crony capitalism."

As a result, U.S. taxpayers and aid organizations are investing billions of dollars in Afghanistan, but the leaders of the country are investing in real estate in Dubai. We care about democracy. Try building democracy in a place which is rife with narcotraffic, crony capitalism, and villas in Dubai. What is this about? Why are we there? I mean, I am from Cleveland, Ohio. The people I represent are very basic people. When you tell them that the head of Afghanistan has his hands in all of these crooked deals, you start to wonder, we are going to build a democracy on this person's shoulders? I don't think so.

We are supporting a government where corruption is epidemic. Last year, USAID [U.S. Agency for International Development] reported that corruption in Afghanistan is significant, a growing problem, and that pervasive, systemic corruption was at an unprecedented scope in the country's history. On November 17, Transparency International ranked Afghanistan as the second most corrupt nation in the world. And to compound the fears, in President Karzai's fraud-filled election late last year, he recently took over the country's election watchdog group. Is this the kind of person that we can trust to have a partnership with for democracy? I don't think so.

A January 2010 report by the United Nations Office on Drugs and Crime reveals that Afghan citizens were forced to pay an estimated $2.5 billion a year in bribes. According to evidence collected through wiretaps and bank records, a senior border police official in Kandahar allegedly collected salaries of hundreds of ghost policemen and stole money from a government fund intended to pay orphans and widows. Is this the kind of environment where we can build a democracy? Our troops in Afghanistan have to deal with corrupt officials on a daily basis. A commander of the Afghan border police offered to give the U.S. military prime land at a crossing with Pakistan to build a waiting area for supply vehicles needed for President Obama's troop increase. The same man, U.S. officials believe, earns tens of millions of dollars a year trafficking opium and extorting cargo truck drivers. Is this the kind of person that we can create movement toward a democracy with? . . .

One of the areas of concern that I have about our presence in Afghanistan that I haven't seen discussed that much deals with the role of oil and gas, particularly in Afghanistan. Paul Craig Roberts, who was an Assistant Secretary of Treasury under the Reagan administration, reported in November of last year on a former British ambassador to Uzbekistan, Craig Murray, who was fired from his job when he spoke out about documents he saw "proving that the motivation for U.S. and U.K. military aggression in Afghanistan had something to do with the natural gas deposits in Uzbekistan and Turkmenistan." He continues, and these are his words, "The Americans wanted a pipeline that bypassed Russia and Iran and went through Afghanistan. To ensure this, an invasion was necessary."

I did some additional research on that and I found an article by Craig Murray where he claims that Mr. Karzai "was put in place because of his role with Unocal [Union Oil of California] in developing the Trans-Afghanistan Gas Pipeline project. That remains a chief strategic goal. The Asian Development Bank has agreed finance to start construction in spring, 2011. It is, of course, a total coincidence that 30,000 extra U.S. troops will arrive 6 months before, and that the U.S. (as opposed to other NATO forces) deployment area corresponds with the pipeline route." It starts on the west in Turkmenistan, goes through Afghanistan, south to Pakistan and India, and it touches near both Helmand and Kandahar provinces, which is exactly where our troop buildup is occurring.

I will also have an article [by Murray] . . . , "Unocal and the Afghanistan Pipeline," [that] talks about how . . . "Capturing the region's oil wealth and carving out territory in order to build a network of transit routes was a primary objective of U.S. military interventions throughout the 1990s in the Balkans, the Caucasus, and Caspian Sea." . . .

I would like to speak for a moment about civilian casualties in Afghanistan.

According to the United Nations, air strikes continue to be a leading cause of civilian casualties. Days into the Marjah [a Taliban stronghold] military offensive, 12 Afghans died when two rockets fired by NATO forces hit the wrong house. Ten of the 12 Afghans killed were from the same family. U.S. military officials initially apologized for the death of the civilians, but later backtracked, claiming they were insurgents. An Italian aid group working at a hospital just outside of Marjah accused allied forces of blocking dozens of critically wounded citizens from receiving medical attention at the hospital. A February 21 NATO air strike conducted by U.S. Special Forces helicopters killed over 27 civilians and wounded dozens more after minibuses were hit by helicopters "patrolling the area hunting for insurgents who had escaped the NATO offensive in the Marjah area," over 100 miles outside of Marjah in the southern province of Uruzgan.

The Wall Street Journal cited Afghan and NATO representatives, explaining that the air strike was ordered because it was believed that the minibus carried fresh Taliban fighters who were sent to help those under attack. However, the source of intelligence used to determine that the minibus carried insurgents has not been made known. Admiral Mike Mullen, Chair of the Joint Chiefs of Staff, claimed the goal of the Marjah operation was to have no civilian casualties. [There is] a Brookings Institution 2009 report estimate that 10 civilians die for every militant killed in a drone strike. . . .

I would [also] like to speak about the failure of the counterinsurgency strategy.

The Brookings Institution recently reported that, in terms of raw violence, the situation is at an historic worst level, with early 2010 levels of various types of attacks much higher than even last year at this time. Much of that is due to the recent Marjah campaign and, more generally, to the deployment of additional U.S. and Afghan troops to parts of the country where they have not been present before. The president has called this war a just war. The framing of war as "just" is served to legitimize the slaughter of innocent civilians in Iraq and Afghanistan.

A 200-page report by the RAND Corporation is entitled, *Counterintelligence in Afghanistan Deals a Huge Blow to Our Ideas of Counterinsurgency*. It reads. "In many cases, a significant direct intervention by U.S. military forces may undermine popular support and legitimacy. The United States is also unlikely to remain for the duration of most insurgencies." This study's assessment of 90 insurgencies indicates that it takes an average of 14 years to defeat insurgents once an insurgency develops. Occupations fuel insurgencies. In other words, this assessment does not fit into the president's supposed rapid increase and the shaky plan to withdraw by the summer of 2011.

The Brookings report continues:

> Second, the United States and other international actors need to improve the quality of local governance, especially in rural areas of Afghanistan. Field research in the east and south show that development and reconstruction did not reach most rural areas because of the deteriorating security environment. Even the provincial reconstruction teams, which were specifically designed to assist in the development of reconstruction projects, operate inside pockets in east and south because of security concerns.

NGOs [nongovernmental organizations, this is private ones] and [government] agencies, such as USAID and the Canadian International Development Agency, were also not involved in the reconstruction and development in many areas of the south and east.

The irony of this situation is that rural areas which were at most risk from the Taliban, which were unhappy with the slow pace of change, a population with the greatest unhappiness, received little assistance. The counterinsurgency in Afghanistan will be won or lost in the local communities of rural Afghanistan, not in urban centers such as Kabul, says the Brookings Institution.

Now, someone I'm not used to quoting, conservative columnist George Will, wrote in *The Washington Post* that the counterinsurgency theory concerning the time and level of forces required to protect the population indicates that, nationwide, Afghanistan would need hundreds of thousands of coalition troops, perhaps, for a decade or more. That is inconceivable.

For how long are we willing to dedicate billions of dollars and thousands of lives before we realize that we can't win Afghanistan militarily? Our biggest mistake in the Afghanistan strategy is to think that we can separate the Taliban from the rest of the population. We cannot. The Taliban is a local resistance movement that is part and parcel of an indigenous population. We lost Vietnam because we failed to win the hearts and minds of local populations without providing them with a competent government that provided them with basic security and with a decent living. That message can and should be applied to Afghanistan.

The strategy for winning Afghanistan is simple: Stop killing the people and they will stop killing you. . . .

The more troops we send into Afghanistan, the more support the Taliban gains as resistors of foreign occupation. We say we want to negotiate with the Taliban in the future while, at the same time, conducting air strikes to take out Taliban strongholds across the country.

Just yesterday, *The Washington Post* published an article about the Zabul province and the pouring in of Taliban fighters following a retreat of U.S. Armed Forces from Zabul in December [2009]. If we accept the premise that we can never leave Afghanistan until the Taliban is eradicated, we may be there for a very long time.

The justification for our continued military presence in Afghanistan is that the Taliban, in the past, has provided a safe haven for al Qaeda, or could do so in the future. General [David] Petraeus has already admitted that al Qaeda has little or no presence in Afghanistan.

We have to be careful about branding al Qaeda and the Taliban as a single terrorist movement. Al Qaeda is an international organization, and, yes, they are a threat to the United States. The Taliban is only a threat to us as long as we continue our military occupation of Afghanistan.

At the current estimated deployment rate, the number of troops in Afghanistan will increase from about 70,000 at the end of 2009 to the stated goal of 100,000 by July of this year. My resolution calls for the withdrawal of all U.S. Armed Forces from Afghanistan no later than December 31 of this year [2010]. And it can be done. Unlike Iraq, where we have significant infrastructure built in and around the country to support our presence there, prior to last year, the United States invested very little in permanent infrastructure for U.S. Armed Forces in Afghanistan.

President Obama has called on the logisticians for the U.S. military to triple the amount of troops we have had in the country since the war started. If the administration expects the U.S. military to figure out a way for a rapid increase of troops on the ground, we can figure out how to have a method of rapid withdrawal.

Getting supplies into Afghanistan is one of the biggest obstacles to providing adequate support for troops on the ground. Due to frequent attacks on U.S. convoys traveling to Afghanistan through Pakistan, the U.S. is forced to deliver most of the supplies by air. Madam Speaker, we have, in the last 3 hours, talked about 1,000 troop casualties; we have talked about a cost of a quarter of a trillion dollars and rising; we have spoken of civilian casualties and about the incredible amount of corruption that is going on in Afghanistan; we have spoken of the role of the pipeline, which is sure to deserve more critical inquiry; and we have talked about the failure of doctrines of counterinsurgency. That strategy doesn't work, and there are logistics of withdrawal that we can pursue.

The question is should the United States' people continue to bear the burden of this war when we have so many problems at home, with 15 million people unemployed, with millions of people losing their homes, with so many people without health care, with so many people not being able to send their children to good schools.

We have to reset our priorities. Our priorities should begin by getting out of Afghanistan. . . .

POSTSCRIPT

Should U.S. Forces Continue to Fight in Afghanistan?

Representative Kucinich's legislation, House Concurrent Resolution 248, was overwhelmingly defeated, drawing only 65 yes votes, compared to 356 no votes, with 9 members of the House not voting. That more 5 to 1 defeat did not accurately reflect sentiments in the House about the war, though, because many members who noted no did not want to seem to be undercutting U.S. troops in the field or, among Democrats, did not want to add to President Obama's travails.

Among the American public, as in Congress, concern over Afghanistan has not reached the boiling point. American attention during 2010 was focused on the economy, with other stories such as the BP oil spill in the Gulf of Mexico sometimes grabbing center stage in the news, while only 5 percent to 11 percent of respondents to various polls listed it as the story that they were following the most. Still, the year brought no relief from the growing sense of frustration. Casualties grew, and based on the first 8 months of 2010, American deaths should reach over 500 for the year. Nor was 2010 a good year politically for President Obama's policy in Afghanistan. In June he fired General Stanley McChrystal, the U.S. commander in Afghanistan, after the general made derisive comments about the president, vice president, and other top civilian officials. The following month, there was a leak of about 77,000 classified documents about Afghanistan to the public. Although most were old and none was sensational, they generally portrayed a negative image of the war and political effort. Ongoing news accounts of ineptitude and corruption in the government of President Hamid Karzai further gnawed at American public support. Illustrating this, the share of Americans willing to say the war was "worth fighting" dropped from 52 percent in December 2009 to 42 percent in July 2010. And in this debate, August found 47 percent of the public in support of keeping the U.S. troops in Afghanistan until it is stabilized, 42 percent in favor of removing the troops, and 11 percent were unsure.

To find out more about Afghanistan, go to the Web site of the government of Afghanistan at http://www.afghangovernment.com/ or to http://www.afghanweb .com/. A source for U.S. policy is the White House's Web page at http://www .whitehouse.gov. Keyboard "Afghanistan" into the search window. Using the search window at the Department of Defense site, http://www.defenselink.mil/, will yield more on the military side. Casualty data for Afghanistan, and Iraq also, are at http://icasualties.org/. For a general background, read David Loyn, *In Afghanistan: Two Hundred Years of British, Russian and American Occupation* (Palgrave Macmillan, 2009).

Questions for Critical Thinking and Reflection

1. If the war in Afghanistan was worth undertaking in 2001, why is it still not worth "winning"?
2. How in a situation does one determine when one has won enough to begin to bring troops home?
3. What do you think of the argument of some people that if the Taliban were to surrender Osama bin Laden to the United States and agree to not support terrorism, then the United States should step aside in Afghanistan and let the Taliban assert control once again if they can?

ISSUE 15

Does Using Drones to Attack Terrorists Globally Violate International Law?

YES: Mary Ellen O'Connell, from "Lawful Use of Combat Drones," Testimony during Hearings on "Rise of the Drones II: Examining the Legality of Unmanned Targeting," before the Subcommittee on National Security and Foreign Affairs, Committee on Oversight and Government Reform, U.S. House of Representatives (April 28, 2010)

NO: Michael W. Lewis, from "Examining the Legality of Unmanned Targeting," Testimony during Hearings on "Rise of the Drones II: Examining the Legality of Unmanned Targeting," before the Subcommittee on National Security and Foreign Affairs, Committee on Oversight and Government Reform, U.S. House of Representatives (April 28, 2010)

ISSUE SUMMARY

YES: Mary Ellen O'Connell, a research professor at the Kroc Institute, University of Notre Dame, and the Robert and Marion Short Professor of Law at the School of Law, University of Notre Dame, tells a congressional committee that the United States is failing more often than not to follow the most important single rule governing drones: restricting their use to the battlefield.

NO: Michael W. Lewis, a professor of law at Ohio Northern University's Pettit College of Law, disagrees, contending that there is nothing inherently illegal about using drones to target specific terrorists or groups of terrorists on or away from the battlefield.

Duringuring March and April 2010, the Subcommittee on National Security and Foreign Affairs of the Committee on Oversight and Government Reform in the U.S. House of Representatives held a series of hearings to look into the military use of unmanned aerial vehicles (UAVs, drones). These remotely piloted aircraft are capable of launching missiles and otherwise attacking targets, of using cameras and other sensors to gather intelligence, of facilitating communications, and of performing other tasks. The characteristics of the numerous types of UAVs in the U.S. military inventory vary considerably by mission, but one of the best known is the Predator. It is propeller driven, has a top speed of 135 mph, has a 450-mile range, is 27 feet long, has a 48-foot wingspan, can stay aloft for 20 hours, and is armed with two air-to-surface Hellfire missiles, each tipped with a warhead carrying 20 pounds of high explosives. Relative to piloted warplanes, UAVs are inexpensive, costing about one-tenth as much each. There are also great differences in the time and money spent creating pilots.

During the first session of the hearings on March 23, 2010, the subcommittee's chair, Representative John F. Tierney (D-MA), opened the inquiry by outlining its purpose. As Tierney put it with regard to the subject of this debate:

> . . . Over the last decade, the number of unmanned systems and their applications has grown rapidly. So too has the number of operational, political, and legal questions associated with this technology. The growing demand for and reliance on unmanned systems has serious implications, . . . As the United States is engaged in two wars abroad, unmanned systems, particularly unmanned aerial vehicles, have become a centerpiece of that war effort. In recent years, the Department of Defense's UAV inventory has rapidly grown in size, from 167 in 2002 to over 7000 today. Last year, for the first time, the U.S. Air Force trained more unmanned pilots than traditional fighter pilots.
>
> Some express no doubt that unmanned systems have been a boost to U.S. war efforts in the Middle East and South Asia. CIA Director Leon Panetta said last May that "drone strikes are the only game in town in terms of confronting or trying to disrupt the al Qaeda leadership." Media reports over the last year that the top two leaders of the Pakistani Taliban were killed by drone strikes also support this argument.
>
> But some critics argue that drone strikes are unethical at best and counter-productive at worst. They point to the reportedly high rate of civilian casualties . . . and argue that the strikes do more to stoke anti-Americanism than they do to weaken our enemies. . . . This is particularly relevant in the era of counter-insurgency doctrine, a central tenet of which is, "first, do no harm."
>
> It also may be the case that we are fighting wars with modern technology under an antiquated set of laws. For example, if the United States uses unmanned weapons systems, does that require an official declaration of war or an authorization for the use of force? . . .
>
> These trends are already forcing us to ask new questions about domestic airspace regulation: who is allowed to own unmanned systems, and where they are allowed to operate them?
>
> These are some of the questions that we will begin to answer in this hearing. Surely we will not conclude this conversation in one afternoon, . . .

In the following readings, two experts on international law relating to war take up the use of UAVs to attack targets away from an immediate war zone or "battlefield." Ellen O'Connell argues that such attacks violate international law. Michael Lewis disagrees.

YES

Mary Ellen O'Connell

Lawful Use of Combat Drones

Combat drones are battlefield weapons. They fire missiles or drop bombs capable of inflicting very serious damage. Drones are not lawful for use outside combat zones. Outside such zones, police are the proper law enforcement agents and police are generally required to warn before using lethal force. Restricting drones to the battlefield is the most important single rule governing their use. Yet, the United States is failing to follow it more often than not. At the very time we are trying to win hearts and minds to respect the rule of law, we are ourselves failing to respect a very basic rule: remote weapons systems belong on the battlefield.

I. A Lawful Battlefield Weapon

The United States first used weaponized drones during the combat in Afghanistan that began on October 7, 2001. We requested permission from Uzbekistan, which was then hosting the U.S. air base where drones were kept. We also used combat drones in the battles with Iraq's armed forces in the effort to topple Saddam Hussein's government that began in March 2003. We are still using drones lawfully in the ongoing combat in Afghanistan. Drones spare the lives of pilots, since the unmanned aerial vehicle is flown from a site far from the attack zone. If a drone is shot down, there is no loss of human life. Moreover, on the battlefield drones can be more protective of civilian lives than high aerial bombing or long-range artillery. Their cameras can pick up details about the presence of civilians. Drones can fly low and target more precisely using this information. [The U.S. commander in Afghanistan] General [Stanley] McChrystal has wisely insisted on zero-tolerance for civilian deaths in Afghanistan. The use of drones can help us achieve that. What drones cannot do is comply with police rules for the use of lethal force away from the battlefield. In law enforcement it must be possible to warn before using lethal force, in war-fighting this is not necessary, making the use of bombs and missiles lawful. The United Nations Basic Principles for the Use of Force and Firearms by Law Enforcement Officials (*UN Basic Principles*) set out the international legal standard for the use of force by police:

> Law enforcement officials shall not use firearms against persons except in self-defense or defense of others against the imminent threat of death or serious injury, to prevent the perpetration of a particularly

U.S. House of Representatives, April 28, 2010.

serious crime involving grave threat to life, to arrest a person present-
ing such a danger and resisting their authority, or to prevent his or her
escape, and only when less extreme means are insufficient to achieve
these objectives. In any event, intentional lethal use of firearms may
only be made when strictly unavoidable in order to protect life.

The United States has failed to follow these rules by using combat drones
in places where no actual armed conflict was occurring or where the U.S. was
not involved in the armed conflict. On November 3, 2002, the CIA used a
drone to fire laser-guided Hellfire missiles at a passenger vehicle traveling in a
thinly populated region of Yemen. At that time, the Air Force controlled the
entire drone fleet, but the Air Force rightly raised concerns about the legality
of attacking in a place where there was no armed conflict. CIA agents based in
Djibouti carried out the killing. All six passengers in the vehicle were killed,
including an American. In January 2003, the United Nations Commission on
Human Rights received a report on the Yemen strike from its special rapporteur on extrajudicial, summary, or arbitrary killing. The rapporteur concluded
that the strike constituted "a clear case of extrajudicial killing."

Apparently, Yemen gave tacit consent for the strike. States [countries]
cannot, however, give consent to a right they do not have. States may not
use military force against individuals on their territory when law enforcement
measures are appropriate. At the time of the strike, Yemen was not using military force anywhere on its territory. More recently, Yemen has been using military force to suppress militants in two parts of the country. The U.S.'s ongoing
drone use, however, has not been part of those campaigns.

The United States has also used combat drones in Somalia probably starting in late 2006 during the Ethiopian invasion when the U.S. assisted Ethiopia
in its attempt to install a new government in that volatile country. Ethiopia's
effort had some support from the UN and the African Union. To the extent that
the U.S. was assisting Ethiopia, our actions had some justification. It is clear,
however, that the U.S. has used drone strikes independently of the attempt to
restore order in Somalia. The U.S. has continued to target and kill individuals
in Somalia following Ethiopia's pullout from the country.

The U.S. use of drones in Pakistan has similar problems to the uses in
Yemen and Somalia. Where military force *is* warranted to address internal violence, governments have widely resorted to the practice of inviting in another
state to assist. This is the legal justification the U.S. cites for its use of military
force today in Afghanistan and Iraq. Yet, the U.S. cannot point to invitations
from Pakistan for most of its drone attacks. Indeed, for much of the period
that the United States has used drones on the territory of Pakistan, there has
been no armed conflict. Therefore, even express consent by Pakistan would
not justify their use.

The United States has been carrying out drone attacks in Pakistan since
2004. Pakistani authorities only began to use major military force to suppress
militancy in May 2009, in Buner Province. Some U.S. drone strikes have been
coordinated with Islamabad's efforts, but some have not. Some strikes have
apparently even targeted groups allied with Islamabad.

II. The Battlefield Defined

The Bush administration justified the 2002 Yemen strike and others as justified under the law of armed conflict in the "Global War on Terror." The current State Department Legal Adviser, Harold Koh, has rejected the term "Global War on Terror," preferring to base our actions on the view that the U.S. is in an "armed conflict with al-Qaeda, the Taliban and associated forces." Under the new label, the U.S. is carrying out many of the same actions as the Bush administration under the old one: using lethal force without warning, far from any actual battlefield.

Armed conflict, however, is a real thing. The United States is currently engaged in an armed conflict in Afghanistan. The United States has tens of thousands of highly trained troops fighting a well-organized opponent that is able to hold territory. The situation in Afghanistan today conforms to the definition of armed conflict in international law. The International Law Association's Committee on the Use of Force issued a report in 2008 confirming the basic characteristics of all armed conflict: (1) the presence of organized armed groups that are (2) engaged in intense inter-group fighting. The fighting or hostilities of an armed conflict occur within limited zones, referred to as combat or conflict zones. It is only in such zones that killing enemy combatants or those taking a direct part in hostilities is permissible.

Because armed conflict requires a certain intensity of fighting, the isolated terrorist attack, regardless of how serious the consequences, is not an armed conflict. Terrorism is crime. Members of al Qaeda or other terrorist groups are active in Canada, France, Germany, Indonesia, Morocco, Saudi Arabia, Spain, the United Kingdom, Yemen and elsewhere. Still, these countries do not consider themselves in a war with al Qaeda. In the words of a leading expert on the law of armed conflict, the British Judge on the International Court of Justice, Sir Christopher Greenwood:

> In the language of international law there is no basis for speaking of a war on Al-Qaeda or any other terrorist group, for such a group cannot be a belligerent, it is merely a band of criminals, and to treat it as anything else risks distorting the law while giving that group a status which to some implies a degree of legitimacy.

To label terrorists "enemy combatants" lifts them out of the status of *criminal* to that of *combatant,* the same category as America's own troops on the battlefield. This move to label terrorists combatants is contrary to strong historic trends. From earliest times, governments have struggled to prevent their enemies from approaching a status of equality. Even governments on the verge of collapse due to the pressure of a rebel advance have vehemently denied that the violence inflicted by their enemies was anything but criminal violence. Governments fear the psychological and legal advantages to opponents of calling them "combatants" and their struggle a "war."

President Ronald Reagan strongly opposed labeling terrorists combatants. He said that to "grant combatant status to irregular forces even if they do not satisfy the traditional requirements . . . would endanger civilians among whom terrorists and other irregulars attempt to conceal themselves."

The United Kingdom and other allies take the same position as President Reagan: "It is the understanding of the United Kingdom that the term 'armed conflict' of itself and in its context denotes a situation of a kind which is not constituted by the commission of ordinary crimes including acts of terrorism whether concerted or in isolation."

In the United States and other countries plagued by al Qaeda, institutions are functioning normally. No one has declared martial law. The International Committee of the Red Cross is not active. Criminal trials of suspected terrorists are being held in regular criminal courts. The police use lethal force only in situations of necessity. The U.S.'s actions today are generally consistent with its long-term policy of separating acts of terrorism from armed conflict—except when it comes to drones.

III. Battlefield Restraints

Even when the U.S. is using drones at the request of Pakistan in battles it is waging, we are failing to follow important battlefield rules. The U.S. must respect the principles of necessity, proportionality and humanity in carrying out drone attacks. "Necessity" refers to military necessity, and the obligation that force is used only if necessary to accomplish a reasonable military objective. "Proportionality" prohibits that "which may be expected to cause incidental loss of civilian life, injury to civilians, damage to civilian objects, or a combination thereof, which would be excessive in relation to concrete and direct military advantage anticipated." These limitations on permissible force extend to both the quantity of force used and the geographic scope of its use.

Far from suppressing militancy in Pakistan, drone attacks are fueling the interest in fighting against the United States. This impact makes the use of drones difficult to justify under the terms of military necessity. Most serious of all, perhaps, is the disproportionate impact of drone attacks. A principle that provides context for all decisions in armed conflict is the principle of humanity. The principle of humanity supports decisions in favor of sparing life and avoiding destruction in close cases under either the principles of necessity or proportionality. According to the International Committee of the Red Cross, the principles of necessity and humanity are particularly important in situations such as Pakistan:

> In classic large-scale confrontations between well-equipped and organized armed forces or groups, the principles of military necessity and of humanity are unlikely to restrict the use of force against legitimate military targets beyond what is already required by specific provisions of IHL [international humanitarian law]. The practical importance of their restraining function will increase with the ability of the conflict to control the circumstances and area in which its military operations are conducted, may become decisive where armed forces operate against selected individuals in situations comparable to peacetime policing. In practice, such considerations are likely to become particularly relevant where a party to the conflict exercises effective territorial control, most notably in occupied territories and non-international armed conflicts.

Another issue in drone use is the fact that strikes are carried out in Pakistan by the CIA and civilian contractors. Only members of the United States armed forces have the combatant's privilege to use lethal force without facing prosecution. CIA operatives are not trained in the law of armed conflict. They are not bound by the Uniform Code of Military Justice to respect the laws and customs of war. They are not subject to the military chain of command. This fact became abundantly clear during the revelation of U.S. use of harsh interrogation tactics. Given the negative impact of that unlawful conduct on America's standing in the world and our ability to promote the rule of law, it is difficult to fathom why the Obama administration is using the CIA to carry out drone attacks, let alone civilian contractors.

Conclusion

The use of military force in counter-terrorism operations has been counter-productive. Military force is a blunt instrument. Inevitably unintended victims are the result of almost any military action. Drone attacks in Pakistan have resulted in large numbers of deaths and are generally seen as fueling terrorism, not abating it. In congressional testimony in March 2009, counter-terrorism expert, David Kilcullen, said drones in Pakistan are giving "rise to a feeling of anger that coalesces the population around the extremists and leads to spikes of extremism well outside the parts of the country where we are mounting those attacks." Another expert told the *New York Times,* "The more the drone campaign works, the more it fails—as increased attacks only make the Pakistanis angrier at the collateral damage and sustained violation of their sovereignty." A National Public Radio Report on April 26, 2010, pointed out that al Qaeda is losing support in the Muslim world because of its violent, lawless tactics. We can help eliminate the last of that support by distinguishing ourselves through commitment to the rule of law, especially by strict compliance with the rules governing lethal force.

Michael W. Lewis  **NO**

Examining the Legality of Unmanned Targeting

Introduction

I am a professor of law at Ohio Northern University's Pettit College of Law where I teach International Law and the Law of Armed Conflict. I spent over 7 years in the U.S. Navy as a Naval Flight Officer flying F-14s. I flew missions over the Persian Gulf and Iraq as part of Operations Desert Shield/Desert Storm and I graduated from Top Gun [the U.S. Navy Fighter Weapons School] in 1992. After my military service I attended Harvard Law School and graduated *cum laude* in 1998. Subsequently I have lectured on a variety of aspects of the laws of war, with an emphasis on aerial bombardment, at dozens of institutions including Harvard, NYU, Columbia and the University of Chicago. I have published several articles and co-authored a book on the laws of war relating to the war on terror. My prior experience as a combat pilot and strike planner provides me with a different perspective from most other legal scholars on the interaction between law and combat.

The Current Laws of War Are Sufficient to Address the Drone Question

There is nothing inherently illegal about using drones to target specific individuals. Nor is there anything legally unique about the use of unmanned drones as a weapons delivery platform that requires the creation of new or different laws to govern their use.

As with any other attack launched against enemy forces during an armed conflict, the use of drones is governed by International Humanitarian Law (IHL). Compliance with current IHL that governs aerial bombardment and requires that all attacks demonstrate military necessity and comply with the principle of proportionality is sufficient to ensure the legality of drone strikes. In circumstances where a strike by a helicopter or an F-16 [a U.S. warplane] would be legal, the use of a drone would be equally legitimate. However, this legal parity does not answer three fundamental questions that have been raised by these hearings. Who may be targeted? Where may they be targeted? And finally who is allowed to pilot the drones and determine which targets are legally appropriate?

U.S. House of Representatives, April 28, 2010.

Who May Be Targeted?

In order to understand the rules governing the targeting of individuals, it is necessary to understand the various categories that IHL assigns to individuals. To best understand how they relate to one another it is useful to start from the beginning.

All people are civilians and are not subjected to targeting unless they take affirmative steps to either become combatants or to otherwise lose their civilian immunity. It is important to recognize that a civilian does not become a combatant by merely picking up a weapon. In order to become a combatant an individual must be a member of the "armed forces of a Party to a conflict." This definition is found in Article 43 of Additional Protocol I to the Geneva Conventions. It goes on to define the term "armed forces" as:

> The armed forces of a Party to a conflict consist of all organized armed forces, groups and units which are under a command responsible to that Party for the conduct of its subordinates, even if that Party is represented by a government or an authority not recognized by an adverse Party. Such armed forces shall be subject to an internal disciplinary system which, *inter alia*, shall enforce compliance with the rules of international law applicable in armed conflict.

The status of combatant is important because combatants "have the right to participate directly in hostilities." This "combatants' privilege" allows privileged individuals to participate in an armed conflict without violating domestic laws prohibiting the destruction of property, assault, murder, etc. The combatant's conduct is therefore regulated by IHL rather than [by] domestic law.

Combatant status is something of a double-edged sword, however. While it bestows the combatant privilege on the individual, it also subjects that individual to attack at any time by other parties to the conflict. A combatant may be lawfully targeted whether or not they pose a current threat to their opponents, whether or not they are armed, or even awake. The only occasion on which IHL prohibits attacking a combatant is when that combatant has surrendered or been rendered *hors de combat*. Professor Geoff Corn has argued compellingly that this ability to target based upon status, rather than on the threat posed by an individual, is the defining feature of an armed conflict.

After examining the definition of combatant, it becomes apparent that combatant status is based upon group conduct, not individual conduct. Members of al Qaeda are not combatants because as a group they are not "subject to an internal disciplinary system which [enforces] compliance with the rules of international law applicable in armed conflict." It does not matter whether an individual al Qaeda member may have behaved properly; he can never obtain the combatants' privilege because the group he belongs to does not meet IHL's requirements. Professor [David] Glazier's testimony [before this committee] that al Qaeda and the Taliban could possess "the basic right to engage in combat against us" is mistaken. These groups have clearly and unequivocally forfeited any "right" to be treated as combatants by choosing to employ means and methods of warfare that violate the laws of armed conflict, such as deliberately targeting civilians.

If al Qaeda members are not combatants, then what are they? They must be civilians, and civilians as a general rule are immune from targeting. However, civilians lose this immunity "for such time as they take a direct part in hostilities." The question of what constitutes direct participation in hostilities (DPH) has been much debated. While DOD [the U.S. Department of Defense] has yet to offer its definition of DPH, the International Committee of the Red Cross (ICRC) recently completed a six-year study on the matter and has offered interpretive guidance that, while not binding on the United States, provides a useful starting point. The ICRC guidance states that "members of organized armed groups [which do not qualify as combatants] belonging to a party to the conflict lose protection against direct attack for the duration of their membership (i.e., for as long as they assume a continuous combat function)."

The concept of a "continuous combat function" within DPH is a reaction to the "farmer by day, fighter by night" tactic that a number of organized armed terrorist groups have employed to retain their civilian immunity from attack for as long as possible. Because such individuals (be they fighters, bomb makers, planners or leaders) perform a continuous combat function, they may be directly targeted for as long as they remain members of the group. The only way for such individuals to reacquire their civilian immunity is to disavow membership in the group.

So the answer to "Who may be targeted?" is any member of al Qaeda or the Taliban, or any other individuals that have directly participated in hostilities against the United States. This would certainly include individuals that directly or indirectly (e.g. by planting IEDs) [improvised explosive devices] attacked Coalition forces as well as any leadership within these organizations. Significantly, the targeting of these individuals does not involve their elevation to combatant status as Professor O'Connell implied in her testimony [found in the first reading]. These individuals are civilians who have forfeited their civilian immunity by directly participating in hostilities. They are not, and cannot become, combatants until they join an organized armed group that complies with the laws of armed conflict, but they nevertheless remain legitimate targets until they clearly disassociate themselves from al Qaeda or the Taliban.

Where May Attacks Take Place?

Some witnesses have testified to this subcommittee that the law of armed conflict only applies to our ongoing conflict with al Qaeda in certain defined geographic areas. Professor O'Connell states that the geographic limit of the armed conflict is within the borders of Afghanistan while others include the border areas of Pakistan and Iraq. They take the position that any operations against al Qaeda outside of this defined geography are solely the province of law enforcement, which requires that the target be warned before lethal force is employed. Because drones cannot meet this requirement they conclude that drone strikes outside of this geographical area should be prohibited. The geographical boundaries proposed are based upon the infrequency of armed assaults that take place outside of Afghanistan, Iraq and the border region of Pakistan. Because IHL does not specifically address the geographic scope of armed conflicts, to assess these proposed requirements it is necessary to step back and consider the law of armed conflict as a whole and the realities of warfare as they apply to this conflict.

One of the principal goals of IHL is to protect the civilian population from harm during an armed conflict. To further this goal IHL prohibits direct attacks on civilians and requires that parties to the conflict distinguish themselves from the civilian population. As a result, it would seem anomalous for IHL to be read in such a way as to reward a party that regularly targets civilians, and yet that is what is being proposed. As discussed above, a civilian member of al Qaeda who is performing a continuous combat function may be legitimately targeted with lethal force without any warning. But the proposed geographic limitations on IHL's application offer this individual a renewed immunity from attack. Rather than disavowing an organization that targets civilians, IHL's preferred result, the proposed geographic restrictions allow the individual to obtain the same immunity by crossing an international border and avoiding law enforcement while remaining active in an organization that targets civilians. When law enforcement's logistical limitations are considered, along with the host state's ambivalence for actively pursuing al Qaeda within its borders, it becomes clear that the proposed geographical limitations on IHL are tantamount to the creation of a safe haven for al Qaeda.

More importantly these proposed limitations would hand the initiative in this conflict over to al Qaeda. Militarily the ability to establish and maintain the initiative during a conflict is one of the most important strategic and operational advantages that a party can possess. To the extent that one side's forces are able to decide when, where and how a conflict is conducted, the likelihood of a favorable outcome is greatly increased. If IHL is interpreted to allow al Qaeda's leadership to marshal its forces in Yemen or the Sudan, or any number of other places that are effectively beyond the reach of law enforcement and to then strike at its next target of choice, whether it be New York, Madrid, London, Bali, Washington, DC or Detroit, then IHL is being read to hand the initiative in the conflict to al Qaeda. IHL should not be read to reward a party that consistently violates IHL's core principles and as Professor Glazier points out in his reference to the Cambodian incursion, it was not read that way in the past.

Those opposed to the position that IHL governs the conflict with al Qaeda regardless of geography, and therefore allows strikes like the one conducted in Yemen in 2002, have voiced three main concerns. The first concern is that the United States may be violating the sovereignty of other nations by conducting drone strikes on their territory. It is true that such attacks may only be conducted with the permission of the state on whose territory the attack takes place and questions have been raised about whether Pakistan, Yemen and other states have consented to this use of force. This is a legitimate concern that must be satisfactorily answered while accounting for the obvious sensitivity associated with granting such permission. The fact that Harold Koh, the State Department's Legal Advisor, specifically mentioned [in his testimony] the "sovereignty of the other states involved" in his discussion of drone strikes is evidence that the Administration takes this requirement seriously.

The second concern is that such a geographically unbounded conflict could lead to drone strikes in Paris or London, or to setting the precedent for other nations to employ lethal force in the United States against its enemies that have taken refuge here. These concerns are overstated. The existence of the permission requirement mentioned above means that any strikes conducted in London or Paris could only take place with the approval of the British or French governments. Further, any such strike would have to meet the requirements of military necessity and proportionality and it is difficult to imagine how these requirements could be satisfactorily met in such a congested urban setting.

Lastly, there is a legitimate concern that mistakes could be made. An individual could be inappropriately placed on the list and killed without being given any opportunity to challenge his placement on the list. Again, Mr. Koh's assurances that the procedures for identifying lawful targets "are extremely robust" are in some measure reassuring, particularly given his stature in the international legal community. However, some oversight of these procedures is clearly warranted. While *ex ante* [before the fact/event] review must obviously be balanced against secrecy and national security concerns, *ex post* review can be more thorough. When the Israeli Supreme Court approved the use of targeted killings, one of its requirements was for transparency after the fact coupled with an independent investigation of the precision of the identification and the circumstances of the attack. A similar *ex post* transparency would be appropriate here to ensure that "extremely robust" means something.

Who May Do the Targeting?

Another question raised in the hearings was the propriety of allowing the CIA to control drone strikes. Professor Glazier opined that CIA drone pilots conducting strikes are civilians directly participating in hostilities and suggested that they might be committing war crimes by engaging in such conduct. Even if these are not considered war crimes, if the CIA members are civilians performing a continuous combat function then they are not entitled to the combatants' privilege and could potentially be liable for domestic law violations.

Therefore, if CIA members are going to continue piloting drones and planning strikes, then they must obtain combatant status. Article 43(3) of Protocol I [to the Geneva Convention of 1949] allows a party to "incorporate a paramilitary or armed law enforcement agency into its armed forces" after notifying other parties to the conflict. For such an incorporation to be effective a clear chain of command would have to be established (if it does not already exist) that enforces compliance with the laws of armed conflict. Without this incorporation or some other measure clearly establishing the CIA's accountability for law of armed conflict violations, the continued use of CIA drone pilots and strike planners will be legally problematic.

Conclusion

Drones are legitimate weapons platforms whose use is effectively governed by current IHL applicable to aerial bombardment. Like other forms of aircraft they may be used to target enemy forces, whether specifically identifiable individuals or armed formations.

IHL permits the targeting of both combatants and civilians that are directly participating in hostilities. Because of the means and methods of warfare that they employ, al Qaeda and Taliban forces are not combatants and are not entitled to the combatants' privilege. They are instead civilians that have forfeited their immunity because of their participation in hostilities. Members of al Qaeda and the Taliban that perform continuous combat functions may be targeted at any time, subject to the standard requirements of distinction and proportionality.

Placing blanket geographical restrictions on the use of drone strikes turns IHL on its head by allowing individuals an alternative means for reacquiring effective immunity from attack without disavowing al Qaeda and its methods of warfare. It further bolsters al Qaeda by providing them with a safe haven that allows them to regain the initiative in their conflict with the United States. The geographical limitations on drone strikes imposed by sovereignty requirements, along with the ubiquitous requirements of distinction and proportionality, are sufficient to prevent these strikes from violating international law. However, some form of *ex post* [after the fact/event] transparency and oversight is necessary to review the identification criteria and strike circumstances to ensure that they remain "extremely robust."

POSTSCRIPT

Does Using Drones to Attack Terrorists Globally Violate International Law?

A UAV attack on May 31, 2010, illustrates a number of issues involved in this debate. The strike killed Mustafa Abu al-Yazid, a founding member of al Qaeda and its third-raking leader after Osama bin Laden and Ayman al-Zawahiri. However, the attack also killed Yazid's wife, three of his daughters, and a granddaughter. Moreover, the attack occurred in the area of Miramshah, Pakistan, close to the border with, but not in, Afghanistan.

Drone attacks undoubtedly often kill and wound noncombatants and/ or destroy their property. But how much this occurs is open to debate. One study (Brookings Institution, 2009) of U.S. drone attacks in Pakistan estimated that they killed 10 noncombatants for every Taliban or al Qaeda combatant, but another study (New America Foundation, 2010) estimated only one civilian died for every two combatants killed. Inasmuch as zero-collateral damage in all military operations is neither an achievable standard nor required under *jus in bello* (just conduct of war) by international law, the issue of collateral damage remains highly debatable. So do the boundaries of the battlefield. President Obama has authorized several increases in the geographic use of drones and permissible targets, and State Department legal adviser Harold Koh has defended those extensions, arguing that the war of terrorism is global, not confined to Afghanistan or any other battle zone and that the United States has a right of self-defense to attack terrorists and their supporters anywhere. Koh also described U.S. procedures for identifying and hitting legal targets as "extremely robust" and becoming "even more precise." A different view was given to the United Nations Human Rights Council in a June 2010 report by UN special investigator Philip Alston. He criticized U.S. UAV attacks as having displaced "clear legal standards with a vaguely defined license to kill," and also for creating a "risk of developing a 'Playstation' mentality to killing."

For a background on drones and other unmanned weapons systems, read Peter W. Singer, *Wired for War: The Robotics Revolution and Conflict in the 21st Century* (Penguin Press, 2009). Details on part of the U.S. arsenal of drones can be found at http://www.airforce-technology.com/projects/predator/. Two recent looks at how terrorism has impacted the law of war are Myra Williamson, *Terrorism, War and International Law* (Ashgate, 2009) and Michael Lewis et al., *The War on Terror and the Laws of War: A Military Perspective* (Oxford University Press, 2009).

Questions for Critical Thinking and Reflection

1. If al Qaeda were able to attack the White House using a small airplane with suicide bombers that killed Barack, Michelle, Sasha, and Melia Obama, would that strike be different in terms of *jus in bello* than the missile strike that specifically targeted Mustafa Abu al-Yazid and also killed his family members?

2. What do you think of the implication in the remarks of UN investigator Philip Alston that the ability to kill from a far distance, including now using robotic weapons system, is causing a "disconnect" from the death and suffering caused.

3. In April 2010, President Obama reportedly authorized a drone attack, if possible, on an American citizen living in Yemen. The individual, Muslim cleric Anwar al-Aulaqi, is alleged, but not proven, to have been involved in several terrorist plots against the United States. Do you support President Obama's decision, and, if so, are there other circumstances in which the president can justifiably authorize the *de facto* execution of an American without judicial sanction?

Internet References . . .

United Nations Department of Peacekeeping Operations

This UN site is the gateway to all the peacekeeping functions of the United Nations.

http://www.un.org/en/peacekeeping/

International Law Association

The International Law Association, which is currently headquartered in London, was founded in Brussels in 1873. Its objectives, under its constitution, include the "study, elucidation and advancement of international law, public and private, the study of comparative law, the making of proposals for the solution of conflicts of law and for the unification of law, and the furthering of international understanding and goodwill."

http://www.ila-hq.org

United Nations Treaty Collection

The United Nations Treaty Collection is a collection of 30,000 treaties, addenda, and other items related to treaties and international agreements that have been field with the UN Secretariat since 1946. The collection includes the texts of treaties in their original language(s) and English and French translations.

http://untreaty.un.org

Jurist: Terrorism Law and Policy

This site maintained by the University of Pittsburgh is a good source for the many complex legal issues involved in defining and combating terrorism.

http://jurist.law.pitt.edu/

International Law and Organization Issues

*P*art of the process of globalization is the increase in scope and importance of both international law and international organizations. The issues in this section represent some of the controversies involved with the expansion of international law and organizations into the realm of military security. Issues here relate to increasing international organizations' responsibility for security, the effectiveness of international financial organizations, and the proposal to authorize international courts to judge those who are accused of war crimes.

- Is UN Peacekeeping Seriously Flawed?

- Is U.S. Refusal to Join the International Criminal Court Wise?

- Should the United States Ratify the Convention to Eliminate All Forms of Discrimination Against Women?

ISSUE 16

Is UN Peacekeeping Seriously Flawed?

YES: Brett D. Schaefer, from Testimony during Hearings on "United Nations Peacekeeping: Challenges and Opportunities," before the Subcommittee on International Operations and Organizations, Democracy, and Human Rights, Committee on Foreign Relations, U.S. Senate (July 23, 2008)

NO: William J. Durch, from "Peace and Stability Operations: Challenges and Opportunities for the Next U.S. Administration," Testimony during Hearings on "United Nations Peacekeeping: Challenges and Opportunities," before the Subcommittee on International Operations and Organizations, Committee on Foreign Relations, U.S. Senate (July 23, 2008)

ISSUE SUMMARY

YES: Brett D. Schaefer, the Jay Kingham Fellow in International Regulatory Affairs at the Heritage Foundation, a conservative think tank in Washington, DC, contends that the increased number and size of recent UN deployments have overwhelmed the capabilities of the UN Department of Peacekeeping Operations, leading to problems that make support of UN peacekeeping questionable.

NO: William J. Durch, senior associate at the Henry L. Stimson Center, an internationalist-oriented think tank in Washington, DC, acknowledges that UN peacekeeping has had problems, but argues that the UN is making major reforms and deserves strong support.

The United Nations was established in 1945 as a reaction to World War II with its horrendous destruction of life and property. In an effort to avoid a repeat of that calamity, most of the victorious and neutral countries agreed to a UN Charter that outlined a number of steps to maintain or restore peace. One was a pledge by all member countries not to resort unilaterally to war or other international violence except for self-defense. In all other cases where violence threatened or was occurring, the issue is supposed to be brought to the Security Council for its decision about how to respond.

One option involving military force is for the Security Council to authorize member countries to take military action against an aggressor. This has happened only twice: the UN authorized interventions in Korea (1950–1953) and in the Persian Gulf (1990–1991). The United States tried but failed to convince the Security Council in 2003 that the situation in Iraq warranted a third such collective security action.

Peacekeeping is the other military option available to the Security Council. In contrast to option one, which identifies an aggressor authorizes others to defeat it, peacekeeping deploys a military force under UN command that is made up of units contributed by member countries. Since UN forces are traditionally fairly small and lightly armed, the idea of peacekeeping is not to defeat one side or another but to prevent fighting, usually by acting as a buffer.

From 1945 to 2007, the United Nations sent over 9 million soldiers, police officers, and unarmed observers drawn from two-thirds of the world's countries to conduct 61 peacekeeping or truce observation missions. The frequency of such UN missions has risen sharply since the end of the cold war also ended the frequent veto of using peacekeeping forces by the Soviet Union and, to a lesser degree, the United States. To a degree, the difficulty of the missions has grown also as the Security Council has increasingly sent peacekeepers into unstable situations such as the Balkans, Democratic Republic of the Congo, and Darfur in western Sudan where the mission has had to try to establish peace or protect one or more groups.

A candid review of the success of UN peacekeeping missions would give them only mixed reviews. Some have worked well, but others have proven ineffective. There are several reasons for the limited effectiveness of UN forces, and to a degree, the debate in this issue is about the relative importance of the problems that beset UN peacekeeping and what to do about them.

Those who support peacekeeping focus on two problems. First, countries frequently do not meet their financial obligation to support UN forces, thereby limiting what they can do. As of late 2007, the UN's members were $3.2 billion behind on their peacekeeping payments. The largest debtor, the United States, owed about a third of this total. Second, it is often difficult to get the self-interested Security Council members to agree to authorize a UN mission. Even when the mission is authorized, it is often given little authority to act and a troop contingent that is too small and too poorly armed to make a difference. When, for example, the UN initially sent forces to the Balkans in 1992, the secretary-general asked for 35,000 peacekeepers. However, the Security Council authorized only 7,000 troops, with restrictions and limitations. These limits prevented the peacekeepers from being effective and even led, at one point, to UN troops being taken hostage and publicly humiliated.

Those who are skeptical of UN peacekeeping often focus, as does Brett D. Schaefer in the first reading, on a third problem that it is the internal problems and scandals that have cast a shadow on the UN's peacekeeping efforts. He responds to these problems by urging the U.S. government to be wary of funding UN peacekeeping and by advocating fewer, less ambitious peacekeeping missions. William J. Durch in the second reading argues that needed reforms are being instituted and that the United States should give strong financial and military support for UN peace operations, thus setting an example for others.

YES

United Nations Peacekeeping: Challenges and Opportunities

UN Peacekeeping

One of the United Nations' primary responsibilities—and the one that Americans most agree with—is to help maintain international peace and security, but the UN has come under increasing criticism, both within the United States and around the world, for its inability to keep the peace where it is asked to do so. The UN Charter places principal responsibility for maintaining international peace and security within the UN system on the Security Council. The Charter gives the Security Council extensive powers to investigate disputes to determine whether they endanger international peace and security; to call on participants in a dispute to settle the conflict through peaceful negotiation; to impose mandatory economic, travel, and diplomatic sanctions; and ultimately to authorize the use of military force. This robust vision of the UN as a key vehicle for maintaining international peace and security quickly ran athwart the interests of the member states, particularly during the Cold War when opposing alliances prevented the UN from taking decisive action except when the interests of the major powers were minimal.

As a result, between 1945 and 1990, the Security Council established only 18 peace operations, despite a multitude of conflicts during that period that threatened international peace and security to greater or lesser degree. Traditionally, Security Council authorizations of military force have involved deployments into relatively low-risk situations such as truce monitoring. The bulk of these peace operations were fact-finding missions, observer missions, and other roles in assisting peace processes in which the parties had agreed to cease hostilities. UN peace operations were rarely authorized with the expectation of the use of force.

Since the end of the Cold War, the UN Security Council has been far more active in establishing peace operations. In the early 1990s, crises in the Balkans, Somalia, and Cambodia led to a dramatic increase in missions. However, the debacle in Somalia and the failure of UN peacekeepers to intervene and prevent the 1994 genocide in Rwanda and or to stop the 1995 massacre in Srebrenica, Bosnia, led to a necessary skepticism about UN peacekeeping. With a number of troubling situations, many in Africa, receiving increasing attention in the media in recent years, however, the Security Council has found

U.S. Senate, July 23, 2008.

itself under pressure to respond and "do something." The response, for better or worse, has often been to establish a new peacekeeping operation.

The Security Council has approved over 40 new peace operations since 1990. Half of all current peacekeeping operations have been authorized by the Security Council since 2000. These post-1990 operations involved a dramatic expansion in scope, purpose, and responsibilities beyond traditional peace operations. Moreover, these missions reflected a change in the nature of conflict from interstate conflict between nations to intrastate conflict within states by authorizing missions focused on quelling civil wars.

This expansion of risk and responsibilities was justified by pointing out the international consequences of the conflict, such as refugees or preventing widespread conflict and instability. While such actions may be justified in some cases, they represent a dramatic shift from earlier doctrine. As a result, from a rather modest history of monitoring cease-fires, demilitarized zones, and post-conflict security, UN peace operations have expanded to include multiple responsibilities including more complex military interventions, civilian police duties, human rights interventions, reconstruction, overseeing elections, and post-conflict reconstruction.

At the end of May 2008, there were 17 active UN peacekeeping operations and another three political or peace-building operations directed and supported by the UN Department of Peacekeeping Operations (UNDPKO). Ten of these operations, including political missions, were in Africa (Burundi, Central African Republic and Chad, Côte d'Ivoire, Darfur, Democratic Republic of Congo, Ethiopia and Eritrea, Liberia, Sierra Leone, Sudan, Western Sahara); one was in the Caribbean (Haiti); three were in Europe (Cyprus, Georgia, and Kosovo); and the remaining six missions were in the Middle East (the Middle East, Lebanon, the Syrian Golan Heights) and in Asia (Afghanistan, East Timor, and India and Pakistan).

The size and expense of UN peace operations have risen to unprecedented levels. The 17 peacekeeping missions cited above involved some 88,000 uniformed personnel from 117 countries, including over 74,000 troops, 2,500 military observers, and 11,000 police personnel. There were also over 19,500 UN volunteers and other international and local civilian personnel employed in these 17 operations. Additionally, over 2,000 military observers, police, international and local civilians, and UN volunteers were involved in the three political or peace-building missions directed and supported by UNDPKO.

All told, including international and local civilian personnel and UN volunteers, the personnel involved in UN peacekeeping, political, or peace-building operations overseen by UNDPKO totaled more than 109,500 at the end of May 2008. These operations involved the deployment of more uniformed personnel than were deployed by any single nation in the world other than the United States.

This activity has also led to a dramatically increased budget. The approved budget for UNDPKO—just one department in the UN Secretariat—from July 1, 2007, to June 30, 2008, was approximately $6.8 billion. The projected budget for UN peacekeeping operations is $7.4 billion for the July 1, 2008, to June 30, 2009, fiscal year. This is a 10 percent increase over the previous budget and nearly a threefold increase in budget and personnel since 2003. By comparison, the annual peacekeeping budget is now triple the size of the annualized UN regular biennial 2008/2009 budget for the rest of the Secretariat.

In general, the U.S. has supported the expansion of UN peacekeeping. Multiple Administrations have concluded that it is in America's interest to support UN operations as a useful, cost-effective way to influence situations that affect the U.S. national interest but do not rise to the level of requiring direct U.S. intervention. Although the UN peacekeeping record includes significant failures, UN peace operations overall have proven to be a convenient multilateral means for addressing humanitarian concerns in situations where conflict or instability makes civilians vulnerable to atrocities, for promoting peace efforts, and for supporting the transition to democracy and post-conflict rebuilding.

The U.S. contributes the greatest share of funding for peacekeeping operations. The U.S. is assessed 22 percent of the UN regular budget, but is assessed over 26 percent of the UN peacekeeping budget. All permanent members of the Security Council—China, France, Russia, the United Kingdom, and the United States—are charged a premium above their regular assessment rate. However, none pay nearly what the U.S. is assessed. In 2008–2009, the UN assessment for the U.S. is just under 26 percent. China is assessed 3.15 percent, France is assessed 7.4 percent, Russia is assessed 1.4 percent, and the U.K. is assessed 7.8 percent. Thus, the U.S. is assessed more than all of the other permanent members combined. Japan and Germany, even though they are not permanent members of the Security Council, rank second and third in assessments at 16.6 percent and 8.6 percent, respectively.

Based on the UN's July 1, 2008, to June 30, 2008, budget projection for peacekeeping, the U.S. will be asked to pay over $1.9 billion for UN peacekeeping activities over that time. As a means of comparison, the 30-plus countries assessed the lowest rate of 0.0001 percent of the peacekeeping budget for 2008–2009 will be assessed $7,352 based on that projection.

Although the U.S. and other developed countries regularly provide lift and logistics support, many developed countries that possess trained personnel and other essential resources are generally reluctant to participate directly in UN peace operations. The five permanent members contribute a total of less than 6 percent of UN uniformed personnel. The U.S. contribution totaled 14 troops, 16 military observers, and 259 police. This is roughly comparable to Russia and the U.K., which contributed 358 and 299 uniformed personnel, respectively. China and France contributed more at 1,977 and 2,090 personnel.

The top 10 contributors of uniformed personnel to UN operations are nearly all developing countries: Pakistan (10,623); Bangladesh (9,037); India (8,862); Nigeria (5,218); Nepal (3,711); Ghana (3,239); Jordan (3,017); Rwanda (3,001); Italy (2,864); and Uruguay (2,617). A number of reasons account for this situation, including the fact that major contributors use UN participation as a form of training and income.

While the U.S. clearly should support UN peacekeeping operations when they support America's national interests, broadening UN peace operations into nontraditional missions like peace enforcement and the inability to garner broad international support in terms of troop contributions, logistics support, and funding raise legitimate questions as to whether or not the UN should be engaged in the current number of missions and whether these situations are best addressed through the UN or through regional, multilateral, or ad hoc efforts with Security Council support. Concerns are growing that the system for assessing the UN peacekeeping budget is inappropriate, given the far larger financial demands of this expanded role for UN peacekeeping. Such questions are primarily political questions that can be resolved only by the member states.

Outside of the political realm, however, is the fundamental question of whether the system as currently structured is capable of meeting its responsibilities. Indisputably, the unprecedented frequency and size of recent UN deployments and the resulting financial demands have challenged and overwhelmed the capabilities of the UN Department of Peacekeeping Operations, leading to serious problems of mismanagement, misconduct, poor planning, corruption, sexual abuse, unclear mandates, and other weaknesses. Let me highlight two notable problems.

Mismanagement, Fraud, and Corruption

The UN, as illustrated by the Oil-for-Food scandals and the more recent instances of mismanagement by UNDP [UN Development Programme] in North Korea, has proven to be susceptible to mismanagement, fraud, and corruption. [The food-for-oil scandal involved UN administrators profiting from the UN's oversight of the use of Iraq's oil revenues to buy food and medicine for Iraq.] This also applies to UN peacekeeping. The Secretariat procured over $1.6 billion in goods and services in 2005, mostly to support peacekeeping, which has more than quadrupled in size since 1999. An Office of Internal Oversight Services (OIOS) audit of $1 billion in DPKO procurement contracts over a six-year period found that at least $265 million was subject to waste, fraud, or abuse. The U.S. Government Accountability Office concluded:

> While the U.N. Department of Management is responsible for U.N. procurement, field procurement staff are instead supervised by the U.N. Department of Peacekeeping Operations, which currently lacks the expertise and capacities needed to manage field procurement activities.

In reaction to the OIOS audit, the Department of Management and the DPKO accepted a majority of the 32 OIOS audit recommendations for addressing the findings. However, a more recent report from earlier this year indicates that these new procedures may not be sufficient to prevent a recurrence of fraud and corruption. Specifically, the OIOS revealed earlier this year that it is investigating about 250 corruption cases ranging from sexual abuse by peacekeepers to financial irregularities. According to Inga-Britt Ahlenius, head of the OIOS, "We can say that we found mismanagement and fraud and corruption to an extent we didn't really expect." According to the report, $1.4 billion worth of peacekeeping contracts turned up "significant" corruption schemes involving more than $619 million, or 44 percent of the total value of the contracts. At the time of the report, the task force had looked at only seven of the 18 UN peacekeeping missions that were operational over the period of the investigation. A 2008 report on the audit of the UN mission in Sudan revealed tens of millions lost to mismanagement and waste and substantial indications of fraud and corruption.

Worse, even the OIOS seems to be susceptible to improper influence. Allegations were made in 2006 that UN peacekeepers had illegal dealings with Congolese militias, including gold smuggling and arms trafficking. According to the lead OIOS investigator in charge of investigating the charges against the UN peacekeepers in the Congo, he had found the allegations of abuses by Pakistani peacekeepers to be "credible," but the "the investigation was taken away from my team after we resisted what we saw as attempts to influence the outcome. My fellow team members and I were appalled to see that the oversight office's final report was little short of a whitewash." The BBC and Human Rights Watch have provided evidence that the UN covered up evidence of wrongdoing by its peacekeepers in Congo.

Sexual Misconduct

In recent years, there have been several harrowing reports of crimes committed by UN personnel, from rape to the forced prostitution of women and young girls, the most notorious of which have involved the UN Mission in the Democratic Republic of Congo. Indeed, allegations and confirmed incidents of sexual exploitation and abuse by UN personnel have become depressingly routine in Bosnia, Burundi, Cambodia, Congo, Guinea, Haiti, Kosovo, Liberia, Sierra Leone, and Sudan.

The alleged perpetrators of these abuses include UN military and civilian personnel from a number of UN member states involved in peace operations and from UN funds and programs. The victims are refugees—many of them children—who have been terrorized by years of war and look to the UN for safety and protection. In addition to the horrible mistreatment of those who are under the protection of the UN, sexual exploitation and abuse undermine the credibility of UN peace operations and must be addressed through an effective plan and commitment to end abuses and ensure accountability.

After intense lobbying by the U.S. Department of State and U.S. Mission to the United Nations since early 2004, as well as pressure from several key Members of Congress, the UN Secretariat agreed to adopt stricter requirements for peacekeeping troops and their contributing countries. The U.S. also helped the DPKO to publish a resource manual on trafficking for UN peacekeepers. In 2005, Prince Zeid Ra'ad Al-Hussein of Jordan, the Secretary-General's adviser on sexual exploitation and abuse by UN peacekeeping personnel, submitted his report to the Secretary-General with recommendations on how to address the sexual abuse problem, including imposing a uniform standard of conduct, conducting professional investigations, and holding troop-contributing countries accountable for the actions of their soldiers and for proper disciplinary action. In June 2005, the General Assembly adopted the recommendations in principle, and some recommendations have been implemented. For instance, contact and discipline teams are now present in most missions, and troops are now required to undergo briefing and training on behavior and conduct. Tragically, this does not seem to have addressed the problem adequately.

Only this past May, Save the Children accused aid workers and peace-keepers of sexually abusing young children in war zones and disaster zones in Ivory Coast, southern Sudan, and Haiti and going largely unpunished. UN peacekeepers were most likely to be responsible for abuse. According to a report by Save the Children, "Children as young as six are trading sex with aid workers and peacekeepers in exchange for food, money, soap and, in very few cases, luxury items such as mobile phones."

However, despite this action and then-Secretary-General Kofi Annan's announcement of a "zero tolerance" policy, the perpetrators of these crimes are very rarely punished, as was revealed in a January 2007 news report on UN abuses in southern Sudan. The standard memorandum of understanding between the UN and troop contributors clearly grants troop-contributing countries jurisdiction over military members participating in UN peace operations, but little is done if these countries fail to investigate, try, and punish those guilty of such crimes.

The problems of mismanagement, corruption, and misconduct cry out for fundamental reform of the UN peacekeeping structure to improve account-ability and transparency. However, corruption, mismanagement and sexual misconduct by UN peacekeepers are not the only problems with UN peace-keeping. The other problem is a political problem. The vast expansion of UN peacekeeping—with the possibility of even more operations on the horizon like the proposal for a new Somalia mission with up to 27,000 peacekeepers—has led some to point out that the UN Security Council has gone "mandate crazy" in its attempts to be seen as effective and "doing something." The will-ingness of the Security Council to approve missions where "there is no peace to keep"—such as Darfur, Somalia, or Chad—violates a dearly learned lesson that UN peacekeepers are not war fighters.

In general, the UN and its member states had accepted the fact—in the wake of the Somalia, Yugoslavia, Rwanda, and Sierra Leone missions in which there was no peace to keep—that UN peace operations should not include a mandate to enforce peace outside of limited circumstances and should focus instead on assisting countries to shift from conflict to a negotiated peace and from peace agreements to legitimate governance and development. As noted in the *Report of the Panel on United Nations Peace Operations* (the Brahimi Report)

> The United Nations does not wage war. Where enforcement action is required, it has consistently been entrusted to coalitions of willing States, with the authorization of the Security Council, acting under Chapter VII of the Charter.

Yet even situations short of war that may require a UN peace operation are still rife with danger, as illustrated by the nearly 2,500 peacekeepers that have been killed in operations since 1948. They also involve great demands in resources, management, and personnel. Indeed, it has increasingly strained the ability of countries willing to provide peacekeepers, especially in Darfur. Worse, this investment may not be helping the situation.

Dr. Greg Mills, Director of the Johannesburg-based Brenthurst Foundation, and Dr. Terence McNamee, Director of Publications at the Royal United Services Institute for Defence and Security Studies (RUSI), have conducted several cases studies of UN peacekeeping operations in a chapter in a forthcoming book. They have concluded that, in the cases of the Democratic Republic of Congo and Lebanon, it is an open question whether the UN peacekeeping mission has contributed to resolving the situation or exacerbating it.

- Mills and McNamee note that a 30-year United Nations presence has failed to resolve the deep-seated problems in Lebanon. The UN operation has failed to prevent a succession of Israeli incursions. Nor was the mission able to stop Hezbollah and other groups from using the Lebanese border to launch raids and rockets into Israel. The 12,000-plus UN troops currently in place following the 2006 Israeli intervention have not been instructed specifically to disarm the group. Ironically, Hezbollah is now in a stronger position, and the UN mission acts as a buffer to prevent any Israeli assault. Mills and McNamee note, "The problem in Lebanon is more profound than any deal-making or UN force can solve however. It goes to the heart of reconfiguring the state and its role in Lebanon."
- The Democratic Republic of Congo [DRC] is a state in name only. Decades of instability and insecurity have entrenched the view in Kinshasa that anything benefiting the periphery of the country is a threat. Instability is viewed as a political advantage in Kinshasa because it keeps potential rivals focused on each other rather than on the central government. As such, Kinshasa does little to aid the UN effort. Despite more than 19,000 UN military and civilian peacekeepers in Congo at an annual cost of over $1 billion, MONUC has not brought peace or stability. Eastern Congo, bordering Rwanda, Burundi, and Uganda, remains violent. According to Mills and McNamee, "Disarmament, pacification, demobilization and repatriation/reintegration programs could help to dilute the extent of the security threat to the civilian population. But this will require holding [DRC President] Kabila to task . . . removing the fig-leaf of respectability to his indecision and weakness in filling the vacuum with UN troops. But it will require fundamental, root-and-branch reform, with decentralization at its core."

In other cases, such as the UN missions in Cyprus and the Western Sahara established in 1964 and 1991, respectively, the UN presence is simply an historical palliative. The peacekeepers perform little in the way of keeping the peace. Nor does their presence seem to have contributed to the process for resolving the decades-long political standoff. Instead, the missions continue out of inertia and requests by parties to the conflict that they remain in place. It is an open question whether the UN presence has actually contributed to the intractability of the situation by providing the excuse not to develop a resolution to what is largely a political problem.

The next Administration should fundamentally re-evaluate all UN operations that date back to the early 1990s or earlier—some, like UNTSO in the Middle East and UNMOGIP in Kashmir, date back to the 1940s—to determine whether the UN is contributing to resolving the situation or retarding that process. These missions are generally small and among the least costly, but such a re-evaluation would send a welcome message of accountability and assessment that too often has been lacking in the rubber-stamp process of reauthorizing peacekeeping operations.

This is not to say that UN missions are never useful and should be rejected out of hand. UN missions have been successful in situations like Cambodia where it helped to restore stability following dictatorship and civil war. Indeed, no one wants another Rwanda, and the consequences of doing nothing may be unpalatable. But a long list of operations that have been less than successful indicates that the Security Council should be far more judicious when adopting decisions to intervene.

The situation in Darfur is particularly relevant. The U.S. has called the situation in Darfur "genocide." The UN did not come to that conclusion, but it did recognize the widespread human rights violations and suffering. After the African Union mission failed to curtail the violence and suffering, the UN adopted a resolution authorizing a joint AU/UN peacekeeping force despite ongoing conflict and considerable evidence that neither the rebels nor the government-backed forces were prepared to abide by a peace agreement. Protected by China's veto, Sudan also demanded that the peacekeepers be African. This has led to a severe constraint of available troops: There simply are not enough trained and capable African troops to meet the demand. As a result, Jan Eliasson, the Secretary-General's Special Envoy for Darfur, told the Security Council that the situation in Darfur had deteriorated despite the efforts of UN and African Union troops. The recent decision of the International Criminal Court to seek an indictment against Sudanese President Omar Al-Bashir may, if approved by the ICC pretrial chamber, lead to further complications.

In Darfur, the UN Security Council yielded to the pressure to act. Massive suffering was occurring and would likely have grown worse without UN backing and support for the AU peacekeeping effort. However, the Council accepted demands from Sudan that vastly complicate their efforts, such as restricting peacekeepers to African nations. It also entered a conflict situation against the lessons of its own experience. It compounded the error by failing to adopt clear objectives, metrics for success, and an exit strategy. Because of these failings, not to mention the potential for deterioration toward broader conflict or a stiffening of resolve by President Bashir if the ICC proceeds with its indictment, Darfur could very easily become the UN's next spectacular failure.

Recommendations

There are a number of steps the UN and the Security Council should adopt to address the weaknesses identified above.

- **Be more judicious in decisions to authorize UN peacekeeping operations.** The pressure to "do something" must not trump sensible consideration of whether a UN presence will improve or destabilize the situation, clearly establishing the objectives of the operations and ensuring that they are achievable, carefully planning the requirements for achieving those objectives and securing pledges for providing them prior to authorizing the operation, and demanding that an exit strategy be included to prevent the "perpetual mission" trap.

    This process should also apply in reauthorization of existing missions where there is often a rubber-stamp approach. If a mission has not achieved its objective or made evident progress toward that end after a lengthy period, the Council should assess whether it is serving a positive function. In its deliberations, however, the Council should recognize that short, easy missions are extremely rare. When authorizing a mission, the Council should recognize that it may be there for a lengthy period. If the Council seems unlikely to persevere, it should consider not approving the mission.

    Critically, this recommendation should not be construed as implying that all UN peacekeeping operations should or can be identical. On the contrary, differing circumstances often require differing approaches. Indeed, if peacekeeping missions are to be successful, the Council must be flexible in the makeup and composition of UN peacekeeping operations or in choosing to stand back in favor of a regional intervention or an ad hoc coalition if those approaches better fit the immediate situation. However, in the process of deciding to authorize a mission, the Council should not let an "emergency" override the prudent evaluation and assessment process necessary to make sure the prospective mission has the largest chance of success.

- **Transform the DPKO organizational structure to enable it to handle increased peace operations demands and plan for future operations more effectively.** This requires more direct involvement of the Security Council; more resources for staff, supplies, and training; and greatly improved oversight by a capable inspector general dedicated to peace operations.

    A key element of this should include transforming the DPKO to incorporate greater flexibility so that it can rapidly expand and contract to meet varying levels of peace operations activity. Current UN rules do not permit the necessary authority and discretion in hiring and shifting resources to meet priorities. A core professional military staff must be maintained and utilized, but the DPKO should also be able to rely on gratis military and other seconded professionals to meet exceptional demands on UN peace operations. This would readily provide the expertise and experience needed to assess the requirements of mandates under consideration, including troop numbers, equipment, timeline, and rules of engagement, both efficiently and realistically.

- **Build up peacekeeping capabilities around the world, particularly in Africa, and further develop a UN database of qualified, trained, pre-screened uniformed and civilian personnel available for UN operations.** The UN has no standing armed forces and is entirely dependent on member states to donate troops and other personnel to fulfill peace operation mandates. This is appropriate. Nations should maintain control of their armed forces and refuse to support the establishment of armed forces outside of direct national oversight and responsibility. However, the current arrangement results in an ad hoc system plagued by delays; inadequately trained personnel; insufficient numbers of military troops, military observers, civilian police, and civilian staff; inadequate planning; inadequate or non-functional equipment; and logistical gaps.

  The UN has established a Stand-by Arrangements System (UNSAS), wherein member states make conditional commitments to prepare and maintain specified resources (military formations, specialized personnel, services, material, and equipment) on "stand-by" in their home countries to fulfill specified tasks or functions for UN peace operations. This is their prerogative, but the resources committed under the UNSAS fall short of needs. To speed up deployment on missions, the UN would be well served to further develop a database of information on individuals' and units' past experience in UN operations; disciplinary issues; performance evaluations; expertise (e.g., language, engineering, and combat skills); and availability for deployment. In addition, U.S. efforts under the Global Peace Operations Initiative (GPOI) contribute significantly to bolstering the capacity and capabilities of regional troops, particularly in Africa, to serve as peacekeepers through the UN or regional organizations like the African Union.

- **Implement a modern logistics system and streamline procurement procedures so that missions receive what they need when they need it.** To be effective, procurement and contracting must "have a formal governance structure responsible for its oversight and direction," as former Under-Secretary-General for Management Catherine Bertini advised Congress in 2005. Critically, the new logistics system and the procurement system must be subject to appropriate transparency, rigorous accountability, and independent oversight accompanied by robust investigatory capabilities and a reliable system of internal justice.

  The new restructuring of UNDPKO into a Department of Peacekeeping Operations and a Department of Field Support, as proposed by Secretary-General Ban Ki-Moon and approved by the General Assembly, does not appear to have substantially improved peacekeeping procurement. This may be due to the fact that the new department did not receive requested positions or budget, but it also appears to be a case of a "paper reform" rather than an actual reform. Most of the same people remain in place, and it is uncertain that tasking or procedures have changed.

- **Implement mandatory, uniform standards of conduct for civilian and military personnel participating in UN peace operations.** If the UN is to take serious steps to end sexual exploitation, abuse, and other misconduct by peacekeepers, it must do more than adopt a UN code of conduct, issue manuals, and send abusers home. It should not necessarily involve yielding jurisdiction over personnel to the UN or non-national judicial authority, but it should entail commitments by member states to investigate, try, and punish their personnel in cases of misconduct.

Investigators should be granted full cooperation and access to witnesses, records, and sites where alleged crimes occurred so that trials can proceed. Equally important, the UN must be more willing to hold member countries to these standards. States that fail to fulfill their commitments to discipline their troops should be barred from providing troops for peace operations.

Conclusion

Today's hearing is very pertinent. UN peacekeeping is being conducted at unprecedented pace, scope, and ambition. Unsurprisingly, this activity has revealed numerous flaws, limitations, and weaknesses inherent in UN peacekeeping. Problems with UN peacekeeping are serious and need to be addressed, and the Administration and Congress need to consider carefully any requests by the United Nations for additional funding for a system in which procurement problems have wasted millions of dollars and sexual abuse by peacekeepers is still occurring. Without fundamental reform, these problems will likely continue and expand, undermining the UN's credibility and ability to accomplish one of its primary missions—maintaining international peace and security.

UN peacekeeping operations can be useful and successful if entered into with an awareness of the limitations and weaknesses of UN peacekeeping. This awareness is crucial, because there seems little indication that the demand for UN peacekeeping will fall in the foreseeable future.

William J. Durch

Peace and Stability Operations: Challenges and Opportunities for the Next U.S. Administration

Introduction

Peace seems like it ought to be self-enforcing, but the most peaceful states are those with effective police—and fair laws, competent courts, and consent of the governed. States emerging from civil war usually have none of these. Sustaining whatever fragile peace they initially achieve may require outside help, and that help may be needed for several years. In 1995, for example, the North Atlantic Treaty Organization (NATO) poured 60,000 troops into Bosnia to cement the Dayton Accords; today, 2,300 troops and police remain, under European Union (EU) command. So the effort is less but the presence remains. Other places where peacekeepers go are much bigger and more dangerous than Bosnia was when NATO deployed there. Bosnia itself was a very danger-ous place before U.S. pressure and NATO air strikes brought its own civil war to a halt, a war where UN peacekeepers had earlier been deployed with nei-ther the power nor the mandate to create and sustain peace. Yet that earlier operation was authorized by unanimous votes of the UN Security Council, votes in which the United States participated; votes that helped to discredit UN peacekeeping in the West for the remainder of the 1990s, because they sent UN forces into dangerous combat environments with which the United Nations cannot cope.

In this decade, the UN found its feet once again as major reforms in how peacekeeping is managed and mandated began to take hold. But in recent years, and especially the past twelve months, the Security Council has again begun to overuse its tools, with the result that UN peacekeepers find them-selves in situations better suited to combat forces. One of the lessons of the 1990s is that peacekeepers *must* be able to defend themselves and their man-dates when subject to violent tactical challenge, but such challenges must be balanced by high-level, political acceptance of the UN's presence. The Demo-cratic Republic of Congo (or DRC) is one such dangerous place where the UN nonetheless has the support of the elected government and works closely with it against various violent opponents of the peace, especially in this large coun-try's lawless east. Darfur, Sudan, on the other hand, is a dangerous place where

U.S. Senate, July 23, 2008.

the government gives little more than lip service to the UN presence and does everything it can to delay and obstruct its deployment, up to the possible use of proxy forces to attack UN personnel.

Most peace operations in difficult places struggle to attract the man-power and funds they need to create real change over time. The United Nations promotes stability in the DRC, for example, with one-third as many troops as NATO started with in Bosnia, spread over an area six times as large that is teeming with well-armed and vicious militias. At the end of May, the UN deployed 88,000 troops and police globally. Few of those deployed in its toughest operations (which are mostly in Africa) come from developed states, which are the UN's major funders. Not only are in-kind contributions to UN operations from these states rather rare but late payments keep UN operations perennially underfunded. At the end of May, 11 months into its peacekeeping fiscal year, the UN was still short $1.6 billion on a $6.8 billion peacekeeping budget. In one of life's greater ironies, the UN may not borrow funds to cover that shortfall, a rule enforced by the most indebted government on the planet: our own.

As imperfect as the United Nations may be, people around the globe understand, accept, and applaud most UN actions. Compared to regional organizations and ad hoc coalitions, the UN has both broader political legiti-macy, greater political reach, and a deeper logistics network supporting both humanitarian relief and peace operations—a network that leans heavily on private sector service providers. But the United Nations also needs consistent U.S. political, financial, and material support to make its operations work. Each of these is well worth strengthening.

Early in the next Administration, the President should begin that strengthening process by:

- Affirming that the United States and the United Nations share com-mon goals in expanding the writ of human rights and realizing human dignity, which in turn requires international peace and individual human security.
- Offering strong support—in cash and in kind—to every UN peace operation for which it casts its vote in the Security Council, setting an example for others by promptly contributing the U.S. share of UN peacekeeping costs.
- Supporting the continued restructuring and strengthening of UN headquarters offices that plan and support peace operations.
- Pledging strong and sustained U.S. diplomatic and political sup-port to UN peacekeeping operations, especially in volatile states and regions.
- Promising temporary U.S. military support, in collaboration with its NATO allies, for UN operations that experience trouble from local spoilers or terrorist action.
- Continuing to train foreign peacekeepers, contingent on their gov-ernments' willingness to discipline troops who violate international humanitarian law.
- Announcing that the United States will expand its own capacity to con-tribute to the non-military elements of peace and stability operations.

A Brief History of Peace and Stability Operations

Contemporary peace operations got their start after World War II, when some 200 unarmed military observers wearing UN armbands patrolled cease-fire lines between India and Pakistan and armistice lines around the new state of Israel. Six decades later, 110,000 troops, police, and civilian personnel in 20 UN missions on four continents use presence, persuasion, and modern weapons to support the rebuilding of peace under tough conditions. The African Union-UN "hybrid" mission in Darfur (UNAMID) will, when fully deployed, drive that total near 130,000. NATO manages a further 50,000 peacekeepers in Kosovo and Afghanistan, the EU manages 2,300 in Bosnia, and the African Union (AU) managed about 7,000 in Darfur through the end of 2007, when that force merged into UNAMID. Washington has authorized, endorsed, or supported all of these operations through its votes in the UN Security Council or on NATO's North Atlantic Council.

In the past two years, in fact, the United States has supported a substantial increase in the size, use, and deployment of UN peacekeeping around the globe, including:

- A new peacekeeping mission in Somalia;
- A seven-fold expansion of the UN's peacekeeping mission in Lebanon;
- The four-fold expansion of the peacekeeping mission in Darfur;
- Reauthorization of the UN's large peacekeeping missions in Haiti and Liberia;
- A renewed peacekeeping mission for East Timor; and
- New missions in Chad, the Central African Republic, and Nepal.

Peacekeeping today costs $10 to $12 billion annually, not including counterinsurgency in Iraq or Afghanistan. The UN's peacekeeping budget accounts for just over half of that total and Washington pays for roughly one-quarter of the UN peacekeeping budget.

The costs of UN peacekeeping operations are pro-rated among member states according to a "peacekeeping scale of assessment," which is based on states' shares of the regular UN budget. The five permanent members of the Security Council each pay a 20% larger share of peacekeeping costs than they do of the UN Regular Budget, given their special responsibility under the UN Charter for international peace and security, and because they can veto any operation they dislike. UN operations, as currently conducted, are a relative bargain for their major funders, costing less than one-fifth of what they would cost if conducted exclusively by the funders' own military forces.

The costs of other peacekeeping missions are borne primarily by the troop contributors. NATO and the EU collectively fund mostly minor "common costs" for their missions. Occasional subsidies from wealthy states allow less-wealthy states to send troops to non-UN operations. Substantial outside cash and in-kind support (airlift and civilian contractors) have enabled the AU, for example, to deploy and support its observer force in Darfur.

The Case for International Cooperation

In deciding how best to defend themselves and their interests, all states face tough policy choices. Small, poor states have few options and often find their choices dictated by others. Big, rich states have more choices—but each choice comes with consequences. America can act on its own in many matters of peace and security, but there are times when acting in concert—through coalitions, alliances, regional groupings, or global institutions—is not only useful but necessary, because even a superpower has finite resources, as the US experience in Iraq and Afghanistan continue to demonstrate. And where resources needed to shore up the peace can be found among many implementing partners and organizations, smart engagement argues for leveraging those resources to accomplish common goals and to better manage hard problems multilaterally.

The United States has found it increasingly cost-effective and politically helpful to lean on other states and organizations to help it advance shared strategic interests in international peace, security, justice, and prosperity. The available forms of collaboration have complementary strengths: Coalitions of the willing are better at suppressing violence but typically lack staying power and means of joint finance. Regional organizations have greater legitimacy and cohesion when working within their regions but risk losing both when they venture farther afield. The UN cannot handle full-scale combat since it lacks both full control over the forces it receives and the cohesion of the best alliances and coalitions, but what it lacks in combat power, the UN makes up for in its legitimacy and staying power.

Compared to regional organizations and ad hoc alliances of states, the UN has greater political reach and a deeper network supporting humanitarian relief as well as peace operations. Those who think of the UN system as desk-bound should witness its fieldwork firsthand, since more UN staff members work in field postings than in headquarters. Peacekeeping operations are supported by a global system of financial assessments that enable the UN to tap the strengths of the private sector, with more than 100 "systems contracts" in place for essential mission support. Given the growth in this area, it is a sure bet that the next Administration will face serious questions of resource allocation regarding the UN and global peace and stability operations.

Coping with Growth in Peacekeeping Operations

In the face of explosive growth in UN peacekeeping over the past decade, the first question is whether the world, and the United States in particular, are providing sufficient resources to support this growth—which they have promoted. The answer to this question would have to be "no." The surge in UN peacekeeping has not been met with steady funding, by commensurate increases in the number of staff in the UN Department of Peacekeeping Operations (DPKO), or in the number of troops or police volunteered to the UN by its richest members for the UN's toughest missions. The result has been forces of highly variable professionalism. In the past three years, the UN has asked

states to take back hundreds of troops and police as investigations have implicated them in sexual abuse and exploitation of local populations.

The United States chronically under-budgets its share of UN peacekeeping costs, even as it votes for more and expanded peacekeeping missions on
the Security Council. As of February 2008, the U.S. had built up $1.2 billion in
essentially permanent prior-year debt for UN peacekeeping and was likely to
fall at least another $500 million short in its peacekeeping dues for 2007–08.

Beyond this challenge, ever since operations in Somalia (1992–93), the
United States has declined to provide troops for the riskier UN peacekeeping
forces. The Force Commander and majority of UN forces in Haiti (1995–96)
were American but the last U.S. military unit to serve in a UN-led mission came
home in 1999. Subsequent U.S. non-participation means that our government
has no military commanders in any current UN field missions and dwindling institutional memory of how UN operations work. U.S. contributions
of police officers to UN operations also have dwindled in this decade, from
849 in December 2000 to 230 this June. The second big question is whether
the world and the United States are lining up the right kinds of capabilities
to meet the world's needs in the peace and stability arena. In peace operations, the military's real exit strategy is successful peacebuilding, or "transition
and reconstruction." This involves many tasks—from arranging and supervis-
ing elections, training novice lawmakers, and jumpstarting economic activity
to rebuilding police forces and promoting independent judiciaries—all tasks
for which armed forces are poorly suited or totally inappropriate. Successful
peacebuilding, and therefore a successful exit strategy, require complementary
civilian capacity working alongside the military.

What Washington Should Do:
Recommendations for Action

As UN peacekeeping's largest and most influential donor, the U.S. government,
under a new Administration, should make it clear, very early on, that it supports an effective UN that, in turn, supports international peace and security
in irreplaceable ways—not as a tool of U.S. policy but as a venue for leveraging
scarce funds and people toward a just public order that improves people's lives
and contributes to our national security. Early in the new term, while the UN
Special Committee on Peacekeeping Operations is in session, the President
should set out the following principles and policy goals:

- **Affirm that the United States and the United Nations share
  common goals in expanding the writ of human rights and realizing human dignity, which in turn requires international peace
  and individual human security.** The majority of UN member states
  are poor, less than free, and often difficult to deal with. As a global
  institution, the UN includes the world's worst human rights offend-
  ers but also its strongest human rights proponents. Moreover, the UN
  Charter and the Covenant on Civil and Political Rights reflect Western
  values on a global stage.

The General Assembly regularly votes budgets for peace operations that Washington sees fit to support in the Security Council, and those budgets are cleared first by a committee of 16 states on which the United States has nearly always had a strong voice. The UN system also provides a wide range of services through its operational agencies that work beyond the realm of high politics and security, in food aid, refugee support, human rights support, global public health, vaccinations against childhood diseases, and nuclear non-proliferation.

- **Offer strong support—in cash and in kind—to every UN peace operation for which it casts its vote in the Security Council and set an example for others by promptly contributing the U.S. share of UN peacekeeping costs.** The UN is precluded from borrowing to finance its operations, so when the Security Council votes to support a mission, the UN must rely on Member States' payments toward the mission's "assessed" budget to get things underway. The Administration frequently under-budgets for UN peacekeeping operations, and the Office of Management and Budget in recent years has cut State Department requests, making it up later with "supplemental" requests. This sleight-of-hand approach means that money shortages have driven U.S. dealings with the UN on matters of peace and security that should have been driven by U.S. interests. Even UN missions launched with urgent U.S. backing may not receive U.S. funds for months unless they can hitch a ride on a timely supplemental in the Congress. U.S. delays encourage other member nations to hold back funds. The bottom line? Mission deployments slow down to match the flow of funds, jeopardizing the people, places, and peace they are intended to protect.
- **Support the continued restructuring and strengthening of the UN headquarters offices that plan and support peace operations.** Secretary-General Ban-Ki Moon proposed, and the General Assembly approved, splitting the Department of Peacekeeping Operations into two parts, one (which keeps the old name) that is focused on policy, strategy, and planning, and another (the Department of Field Support) that is focused on finance, personnel, logistics, and communications. The General Assembly also agreed to add 287 staff to UN Headquarters support of peacekeeping, bringing the total New York staff to about 1,200, to manage up to 130,000 personnel in the field. Its cost, together with that of the UN's main peacekeeping logistics base at Brindisi, Italy, is five percent of the UN's peacekeeping budget. It is difficult to find any other agency (or company) in defense and security that runs on five percent overhead.
- **Pledge strong and sustained U.S. diplomatic and political support to UN peacekeeping operations, especially in volatile states and regions.** Every successful peace operation has had the strong support of at least one great power. Such support does not guarantee success, but its absence is a near guarantee of failure.
- **Promise temporary U.S. military support, in collaboration with its NATO allies, for UN operations that experience trouble from local spoilers or terrorist activities.** In spring 2000, in Sierra Leone, Britain turned a non-combatant evacuation operation into a mini-counterinsurgency campaign against the armed gangs who had

threatened both the country's fragile peace and a wobbly UN peace-keeping operation. Most of the British troops withdrew within four months, leaving behind a training mission to rebuild Sierra Leone's army. The UN operation restructured itself and ended up doing a creditable job, withdrawing in 2005. In 2004, in Haiti, U.S. armed forces led a coalition of the willing that preceded a UN operation, instead of serving in parallel. There is no good reason why such U.S. deployments could not be made in parallel, however, as Britain and the EU have done, should a UN operation run into trouble.

- **Continue training foreign peacekeepers, contingent on their governments' willingness to discipline troops who violate international humanitarian law.** The U.S. supports the G8's Global Peace Operations Initiative, which aims to train 75,000 peacekeepers, primarily in Africa, by 2010. This is a valuable program worth sustaining and extending, but it could also be used to give the UN better leverage over troop-contributing states whose troops commit crimes while on UN duty. The U.S. government should tie continued assistance under this and similar initiatives to recipients' demonstrated willingness to discipline troops who violate their own military codes of justice or UN standards of conduct while serving in UN operations.

- **Announce that the United States will expand its own capacity to contribute to the non-military elements of peace and stability operations.** This includes police personnel, political advisors, and civilian substantive experts who specialize, for example, in infrastructure repair, human rights, or de-mining. In the past two years, the US government has taken important steps toward the goal of building its non-military capabilities for stabilization and reconstruction. The next Administration should reinforce this nascent interagency process for recruiting, training, and deploying civilian personnel, acting on the knowledge that effective "transition and reconstruction" programs are the best exit strategy for peacekeepers—our own and everyone else's.

Lives and Leadership: Both on the Line

For nearly half a century, Washington was the recognized leader of the free world, earning that distinction by investing in and protecting the freedom of others. In the new century, as in the last, alternatives to western-style liberty and self rule are being offered to—or forced upon—peoples in Asia, Africa, Latin America, and the borderlands of Europe, especially in countries recently torn apart by war. Preserving liberty and fostering democracy among such countries is critical to America's interests. It is too big a job for any one country to shoulder alone, but by working with allies and institutions like the UN, we can share that burden and earn back the respect of the world.

POSTSCRIPT

Is UN Peacekeeping Seriously Flawed?

The year 2010 marked the 62nd anniversary of UN peacekeeping operations. The first UN peacekeepers were sent to the Middle East to monitor the truce between Israel and the Arab countries in 1948, and between then and late 2010, 64 more missions were created. These efforts drew more than 9 million troops, police, and other participants from 118 countries. More than 2400 have been killed during UN service. With 16 missions under way and about 124,000 armed peacekeepers and supporting civilian staff in the field, 2008 was also a record year for the number of UN peacekeeping operations. The UN peacekeeping budget for 2010 was approximately $8 billion. The U.S. assessment according to the UN's formula based on national wealth was 27 percent of that total, or nearly $2.2 billion. That is actually lower than it would be, but despite a legal obligation under the UN Charter to pay, Congress as of 2008 capped the U.S. payment at 27 percent (up from 25 percent). Moreover, Congress sometimes appropriates less than what is due, and the United States is about $1 billion in arrears on its payments. There are some complaints about the size of the UN peacekeeping budget and the UN contribution. However, the UN peacekeeping budget for 2010 equaled only about 50 cents for every $100 spent that year by countries of their own militaries. As for the U.S. contribution, even if fully funded it would have equaled less than what Washington spends every day on the U.S. military.

UN peacekeeping also continues to struggle with the political realities that so often limit its effectiveness. The reluctance of China and Russia to vote for a large, well-equipped, substantially empowered force is one. The reluctance of countries to contribute troops, financial restraints, and other problems also persist. Although the Security Council has authorized a UN force of over 32,000 troops and police for Darfur to aid the African Union peacekeeping effort there, as of August 2010, only a bit more than 15,000 troops and police were on duty. Equipment is especially hard to come by. The UN force is said to need 19 heavy-lift helicopters. Not a single one has been offered by a member country.

What needs to be done continues to be the main UN peacekeeping issue. There are many proposals, but not the political will to implement them. The veto-related difficulty of getting Security Council agreement is one major hurdle, but neither the United States nor any of the other countries with a veto is willing to give up their veto powers. A permanent UN force is another proposal, but few countries are willing to fund or permanently attach troop units to it. Whatever one thinks of UN peacekeeping, another issue is alternatives. If it is inadequate and substantial improvements are politically impossible, then what? Would the world be better off without UN peacekeepers?

To learn more, one "must" Web site is that of the UN's Department of Peacekeeping Operations at http://www.un.org/Depts/dpko/dpko/. A source of current research is *International Peacekeeping,* a journal published quarterly by Routledge. Beginning in 2009, the annual *International Peacekeeping: The Yearbook of International Peace Operations* published by Martinus Mijhoff was transformed into the quarterly *Journal of International Peacekeeping.* An overview of peacekeeping is available in Alex J. Bellamy, Paul Williams, and Stuart Griffin, *Understanding Peacekeeping* (Polity, 2010). A recent look at how to properly judge the success or failure of UN peacekeeping operations is Paul F. Diehl and Daniel Druckman, *Evaluating Peace Operations* (Lynne Rienner, 2010). Two of the most recent scholarly books on this topic are Donald C. F. Daniel, Patricia Taft, and Sharon Wiharta (eds.), *Peace Operations: Trends, Progress, and Prospects* (Georgetown University Press, 2008); and Virginia Page Fortna, *Does Peacekeeping Work?: Shaping Belligerents' Choices after Civil War* (Princeton University Press, 2008), which concludes that indeed peacekeeping does work.

Questions for Critical Thinking and Reflection

1. President Obama has asked Congress not only to fully meet U.S. peacekeeping dues but also to pay off the U.S. arrears. Do you support that?
2. It is currently against U.S. law for U.S. troops to serve in any UN peacekeeping operation that is not commanded by an American officer. Is that a good policy?
3. Would it be a good idea to create a standing UN military force of perhaps 10,000 troops that could quickly be dispatched to prevent conflict or restore peace?

ISSUE 17

Is U.S. Refusal to Join the International Criminal Court Wise?

YES: Brett Schaefer and Steven Groves, from "The U.S. Should Not Join the International Criminal Court," Backgrounder on International Organization, The Heritage Foundation (August 18, 2009)

NO: Jonathan F. Fanton, from "The Challenge of International Justice," Remarks to the U.S. Military Academy at West Point, New York (May 5, 2008)

ISSUE SUMMARY

YES: Brett D. Schaefer, the Jay Kingham fellow in international regulatory affairs at the Heritage Foundation, and Steven Groves, the Bernard and Barbara Lomas fellow in the Margaret Thatcher Center for Freedom, a division of the Kathryn and Shelby Cullom Davis Institute for International Studies at The Heritage Foundation, contend that although the court's supporters have a noble purpose, there are a number of reasons to be cautious and concerned about how ratification of the Rome Statute would affect U.S. sovereignty and how ICC action could affect politically precarious situations around the world.

NO: Jonathan F. Fanton, president of the John D. and Catherine T. MacArthur Foundation, which is headquartered in Chicago, IL, and is among the world's largest independent foundations, maintains that creation of the International Court of Justice is an important step toward creating a more just world, and that the fear that many Americans have expressed about the court has not materialized.

Historically, international law has focused primarily on countries. More recently, individuals have increasingly become subject to international law. The first major step in this direction was the convening of the Nuremberg and Tokyo war crimes trials after World War II to try German and Japanese military and civilian leaders charged with various war crimes. There were no subsequent war crimes tribunals until the 1990s when the United Nations (UN) established two of them. One sits in The Hague, the Netherlands, and deals with the horrific events in Bosnia. The other tribunal is in Arusha, Tanzania, and provides justice for the genocidal massacres in Rwanda. These tribunals have indicted numerous people for war crimes and have convicted and imprisoned many of them. Nevertheless, there was a widespread feeling that such ad hoc tribunals needed to be replaced by a permanent international criminal tribunal.

In 1996, the UN convened a conference in Rome to do just that. At first the United States was supportive, but it favored a very limited court that could only prosecute and hear cases referred to it by the UN Security Council (where the United States had a veto) and, even then, could only try individuals with the permission of the defendant's home government. Most countries disagreed, but in 1998 the Rome conference voted overwhelmingly to create a relatively strong court. The Rome Statute of the International Criminal Court (ICC) gives the ICC jurisdiction over wars of aggression, genocide, and other crimes, but only if the home country of an alleged perpetrator fails to act.

Although the ICC treaty was open for signature in July 1998, President Bill Clinton showed either ambivalence or a desire not to have it injected as an issue into the 2000 presidential election by waiting until December 31, 2000, to have a U.S. official sign the treaty. If Clinton had his doubts, his successor, George W. Bush, did not. He was adamantly opposed to the treaty. As directed by the White House, State Department official John R. Bolton sent a letter dated May 6, 2002, to UN Secretary General Kofi Annan informing him that "in connection with the Rome Statute of the International Criminal Court . . . , the United States does not intend to become a party to the treaty . . . [and] has no legal obligations arising from its signature on December 31, 2000." The Bush administration also launched an effort to persuade other countries to sign "Article 98" agreements by which countries agree not to surrender U.S. citizens to the ICC.

The letter formally notifying the UN that the United States does not intend to become a party to the Rome Statute also ended any U.S. participation in the workings of the court. In the first reading, Brett Schaefer and Steven Groves review the ICC's legal implications and assess its operation so far. As a result, they conclude that although the court reflects an admirable desire to hold war criminals accountable for their terrible crimes, the ICC is so flawed that it would be unwise for the United States to join it. In the second reading Jonathan F. Fanton also reviews the evolution of the ICC and comes to a different conclusion. He says he is convinced that the United States and its armed forces have nothing to fear from the ICC and much to both offer to and gain from its success.

YES

Brett Schaefer and
Steven Groves

The U.S. Should Not Join the International Criminal Court

The idea of establishing an international court to prosecute serious international crimes—war crimes, crimes against humanity, and genocide—has long held a special place in the hearts of human rights activists and those hoping to hold perpetrators of terrible crimes to account. In 1998, that idea became reality when the Rome Statute of the International Criminal Court was adopted at a diplomatic conference convened by the U.N. General Assembly. The International Criminal Court (ICC) was formally established in 2002 after 60 countries ratified the statute. The ICC was created to prosecute war crimes, crimes against humanity, genocide, and the as yet undefined crime of aggression. Regrettably, although the court's supporters have a noble purpose, there are a number of reasons to be cautious and concerned about how ratification of the Rome Statute would affect U.S. sovereignty and how ICC action could affect politically precarious situations around the world.

Among other concerns, past U.S. Administrations concluded that the Rome Statute created a seriously flawed institution that lacks prudent safeguards against political manipulation, possesses sweeping authority without accountability to the U.N. Security Council, and violates national sovereignty by claiming jurisdiction over the nationals and military personnel of non-party states in some circumstances. These concerns led President Bill Clinton to urge President George W. Bush not to submit the treaty to the Senate for advice and consent necessary for ratification. After extensive efforts to change the statute to address key U.S. concerns failed, President Bush felt it necessary to "un-sign" the Rome Statute by formally notifying the U.N. Secretary-General that the U.S. did not intend to ratify the treaty and was no longer bound under international law to avoid actions that would run counter to the intent and purpose of the treaty. Subsequently, the U.S. took a number of steps to protect its military personnel, officials, and nationals from ICC claims of jurisdiction.

Until these and other concerns are fully addressed, the Obama Administration should resist pressure to "re-sign" the Rome Statute, eschew cooperation with the ICC except when U.S. interests are affected, and maintain the existing policy of protecting U.S. military personnel, officials, and nationals from the court's illegitimate claims of jurisdiction. Nor should the Obama Administration seek ratification of the Rome Statute prior to the 2010 review, and

From *The Heritage Foundation Backgrounder*, August 18, 2009. Copyright © 2009 by The Heritage Foundation. Reprinted by permission.

then only if the Rome Statute and the ICC and its procedures are amended to address all of the serious concerns that led past U.S. Administrations to oppose ratification of the Rome Statute.

Background

The United States has long championed human rights and supported the ideal that those who commit serious human rights violations should be held accountable. Indeed, it was the United States that insisted—over Soviet objections—that promoting basic human rights and fundamental freedoms be included among the purposes of the United Nations. The United States also played a lead role in championing major international efforts in international humanitarian law, such as the Geneva Conventions.

The U.S. has supported the creation of international courts to prosecute gross human rights abuses. It pioneered the Nuremburg and Tokyo tribunals to prosecute atrocities committed during World War II. Since then, the U.S. was a key supporter of establishing the ad hoc International Criminal Tribunal for the former Yugoslavia (ICTY) and International Criminal Tribunal for Rwanda (ICTR), which were both approved by the Security Council.

Continuing its long support for these efforts, the U.S. initially was an eager participant in the effort to create an International Criminal Court in the 1990s. However, once negotiations began [in 1998] on the final version of the Rome Statute, America's support waned because many of its concerns were ignored or opposed outright. According to David J. Scheffer, chief U.S. negotiator at the 1998 Rome conference:

> In Rome, we indicated our willingness to be flexible. . . . Unfortunately, a small group of countries, meeting behind closed doors in the final days of the Rome conference, produced a seriously flawed take-it-or-leave-it text, one that provides a recipe for politicization of the court and risks deterring responsible international action to promote peace and security.

In the end, despite persistent efforts to amend the Rome Statute to alleviate U.S. concerns, the conference rejected most of the changes proposed by the U.S., and the final document was approved over U.S. opposition.

Since the approval of the Rome Statute in 1998, U.S. policy toward the ICC has been clear and consistent: The U.S. has refused to join the ICC because it lacks prudent safeguards against political manipulation, possesses sweeping authority without accountability to the U.N. Security Council, and violates national sovereignty by claiming jurisdiction over the nationals and military personnel of non-party states in some circumstances.

The United States is not alone in its concerns about the ICC. As of August 6, 2009, only 110 of the 192 U.N. member states had ratified the Rome Statute. In fact, China, India, and Russia are among the other major powers that have refused to ratify the Rome Statute out of concern that it unduly infringes on their foreign and security policy decisions—issues rightly reserved to sovereign governments and over which the ICC should not claim authority.

The ICC's Record

The International Criminal Court has a clear legal lineage extending back to the Nuremburg and Tokyo trials and ad hoc tribunals, such as the ICTY and the ICTR, which were established by the U.N. Security Council in 1993 and 1994, respectively. However, the ICC is much broader and more independent than these limited precedents. Its authority is not limited to disputes between governments as is the case with the International Court of Justice (ICJ) or to a particular jurisdiction as is the case with national judiciaries. Nor is its authority limited to particular crimes committed in a certain place or period of time as was the case with the post-World War II trials and the Yugoslavian and Rwandan tribunals.

Instead, the ICC claims jurisdiction over individuals committing genocide, crimes against humanity, war crimes, and the undefined crime of aggression. This jurisdiction extends from the entry into force of the Rome Statute in July 2002 and applies to all citizens of states that have ratified the Rome Statute. However, it also extends to individuals from countries that are not party to the Rome Statute if the alleged crimes occur on the territory of an ICC party state, the non-party government invites ICC jurisdiction, or the U.N. Security Council refers the case to the ICC.

International lawyers Lee Casey and David Rivkin point out that the ICC is a radical departure from previous international courts [because] "It has jurisdiction over individuals, including elected or appointed government officials, and its judgments may be directly enforced against them, regardless of their own national constitutions or court systems."

> Moreover, the court's structure establishes few, if any, practical external checks on the ICC's authority. Among the judges' responsibilities are determining whether the prosecutor may proceed with a case and whether a member state has been "unwilling or unable genuinely to carry out the investigation or prosecution," which would trigger the ICC's jurisdiction under the principle of "complementarity," which is designed to limit the court's power and avoid political abuse of its authority. Thus, the various arms of the ICC are themselves the only real check on its authority.

Even though the Rome Statute entered into force in July 2002, there is little concrete basis for judging the ICC's performance. Shortly after its formal establishment, the ICC began receiving its first referrals. Currently, the ICC has opened four cases, involving situations in the Democratic Republic of Congo (DRC), Uganda, the Central African Republic, and Darfur, Sudan.

As an institution, the ICC has performed little, if any, better than the ad hoc tribunals that it was created to replace. Like the Rwandan and Yugoslavian tribunals, the ICC is slow to act. The ICC prosecutor took six months to open an investigation in Uganda, two months with the DRC, over a year with Darfur, and nearly two years with the Central African Republic. It has yet to conclude a full trial cycle more than seven years after being created. Moreover, like the ad hoc tribunals, the ICC can investigate and prosecute crimes only after the fact. The alleged deterrent effect of a standing international criminal court has not ended atrocities in the DRC, Uganda, the Central African Republic, or Darfur, where cases are ongoing. Nor has it deterred atrocities by Burma against its own people, crimes committed during Russia's 2008 invasion of Georgia (an ICC party), ICC party Venezuela's support of leftist guerillas in Colombia, or any of a number of other situations around the world where war crimes or crimes against humanity may be occurring.

Another problem is that the ICC lacks a mechanism to enforce its rulings and is, therefore, entirely dependent on governments to arrest and transfer perpetrators to the court. However, such arrests can have significant diplomatic consequences, which can greatly inhibit the efficacy of the court in pursuing its warrants and prosecuting outstanding cases. The most prominent example is Sudanese President Bashir's willingness to travel to other countries on official visits—thus far only to non-ICC states—despite the ICC arrest warrant. This flaw was also present with the ICTY and the ICTR, although they could at least rely on a Security Council resolution mandating international cooperation in enforcing their arrest warrants. In contrast, the Nuremburg and Tokyo tribunals were established where the authority of the judicial proceedings could rely on Allied occupation forces to search out, arrest, and detain the accused.

The Myth of Bush Administration Intransigence

The U.S. refusal to ratify the Rome Statute has been mischaracterized by ICC proponents as solely a Bush Administration policy. In fact, the Clinton Administration initiated the U.S. policy of distancing itself from the ICC. According to David J. Scheffer, Ambassador-at-Large for War Crimes Issues under the Clinton Administration:

> Foreign officials and representatives of non-governmental organizations tried to assure us in Rome that procedural safeguards built into the treaty—many sought successfully by the United States—meant that there would be no plausible risk to U.S. soldiers. We could not share in such an optimistic view of the infallibility of an untried institution. . . .

President Clinton himself acknowledged the treaty's "significant flaws" and recommended that President Bush not submit the treaty to the Senate for advice and consent. When President Clinton authorized the U.S. delegation to sign the Rome Statute on December 31, 2000, it was not to pave the way for U.S. ratification, but solely to give the U.S. an opportunity to address American concerns about the ICC. As Clinton said at the time in his signing statement:

> In signing, however, we are not abandoning our concerns about significant flaws in the treaty. In particular, we are concerned that when the court comes into existence, it will not only exercise authority over personnel of states that have ratified the treaty but also claim jurisdiction over personnel of states that have not. With signature, however, we will be in a position to influence the evolution of the court. Without signature, we will not.

After adoption of the Rome Statute in 1998, both the Clinton and Bush Administrations sought to rectify the parts of the statute that precluded U.S. participation. Specifically, the U.S. actively participated in the post-Rome preparatory commissions, hoping to address its concerns. As former U.S. Under Secretary for Political Affairs Marc Grossman noted:

> After the United States voted against the treaty in Rome, the U.S. remained committed and engaged—working for two years to help shape the court and to seek the necessary safeguards to prevent a politicization of the process. While we were able to make some improvements during our active participation in the UN Preparatory Commission meetings in New York, we were ultimately unable [to] obtain the remedies necessary to overcome our fundamental concerns. . . .

The consequences of failing to change the objectionable provisions of the Rome Statute became acute when the 60th country ratified the treaty, causing the statute to enter into force in July 2002. Faced with the prospect of a functioning International Criminal Court that could assert jurisdiction over U.S. soldiers and officials in certain circumstances, the Bush Administration and Congress took steps to protect Americans from the court's jurisdiction, which the U.S. did not recognize. For instance, Congress passed the American Service-Members' Protection Act of 2002 (ASPA), which restricts U.S. interaction with the ICC and its state parties by:

- Prohibiting cooperation with the ICC by any official U.S. entity, including providing support or funds to the ICC, extraditing or transferring U.S. citizens or permanent resident aliens to the ICC, or permitting ICC investigations on U.S. territory.
- Prohibiting participation by U.S. military or officials in U.N. peacekeeping operations unless they are shielded from the ICC's jurisdiction.
- Prohibiting the sharing of classified national security information or other law enforcement information with the ICC.
- Constraining military assistance to ICC member states, except NATO countries and major non-NATO allies and Taiwan, unless they entered into an agreement with the U.S. not to surrender U.S. persons to the ICC without U.S. permission.
- Authorizing the President to use "all means necessary and appropriate" to free U.S. military personnel or officials detained by the ICC.

Congress also approved the Nethercutt Amendment to the foreign operations appropriations bill for fiscal year 2005, which prohibited disbursement of selected U.S. assistance to an ICC party unless the country has entered into a bilateral agreement not to surrender U.S. persons to the ICC (commonly known as an Article 98 agreement) or is specifically exempted in the legislation. Both ASPA and the Nethercutt Amendment contained waiver provisions allowing the President to ignore these restrictions with notification to Congress. In recent years, Congress has repealed or loosened restrictions on providing assistance to ICC state parties that have not entered into Article 98 agreements with the U.S. However, other ASPA restrictions remain in effect.

The Bush Administration signed these legislative measures and undertook several specific efforts to fulfill the mandates of the legislation and to protect U.S. military personnel and officials from potential ICC prosecution.

Possible Legal Obligations from Signing the Rome Statute

Under Article 18 of the Vienna Convention on the Law of Treaties, the Bush Administration determined that its efforts to protect U.S. persons from the ICC could be construed as "acts which would defeat the object and purpose of a treaty." To resolve this potential conflict, the U.S. sent a letter to U.N. Secretary-General Kofi Annan, the depositor for the Rome Statute, stating that it did not intend to become a party to the Rome Statute and declaring that "the United States has no legal obligations arising from its signature" of the Rome Statute. This act has been described as "un-signing" the Rome Statute. As John Bellinger, former Legal Advisor to Secretary of State Condoleezza Rice, made clear in a 2008 speech, "the central motivation was to resolve any confusion whether, as a matter of treaty law, the United States had residual legal obligations arising from its signature of the Rome Statute."

Article 98 Agreements

Because the ICC could claim jurisdiction over non-parties to the Rome Statute—an assertion unprecedented in international legal jurisdiction—the Bush Administration sought legal protections to preclude nations from surrendering, extraditing, or transferring U.S. persons to the ICC or third countries for that purpose without U.S. consent. Under an Article 98 agreement, a country agrees not to turn U.S. persons over to the ICC without U.S. consent.

Contrary to the claims of the more strident critics, who label the Article 98 agreements as "bilateral immunity agreements" or "impunity agreements," the agreements neither absolve the U.S. of its obligation to investigate and prosecute alleged crimes, constrain the other nation's ability to investigate and prosecute crimes committed by an American person within its jurisdiction, nor constrain an international tribunal established by the Security Council from investigating or prosecuting crimes committed by U.S. persons. The agreements simply prevent other countries from turning U.S. persons over to an international court that does not have jurisdiction recognized by the United States.

The limited nature of the agreements is entirely consistent with international law, which supports the principle that a state cannot be bound by a treaty to which it is not a party. The agreements are also consistent with customary international law because the issue of ICC jurisdiction is very much in dispute. Moreover, they are consistent with the Rome Statute itself, which contemplates such agreements in Article 98:

> The Court may not proceed with a request for surrender which would require the requested State to act inconsistently with its obligations under international agreements pursuant to which the consent of a sending State is required to surrender a person of that State to the Court, unless the Court can first obtain the cooperation of the sending State for the giving of consent for the surrender.

Although the U.S. is not currently seeking to negotiate additional Article 98 agreements, there are no known plans to terminate existing agreements. Reportedly, 104 countries have signed Article 98 agreements with the U.S., of which 97 agreements remain in effect.

Language to Protect U.S. Persons

In 2002, the U.S. sought a Security Council resolution to indefinitely exempt from ICC jurisdiction U.S. troops and officials participating in U.N. peacekeeping operations. The effort failed in the face of arguments that the Security Council lacked the authority to rewrite the terms of the Rome Statute, but the Security Council did adopt Resolution 1422, which deferred ICC prosecution of U.N. peacekeeping personnel for one year under Article 16 of the Rome Statute. The deferral was renewed once and expired in June 2004. The U.S. also successfully included language in Resolution 1497 on the U.N. Mission to Liberia granting exclusive jurisdiction over "current or former officials or personnel from a contributing State" to the contributing state if it is not a party to the Rome Statute.

Persistent Barriers to U.S. Ratification

ICC supporters have called for the Obama Administration to re-sign the Rome Statute, reverse protective measures secured during the Bush Administration (Article 98 agreements), and fully embrace the ICC. Indeed, the Obama Administration may be considering some or all of those actions. However, the ICC's flaws advise caution and concern, particularly in how the ICC could affect national sovereignty and politically precarious situations around the globe.

When it decided to un-sign the Rome Statute, the Bush Administration voiced five concerns regarding the Rome Statute. These critical concerns have not been addressed.

The ICC's Unchecked Power

The U.S. system of government is based on the principle that power must be checked by other power or it will be abused and misused. With this in mind, the Founding Fathers divided the national government into three branches, giving each the means to influence and restrain excesses of the other branches. For instance, Congress confirms and can impeach federal judges and has the sole authority to authorize spending, the President nominates judges and can veto legislation, and the courts can nullify laws passed by Congress and overturn presidential actions if it judges them unconstitutional.

> The ICC lacks robust checks on its authority, despite strong efforts by U.S. delegates to insert them during the treaty negotiations. The court is an independent treaty body. In theory, the states that have ratified the Rome Statute and accepted the court's authority control the ICC. In practice, the role of the Assembly of State Parties is limited. The judges themselves settle any dispute over the court's "judicial functions." The

prosecutor can initiate an investigation on his own authority, and the ICC judges determine whether the investigation may proceed. The U.N. Security Council can delay an investigation for a year—a delay that can be renewed—but it cannot stop an investigation.

The Challenges to the Security Council's Authority

The Rome Statute empowers the ICC to investigate, prosecute, and punish individuals for the as yet undefined crime of "aggression." This directly challenges the authority and prerogatives of the U.N. Security Council, which the U.N. Charter gives "primary responsibility for the maintenance of international peace and security" and which is the only U.N. institution empowered to determine when a nation has committed an act of aggression. Yet, the Rome Statute "empowers the court to decide on this matter and lets the prosecutor investigate and prosecute this undefined crime" free of any oversight from the Security Council.

A Threat to National Sovereignty

A bedrock principle of the international system is that treaties and the judgments and decisions of treaty organizations cannot be imposed on states without their consent. In certain circumstances, the ICC claims the authority to detain and try U.S. military personnel, U.S. officials, and other U.S. nationals even though the U.S. has not ratified the Rome Statute and has declared that it does not consider itself bound by its signature on the treaty. As Grossman noted, "While sovereign nations have the authority to try non-citizens who have committed crimes against their citizens or in their territory, the United States has never recognized the right of an international organization to do so absent consent or a U.N. Security Council mandate."

As such, the Rome Statute violates international law as it has been traditionally understood by empowering the ICC to prosecute and punish the nationals of countries that are not party to it. In fact, Article 34 of the Vienna Convention on the Law of Treaties unequivocally states: "A treaty does not create either obligations or rights for a third State without its consent."

> Protestations by ICC proponents that the court would seek such prosecutions only if a country is unwilling or unable to prosecute those accused of crimes within the court's jurisdiction—the principle of complementarity—are insufficient to alleviate sovereignty concerns.

For example, the Obama Administration recently declared that no employee of the Central Intelligence Agency (CIA) who engaged in the use of "enhanced interrogation techniques" on detainees would be criminally prosecuted. That decision was presumably the result of an analysis of U.S. law, legal advice provided to the CIA by Justice Department lawyers, and the particular actions of the interrogators. Yet if the U.S. were a party to the Rome Statute, the Administration's announced decision not to prosecute would fulfill a prerequisite for possible prosecution by the ICC under the principle of complementarity. That is, because the U.S. has no plans to prosecute its operatives for acts that many in the international community consider torture, the ICC prosecutor would be empowered (and possibly compelled) to pursue charges against the interrogators.

Erosion of Fundamental Elements of the U.N. Charter

The ICC's jurisdiction over war crimes, crimes against humanity, genocide, and aggression directly involves the court in fundamental issues traditionally reserved to sovereign states, such as when a state can lawfully use armed force to defend itself, its citizens, or its interests; how and to what extent armed force may be applied; and the point at which particular actions constitute serious crimes. Blurring the lines of authority and responsibility in these decisions has serious consequences. As Grossman notes, "with the ICC prosecutor and judges presuming to sit in judgment of the security decisions of States without their assent, the ICC could have a chilling effect on the willingness of States to project power in defense of their moral and security interests." The ability to project power must be protected, not only for America's own national security interests, but also for those individuals threatened by genocide and despotism who can only be protected through the use of force.

Complications to Military Cooperation Between the U.S. and Its Allies

The treaty creates an obligation to hand over U.S. nationals to the court, regardless of U.S. objections, absent a competing obligation such as that created through an Article 98 agreement. The United States has a unique role and responsibility in preserving international peace and security. At any given time, U.S. forces are located in approximately 100 nations around the world, standing ready to defend the interests of the U.S. and its allies, engaging in peacekeeping and humanitarian operations, conducting military exercises, or protecting U.S. interests through military intervention. The worldwide extension of U.S. armed forces is internationally unique. The U.S. must ensure that its soldiers and government officials are not exposed to politically motivated investigations and prosecutions.

Ongoing Causes for Concern

Supporters of U.S. ratification of the Rome Statute often dismiss these concerns as unjustified, disproved by the ICC's conduct during its first seven years in operation, or as insufficient to overcome the need for an international court to hold perpetrators of serious crimes to account. Considering the other options that exist or could be created to fill the ICC's role of holding perpetrators of war crimes, crimes against humanity, genocide, and aggression to account, the benefits from joining such a flawed institution do not justify the risks.

Furthermore, based on the ICC's record and the trend in international legal norms, they are being disingenuous in dismissing concerns about over-politicization of the ICC, its impact on diplomatic initiatives and sovereign decisions on the use of force, its expansive claim of jurisdiction over the citizens of non-states parties, and incompatibility with U.S. legal norms and traditions. A number of specific risks are obvious.

Politicization of the Court

Unscrupulous individuals and groups and nations seeking to influence foreign policy and security decisions of other nations have and will continue to seek to misuse the ICC for politically motivated purposes. Without appropriate checks and balances to prevent its misuse, the ICC represents a dangerous temptation for those with political axes to grind. The prosecutor's *proprio motu* authority to initiate an investigation based solely on his own authority or on information provided by a government, a nongovernmental organization (NGO), or individuals is an open invitation for political manipulation.

One example is the multitude of complaints submitted to the ICC urging the court to indict Bush Administration officials for alleged crimes in Iraq and Afghanistan. The Office of the Prosecutor received more than 240 communications alleging crimes related to the situation in Iraq. Thus far, the prosecutor has demonstrated considerable restraint, declining to pursue these cases for various reasons, including that the ICC does not have "jurisdiction with respect to actions of non-State Party nationals on the territory of Iraq," which is also not a party to the Rome Statute.

All current ICC cases were referred to the ICC by the governments of the territories in which the alleged crimes occurred or by the Security Council. Comparatively speaking, these cases are low-hanging fruit—situations clearly envisioned to be within the authority of the court by all states. Even so, they have not been without controversy, as demonstrated by the AU reaction to the arrest warrant for President Bashir and attempts to have the Security Council defer the case.

However, the ICC's brief track record is no assurance that future cases will be similarly resolved, especially given the increasing appetite for lodging charges with the ICC. A far more significant test will arise if the prosecutor decides to investigate (and the court's pre-trial chamber authorizes) a case involving a non-ICC party without a Security Council referral or against the objections of the government of the involved territory.

This could arise from the prosecutor's monitoring of the situation in Palestine. Even though Israel is not a party to the Rome Statute, the ICC prosecutor is exploring a request by the Palestinian National Authority to prosecute Israeli commanders for alleged war crimes committed during the recent actions in Gaza. The request is supported by 200 complaints from individuals and NGOs alleging war crimes by the Israeli military and civilian leaders related to military actions in Gaza.

Palestinian lawyers maintain that the Palestinian National Authority can request ICC jurisdiction as the de facto sovereign even though it is not an internationally recognized state. By countenancing Palestine's claims, the ICC prosecutor has enabled pressure to be applied to Israel over alleged war crimes, while ignoring Hamas's incitement of the military action and its commission of war crimes against Israeli civilians. Furthermore, by seemingly recognizing

Palestine as a sovereign entity, the prosecutor's action has arguably created a pathway for Palestinian statehood without first reaching a comprehensive peace deal with Israel. This determination is an inherently political issue beyond the ICC's authority, yet the prosecutor has yet to reject the possibility that the ICC may open a case on the situation.

Alternatively, the prosecutor could raise ire by making a legal judgment call on a crime under the court's jurisdiction that lacks a firm, universal interpretation, such as:

- "Committing outrages upon personal dignity, in particular humiliating and degrading treatment";
- "Intentionally launching an attack in the knowledge that such attack will cause incidental loss of life or injury to civilians or damage to civilian objects or widespread, long-term and severe damage to the natural environment which would be clearly excessive in relation to the concrete and direct overall military advantage anticipated"; or
- Using weapons "which are of a nature to cause superfluous injury or unnecessary suffering or which are inherently indiscriminate in violation of the international law of armed conflict."

In each of these cases, a reasonable conclusion could be made to determine whether a crime was committed. For instance, many human rights groups allege outrages on personal dignity and "humiliating and degrading treatment" were committed at the detention facility at Guantanamo Bay, Cuba. The U.S. disputes these claims. Excessive use of force has been alleged in Israel's attacks in Gaza, while others insist Israel demonstrated forbearance and consideration in trying to prevent civilian casualties. There is also an ongoing international effort to ban landmines and cluster munitions. If the ICC member states agree to add them to the annex of banned weapons, it could lead to a confrontation over their use by non-party states, such as the U.S., which opposes banning these weapons. These are merely some scenarios in which politicization could become an issue for the ICC.

The Undefined Crime of Aggression

It would be irresponsible for the U.S. to expose its military personnel and civilian officials to a court that has yet to define the very crimes over which it claims jurisdiction. Yet that is the situation the U.S. would face if it ratified the Rome Statute. The Statute includes the crime of aggression as one of its enumerated crimes, but the crime has yet to be defined, despite a special working group that has been debating the issue for more than five years.

For instance, some argue that any military action conducted without Security Council authorization violates international law and is, therefore, an act of aggression that could warrant an ICC indictment. The U.S. has been the aggressor in several recent military actions, including military invasions of the sovereign territories of Afghanistan and Iraq, albeit with the U.N. Security Council's blessing in the case of Afghanistan. U.S. forces bombed Serbia in 1999 and launched dozens of cruise missiles at targets in Afghanistan and the Sudan in

1998 without explicit Security Council authorization. While charges of aggression are unlikely to be brought against U.S. officials *ex post facto* for military actions in Iraq and elsewhere—certainly not for actions before July 2002 as limited by the Rome Statute—submitting to the jurisdiction of an international court that judges undefined crimes would be highly irresponsible and an open invitation to levy such charges against U.S. officials in future conflicts.

If the U.S. becomes an ICC party, every decision by the U.S. to use force, every civilian death resulting from U.S. military action and every allegedly abused detainee could conceivably give cause to America's enemies to file charges against U.S. soldiers and officials. Indeed, any U.S. "failure" to prosecute a high-ranking U.S. official in such instances would give a cause of action at the ICC. For example, the principle of complementarity will not prevent a politicized prosecutor from bringing charges against a sitting U.S. President or Secretary of Defense. That is, the U.S. Department of Justice is unlikely to file criminal charges against such officials for their decisions involving the use of military force. This decision not to prosecute would be a prerequisite for the ICC taking up the case.

At best, the U.S. would find itself defending its military and civilian officials against frivolous and politically motivated charges submitted to the ICC prosecutor. At worst, international political pressure could compel the ICC's prosecutor to file charges against current or former U.S. officials. Until the crime of aggression is defined, U.S. membership in the ICC is premature.

What the U.S. Should Do

The serious flaws that existed when President Clinton signed the Rome Statute in December 2000 continue to exist today. The Bush Administration's policy toward the ICC was prudent and in the best interests of the U.S., its officials, and particularly its armed forces. Since the ICC came into existence, the U.S. has treaded carefully by supporting the ICC on an ad hoc basis without backing away from its long-standing objections to the court. The U.S. has simultaneously taken the necessary steps to protect U.S. persons from the court's illegitimate claims of jurisdiction.

Despite intense pressure to overturn U.S. policies toward the ICC, the Obama Administration appears to appreciate the possible ramifications of joining the court. Indeed, as a candidate, Obama expressed the need to ensure that U.S. troops have "maximum protection" from politically motivated indictments by the ICC and did not openly support ratification of the Rome Statute. However, the Obama Administration has expressed less caution than either the Bush or Clinton Administrations did about the ICC. Specifically, during her confirmation hearing as Secretary of State Hillary Clinton stated:

> The President-Elect believes as I do that we should support the ICC's investigations. . . .
>
> But at the same time, we must also keep in mind that the U.S. has more troops deployed overseas than any nation. As Commander-in-Chief, the President-Elect will want to make sure they continue to

have the maximum protection. . . . Whether we work toward joining or not, we will end hostility towards the ICC, and look for opportunities to encourage effective ICC action in ways that promote U.S. interests by bringing war criminals to justice.

News reports indicate that the Obama Administration is close to announcing a change in U.S. policy toward the ICC, including affirming the 2000 signature on the Rome Statute and increasing U.S. cooperation with the court. On her recent trip to Africa, Secretary of State Clinton stated that it was "a great regret but it is a fact that we are not yet a signatory [to the Rome Statute]. But we have supported the court and continue to do so."

These steps are premature if the Administration seriously wishes to provide "maximum protection" for U.S. troops. Instead, to protect U.S. military personnel and other U.S. persons and to encourage other member states to support reforms to the Rome Statute that would address U.S. concerns, the Obama Administration should:

- *Not re-sign the Rome Statute.* The Obama Administration is under pressure to "re-sign" the Rome Statute, reversing the Bush Administration's decision. In critical ways, this would be tantamount to signing a blank check. The Rome Statute is up for review by the Assembly of States Parties in 2010, and key crimes within the court's jurisdiction have yet to be defined and long-standing U.S. objections to the treaty have yet to be addressed. The Obama Administration should use the possibility of U.S. membership as an incentive to encourage the state parties to remedy the key flaws in the Rome Statute.
- *Maintain existing Article 98 agreements.* Until the Rome Statute is reformed to address all of the U.S. concerns, the Obama Administration should confirm and endorse all existing Article 98 agreements. The U.S. is militarily engaged in Iraq and Afghanistan, has troops stationed and in transit around the globe, and in all likelihood will be involved in anti-terror activities around the world for many years. Now is not the time to terminate the legal protections enjoyed by U.S. military personnel and officials deployed in foreign nations. Even if the U.S. joins the ICC at some future date, the U.S. should not terminate the Article 98 agreements because they are consistent with the Rome Statute and would serve as a useful protection if the court overreaches.
- *Establish clear objectives for changes to the Rome Statute for the 2010 review conference that would help to reduce current and potential problems posed by the ICC.* In 2010, the Assembly of States Parties is scheduled to hold the first review conference to consider amendments to the Rome Statute. A key issue on the agenda is agreeing to a definition of the crime of aggression, which is technically under the ICC's jurisdiction, but remains latent due to the states parties' inability to agree to a definition. Rather than accede to an anodyne definition, the U.S. should either seek an explicit, narrow definition to prevent politicization of this crime or, even better, seek to excise the crime from the Rome Statute entirely, on the grounds that it infringes on the Security Council's authority. Moreover, the review conference should reverse the

Rome Statute's violation of customary international law by explicitly limiting the ICC's jurisdiction only to nationals of those states that have ratified or acceded to the Rome Statute and to nationals of non-party states when the U.N. Security Council has explicitly referred a situation to the ICC.

- *Approach Security Council recommendations to the ICC on their merits and oppose those deemed detrimental to U.S. interests.* The U.S. abstentions on Security Council resolutions on Darfur indicate only that it is not U.S. policy to block all mentions of the ICC. However, accepting the reality of the ICC does not mean that the U.S. should acquiesce on substantive issues when they may directly or indirectly affect U.S. interests, U.S. troops, U.S. officials, or other U.S. nationals. Many concerns about the Rome Statute have not yet been adequately addressed. The U.S. should abstain if the resolution addresses issues critical to U.S. interests and would not directly or indirectly undermine the U.S. policy of opposing ICC claims of jurisdiction over U.S. military personnel and its nationals. Moreover, the U.S. should insist that all resolutions include language protecting military and officials from non-ICC states participating in U.N. peacekeeping operations.

Conclusion

While the International Criminal Court represents an admirable desire to hold war criminals accountable for their terrible crimes, the court is flawed notionally and operationally. The ICC has not overcome many of the problems plaguing the ad hoc tribunals established for Yugoslavia and Rwanda. It remains slow and inefficient. Worse, unlike ad hoc tribunals, it includes a drive to justify its budget and existence in perpetuity rather than simply completing a finite mission.

Its broad autonomy and jurisdiction invite politically motivated indictments. Its inflexibility can impede political resolution of problems, and its insulation from political considerations can complicate diplomatic efforts. Efforts to use the court to apply pressure to inherently political issues and supersede the foreign policy prerogatives of sovereign nations—such as the prosecutor's decision to consider Israel's actions in Gaza—undermine the court's credibility and threaten its future as a useful tool for holding accountable the perpetrators of genocide, war crimes, and crimes against humanity.

President Clinton considered the ICC's flaws serious enough to recommend against U.S. ratification of the Rome Statute unless they were resolved, and President Bush concurred. These issues remain unresolved and continue to pose serious challenges to U.S. sovereignty and its national interests. Unless the serious flaws are addressed fully, President Obama should similarly hold the ICC at arm's length. To protect its own interests and to advance the notion of a properly instituted international criminal court, the U.S. should continue to insist that it is not bound by the Rome Statute and does not recognize the ICC's authority over U.S. persons and should exercise great care when deciding to support the court's actions.

Jonathan F. Fanton  **NO**

The Challenge of International Justice

I am glad to be here at the U.S. Military Academy, an institution deeply woven into the fabric of this country's history. In 1902, President Theodore Roosevelt said, "No other educational institution in the land has contributed as many names as West Point to the honor roll of the nation's greatest citizens." After more than a century, that statement remains true – a compelling testimony to the enduring value of the Academy and its high ideals.

The John D. and Catherine T. MacArthur Foundation, has a shorter tradition: we were established in 1978. . . . With an endowment of $6.5 billion, MacArthur will give $300 million in grants and program-related investments to individuals and organizations in the U.S. and abroad this year. . . . The Foundation aims to help build a more just, peaceful, and sustainable world. We do so through sponsoring research, educating the public, and supporting organizations that work in fields that range from conservation to international nuclear disarmament, from renewing America's cities to creating high-quality documentaries for public television. In 2006, we made a grant that was unusual for us – $750,000 to West Point's Program in Conflict and Human Security Studies to support coursework and overseas cadet internships with non-governmental organizations (or NGOs).

I have been impressed by the content and quality of the courses offered in Conflict and Human Security Studies – such as "International Conflict and Negotiation," "Winning the Peace," and "International Security Strategy." The breadth of their approach, their awareness of the human dimension of conflict and restoring peace are impressive and encouraging. . . .

There is no shortage of NGOs with which to work – by one count, there are already five million of them, and new organizations are founded each year. The vision and engagement of these groups – together, called "civil society" – is helping to change the world for the better. Many of them concentrate on issues of human rights, justice for all citizens, and the rule of law – causes MacArthur has supported from our very first grant, which went to Amnesty International.

We fund large organizations that monitor abuses around the world, like Human Rights Watch, and small local institutions that tackle issues like child marriage in India, police abuse in Russia, and the rights of prisoners in Nigeria.

MacArthur holds passionately that individuals everywhere have intrinsic rights that should be enshrined in law and defended by due process. The U.S.

has a Bill of Rights and courts that are responsive to wronged individuals, other countries have similarly clear and effective justice systems – but many nations do not.

Where are individuals to turn when they are denied freedom of speech, beaten by the police, subjected to harsh discrimination, or forcibly conscripted into rebel armies and there are no independent national courts to hear them? And how is the world to deal with genocide, war crimes, and the brutal acts called "crimes against humanity"?

MacArthur believes that the answer lies in an international system of justice that will supplement unresponsive local courts and provide a forum for those who have suffered the worst abuses. The international community has courts for other purposes, for example the International Court of Justice, International Tribunal for the Law of the Sea, or Dispute Settlement System of the World Trade Organization. These bodies have been functioning over many decades and are central to international relations.

But the time has come to develop an international system of justice with the International Criminal Court as the centerpiece. Let me describe the evolution and objectives of this movement.

The first Geneva Conventions of 1864 and the Hague Conventions of 1899 serve as the foundations for modern attempts to stop wartime atrocities. Tribunals for war crimes were proposed, but not effectively implemented, after WWI. The Nuremberg and Far East tribunals after WWII tried and convicted the most prominent Axis leaders, at last holding individuals accountable for their criminal acts – even when following orders.

The WWII tribunals were possible because there was international consensus among the Allied powers. The Cold War ended that consensus. Only when the Soviet Union had collapsed was there a new impetus toward establishing an international system of criminal justice, prompted by the disintegration of Yugoslavia and the infamous "ethnic cleansing" that followed.

NGOs, human rights activists, and diplomats called for a forum to deal specifically with such crimes against humanity when national systems failed to do so. The UN Security Council responded, establishing an ad hoc Criminal Tribunal for Yugoslavia in 1993 and another in response to the Rwandan genocide in 1994.

The results were encouraging. [President] Slobodan Milosovic of Serbia was the first sitting head of state ever indicted; Jean Kambanda, former prime minister of Rwanda, faced charges of genocide, pled guilty, and is now serving a life sentence in Mali. With trials and appeals continuing, 239 people have been indicted and 78 convicted so far. New tribunals are now at work dealing with the atrocities committed in Sierra Leone's civil war and Cambodia's "killing fields."

The early tribunals helped establish the feasibility of a permanent International Criminal Court (ICC). In 1989, preparation and drafting had begun for a Statute that would establish such a Court; it was completed in 1998 and is commonly called "the Rome Statute." States were asked to ratify the Statute individually; by 2002 the required 60 had done so, allowing the Court to have jurisdiction. To date, 106 countries have ratified and joined the Court; the United States has not.

The Court, based in The Hague, is permanent and independent, dedicated to prosecuting only the most serious crimes against humanity. It has jurisdiction over acts committed on the territory, or by nationals, of States Party to the Statute. Also, the UN Security Council may refer a situation to the Court, regardless of the nationality of the accused or the location of their crimes.

The ICC is a "court of last resort," which means that it has authority only when national courts are unable or unwilling to act. All member nations retain the primary right and responsibility to investigate their own citizens – the principle of complementarity, which the U.S. helped embed in the Treaty.

How is the Court performing so far? It issued warrants, beginning in 2005, against Joseph Kony, head of the Lord's Resistance Army in Uganda, for the murder and torture of civilians; against Thomas Lubanga, leader of the UPF militia in the Democratic Republic of the Congo, for kidnapping children to become soldiers; and against Ahmad Mohammad Harun, formerly Sudan's Minister of State for the Interior, and Ali Kushayb, leader of the Janjaweed militia, for their crimes in Darfur – the forced displacement of millions, and a campaign of terror including abduction, rape, and murder.

Lubanga is in custody and his trial expected to begin in June. It will be the first in the Court's history. Two other militia leaders from the Congo are also in The Hague awaiting trial.

The two other cases exemplify the problems of international justice in practice. Joseph Kony of Uganda is still at large and his rebel movement active. The government of Sudan has no incentive to turn over either Kushayb or Harun. Indeed, it has appointed Harun Minister of Humanitarian Affairs, responsible for hearing human rights complaints from the victims of Darfur.

Unless the international community is prepared to act on the Court's warrants, it cannot be effective. More needs to be done to establish responsibility for apprehending and arresting those charged.

There has been debate about whether the threat of prosecution will be an obstacle in negotiating settlements to violent situations. Leaders who fear indictment, it is argued, will be less likely to relinquish power or end conflicts. This is a valid concern. A 2006 peace accord between the Lord's Resistance Army and the Ugandan government rejected the LRA's demand for amnesty. This may explain why Joseph Kony did not appear to sign the treaty earlier this month. But peace and justice, I believe, complement and reinforce one another. Societies that have been torn apart by atrocities are unlikely to heal unless there is resolution for those who have been harmed and some penalty for the perpetrators.

There is evidence also that the Court has a deterrent effect. In late 2004, there was a wave of violence in Côte d'Ivoire, accompanied by radio broadcasts of hate speech reminiscent of the Rwandan genocide. Juan Mendez, the UN's Special Adviser on the Prevention of Genocide, wrote to remind the Security Council that the ICC has jurisdiction over acts that may lead to crimes against humanity. His intervention was widely reported, and the message was heard in Côte d'Ivoire: the hate speech and threats subsided.

I should note that, while the ICC is the centerpiece of the system of international justice, there are other venues for ordinary people to seek redress when they have exhausted remedies in their own countries.

Regional human rights courts and commissions for Africa, Latin America, and Europe deal with cases that range from freedom of speech to discrimination to police brutality. Often, the courts' decisions have the effect of compelling countries to recognize rights that exist under their own laws or in international treaties they have signed. At present, 80,000 such cases from 70 nations are pending. Perhaps the most significant contribution of the regional courts and the ICC will be strengthening national courts and bringing national laws up to international standards.

So far, MacArthur's staff has been impressed with the early record of the ICC, but the Court is not without its critics. The U.S., as I have noted, is not party to the Rome Statute. This broke with America's record of leading the way in international justice since the Nuremberg and Far East tribunals. The U.S. actively supported the tribunals for the former Yugoslavia, Rwanda, and Sierra Leone and assisted in drafting the Rome Statute. But fears that membership in the ICC would expose Americans to politically-motivated cases have persuaded two successive administrations not to ratify.

Opponents of the Court also object that the Rome Statute impinges on U.S. sovereignty, that it overrides the Constitutional due-process protections afforded to U.S. citizens, and that it would limit America's ability to operate abroad – even in joint humanitarian operations.

So far, those fears have not materialized. And I do not believe they are likely to. ICC procedures have all the same due-process protections as U.S. courts, except that of trial by jury. And the Court has been rigorous in pursuing only those cases that are sufficiently grave and over which it clearly has jurisdiction. The Court has received almost 3,000 communications from 140 nations. The vast majority has been rejected outright, only four investigations have been opened by the Prosecutor, and all charges involving Americans have been dismissed.

The Court would certainly be stronger if the U.S. were a member. American legal expertise would strengthen the early cases and shape the Court's future jurisprudence; American intelligence agencies could provide evidence to ensure successful prosecutions.

Many in the U.S. military have concerns about the ICC. In 2006, MacArthur sponsored the Stimson Center to survey and assess how professional officers, some from the military justice system, perceived the Court and its impact.

Stimson found a range of opinion – much of it positive, some strongly negative – but also that many officers knew little about the Court or the Rome Statute. The most common objections were that the Court "second-guessed" decisions taken in action that were thought to fall within the rules of combat, that American service personnel would be unfairly targeted when abroad, that ignorance of the provisions of the Rome Statute would lead to inadvertent infractions, and that field operations and military alliances would be hampered by further layers of legal restrictions. Others felt the Court would simply be ineffective, unable to bring criminals to justice.

Specific problems were cited: Would the U.S.'s deployment of cluster bombs and landmines, outlawed by the 140 countries party to the Ottawa Convention, give grounds for prosecution? Would decisions taken on faulty intelligence, such as the accidental bombing of the Chinese Embassy in Belgrade in 1999, make officers liable?

Officers with legal expertise pointed out gaps between U.S. domestic law and the Uniform Code of Military Justice and the Rome Statute, which they saw opening the possibility of prosecution for offences that were unclearly defined, or not addressed at all, in American legislation.

These are cogent objections, but I believe they are not insurmountable. Most of the acts prohibited by the Rome Statute are already illegal under U.S. military and civilian codes; where there are gaps or more clarity is needed, further legal work could harmonize the legislation and sharpen definitions. A simple program of education would give service personnel adequate working knowledge of the Statute. As there are few areas in which the Statute differs from existing U.S. codes, there would be little practical difference in field operations.

The specific objections may be met by noting that the use of certain weapons and specific operational decisions do not come under the remit of the Court, whose role is to deal with only the most egregious crimes. If the U.S. joined the Court, the principle of complementarity requires that its military personnel charged with misconduct would be subject to existing U.S. laws and procedures, which are robust and high-functioning.

It is worth noting that, between 2003 and 2006, the Prosecutor received almost 250 submissions related to the conflict in Iraq, the majority concerned with military operations by U.S. and allied troops. In his 2006 response, Prosecutor Luis Moreno Ocampo declined to pursue any of them further, ruling that the Court had no jurisdiction in most cases, that the individual instances did not rise to the level of gravity required, and that there were adequate national judicial systems in place to deal with the alleged offences.

Most of those who participated in the Stimson project supported the overall goals of the Court as being consistent with fundamental American values and the legal standards to which U.S. military personnel are already held. Some also saw the advantages for U.S. personnel of an international court that would strengthen the rule of law within countries that, in the past, would have ignored international standards altogether.

The ICC is arguably the most important new international institution since the founding of the United Nations itself. It is destined to have a considerable and lasting impact on how justice and human rights are defined and enforced. I urge you to acquaint yourselves with the Court, to investigate how it works, and to debate its future. How do you, as citizens, evaluate America's relationship to the ICC? How should your training, and your conduct in operations, take account of the Court's mission to protect the world's most vulnerable people and bring perpetrators of atrocities to justice?

MacArthur will continue to educate the public about the Court, fund groups that further its work, and support an integrated system of international justice. We are convinced that America and its armed forces have nothing to fear from such a system, and much to offer to its success. And we are sure that lively and free-ranging discussion of the issues involved will help build a consensus that the world needs clear, universal, and humane standards of justice for all.

POSTSCRIPT

Is U.S. Refusal to Join the International Criminal Court Wise?

With the ICC treaty in effect, the countries that were a party to it met in 2003 and elected the court's 18 judges and its chief prosecutor. The following year the ICC began operations at its seat in The Hague, the Netherlands. Soon thereafter, the ICC prosecutor launched several investigations, mostly focusing on conflicts in central Africa and in the Darfur region of Sudan in northeast Africa. As of late 2008, the ICC indicted nine individuals from Sudan, Uganda, the Democratic Republic of the Congo, and the Central African Republic and had four in custody awaiting trial. Most significantly, the ICC on application of its chief prosecutor, Luis Moreno-Ocampo of Argentina, indicted President Omar al-Bashir of Sudan for 10 counts of genocide, war crimes, and crimes against humanity, and in July 2009 issued an instrumental warrant for his arrest. The indictment of a sitting head of state was supported by many but also set off a storm of protest. Some believed that the effort to indict Bashir would complicate the search for a solution in Darfur. Others worried about the ICC's focus on Africa. As of late 2010, Bashir remains in power in Sudan. In other activity, the court' first trials, both against individuals accused of war crimes in the Democratic Republic of the Congo, began in 2009 and are ongoing. In October 2008, the judges of the ICC had not decided on Moreno-Ocampo's request for the indictment. The Web site of the ICC at http://www.icc-cpi.int/ is an excellent source of information about its organization, personnel, and activities.

As of September 2010, 113 countries had formally agreed to the Rome Statute and joined the Assembly of State Parties that constitutes the ICC's governing board. Most of the major countries of Western Europe, Africa, and South and Central America are now parties to the ICC, as are Canada and Japan. China, Russia, India, Iran, Israel, and most of the Arab countries are among the prominent nonadherents. The United States has also remained among the absent. It is unlikely that will change. Barack Obama has taken a more positive approach to the ICC than President Bush did but still has made no move to ask the Senate to ratify the Treaty of Rome. Even if Obama did so, ratification would be unlikely without, at the least, much greater protections for U.S. troops abroad against possible ICC indictments. A way to begin learning more about the evolution of the ICC is by reading Erna Paris, *The Sun Climbs Slow: The International Criminal Court and the Struggle for Justice* (Steven Stories Press, 2009). Excellent as a general resource is the *Journal of International Criminal Justice,* published quarterly.

Americans' concern with diminishing U.S. sovereignty is one barrier to U.S. ratification of the Treaty of Rome. A study that explains why most countries have chosen to support the ICC is Beth A. Simmons and Allison Danner, "Credible Commitments and the International Criminal Court," *International Organization* (2010).

Questions for Critical Thinking and Reflection

1. If you are opposed to the United States being subject to the ICC, what changes in the ICC's procedures and jurisdiction would change your mind?
2. What do you make of the following results of two surveys taken just a few months apart in 2002–2003. In the first, 71 percent of Americans said the United States should agree to the ICC as a court that could try individuals for war crimes "if their own country won't try them." The second survey asked about support of the ICC given that it could try U.S. soldiers accused of war crimes "if the United States government refuses to try them." Only 37 percent supported the ICC on this question.
3. Small, weak countries sometimes criticize the ICC because all its investigations and indictments have so far have involved small, weak countries. Why has this been the pattern occurred?

ISSUE 18

Should the United States Ratify the Convention to Eliminate All Forms of Discrimination Against Women?

YES: Harold Hongju Koh, from Testimony during Hearings on "Ratification of the Convention on the Elimination of All Forms of Discrimination Against Women," before the Committee on Foreign Relations, U.S. Senate (June 13, 2002)

NO: Grace Smith Melton, from "CEDAW: How U.N. Interference Threatens the Rights of American Women," *Heritage Foundation Backgrounder #2227* (January 9, 2009)

ISSUE SUMMARY

YES: Harold Hongju Koh, the Gerard C. and Bernice Latrobe Smith Professor of International Law at Yale University and former U.S. assistant secretary of state, contends that the United States cannot champion progress for women's human rights around the world unless it is also a party to the global women's treaty.

NO: Grace Smith Melton, an associate for social issues at the United Nations with the Richard and Helen DeVos Center for Religion and Civil Society at The Heritage Foundation, contends that ratifying would neither advance women's equality nor serve American foreign policy interests, including the security and advancement of women around the globe.

Females constitute about half the world population, but they are a distinct economic–political–social minority because of the wide gap in societal power and resources between women and men. Women constitute 70 percent of the world's poor and two-thirds of its literates. They occupy only 14 percent of the managerial jobs, are less than 40 percent of the world's professional and technical workers, and garner only 35 percent of the earned income in the world. Women are also disadvantaged politically. In late 2003, only 17 women were serving as presidents or prime ministers of their countries; women make up just 8 percent of all national cabinet officers; and only one of every six national legislators is a woman.

On average, life for women is not only harder and more poorly compensated than it is for men, it is also more dangerous. "The most painful

315

devaluation of women," the United Nations reports, "is the physical and psychological violence that stalks them from cradle to grave." Signs of violence against women include the fact that about 80 percent of the world's refugees are women and their children. Other assaults on women arguably constitute a form of genocide. According to the U.N. Children's Fund, "In many countries, boys get better care and better food than girls. As a result, an estimated one million girls die each year because they were born female." None of these economic, social, and political inequities is new. Indeed, the global pattern of discrimination against women is ancient. What is new is the global effort to recognize the abuses that occur and to ameliorate and someday end them.

To help accomplish that goal, the U.N. General Assembly in 1979 voted by 130 to 0 to put the Convention on the Elimination of All Forms of Discrimination Against Women (CEDAW) before the world's countries for adoption. Supporters hailed the treaty as a path-breaking step on behalf of advancing the status of women. Many countries agreed, and by September 1981 enough countries had signed and ratified CEDAW to put it into effect. This set a record for the speed with which any human rights convention had gone into force.

CEDAW is a women's international bill of rights. Most of these rights are enumerated in various other treaties as applicable to all humans, but women's rights had not been specifically and fully addressed in any other treaty before CEDAW. Countries that legally adhere to the convention agree to undertake measures to end all the various forms of discrimination against women. Doing so entails accepting legal gender equality and ensuring the practice of gender equality by abolishing all discriminatory laws, enacting laws that prohibit discrimination against women, and establishing agencies protect women's rights.

President Jimmy Carter signed CEDAW in 1980 and submitted it to the Senate for ratification. However, he was soon thereafter defeated for reelection, and the treaty languished in legislative limbo through the presidencies of Ronald Reagan and George H. W. Bush. By contrast, President Bill Clinton made an effort to move CEDAW forward. The Senate Committee on Foreign Relations held hearings on the pact in 1994 and recommended ratification. There the effort on behalf of CEDAW stalled. It did not come up for debate or a vote in the Senate. Ratification requires a two-thirds vote by the Senate, and there was little chance that the measure would garner the required votes.

The testimony that constitutes the first reading here came during hearings in 2002 that were part of yet another effort to gain Senate approval of CEDAW. In that reading, Harold Hongju Koh maintains that failure to ratify the treaty will undermine U.S. efforts to fight for human rights around the world. Nevertheless, the measure never came to a vote in the Senate because the strength of the mostly Republican opposition ensured that the necessary two-thirds support needed for ratification was out of reach. With the election of a Democratic president and an Democratic Congress in 2008, those supporting CEDAW see a renewed possibility of its ratification. However, in the second reading, Grace Smith Melton argues that CEDAW remains unnecessary to protect the right of American women and also opens the United States up to interference by the United Nations and international courts.

YES

Harold Hongju Koh

Ratification of the Convention on the Elimination of All Forms of Discrimination Against Women

In his [2002] State of the Union address, President George W. Bush . . . announced that "America will always stand for the non-negotiable demands of human dignity: the rule of law; limits on the power of the state; respect for women; private property; free speech; equal justice; and religious tolerance." I can imagine no more fitting way for this Administration and this Senate to answer that demand than by moving quickly to ratify this treaty for the rights of women. . . .

My main message today is that this commitment should not stop at the water's edge. Particularly after September 11, America cannot be a world leader in guaranteeing progress for women's human rights, whether in Afghanistan, here in the United States, or around the world, unless it is also a party to the global women's treaty.

Let me first review the background and history of CEDAW [Convention to Eliminate All Forms of Discrimination Against Women]; second, explain why ratifying that treaty would further our national commitments to eliminating gender discrimination, without jeopardizing our national interests; and third, explain why some concerns occasionally voiced about our ratification of this treaty are, upon examination, completely unfounded.

First, some history. The United Nations Charter reaffirms both the faith of the peoples of the United Nations "in the equal rights of men and women," [Preamble], and their determination to promote respect for human rights "for all without distinction as to race, sex, language, or religion." In 1948, the Universal Declaration of Human Rights similarly declared that "everyone" is entitled to the rights declared there "without distinction of any kind, such as race, colour, (or) sex . . ." In 1975, a global call for an international convention specifically to implement those commitments emerged from the First World Conference on Women in Mexico City. But until 1979, when the General Assembly adopted the CEDAW, there was no convention that addressed comprehensively women's rights within political, social, economic, cultural, and family life. After years of drafting, the United Nations adopted the Convention on the Elimination of All Forms of Discrimination Against Women on December 18, 1979, and the Convention entered into force in September 1981.

Committee on Foreign Relations, U.S. Senate, June 13, 2002.

In the more than two decades since, 169 nations other than our own have become parties to the Convention. Only nineteen United Nations member states have not. That list includes such countries as Afghanistan, Bahrain, Iran, Somalia, Sudan, Syria, Qatar, and the United Arab Emirates. To put it another way, the United States is now the only established industrialized democracy in the world that has not yet ratified the CEDAW treaty. Frankly, Senators, this is a national disgrace for a country that views itself as a world leader on human rights.

Why should the United States ratify this treaty? For two simple reasons. First, ratification would make an important global statement regarding the seriousness of our national commitment to these issues. Second, ratification would have a major impact in ensuring both the appearance and the reality that our national practices fully satisfy or exceed international standards.

The CEDAW treaty has been accurately described as an international bill of rights for women. The CEDAW simply affirms that women, like the rest of the human race, have an inalienable right to live and work free of discrimination. The Convention affirms the rights of all women to exercise on an equal basis their "human rights and fundamental freedoms in the political, economic, social, cultural, civil or any other field."

The treaty defines and condemns discrimination against women and announces an agenda for national action to end such discrimination. By ratifying the treaty, states do nothing more than commit themselves to undertaking "appropriate measures" toward ending discrimination against women, steps that our country has already begun in numerous walks of life. The CEDAW then lays a foundation for realizing equality between women and men in these countries by ensuring women's equal access to, and equal opportunities in, public and political life—including the right to vote, to stand for election, to represent their governments at an international level, and to enjoy equal rights "before the law" as well as equal rights in education, employment, health care, marriage and family relations, and other areas of economic and social life. The Convention directs State Parties to "take into account the particular problems faced by rural women," and permits parties to take "temporary special measures aimed at accelerating de facto equality" between men and women, a provision analogous to one also found in the Convention on the Elimination of All Forms of Racial Discrimination, which our country has already ratified.

Ratifying this treaty would send the world the message that we consider eradication of these various forms of discrimination to be solemn, universal obligations. The violent human rights abuses we recently witnessed against women in Afghanistan, Bosnia, Haiti, Kosovo, and Rwanda painfully remind us of the need for all nations to join together to intensify efforts to protect women's rights as human rights. At the State Department, where I supervised the production of the annual country reports on human rights conditions worldwide, I found that a country's ratification of the CEDAW is one of the surest indicators of the strength of its commitment to internalize the universal norm of gender equality into its domestic laws.

Let me emphasize that in light of our ongoing national efforts to address gender equality through state and national legislation, executive action, and judicial decisions, the legal requirements imposed by ratifying this treaty would not be burdensome. Numerous countries with far less impressive practices regarding gender equality than the United States have ratified the treaty, including countries whom we would never consider our equals on such matters, including Iraq, Kuwait, North Korea, and Saudi Arabia.

At the same time, from my direct experience as America's chief human rights official, I can testify that our continuing failure to ratify CEDAW has reduced our global standing, damaged our diplomatic relations, and hindered our ability to lead in the international human rights community. Nations that are otherwise our allies, with strong rule-of-law traditions, histories, and political cultures, simply cannot understand why we have failed to take the obvious step of ratifying this convention. In particular, our European and Latin American allies regularly question and criticize our isolation from this treaty framework both in public diplomatic settings and private diplomatic meetings.

Our nonratification has led our allies and adversaries alike to challenge our claim of moral leadership in international human rights, a devastating challenge in this post-September 11 environment. Even more troubling, I have found, our exclusion from this treaty has provided anti-American diplomatic ammunition to countries who have exhibited far worse records on human rights generally, and women's rights in particular. Persisting in the aberrant practice of nonratification will only further our diplomatic isolation and inevitably harm our other United States foreign policy interests.

Treaty ratification would be far more than just a paper act. The treaty has demonstrated its value as an important policy tool to promote equal rights in many of the foreign countries that have ratified the CEDAW. As a recent, comprehensive world survey issued by the United Nations Development Fund for Women chronicles, numerous countries around the world have experienced positive gains directly attributable to their ratification and implementation of the CEDAW. CEDAW has been empowering women around the globe to change constitutions, pass new legislation, and influence court decisions in their countries. Ratification of the CEDAW by the United States would similarly make clear our national commitment to ensure the equal and nondiscriminatory treatment of American women in such areas as civil and political rights, education, employment, and property rights.

Most fundamentally, ratification of CEDAW would further our national interests. Secretary of State Colin Powell put it well when he said earlier this year: "The worldwide advancement of women's issues is not only in keeping with the deeply held values of the American people; it is strongly in our national interest as well. . . . Women's issues affect not only women; they have profound implications for all humankind. Women's issues are human rights issues. . . . We, as a world community, cannot even begin to tackle the array of problems and challenges confronting us without the full and equal participation of women in all aspects of life."

After careful study, I have found nothing in the substantive provisions of this treaty that even arguably jeopardizes our national interests. Those treaty provisions are entirely consistent with the letter and spirit of the United States Constitution and laws, both state and federal. The United States can and should accept virtually all of CEDAW's obligations and undertakings without qualification. Regrettably, the Administration has not provided a witness here today to set forth its views on the ratification of this treaty. Although past Administrations have proposed that ratification be accompanied by certain reservations, declarations, and understandings, only one of those understandings, relating to limitations of free speech, expression and association, seems to me advisable to protect the integrity of our national law.

Finally, let me address some myths and fallacies that have been circulated about the likely impact of United States ratification of the CEDAW. The most common include the following:

First, that CEDAW supports abortion rights by promoting access to "family planning." This is flatly untrue. There is absolutely no provision in CEDAW that mandates abortion or contraceptives on demand, sex education without parental involvement, or other controversial reproductive rights issues. CEDAW does not create any international right to abortion. To the contrary, on its face, the CEDAW treaty itself is neutral on abortion, allowing policies in this area to be set by signatory states and seeking to ensure equal access for men and women to health care services and family planning information. In fact, several countries in which abortion is illegal—among them Ireland, Rwanda, and Burkina Faso—have ratified CEDAW.

A second fallacy is that CEDAW ratification would somehow undermine the American family by redefining traditional gender roles with regard to the upbringing of children. In fact, CEDAW does not contain any provisions seeking to regulate any constitutionally protected interests with respect to family life. The treaty only requires that parties undertake to adopt measures "prohibiting all discrimination against women" and to "embody the principle of the equality of men and women" in national laws "to ensure, through law and other appropriate means, the practical realization of this principle." How best to implement that obligation consistent with existing United States constitutional protections—which as you know, limit the government's power to interfere in family matters, including most parental decisions regarding childrearing—is left for each country to decide for itself.

Third, some have falsely suggested that ratification of CEDAW would require decriminalization of prostitution. Again, the text of the treaty is to the contrary. CEDAW's Article 6 specifically states that countries that have ratified CEDAW "shall take all appropriate measures, including legislation, to suppress all forms of traffic in women and exploitation of prostitution in women."

Fourth, some claim that if CEDAW were U.S. law, it would outlaw single-sex education and require censorship of school textbooks. In fact, nothing in CEDAW mandates abolition of single-sex education. As one way to encourage equal access to quality education for all children, Article 10 requires parties to take all appropriate measures to eliminate "any stereotyped concept of the roles of men and women at all levels and in all forms of education by encouraging [not requiring] coeducation and other types of education which will help to achieve this aim . . . ," including, presumably, single-sex education that teaches principles of gender equality. CEDAW also encourages the development of equal education material for students of both genders. This provision is plainly designed not to disrupt educational traditions in countries like ours, but rather, to address those many countries in the world (like Afghanistan during Taliban rule) in which educational facilities for girls are either nonexistent or remain separate and unequal.

Fifth, some have suggested that U.S. ratification of CEDAW would require the legalization of same-sex marriage. Whatever view one may hold regarding the desirability of same-sex marriage, this treaty plainly contains no such requirement. Article 10 of CEDAW requires only elimination of discrimination directed against women "in all matters related to marriage and family relations." Thus, for example, the practice of polygamy is inconsistent with the CEDAW because it undermines women's equality with men and potentially fosters severe financial inequities. Article 10 would neither require nor bar any national laws regarding same-sex marriage, which by their very nature, would apply equally to men and women.

Finally, and most pervasively, opponents of CEDAW have claimed that U.S. ratification would diminish our national sovereignty and states' rights by superseding or overriding our national, state or local laws. Given the broad compatibility between the treaty requirements and our existing national laws, however, very few occasions will arise in which this is even arguably an issue. Moreover, the treaty generally requires States to use "appropriate measures" to implement the nondiscrimination principle, which by its terms accords some discretion to member countries to determine what is "appropriate" under the national circumstances. Finally, the Senate is, of course, free to address any material discrepancies between national law and the treaty by placing understandings upon its advice and consent, along the lines of the "freedom of speech" understanding discussed above, or by the Congress passing implementing legislation—as it has done, for example, to effectuate the Genocide Convention—specifying the precise ways in which the Federal legislature will carry out our international obligations under this treaty.

Ironically, many of the unfounded claims about the likely effects of CEDAW ratification have been asserted by self-proclaimed advocates of states' rights. In fact, within our own country, the emerging trend has been the opposite. Broad sentiment has been emerging at both the state and local level to incorporate the CEDAW requirements into local law. As I speak, governmental bodies in some fifteen states and Guam, sixteen counties and forty-two cities have adopted resolutions or instruments endorsing CEDAW or adopting it on behalf of their jurisdictions. Far from CEDAW imposing unwanted obligations on local governments, local governments are in fact responding to the demands of their citizens, who have become impatient at the lack of federal action to implement these universal norms into American law.

Particularly in a time of terror, promoting human rights and eradicating discrimination should not be partisan issues. As President Bush recently reminded us, the United States cannot fight a war on terrorism alone; it needs cooperation not only from its current allies, but also from the rest of the world. "We have a great opportunity during this time of war," he said, "to lead the world toward the values that will bring lasting peace . . . [such as] the non-negotiable demands of human dignity [that include] respect for women. . . ."

First Lady Laura Bush echoed that sentiment on International Women's Day 2002, when she said, "People around the world are looking closely at the roles that women play in society. And Afghanistan under the Taliban gave the world a sobering example of a country where women were denied their rights and their place in society. . . . Today, the world is helping Afghan women return to the lives that they once knew. . . . Our dedication to respect and protect women's rights in all countries must continue if we are to achieve a peaceful, prosperous world. . . . Together, the United States, the United Nations and all of our allies will prove that the forces of terror can't stop the momentum of freedom."

The world looks to America for leadership on human rights, both in our domestic practices and in our international commitments. Ours is a nation conceived in liberty and dedicated to the proposition that all human beings—not just men—are created equal. Our country has fought a civil war and a centuries-long social struggle to eliminate racial discrimination. It is critically important that we seize this opportunity to announce unequivocally to the world that we, of all nations, insist on the equality of all human beings, regardless of gender.

Senators, in closing let me say how much United States ratification of this important treaty means to every American. My mother, Hesung Chun Koh, came to this country more than fifty years ago from the Republic of Korea and found equal opportunity here as a naturalized American citizen. My wife, Mary-Christy Fisher, is a natural-born American citizen and lawyer of Irish and British heritage. I am the father of a young American, Emily Koh, who will turn sixteen years old in ten days' time.

Although I have tried, I simply cannot give my daughter any good reason why her grandmother and mother would have been protected by CEDAW in their ancestral countries, but that she is not protected by it in the United States, which professes to be a world leader in the promotion of women's rights and gender equality. I cannot explain to her why this country we love, and which I have served as Assistant Secretary of State for Human Rights, has for so long failed to ratify the authoritative human rights treaty that sets the universal standard on women's equality. Finally, I cannot explain why, by not ratifying, the United States chooses to keep company with such countries as Afghanistan, Iran, Sudan, and Syria, in which human rights and women's rights have been brutally repressed.

The choice is simple. Our continuing failure to ratify this treaty will hamper and undermine our efforts to fight for democracy and human rights around the world. Ratification now of the CEDAW treaty would be both prudent foreign policy and simple justice.

Grace Smith Melton  **NO**

CEDAW: How U.N. Interference Threatens the Rights of American Women

Introduction

The Convention on the Elimination of All Forms of Discrimination Against Women (CEDAW) was adopted in 1979 by the United Nations General Assembly and initiated in 1981 after its ratification by 20 member states; today 185 countries are party to CEDAW. The United States Senate—under both Democrat and Republican leadership—has consistently chosen not to ratify it, with good reason.

While women's groups and some politicians have lobbied the Senate to ratify CEDAW, arguing that it would be a useful instrument in championing women's rights at home and abroad, the treaty has rarely made it out of the Senate Foreign Relations Committee for full Senate consideration. The reasons that the Senate has historically rejected CEDAW remain relevant, particularly the challenges it would create for the United States' federalized system of government. Furthermore, the 30 years that have passed since CEDAW's inception continue to illustrate how little the treaty has accomplished to improve women's rights in some of the most oppressive nations that have ratified it, such as Saudi Arabia, and how United Nations "experts" have used the treaty to create new rights and to intimidate countries into adopting radical social policies.

The U.S. Constitution has been a far better protector of women's rights in America than has any international treaty, and the Senate should not subject the Constitution to this one. The Senate Foreign Relations Committee, the full Senate, and the White House must more effectively explain to Americans, particularly women, why CEDAW and the United Nations are not protectors of their interests.

CEDAW's Purpose and Politicization

CEDAW contains many points that mirror America's efforts to promote equal opportunity for women, yet it also poses many problems for America's federalist system of government and the rights established in the U.S. Constitution. Many of the issues with which CEDAW concerns itself, such as access to health

From *The Heritage Foundation Backgrounder,* January 9, 2009. Copyright © 2009 by The Heritage Foundation. Reprinted by permission.

care and education, belong under the purview of state or local jurisdiction in the U.S. constitutional order.

CEDAW requires national governments to work toward eliminating gender-based discrimination in every area of life, using this expansive definition of discrimination against women:

> Any distinction, exclusion or restriction made on the basis of sex which has the effect or purpose of impairing or nullifying the recognition, enjoyment or exercise by women, irrespective of their marital status, on a basis of equality of men and women, of human rights and fundamental freedoms in the political, economic, social, cultural, civil or any other field.

Furthermore, countries that have ratified CEDAW are evaluated based on their compliance with CEDAW by the CEDAW Committee, which meets at the United Nations several times a year. The committee consistently oversteps its mandate, acting as a quasi-judicial body issuing forceful instructions to countries that often do not share its radical social agenda, and committee meetings inevitably serve as a forum for reinterpreting the terms agreed upon by the treaty members.

CEDAW is an ineffective and inappropriate instrument for advancing women's rights around the world. In the case of gross abuses of women's rights, such as sex trafficking or female circumcision, it has been less effective than targeted instruments to address them, such as the American led effort to adopt the United Nations Protocol to Prevent, Suppress, and Punish Trafficking in Persons.

In the case of American women, their freedom and personal dignity are best protected by the U.S. Constitution and the rule of law it establishes. The United States should continue to advance the standing of women domestically and abroad by refusing to ratify CEDAW.

The Enforcers: The CEDAW Committee

The CEDAW Committee was created in 1982 to monitor states' implementation of the Convention on the Elimination of All Forms of Discrimination Against Women and issue recommendations for how states can better comply with the treaty. The committee is what is known in U.N. lingo as a "treaty body."

Members of the CEDAW Committee are self-identified gender experts chosen from the various countries that are party to CEDAW—although they serve in their individual capacities, and not as official representatives of their country's governments. Elected by countries participating in CEDAW, they serve terms of four years and are eligible for re-election. Each country that is party to CEDAW must submit written and oral reports to the committee every four years. The committee questions the delegation and issues concluding observations and recommendations for the state party to follow. In practice, the CEDAW Committee habitually bullies the delegations sent to deliver their countries' reports. The committee pressures state parties to change their domestic policies, and most alarmingly, it regularly reads more into the convention than exists in the actual text of the document. Although the committee is not technically a judicial body, its conclusions and recommendations have been cited in court decisions around the world, including the U.S. Supreme Court.

The CEDAW Committee in Session:
A 2008 Example

The committee met for its 41st session from June 30 to July 18, 2008, to review the periodic reports submitted by Yemen, Lithuania, Nigeria, Iceland, Finland, the United Kingdom, Tanzania, and Slovakia. Its questions to the state party delegations generally focused on the following matters: whether national judiciaries are relying on CEDAW to make legislative decisions while bypassing or changing any conflicting domestic law; using quotas and incentives to achieve equal participation of women in business, politics, and academia; the division of labor and domestic responsibilities between men and women in the home; the protection of women's rights from infringement by "conservatives" and "religious people"; and, "sexual and reproductive health."

Domestication of the Convention.   The committee questioned every country under review about the extent to which the convention has been incorporated into the country's domestic law, specifically inquiring about what kind of training is in place for the judiciary about how to refer to CEDAW in its rulings. For example, the committee chair asked the delegation from Slovakia whether there are any cases before Slovak courts in which CEDAW has been invoked. Another committee member asked for proof that the government of Nigeria is taking the convention seriously.

In its concluding observations on Lithuania's report, the committee expressed concern "that the Convention's provisions and the Committee's general recommendations are not sufficiently known by the majority of judges, lawyers, prosecutors [and women] . . . as indicated by the absence of any court decisions that refer to the Convention." Apparently, Lithuania's proof of compliance with CEDAW depends on its judges citing the treaty. A member of the committee asked the Lithuanian representatives whether the Lithuanian constitution has any provisions that would make the application of "temporary special measures" (affirmative action) on behalf of women unconstitutional. If so, she asked, "[Are] there plans to amend the Constitution? In what area [does] Lithuania plan to apply temporary special measures?"

The committee went even further than pushing countries to adopt CEDAW into law, urging them to enact legislation to comply with the committee's "general recommendations." In concluding observations on Tanzania, for example, the committee "call[ed] on the State party to accelerate its law review process and to work effectively with Parliament in ensuring that all discriminatory legislation is amended or repealed to bring it into compliance with the Convention *and the Committee's general recommendations.*" (Emphasis added.) This is an example of the committee behaving as a quasi-judicial body promulgating substantive interpretations of CEDAW, rather than confining itself to the role of a technical body of experts, as was stipulated in the treaty itself.

Quotas and *De Facto* Equality.   Not satisfied with demonstration of equality of the sexes before the law, the CEDAW Committee seeks *de facto* equalization of women's status in every sphere of society, and often advocates quotas or incentives to achieve it. It recommended that Tanzania "pursue sustained policies aimed at the promotion of women's full and equal participation in decisionmaking *as a democratic requirement* in all areas of public and professional life." (Emphasis added.) In its recommendations to Lithuania, the committee urged the government to "systematically adopt such laws on temporary special measures including goals and time-tables or quotas . . . in order to accelerate the realization of women's *de facto* equality with men in the areas of political and public life, education and public and private employment." That is, Lithuania must adopt laws to ensure that the gender of its legislators (and presumably the rest of its government) reflects its population. During the committee review of the United Kingdom's report, one committee member asked the delegation, "how both the equality of opportunity and the equality *of results* would be guaranteed" (emphasis added) for women throughout the country.

While especially interested in achieving gender parity in governing bodies, the committee also monitors women's participation in academia and the private sector. Consider these examples: One committee member praised Iceland for its 30 percent female representation in Parliament, and expressed her disappointment that only 18 percent of the professors at Iceland's largest university are women. Another asked the Finnish delegation whether it had a timeline for increasing the number of women on the governing boards of both private and government-owned companies. Lithuania was asked about what obligations the private sector faced in order to reduce job segregation and the gender pay gap. Another expert voiced her concerns about women's employment in Yemen, telling Yemen's delegation that the government ought "to pursue the equality of results as opposed to the formal equality of laws. Men and women should have the same job security and equal remuneration."

Family Life.   Beyond the public sphere, the committee calls on state parties to enforce CEDAW by intruding into private family and household matters. It aims to modify interactions between spouses and parental decisions regarding children, regardless of how tenuously related such regulation is to the advancement of women's rights. One committee member questioned several country delegations about corporal punishment and the rights of the "girl child." She asked the delegation from Iceland whether the government is "incorporating so-called 'positive disciplining' in its educational booklets on corporal punishment prevention."

Article 5 of CEDAW calls for the elimination of cultural stereotypes that discriminate against women. The CEDAW Committee uses this directive to instruct state parties on such personal matters as the division of domestic responsibilities within the family. The committee called on Yemen "to foster a better understanding of equality between women and men at all levels of society with a view to transforming stereotypical attitudes and negative cultural norms about the responsibilities and roles of women and men in the family and society." It similarly recommended that Finland work "to promote equal sharing of domestic and family tasks between women and men," and that Slovakia strengthen its efforts "to fully sensitize men to their equal participation in family tasks and responsibilities."

Disregard for culturally distinct patterns of pursuing the advancement of women and their preferences for work-life balance was on display in the committee's treatment of Iceland. The country sought to inform the committee about its own societal norms, explaining that women are more likely to seek part-time employment to be able to carry out their family responsibilities. The Icelandic delegation also referenced surveys that revealed that women are more likely than men to take family commitments into account in their decisions on participation in the labor market.

That prompted one committee member to ask the Icelandic delegation what measures the government has taken "to change these patterns of behavior." Her assumption, which the rest of the committee seems to share, is that women do not choose to focus primarily on family responsibilities, and if they do, they must be victims of discrimination.

Sexual Orientation and Nontraditional Families. The CEDAW Committee also uses its mandate to eliminate gender discrimination as an opportunity to advance the homosexual-lobby agenda. Several members of the committee suggested that the status of women in same-sex relationships or nontraditional families ought to receive greater attention from the state parties. . . .

Religion and Morality. The Committee regards religious communities and individuals—particularly conservatives—as a threat to women's freedom.

It regularly recommends that state parties to the convention be vigilant in monitoring such threats, instructing Slovakia, for example, to "adequately regulate the invocation of conscientious objection by health professionals so as to ensure that women's access to health and reproductive health is not limited." In other words, if a Slovakian doctor invokes a conscientious objection to performing an abortion or prescribing a contraceptive, the Slovakian government must "regulate" the invocation of such an objection. The committee wants Slovakia to require doctors to perform abortions regardless of their moral or religious beliefs. The committee expects religious principles and cultural values to accommodate the convention—and the committee's recommendations—not vice versa. . . .

Sexual and Reproductive Health. CEDAW is a much-debated and carefully negotiated document, and access to abortion is not required, nor even mentioned. But the committee's actions are an entirely different matter.

In its discussion of women's health, the committee focuses almost exclusively on contraception and abortion, referencing its own General Recommendation No. 24 to require countries to liberalize their laws regarding abortion. The committee called on Nigeria "to assess the impact of its abortion law on the maternal mortality rate and to give consideration to its reform or modification." Yemen was reminded that "contraceptives should be free or affordable." . . .

Conclusion

Injustice against women around the world is a reality. It is serious and sometimes even life threatening. Regrettably, the Convention on the Elimination of All Forms of Discrimination Against Women and the CEDAW Committee have done a disservice to the cases of abject discrimination against and mistreatment of women, choosing instead to focus on the advancement of a particular radical social agenda.

It is not the responsibility of the United Nations to set social policy for the United States. Americans rely on their elected representatives in state legislatures and Congress to reflect their values and traditions when legislating domestic issues such as health care, education, marriage, and family policy. The American constitutional order protects the sphere of civil society—families, religious organizations, and private associations—from government intrusion, leaving Americans to determine the course of their private lives, including religious expression and family decisions. Other matters that CEDAW addresses, such as gender equality in the workforce and political participation, are generally sorted out in the free market of ideas, without heavy-handed, government-mandated quotas. American women are free, legally and culturally, to pursue opportunities and relationships of their choosing. Americans should continue to fight incidental discrimination, while preserving the security afforded by the U.S. system of rights enshrined in the U.S. Constitution and protected under federal and state laws.

The actions of the CEDAW Committee are a stark reminder of the dangers of being a party to such multilateral treaties. The U.S. Senate should uphold its responsibility to the American people and not subject them to the tyranny of the CEDAW treaty. Ratifying CEDAW, and by extension subjecting the U.S. to the bullying of the CEDAW Committee, would neither advance women's equality nor serve American foreign policy interests, including the security and advancement of women around the globe.

POSTSCRIPT

Should the United States Ratify the Convention to Eliminate All Forms of Discrimination Against Women?

The concentrated effort to promote women's rights internationally within the context of advancing globalism dates back only to 1975, which the UN declared the International Women's Year. There have been many changes that benefit women since that time, but those changes have only begun to ease the problems that advocates of women's rights argue need to be addressed. CEDAW has been a keystone of the international effort to promote women's rights. In 2009, Qatar became the 186th state to adhere to CEDAW, leaving only seven countries (the United States, Iran, Sudan, Somalia, Nauru, Palau, and Tonga) that have not formally adhered to CEDAW. With President Bush opposed to CEDAW and the Republicans controlling the Senate for most of the time during his tenure, there was little chance that the Senate would ratify CEDAW. In 2008, though, the political wheel turned when the Democrats captured the White House and increased the control of the Senate they had gained in the 2006 elections. President Barack Obama, Vice President Joseph Biden, and Secretary of State Hillary Clinton had all advocated ratification of CEDAW during their campaigns for the Democratic presidential nomination. Moreover, once in office, Obama appointed Harold Koh, the author of the first reading, to the post of legal counsel for the State Department.

Nevertheless, the White House has not pushed for ratification, and the measure is not likely to move forward without the president's strong support. Illustrating that, Representative Lynn C. Woolsey (D-CA) and 124 cosponsors introduced a House resolution in early 2009 calling on the Senate to ratify CEDAW, but the House Foreign Affairs Committee has not even held hearings. Similarly, Senator Barbara Boxer (D-CA) chairs the Foreign Relations Committee's subcommittee that oversees global women's issues and is also on record supporting CEDAW, but she has been unable to advance the issue in her chamber. Even if President Obama was to make a concerted effort to get CEDAW ratified, the fate of the treaty in the Senate would be uncertain. When the Senate confirmed Koh in 2009, the vote was 62 to 35. Of the senators who opposed Koh's confirmation, a prime objection was his advocacy of following U.S. treaty obligations even if they conflict with domestic law. The interface with treaty law and other forms of law under the Constitution is complex, but from the view of many conservatives, following CEDAW would be part of what they see as the general diminution of U.S. sovereignty in general, with a particular threat for the United States to determine its own policy in such areas as abortion. Typical of the Republican opposition to Koh's confirmation, Senator

Jim DeMint (R-SC) specifically cited Koh's support of CEDAW and argued that favoring any "international legal regime when it subordinates . . . the American legal regime should cause all of us to stop and think." DeMint went on to say that "everything we are as a country—depends first on our sovereignty. . . . This idea of a global world order of some kind is frightening to many people, including myself." DeMint's view may be in a minority, but with a two-thirds vote needed for ratification, the 35 senators who voted against Koh would be enough to block ratification.

Expressing the same view as DeMint is John Fonte, "Democracy's Trojan Horse," *The National Interest* (Summer 2004). Also on this topic, read Sandra F. VanBurkleo, *Belonging to the World: Women's Rights and American Constitutional Culture* (Oxford University Press, 2000). An analysis of the issues facing Congress related to CEDAW is Luisa Blanchfield, *The U.N. Convention on the Elimination of All Forms of Discrimination Against Women (CEDAW): Issues in the U.S. Ratification Debate,* a Congressional Research Service report (August 7, 2009).

Questions for Critical Thinking and Reflection

1. Start by reading the text of CEDAW at http://www.un.org/womenwatch/daw/cedaw/cedaw.htm, then ask yourself whether it protects any rights that American women should not have. If it does so, which ones?
2. Those who worry about U.S. sovereignty argue that if U.S. law and the U.S. courts refused to uphold the rights women have under CEDAW the women could appeal to international courts for justice. Is that ability to appeal good or bad?
3. Is U.S. ratification of CEDAW superfluous given the extensive range of rights American women already have?

Internet References . . .

United Nations Department of Peacekeeping Operations

This UN site is the gateway to all the peacekeeping functions of the United Nations.

http://www.un.org/en/peacekeeping/

International Law Association

The International Law Association, which is currently headquartered in London, was founded in Brussels in 1873. Its objectives, under its constitution, include the "study, elucidation and advancement of international law, public and private, the study of comparative law, the making of proposals for the solution of conflicts of law and for the unification of law, and the furthering of international understanding and goodwill."

http://www.ila-hq.org

United Nations Treaty Collection

The United Nations Treaty Collection is a collection of 30,000 treaties, addenda, and other items related to treaties and international agreements that have been field with the UN Secretariat since 1946. The collection includes the texts of treaties in their original language(s) and English and French translations.

http://untreaty.un.org

Jurist: Terrorism Law and Policy

This site maintained by the University of Pittsburgh is a good source for the many complex legal issues involved in defining and combating terrorism.

http://jurist.law.pitt.edu/

UNIT 6

The Environment

*W*hen all is said and done, policy is, or at least ought to be, about values. That is, how do we want our world to be? There are choices to make about what to do (and what not to do). It would be easy if these choices were clearly good versus evil. But things are not usually that simple, and the issue in this part shows the disparity of opinions regarding the current state of the environment.

• Are Warnings About Global Warming Unduly Alarmist?

ISSUE 19

Are Warnings About Global Warming Unduly Alarmist?

YES: James Inhofe, from Remarks on the Floor of the U.S. Senate, *Congressional Record* (October 26, 2007)

NO: Barbara Boxer, from Remarks on the Floor of the U.S. Senate, *Congressional Record* (October 29, 2007)

ISSUE SUMMARY

YES: James Inhofe, a Republican member of the U.S. Senate from Oklahoma, tells the Senate that objective, evidence-based science is beginning to show that the predictions of catastrophic human-made global warming are overwought.

NO: Barbara Boxer, a Democratic member of the U.S. Senate from California, responds that Senator Inhofe's is one of the very few isolated and lonely voices that keeps on saying we do not have to worry about global warming, while, in reality, it is a major problem that demands a prompt response.

We live in an era of almost incomprehensible technological boom. In a very short time—less than a long lifetime in many cases—technology has brought some amazing things. But these advances have had negative by-products. A great deal of prosperity has come through industrialization, electrification, the burgeoning of private and commercial vehicles, and a host of other inventions and improvements that, in order to work, consume massive amounts of fossil fuel (mostly coal, petroleum, and natural gas). The burning of fossil fuels gives off carbon dioxide (CO_2) into the atmosphere. The discharge of CO_2 from burning wood, animals exhaling, and some other sources is nearly as old as Earth itself, but the last century's advances have rapidly increased the level of discharge. Since 1950 alone, annual global CO_2 emissions have more than tripled to about 26 billion tons. Much of this is retained in the atmosphere because the ability of nature to cleanse the atmosphere of the CO_2 through plant photosynthesis has been overwhelmed by the vast increases in fossil fuel burning and the simultaneous cutting of vast areas of the world's forests for habitation and agriculture.

Many analysts believe that as a result of this buildup of CO_2, we are experiencing global warming. The reason, they contend, is the greenhouse effect. As CO_2 accumulates in the upper atmosphere, it creates a blanket effect, trapping heat and preventing the nightly cooling of the Earth. Other gases, such as methane, also contribute to creating the thermal blanket. It is estimated that over the last century Earth's average temperature has risen about 1.1 degree Fahrenheit. The 1990s was the warmest decade since temperature records were first kept in 1856, and the first decade of the 2000s is on track to be even warmer. The pattern of global warming over the last millennium or so is sometimes compared to a "hockey stick." Between A.D. 1000 and 1900, the average world temperature pattern was basically flat, resembling the long shaft of a hockey stick. Since 1900, however, the temperature has risen relatively rapidly upward, with the spike compared to the shorter blade of a hockey stick.

This warming of the atmosphere worries many, who believe that rainfall, wind currents, and other climatic patterns are and could be dramatically, and sometimes dangerously, altered. Among other impacts, the polar ice caps will melt more quickly, and sea levels will rise, displacing perhaps over a 100 million people on the continents' coasts during the coming century. Some weather experts also project an increase in the number and intensity of hurricanes and other catastrophic weather events. James Inhofe lays out this argument in the first reading. Those who agree with Inhofe often call for significant changes in the levels of energy use and other changes in human activity that arguably will have a major impact on lifestyle.

As the commentary in the first reading by James Inhofe indicates, not everyone believes that global warming caused by a CO_2 buildup is occurring or worries about it. Some scientists do not believe that future temperature increases will be significant, either because they will not occur or because offsetting factors, such as increased cloudiness, will ease the effect. Others believe that whatever temperature increase is occurring is from natural trends in Earth's warming and cooling process. They point out that the time since 1856 is a mere blip in climatological time and further note that in the last 1,300 years, two marked temperature changes, the Medieval Warm Period (A.D. 800 to 1400) and the Little Ice Age (A.D. 1600 to 1850), have occurred. Another criticism is that there is only mixed scientific evidence of a level of global warming that will have serious negative effects. By contrast, Barbara Boxer depicts grave consequences from global warming in the second reading, and argues that the longer we wait to address global warming, the harder it will be to achieve the emission reductions we know we need to reach.

YES

James Inhofe

Remarks on the Floor of the U.S. Senate

An abundance of new peer-reviewed studies, analyses, and data-error discoveries in the past several months have prompted scientists to declare that fear of catastrophic manmade global warming [are overstated or false]. Objective, evidence-based science is beginning to crush hysteria. Meteorologist Joseph Conklin, who launched the skeptical Web site climatepolice.com in 2007, recently declared the "global warming movement is falling apart."

I will detail how even committed leftwing scientists now believe the environmental movement has been "co-opted" into promoting global warming as a "crisis," and I will expose the manufactured facade of "consensus." I will also address the economic factors of the so-called solutions to global warming and how they will have no measurable impact on the climate. But these so-called solutions will create huge economic harm for American families and the poor residents of the developing world who may see development hindered by unfounded climate fears.

I am convinced the future climate historians will look back on 2007 as the year the global warming fears began to crumble. Today, the greatest irony is that the U.N. and the media's climate hysteria grows louder as the case for alarmism fades away. While the scientific case grows weaker, the political and rhetorical proponents of climate fear are ramping up to offer hefty tax and regulatory solutions, both internationally and domestically, to solve the so-called crisis.

Those who want to blame man for all of these problems that they try to make us believe are happening are saying anthropogenic gases [generated by human activity] are the problem. Debunking catastrophic manmade global warming fears can be reduced to four essential points. Now, what I am going to do is read these points and go back and elaborate on each one.

1. Recent climate changes on Earth lie well within the bounds of natural climate variability—even the *New York Times* concedes this. U.N. temperature data shows that the late 20th century phase of global warming ended in 1998; new data for the Southern Hemisphere shows that a slight cooling is underway.

2. The second thing we will talk about is almost all current public fear of global warming is being driven by unproven and untestable computer model fears of the future, which now even the United Nations

U.S. Congressional Record, October 26, 2007.

concedes that the models—these are computer models; that is what all this stuff is based on—they do not account for half of the variability in nature and, thus, their predictions are not reliable. Even the United Nations agrees with that.

3. The third thing is debunking the relationship that the more CO_2 you have, the warmer the world is. That is very simplistic and it is untrue. Scientists are reporting in peer-reviewed literature that increasing CO_2 in the atmosphere will not have the catastrophic impact doomsters have been predicting. In fact, climate experts are discovering that you cannot distinguish the impact of human-produced greenhouse gases from natural climate variability. That is extremely significant and something that has come around in the last 6 or 7 months.

4. The fourth thing we will talk about is consensus. We hear so much about consensus. The more things that come out of science, where the scientists are saying, wait a minute, we were wrong. In a minute, I will be naming names of scientists who were marching the streets with Al Gore 10 years ago who now say they were wrong. When you talk about that today, those who are promoting this type of fear from the left, they use the word "consensus." The climate change "consensus" exists. Well, it does not exist. Instead, the illusion that it does has been carefully manufactured for political, financial, and ideological purposes.

These four basic points form the foundation of the rational, evidence-based approach to climate science that has come to be called global warming skepticism.

Essential point No. 1 is: The Earth's climate is within the natural variability. On April 23, 2006, the article in the *New York Times* stated, "Few scientists agree with the idea that the recent spate of potent hurricanes, European heat waves, African drought and other weather extremes are, in essence, our fault. . . . There is more than enough natural variability in nature to mask a direct connection, scientists say." The *Times* is essentially conceding that no recent weather events fall outside the range of natural climate variability. On a slightly longer time scale, many scientific studies have shown the medieval and earlier warm periods were as warm or warmer than the Earth's current temperature—when there were no influences that were due to manmade gases.

There have been recent studies refuting claims that the 20th century has seen unprecedented warmth. A June 29, 2007, paper by Gerd Burger of Berlin's Institute of Meteorology in the peer-reviewed *Science Magazine* challenged [the notion] that the 20th century had been unusually warm. Dr. Robert Giegengack, the chair of the Department of Earth and Environmental Science at the University of Pennsylvania, noted on May 27, 2007 that extremely long geologic timescales reveal that "only about 5 percent of that time has been characterized by conditions on Earth that were so cold that the poles could support masses of permanent ice." Giegengack added, "For most of Earth's history, the globe has been warmer than it has been for the last 200 years. It has rarely been cooler."

Even though Greenland has been a "poster boy" for climate alarmists, it is now cooler there than the temperatures were in the 1930s and 1940s. Greenland reached its highest temperatures in 1941, according to a peer-reviewed study published in the June 2006 issue of the *Journal of Geophysical Research.* Keep in mind that 80 percent of the manmade CO_2 came after the 1940s. That is a very interesting thing because, if you look at it, you would say if 80 percent of the CO_2 came after the 1940s, would that not precipitate a warming period—if they are right—in terms of CO_2 affecting warmer climate change? That didn't happen. That precipitated a cooler period.

According to a July 2007 survey of peer-reviewed literature on Greenland:

> Research in 2006 found that Greenland has been warming since the 1880s, but since 1955, temperature averages at Greenland stations have been colder than the period of 1881–1955. Another 2006 peer-reviewed study concluded the rate of warming in Greenland from 1920 to 1930 was about 50 percent higher than the warming from 1995 to 2005.

That is the time [alarmists] say this crisis is taking place. One 2005 study found Greenland gaining ice in the interior higher elevations and thinning ice at the lower elevations. In addition, the often media promoted fears of Greenland's ice completely melting and a subsequent catastrophic sea level rise are directly at odds with the latest scientific studies.

These are scientific facts you will not hear from the U.N. scientists, Gore, or the hysterical liberal left. Yet despite all of this evidence, the media and many others still attempt to distort the science in order to create hysterical fears about Greenland.

Scientists monitoring ice in Antarctica reported on October 1 that the ice has grown to record levels since 1979, when satellite monitoring began. So the ice levels have grown to record levels since that time, according to an announcement by the University of Illinois Polar Research Group Web site. The Southern Hemisphere sea ice area has broken the previous maximum of 16.03 million square kilometers and is currently at 16.26 million square kilometers.

There is more. A February 2007 study reveals Antarctica is not following predicted global warming temperature or precipitation models. [According to the study,] temperatures during the late 20th century did not climb as had been predicted by many global climate models. The study was conducted by David Bromwich, professor of atmospheric sciences at Ohio State University. How inconvenient that the two poster children of alarmism—Greenland and Antarctica—trumpeted by Al Gore and the climate fear mongers have decided not to cooperate with the computer models.

There is much more evidence that the Earth is currently well within natural climate variability. The Southern Hemisphere is cooling, according to U.N. scientist, Dr. Madhav Khandekar. He explained this on August 6, 2007, and these are all new scientific findings:

> In the Southern Hemisphere, the land-area mean temperature has slowly but surely declined in the last few years. The city of Buenes Aires in Argentina received several centimeters of snowfall in early July, and

the last time it snowed in Buenos Aires was in 1918. Most of Australia experienced one of its coldest months in June of this year. Several other locations in the Southern Hemisphere have experienced lower temperatures in the last few years. Further, the sea surface temperatures over world oceans are slowly declining since mid-1998, according to a recent worldwide analysis of ocean surface temperatures.

The media would not report on the historical perspective of Greenland, the ice growing in Antarctica, or the Southern Hemisphere cooling. Instead, the media's current fixation is on hyping Arctic sea ice shifts. What the media is refusing to report about the North Pole is that according to a 2003 study by an Arctic scientist, Igor Polyakov, the warmest period in the Arctic during the 20th century was the late 1930s through the early 1940s. We are talking about the Northern Hemisphere now. Many scientists believe if we had satellite monitoring of the Arctic back then, it may have shown less ice than today.

According to a 2005 peer-reviewed study in the Geophysical Research Letters by an astrophysicist, Dr. Willie Soon, solar irradiance appears to be the key to Arctic temperatures. The study found Arctic temperatures follow the pattern of increasing or decreasing energy received from the sun. In another 2005 study published in the *Journal of Climate,* Brian Hartmann and Gerd Wendler linked the 1976 Pacific climate shift to a very significant one-time shift upward in Alaskan temperatures. These evidence-based scientific studies debunk fears of manmade warming in the Arctic and in Alaska.

I have covered the latest science on both poles. In the Southern Hemisphere, scientists are finding nothing to be alarmed about. It is important to point out that the phase of global warming that started in 1979 has itself been halted since 1998, which is nearly a decade. In other words, the warming that took place, which I believe is from natural causes, stopped in 1998. It is not getting warmer anymore. According to paleoclimate scientist Dr. Bob Carter, this is significant:

> The accepted global average temperature statistics used by the Intergovernmental Panel on Climate Change [IPCC] show that no ground-based warming has occurred since 1998. Oddly, this eight-year-long temperature stability has occurred despite an increase over the same period of 15 parts per million (or 4 percent) in atmospheric CO_2. Second, lower atmospheric satellite-based temperature measurements, if corrected for non-greenhouse influences, such as El Nino events and large volcanic eruptions, show little if any global warming since 1979, a period over which atmospheric CO_2 has increased by 55 parts per million (17 percent).

Another key development in 2007 is the research led by meteorologist Anthony Watts of surfacestation.org which has revealed massive U.S. temperature collection data errors biasing thermometers to have warmer readings. Meteorologist [Joseph] Conklin explained on August 10, 2007:

> The (U.S.) National Climate Data Center is in the middle of a scandal. Their global observing network, the heart and soul of surface weather

measurement, is a disaster. Urbanization has placed many [temperature monitoring] sites in unsuitable locations—on hot black asphalt, next to trash burn barrels, beside heat exhaust vents, even attached to hot chimneys and above outdoor grills. The data and approach taken by many global warming alarmists is seriously flawed. If the global data were properly adjusted for urbanization and station siting, and land use change issues were addressed, what would emerge is a cyclical pattern of rises and falls with much less of any background trend.

I now move to central point No. 2, the unproven computer models that are driving climate fears. Anytime you try to make a projection into the future, you try to have a model you can rely on instead of relying on data that is current and accurate. Of course, you can't prove a prediction of the climate in 2100 wrong today, which reduces the models to speculating on what could or might may happen 50 or 100 years from now. Even the *New York Times* has been forced to acknowledge the overwhelming evidence that the Earth is currently well within natural climate variation. This inconvenient reality means all the climate doomsdayers have to back up their claims, their climate fears are unproven computer models predicting future doom.

But prominent U.N. scientists publicly questioned the reliability of these computer models. Only a few months ago in a candid statement, IPCC scientist Dr. Jim Renwick, a leading author of the U.N. IPCC 4th Assessment Report, publicly admitted "Half of the variability in the climate system is not predictable, so we don't expect to do terrifically well." In June, another high profile IPCC lead author, Dr. Kevin Trenberth, echoed Renwick's sentiments about the climate models by referring to them as nothing more than "story lines."

Dr. Hendrik Tennekes, a former director of research at The Netherlands' Royal National Meteorological Institute, recently took the critique of climate computer models one step further, saying, "I am of the opinion that most scientists engaged in the design, development, and tuning of climate models are, in fact, software engineers. They are unlicensed, hence unqualified to sell their products to society." Meteorologist Augie Auer of the New Zealand Climate Science Coalition, former professor of atmospheric sciences at the University of Wyoming, agreed, describing models this way, "It's virtual science, it's virtual reality." Auer joked, "Most of these climate predictions are models, they are about a half a step ahead of PlayStation." Prominent scientist Professor Nils-Axel Morner also denounced computer models in 2007, saying, "The rapid rise in sea levels predicted by computer models simply cannot happen." Morner is a leading world authority on sea levels and coastal erosion who headed the Department of Paleogeophysics & Geodynamics at Stockholm University. Physicist Dr. Syun-Ichi Akasofu, the former director of both the University of Alaska Fairbanks' Geophysical Institute and International Arctic Research Center, told a congressional hearing in 2006 that highly publicized computer models showing a disappearing Arctic were nothing more than "science fiction." Geologist Morten Hald, an Arctic expert at the University of Tromso in Norway, has also questioned the reliability of computer models that predict a future melting of the Arctic. He says, "The main problem is that these models are often based on relatively new climate data. The thermometer has only been in existence for 150 years and information on temperature which is 150 years old does not capture the large natural changes."

Physicist Freeman Dyson, professor emeritus of the Institute for Advanced Study at Princeton, [who calls] himself a "heretic" on global warming [has also] slammed computer models as unreliable. "The fuss about global warming is grossly exaggerated," writes Dyson in his 2007 book, *Many Colored Glass: Reflections on the Place of Life in the Universe.* Dyson focuses on debunking climate model predictions of climate doom. He said:

> They do not begin to describe the real world that we live in. The real world is muddy and messy and full of things that we do not yet understand. It is much easier for a scientist to sit in an air-conditioned building and run computer models than to put on winter clothes and measure what is really happening outside in the swamps and the clouds. That is why the climate model experts end up believing their own models.

In fact, so much of climate computer modeling is based on taking temperature data from a very short timeframe and extrapolating it out over 50 or 100 years or more and coming up with terrifying, scary scenarios. There is often no attempt to look at the longer geologic record.

But much of this type of modeling has about as much validity as me taking my 5-year-old granddaughter's growth rate from the last 2 years and using that to project her height when she is 25. My projections may show she will be 12 feet high at that time. Yet that is exactly how many of these computer model fears of the future are generated for sea level rise estimates on ice melt projections in places such as Greenland and the Arctic and other locations.

Earlier this month, yet another report was issued based on future computer models finding that polar bear populations are allegedly going to be devastated by 2050 due to global warming. The report was issued as part of the U.S. Fish and Wildlife Service consideration of listing the polar bear under the Endangered Species Act. This is a classic case of reality versus unproven computer model predictions. The Fish and Wildlife Service estimates that the polar bear population is currently at 20,000 to 25,000 bears, whereas in the fifties and sixties, estimates were as low as 5,000 to 10,000 bears. We also have a 2002 U.S. Geological Survey of wildlife in the Arctic Refuge Coastal Plain that noted the polar bear populations "may now be near historic highs."

The bottom line is that the attempt to list the polar bear under the Endangered Species Act is not based on any evidence that the polar bear populations are declining or in trouble. It is based on computer models fraught with uncertainties.

The third critical point on global warming is to debunk the notion that the more CO_2, the warmer the world, as simplistic. Environmental economist Dennis Avery, co-author with climate scientist Dr. Fred Singer of the new book, *Unstoppable Global Warming Every 1500 Years*, details how solar activity is linked to the Earth's natural temperature cycles. These two scientists argue, "The Earth has warmed only a net of 0.2 degrees centigrade of net warming since 1940. Human-emitted CO_2 gets blamed for only half of that."

Perhaps the most inconvenient fact for the promoters of climate doom is the abundance of new peer-reviewed papers echoing these many more scientists' skeptical views. A new peer-reviewed study by Brookhaven National Lab scientist Stephen Schwartz, accepted for publication in the *Journal of Geophysical Research,* finds that even a doubling of atmospheric carbon dioxide would not have the previous predicted dire impacts on global temperatures. In fact, this paper implies that we have already seen almost all of the warming from CO_2 that mankind has put into the atmosphere.

Astronomer Dr. Ian Wilson proclaimed in August of 2007 that the new Schwartz study means "Anthropogenic—that is manmade global warming—bites the dust." A former Harvard physicist, Dr. Lubos Motl, said the new study has reduced proponents of manmade climate fears to "playing the children's game to scare each other."

Now, just look at a sampling of the recent peer review studies debunking the issues. There are many others I could talk about, but I am just going to name a few here, things all happening this year, 2007. A September peer-reviewed study counters global warming theory, by finding carbon dioxide did not end the last Ice Age. The study found, "Deep-sea temperatures rose 1,300 years before atmospheric CO_2, ruling out the greenhouse gas as driver of meltdown." The lead author geologist Lowell Stott, explained, "The climate dynamic is much more complex than simply saying that CO_2 rises and the temperature warms." An October 2007 study by the Danish National Space Center Study concluded, "The Sun still appears to be the main forcing agent in global climate change." This study was authored by Physicist Henrik Svensmark and Eigil Friis-Christensen. The Belgian weather institute's August 2007 study dismissed the decisive role of CO_2 in warming, saying, "CO_2 is not the big bogeyman of climate change and global warming." Climate scientist Luc Debontridder explained: "Not CO_2, but water vapor is the most important greenhouse gas. It is responsible for at least 75 percent of the greenhouse effect." This is a simple scientific fact, but Al Gore's movie has hyped CO_2 so much that nobody seems to take note of it.

In 2007, even the alarmist IPCC reduced its sea level rise estimates significantly, thus reducing man's estimated impact on the climate by 25 percent. Meanwhile, a separate UN report in late 2006 found that cow emissions are more damaging to the planet than all of the CO_2 emissions from cars and trucks. Stating it in a different way, the gasses released by stock actually exceed the CO_2 in the atmosphere from all the cars and trucks in the transportation sector. Again, I stress that these research studies are but a sampling of the new science flowing in that is starting to overwhelm the fear campaigns of the global warming alarmists.

Geophysicist Dr. David Deming, associate professor of arts and sciences at the University of Oklahoma explained in January of this year, "No one has ever died from global warming. What kills people is cold, not heat. For more than 150 years, it has been documented in the medical literature that human mortality rates are highest in the winter when temperatures are the coldest." Perhaps the most scathing indictment of the "more CO_2 equals a warmer world" simplicity comes from Ivy League geologist Dr. Robert Giegengack, the chair of the Department of Earth and Environmental Science at the University of Pennsylvania. He said, "[Al] Gore claims that temperature increases solely because more CO_2 in the atmosphere traps the sun's heat. That's just wrong. It is a natural interplay. It's hard for us to say that CO_2 drives temperature. It's easier to say temperature drives CO_2." Giegengack continued, "The driving mechanism is exactly the opposite of what Al Gore claims, both in his film and in that book. It's the temperature that, through those 650,000 years, controlled the CO_2; not the CO_2 that controlled the temperature."

The global warming scare machine is now so tenuous that other liberal environmental scientists and activists are now joining Giegengack and condemning the entire basis for manmade global warming concerns. Denis Rancourt, a professor of physics and an environmental science researcher at the University of Ottawa. He believes that the global warming campaign does a disservice to the environmental movement. Rancourt wrote, on February 27, 2007:

> Promoting the global warming myth trains people to accept unverified, remote, and abstract dangers in the place of true problems that they can discover for themselves by becoming directly engaged in their workplace and by doing their own research and observations. It trains people to think lifestyle choices, in relation to CO_2 emission, rather than to think activism in the sense of exerting an influence to change societal structures.

Rancourt believes that global warming, "Will not become humankind's greatest threat until the sun has its next hiccup in a billion years or more in the very unlikely scenario that we are still be around." He also noted that even if CO_2 emissions were a grave threat, government action and political will cannot measurably or significantly ameliorate global climate in the present world. Most significantly, however, Rancourt, a committed leftwing activist and scientist, believes environmentalists have been duped into promoting global warming as a crisis. This is a far leftwing environmentalist type. He said:

> I argue that by far the most destructive force on the planet is profit-driven corporations and their cartels backed by military might; and that the global warming myth is a red herring that contributes to hiding this truth. In my opinion, activists who, using any justification, feed the global warming myth have effectively been co-opted, or at best neutralized. Global warming is strictly an imaginary problem for the First World middleclass.

Perhaps the biggest shock to the global warming debate was the conversion of the renowned French geophysicist Dr. Claude Allegre from a believer in the dangerous manmade warming fears to a skeptic just last year. This is a guy who was one of the first scientists around to sound global warming fears 20 years ago. Now he says the cause of climate change is unknown, and he ridiculed what he termed the "prophets of doom of global warming" in a September 2006 article.

I just say bravo for the growing scientific dissent. It is not easy for these guys who took a hard position just a few years ago to change their minds. In October, *Washington Post* staff writer Juliet Eilperin conceded the obvious, writing that the climate skeptics "appear to be expanding rather than shrinking."

Significant scientific advances have been made since the Kyoto protocol was created, many of which are taking us away from a concern about increasing greenhouse gases. If, back in the mid 1990s, we knew what we know today about climate, Kyoto would almost certainly not exist, because we would have concluded it is not necessary.

The fourth and final essential point deals with how the media and the climate doomsters insist that there is an overwhelming scientific consensus of manmade global warming. The notion of a consensus is carefully manufactured for political, financial, and ideological purposes. Its proponents never explain fully what consensus they are referring to. Is it a consensus that future computer models will turn out correct? Is it a consensus that the Earth has warmed? Proving that parts of the Earth have been warming doesn't prove that humans are responsible.

While it may appear to the casual observer that scientists promoting climate fears are in the majority, that is because most of the media wants to believe this. By the way, this sells papers; we all know that. Evidence continues to reveal this is an illusion. Climate skeptics, the emerging silent majority of scientists, receive much smaller shares of university funds. They don't get university research funds, foundation funds.

Climate skeptics also receive smaller shares of government grants and are not plugged into the well-heeled special interest lobby. If you are part of that lobby, you get all these funds. If you are not, they will not play with you. On the other side of the climate debate, you have a comparatively well-funded group of scientists, the activists who participate in the U.N. conferences, receiving foundation moneys, international government support, and fawning media treatment. The number of skeptics at first glance may appear smaller, but the skeptics are increasingly becoming vocal and turning the tables on the Goliath that has become the global warming fear industry.

Key components of the manufactured consensus fade under scrutiny. We often hear how the National Academy of Sciences and the American Meteorological Society issued statements endorsing the so-called consensus view that man is driving global warming. What you don't hear is that both the NAS and the AMS never allowed member scientists to vote on these climate statements because they know that if it doesn't come out this way, they will not get the money they would otherwise get. Essentially, only two dozen or so members on the governing boards of these institutions produced the consensus statements. It appears that the governing boards of these organizations caved in to pressure from those promoting the politically correct view of the United Nations and Gore-inspired science. The Canadian Academy of Sciences reportedly endorsed a consensus global warming statement that was never even approved by its governing board.

Rank-and-file scientists are now openly rebelling. James Spann, a certified meteorologist with the AMS, openly defied the organization when he said in January he does not know a single TV meteorologist who buys into the manmade global warming hype. In February, a panel of meteorologists expressed unanimous climate skepticism, and one panelist estimated 95 percent of his profession rejects global warming fears.

In August 2007, a comprehensive study of peer-reviewed scientific literature from 2004 to 2007 revealed less than half of all published scientists endorsed global warming theory. In addition, a 2007, report from the international group Institute of Physics [IOP] finds no consensus on global warming. According to one news report:

> As world leaders gathered in New York for a high-level UN meeting on climate change, a new report by some of the world's most renowned scientists urged policymakers to keep their eyes on the "science grapevine" arguing that the understanding of global warming is still far from complete. The IOP is also urging world leaders to remain alert to the latest scientific thought on climate change.

There are frequently claims that the U.N. IPCC "Summary for Policymakers" is the voice of hundreds or even thousands of the world's top scientists, but such claims do not hold up even to the light of scrutiny. According to the Associated Press, during the IPCC "Summary for Policymakers" meeting in April of 2007, the most recent, only 52 scientists participated. Many of the so-called hundreds of [other] scientists who have been affiliated with the U.N. as expert reviewers are, in fact, climate skeptics, but were not involved in writing the alarmist summary and its key notion that, "it is very highly likely that greenhouse gas forcing has been the dominant cause of the observed global warming over the last 50 years." An analysis [of the IPCC report] by climate data analyst John McLean says, "The IPCC leads us to believe that this statement is very much supported by a majority of reviewers. The reality is that there is surprisingly little explicit support for the key notion." Among the 23 independent reviewers, just 4 explicitly endorsed the statement that manmade gasses are the primary cause of global warming.

Hurricane expert Christopher Landsea of NOAA's National Hurricane Center was both an author and a reviewer of the IPCC's second assessment report back in 1995 and the third assessment report in 2001 but resigned from the fourth assessment report after charging the U.N. with playing politics with hurricane science. Landsea wrote a 2005, public letter detailing his experience with the U.N:

> I am withdrawing [from the U.N.] because I have come to view the part of the IPCC to which my expertise is relevant as having become politicized. In addition, when I have raised my concerns to the IPCC leadership, their response was simply to dismiss my concerns. I personally cannot in good faith continue to contribute to a process that I view as both being motivated by pre-conceived agendas and being scientifically unsound.

As you continue to scratch beneath the surface of the alleged global warming consensus, more discoveries await. Alabama's State climatologist Dr. John Christy of the University of Alabama in Huntsville served as a U.N. IPCC lead author in 2001 for the third assessment report and detailed how he personally witnessed U.N. scientists attempting to distort the science for political purposes. Christy told CNN on May 2, 2007, just this year:

> I was at the table with three Europeans, and we were having lunch. And they were talking about their role as lead authors. And they were

talking about how they were trying to make the report dramatic that the United States would just have to sign that Kyoto Protocol.

Former Colorado State climatologist, Dr. Roger Pielke, Sr., also detailed the corruption of the U.N. IPCC process. This is what he said on September 1, 2007:

> The same individuals who are doing primary research in the role of humans on the climate system are then permitted to lead the [IPCC] assessment! There should be an outcry on this obvious conflict of interest, but to date either few recognize this conflict, or see that since the recommendations of the IPCC fit their policy and political agenda, they chose to ignore this conflict. In either case, scientific rigor has been sacrificed and poor policy and political decisions will inevitably follow.

Politics appear to be the fuel that runs this process—the U.N. process we have been talking about—from the scientists to the bureaucrats to the delegates, and all the way to many of the world leaders involved in it.

The hysteria created by the U.N. and by Gore and the media have prompted frustrated scientists to finally fight back in the name of a rational approach to science. Climate rationalists or skeptics do not need to engage in smoke and mirrors to state their case, and we will be offering the world a chance to read and decide for themselves, unfiltered from the increasingly activist and shrill lens of media outlets such as NBC, *Newsweek, Time,* CBS, ABC, and CNN.

I have stood on the floor for years detailing all the unfolding science that has debunked climate alarmism. These scientific developments of 2007 are the result of years or decades of hard work by scientists skeptical of manmade climate fears. Finally reaching the point where we can watch the alarm crumble is very satisfying. All these scientists have come up with the same response.

Despite the massive scientific shift in favor of skeptics, proponents of climate fears are increasingly attempting to suppress dissent by skeptics. During Gore's Live Earth concert—which was a dismal failure, I might add—that he had in July, environmental activist Robert F. Kennedy, Jr., said of climate skeptics, "This is treason. And we need to start treating them as traitors."

I would like now to address a question that I am asked repeatedly: "What if you are wrong and the alarmists are right? Isn't it better to adopt carbon restrictions to stop carbon dioxide emissions, just in case?" Let's assume for a moment that the alarmists are right, which, of course, they are not, but let's assume for the sake of discussion they are. It still makes absolutely no sense to join Kyoto or any successor treaty or to adopt climate restrictions on our own. Not only does it not make economic sense, it does not make environmental sense.

First, going on a carbon diet, for us, would do nothing to avert climate change. Let's assume [the United States] signed on to the Kyoto treaty in 1997 and all other developed nations—not China, not Mexico, just the developed nations—signed on to it and lived by the emission requirements. How much would it lower the temperature in 50 years? His answer was 0.07 degrees Celsius by the year 2050–0.07 degrees is not even measurable, and that is if we took all these drastic steps, and we are not going to be doing that.

Now, I think when we come to the significant part of this—and that is the lesson on economics—the high costs that would be borne under carbon constraints are unjustifiable to achieve minuscule temperature reductions, and that is if the alarmists are right about the science. How much more unjustifiable would it be if I and the growing number of skeptical scientists are right, which I believe we are?

Whatever actions we take today, we must safeguard the well-being of America's families now and into the future. The Senate acknowledged this when resolved in 2005 that the United States should address global warming as long as it will not significantly harm the United States economy and encourages comparable action by other nations that are major trading partners and key contributors to global emissions. Neither the Kyoto protocol nor a single bill before Congress meets these criteria. They range from costly to ruinous.

Both the Energy Information Administration—that is the EIA—and the Wharton Econometric Forecasting Associates—that is the Wharton School of Economics—analyzed the cost of Kyoto when it was signed and the costs were staggering. For instance, EIA found that the annual cost would be up to $283 billion a year. That is in 1992 constant dollars. Wharton put the cost even higher— more than $300 billion a year. Now, that equates out to an increase in taxes $2,700 a year for every family of four in the United States.

What few Americans realize is that the impact of these policies would not be evenly distributed. The Congressional Budget Office recently looked at the approach taken by most global warming proposals in Congress, known as cap and trade—cap and trade the CO_2 emissions—that would place a cap on carbon emissions, allocate how much everyone could emit, and then let them trade those emissions. Let me quote from the CBO report:

> Regardless of how the allowances were distributed, most of the cost of meeting a cap on CO_2 emissions would be borne by consumers, who would face persistently higher prices for products such as electric and gasoline. Those price increases would be regressive in that poor households would bear a larger burden relative to their income than wealthier households would.

Think about that. Even relatively modest bills would put enormous burdens on the poor. The poor already face energy costs much higher as a percentage of their income than the wealthy. While most Americans spend about 4 percent of their monthly budget on heating homes and energy needs, the poorest one-fifth of Americans spend 19 percent of their budget on energy. Why would we adopt policies which disproportionately force the poor and working class to shoulder the higher costs?

So what is the path forward? I categorically will oppose legislation or initiatives that will devastate our economy, as well as those that will cost jobs simply to make symbolic gestures. I believe such measures would be defeated because the approach is politically unsustainable. We are seeing the first signs of that in Europe right now. Even if the alarmists were right on the science— which they are not—their command and control approaches sow the seeds of their own failure. As long as their own policies put national economy in the crosshairs, they will stoke the fires of opposition and eventually collapse under their own weight.

Stabilizing emissions cannot happen in 20, 40, 60 years because our world infrastructure is built on fossil fuels and will continue to be so for a long time to come. The power plants and other facilities being built now and in the future will emit carbon for half a century once they are complete. Quite simply, the technology does not exist to cost-effectively power the world without emitting carbon dioxide.

Let me conclude [by pointing] out that climate alarmism has become a cottage industry in this country and many others. But a growing number of scientists and the general public are coming around to the idea that climate change is natural and that there is no reason for alarm. It is time to stop pretending the world around us is headed for certain doom and that Kyoto-style policies would save us—when, in fact, the biggest danger lies in these policies themselves. Again, new studies continue to pile up and debunk alarm and the very foundation for so-called solutions to warming.

Remarks on the Floor of the U.S. Senate

I have been waiting to speak to the Senate to place in the [*Congressional*] *Record* the case that we have to make to take action to ease the impact of unfettered global warming. I think most Americans know by now—at least those who follow environmental issues—that on our committee, we have Senator Inhofe, who is the former chairman, in a very different place than the current chairman, myself. Senator Inhofe spoke for a couple of hours on this subject last week, and I told him I would come down and put forward my thoughts. I am sure he will want to respond to what I say. That is what the Senate should be. We should be able to debate. I have been looking forward to this debate because, frankly, there are very few isolated and lonely voices who keep on saying we do not have to worry about global warming. Those voices are getting fewer and fewer.

The reality is that a growing and diverse group of voices has recognized the importance of addressing global warming. Here are a few calls to action. Some might surprise you. For example, President Bush, on September 28, [2007] said, "Years from now our children are going to look back at the choices we make today, at this deciding moment. . . . [It] will be a moment when we turn the tide against greenhouse gas emissions instead of allowing the problem to grow."

Again, some of these voices are surprising as we build our case for action in the Senate. Gov. Charlie Crist, a Republican Governor from Florida, said, "We're all on the same planet. We need to work together to make sure the environment is an issue at the forefront. It shouldn't be a political issue. It's a global issue. It's not bipartisan. It's nonpartisan." Certainly, in my own State [California], Governor [Arnold] Schwarzenegger and the Democrats in the legislature have worked very closely to make sure we move against unfettered global warming.

"Vatican to Become World's First Carbon-Neutral State"—This is very recent, this year: The Vatican is installing solar panels and purchasing greenhouse gas offsets to become the first carbon-neutral sovereign state. We can see that everyone is working together except for a few. It is unfortunate because in the Senate, a few can stop us from doing our work. We already heard about some of the problems we are having getting the Energy bill through. But I am very optimistic because we have had a bipartisan breakthrough in the Environment and Public Works Committee with [senators from both parties] getting

U.S. Congressional Record, October 29, 2007.

together and putting forward a very solid bill which, if it is enacted, will be the most far-reaching global warming bill in the world today.

Earlier this year, the U.S. Climate Action Partnership, known as USCAP, which includes major corporations, joined together with environmental groups to issue a call for action on global warming, calling for reductions of 60 to 80 percent in greenhouse gas emissions by 2050. I thought I would go over some of the members of U.S. Climate Action Partnership because, again, there are just a few voices out there saying we are putting our head in the sand, this isn't a problem. But mainstream America is with the program. Let me tell my colleagues who they are. I am just going to read a few: Alcoa, Boston Scientific Corporation, BP America, Caterpillar, Inc., Chrysler, ConocoPhillips, Deere, Duke Energy, DuPont, Environmental Defense, Ford Motor Company, General Electric, General Motors, Johnson & Johnson, National Wildlife Federation, Natural Resources Defense Council, PepsiCo, Pew Center on Global Climate Change, PG&E Corporation, Shell, Siemens Corporation, Dow Chemical Company, the Nature Conservancy, World Resources Institute, and Xerox Corporation.

We can see the diverse members of the American family from corporate America to environmental organizations that have gotten together and have urged us to cap greenhouse gas emissions and cut them. It is very important that we think about the amazing coalition that is out there behind us addressing global warming. When we hear some Senators come down to the floor of the Senate and say this is ridiculous, this isn't an issue, just remember this list of mainstream America urging us forward, urging us to act.

Why should so many industries be calling upon us to enact climate legislation? Because they recognize a couple of points. One, the science is strong, it is irrefutable, and a sound business future for America lies in dealing with climate change. We cannot grow, we cannot move forward if we all of a sudden turn around and our planet is under threat. We cannot have a business looking out 50 years that does not think about this. We have to think about our grandkids and our great-grandkids, and corporate America thinks about the people who are going to come forward to continue the work of that corporation. They recognize the threat, but they also recognize the opportunities.

Let's read from USCAP's call for action. It is very clear:

> We believe that a national mandatory policy on climate change will provide the basis for the United States to assert world leadership in environmental and energy technology innovation, a national characteristic for which the United States has no rival. Such leadership will assure U.S. competitiveness in this century and beyond.

This is a very strong call for action from Republicans, from Democrats, from Independents, from corporate America, from the environmental community, and others that have joined together.

All you have to do, is pick up a newspaper, any newspaper—I don't care if it is a Republican editorial board, a Democratic editorial board, or Independent—and you will see an amazing amount of evidence as to global warming and its potential impact. I am going to go through a few recent headlines. I asked my staff—and they do an amazing job for me—to follow the news and let me know what is being written, what the scientists are saying. So I am going to give you just an example of some of these headlines. If we can walk away from this, then it seems to me we are being irresponsible. We have to listen to them.

Early warning signs: "Greenhouse Gases Fueled 2006 U.S. Heat" (Reuters)—According to NOAA—That is the National Oceanic and Atmospheric Administration. That is the Bush administration's NOAA—"the annual average U.S. temperature in 2006 was 2.1 degrees Fahrenheit above the 20th century average and the ninth consecutive year of above-normal U.S. temperatures" and that this was a result of "greenhouse gas emissions—not El Nino or other natural phenomena." This is our American Government under the President who has been very loath to move on global warming, warning us about these high temperatures.

"Scientists Report Severe Retreat of Arctic Ice"—The Cap of floating sea ice on the Arctic Ocean, which retreats under summer's warmth, this year shrank more than one million square miles—or six Californias—below the average minimum area reached in recent decades.

Again, these are scientists from the National Snow and Ice Data Center in Boulder, CO. This is not a matter of opinion; this is fact. They are measuring the ice. I was in Greenland. I saw it myself. Several of us went. It is the most awesome sight to behold, to see these icebergs, the size of a coliseum, bigger than this beautiful Senate floor, taller than this room, floating into the ocean. Each iceberg is an average of 9,000 years old, and they melt within 12 months from the time they get into the ocean. So let's not put our heads in the sand or under the water.

More early warning signs: "China Blames Climate Change for Extreme Weather"—This is China. China doesn't really want to move forward. They have been slow to come to the table. According to an official from Chinese Meteorological Administration's Department of Forecasting Services and Disaster Mitigation, "It should be said that one of the reasons for the weather extremes this year has been unusual atmospheric circulation brought about by global warming." A lot of people around here say: Let's not do anything until the Chinese come to the table. Now the Chinese are telling us we better watch out for this global warming.

"As Sea Level Rises, Disaster Predicted for Va. Wetlands"—My colleague, [Senator] John Warner [R-VA] was present at a very important set of hearings where we looked at the impact of global warming on his State. It says, "At least half, and perhaps as much as 80 percent, of the wetlands would be covered in too much water to survive if sea levels rise 1 1/2 to 2 feet." The analysis was conducted by Wetlands Watch, an environmental group.

"From Greenland to Antarctica, the world is losing its ice faster than anyone thought possible" (*National Geographic*)—Scientists are finding that glaciers and ice sheets are surprisingly touchy. Instead of melting steadily, like an ice cube on a summer day, they are prone to feedbacks, when melting begets more melting and the ice shrinks precipitously.

This is what is happening. You can come down on this floor and you can put a blindfold over your eyes and you can put your hands over your ears and say: I see no problem, I hear no problem. Then you are not really taking in the signs.

"Fires a Consequence of Climate Change"—This is touching my heart because my State has been burning, and all of my colleagues know this and all of them have been most wonderful to us—to Senator Feinstein and to me—about offering help and assistance. In the long run, we need to do something about global warming or we are going to have that horrible combination of drought, low humidity, high temperatures, and terrible winds—weather extremes that you have experienced from time to time. This is what we are going to see. Greek Prime Minister Costas Kerryman said, "The weather phenomena this year favored, as never before, the outbreak of destructive fires. We are already living with the consequences of climate change."

"Climate Change Pollution Rising—Thanks to Overwhelmed Oceans and Plants" (*Scientific American*)—I am not citing articles here to show you where there is bias. The world's oceans and forests are already so full of CO that they are losing their ability to absorb this climate change culprit. This according to the Proceedings of the National Academy of Sciences.

Some come to the floor [of the Senate] and say: Oh, look at this great scientist, Mr. ABC, or whatever his name, and he is challenging this. Well, he is challenging the world's leading scientists. And I think it is very important to say there are always people who will say HIV doesn't cause AIDS; there are always people who will say cigarette smoking doesn't cause cancer; but thank God this government has followed the preponderance of the science and we now are making progress. How sad it would be if America sits on the sidelines while the whole world looks to us for leadership on global warming.

"The Future Is Drying Up"—According to Nobel Laureate Steven Chu, diminished supplies of fresh water might prove a far more serious problem than slowly rising seas. He also remarked, "The most optimistic climate models for the second half of this century suggest that 30 to 70 percent of the snow pack will disappear." No wonder we have people visiting our offices who are already hurting from the recreation industry in this Nation. They see what is happening. They see the handwriting on the wall. We have to act.

"Study Links CO to Demise of Grazing Lands" (*Los Angeles Times*)—Rising levels of carbon dioxide may be contributing to the conversion of the world's grasslands into a landscape of woody shrubs, much less useful for livestock grazing. So this has implications for the very way of life we have here in America.

"Parks Face Climate Threat"—A report shows how climate change could have a huge effect on the Great Smokey Mountains, the Blue Ridge Parkway and other national parks. This according to a new report by the National Parks Conservation Association. Folks, this is mainstream thinking. Mainstream thinking. We have to act.

"Likely Spread of Deserts to Fertile Land Requires Quick Response, U.N. Report Says" (*New York Times*)—Enough fertile land could turn into desert within the next generation to create an "environmental crisis of global proportions" based on a new U.N. report. The report warns of large-scale migrations and political instability in parts of Africa and Central Asia. The report recommends national and international action to address global warming.

Another call to action. And here, from the Intergovernmental Panel on Climate Change [IPCC], which just won the Nobel Peace Prize, along with former Vice President Al Gore: "Projected trends in climate-change-related exposures of importance to human health will increase the number of people suffering from death, disease and injury from heat waves, floods, storms, fires, and droughts."

So to come down here and talk about the polar bear and say the polar bear is fine, the polar bear is not fine, and we will talk about it; but this isn't about the polar bear. This is about God's creation that is in jeopardy. We had testimony from scientists that 40 percent of the species that were created are going to be gone. Now, it is our turn to do our part. That is why I have been working so closely with the religious community, the evangelical community. They are concerned about God's creation, and we ought to be. We talk a good game about it. We talk about values. We talk about it, so let us do something to show we are willing to protect this gift from God we have been given.

"Why Frogs Are Dying" (*Newsweek*)—Climate change is no longer merely a matter of numbers from a computer model. With startling swiftness, it is reordering the natural world.

"Global Warming May Be Behind Increases in Insects and Disease-Carrying Animals" (*Newsday*)—Rising global temperatures may be helping to spark a population boom in insects and disease-carrying animals, creating unexpected threats to human populations, a number of scientific reports say. That is not a pretty future for my new grandson, to think about being exposed to all these vectors that have not attacked us, but this is what lies in our future if we do nothing.

"WHO—the World Health Organization—77,000 People Die Annually in Asia-Pacific Region from Climate Change" and "Pollution Cutting Life Expectancy in Europe" (both [published in] *USA Today*)—According to a Report by the European Environment Agency: "Poor air and water quality, and environmental changes blamed on global warming, have cut Europeans' life expectancy by nearly a year, Europe's environmental agency warned."

"Report Calls on Europe to Move on Global Warming"—The European Commission report warns that unless there is planning, European countries will face "increasingly frequent crises and disasters which will prove much more costly and also threaten Europe's social and economic systems and its security." The point is, when you invest now, you save $5 later.

How about national security? One of the reasons I got so concerned about this is when I learned what our own Pentagon and our own intelligence people are saying to us. And what are they saying to us? A report commissioned by the Department of Defense in 2003 found that the impacts of global warming would cause the U.S. to "find itself in a world where Europe will be struggling internally, with large numbers of refugees washing up on its shores and Asia in serious crisis over food and water. Disruptions and conflict will be endemic features of life." And, of course, our Pentagon and our Department of Defense are very concerned about that happening with our allies in Europe.

"Warming Will Exacerbate Global Water Conflicts"—According to many studies, including the IPCC, changing weather patterns will leave millions of people without dependable supplies of water for drinking, irrigation, and power.

Now, the reason I took so much time is to show the breadth and the depth of the concern in this country, in the world, to make the point that there is a huge movement in this country and in the world to address global warming. We are not going to listen to those who have their heads in the sand or, frankly, have decided they want to leave this for another generation. That would be irresponsible.

When Senator Inhofe came on the floor, he made a number of statements which were not true, and I am going to deal with a couple of them. He used an MIT [Massachusetts Institute of Technology] report in a misleading fashion. Senator Inhofe has frequently claimed an MIT report shows [that my bill to cut carbon emissions] would lead to a $4,500 tax on a family of four. But the author of the MIT report, John Reilly, said:

> Senator Inhofe misread his findings. Rather than impose a tax of $4,500 as Inhofe described it, he said, the study shows the regulation could generate a substantial amount of Federal revenue for the government to give back to Americans. A family of four, Reilly said, could earn an additional $4,500 if the United States adopted a carbon tax or auctioned off carbon credits.

So let us not misquote authors around here, because that is not the right thing to do for them nor is it the right thing to do to mislead our colleagues.

I mentioned the polar bears before, and many of us have been touched to see the polar bears clinging to smaller and smaller pieces of ice in order to survive. Senator Inhofe has claimed—and he claimed it on the floor—that the polar bear populations are increasing. The best-studied population, in Canada's western Hudson Bay, fell by 22 percent from 1,194 animals in 1987 to 935 in 2004, according to the U.S. Fish and Wildlife Service. Our own people are telling us that the polar bear is in trouble. The World Conservation Union projects that the bears' numbers will drop by 30 percent by 2050 due to continued loss of Arctic sea ice.

I think it is important that we talk about facts. Science must dictate what we do, not ideological arguments that don't have any weight behind them. The leading scientists of the world, including the Intergovernmental Panel on Climate Change, which I earlier mentioned, and which won the Nobel prize along with Vice President Gore, and the IPCC included hundreds of scientists, the best scientists from 130 nations—they tell us clearly that global warming is happening now and human activities are the cause. I believe we can meet this challenge, with hope, not fear. I believe when we meet this challenge, we will be stronger as a nation and we will be healthier as a nation.

And, by the way, we will create a whole new array of green-dollar jobs. My own state, a leader in the environment, has proven the point that when you step out and you address the needs of the environment, what comes with it are only good things—prosperity, job creation, and healthier families. We are doing it in our State with global warming and, by the way, many other States are following. If we did nothing, it would be a shame. This is a seminal issue, and we need to do something about it, because doing nothing is not an option we can afford. The potential consequences will be devastating for our families in the future and for the world.

We are seeing the early warning signs. People can come down to this floor and say whatever they want. We have seen melting of snow, we have seen melting of permafrost, increased temperatures, warming of lakes, rivers, oceans, changing in the seasons, shifts in the ranges of plant and animal species, rising sea levels. In the future, we can expect to see more extreme weather events, more severe heat waves, droughts, flooding, increased storm surges and, sadly, an increased incidence of wildfires. We will see extinction of species; we will see freshwater resources at risk. By 2020, between 75 million and 250 million people will be exposed to increased water stress due to climate change in Africa. In Asia there will be problems. Warming in the western mountains of America is projected to cause decreased snow pack and reduced summer flows, resulting in even greater competition for already over allocated water resources.

[During hearings on the environment] we had scientists who were experts on wildlife. I remember sitting there, being so saddened to hear that if we do nothing, 40 percent of God's species on planet Earth could face extinction.

Now we hear our oceans are at risk as well. The British Royal Society projects that progressive acidification of oceans due to increasing carbon dioxide is expected to have terrible impacts on marine life, such as corals and their dependent species. You have heard of coral bleaching. It is caused by increased water temperatures as well as the oceans becoming acidic from storing excess carbon. The water becomes so acidic [that] some marine life, such as shellfish and coral reefs, can no longer form their shell, as it dissolves in the acidic water.

The IPCC found that pests, diseases, and fire are having terrible impacts on forests, with an extended period of high fire risk and large increases in areas burned. Again, I wish to use this moment to thank the firefighters in my State, all of them—local, state, federal—working seamlessly together. We have the most extraordinary heroic firefighters in California, as we do all over this country. Their jobs are becoming more and more dangerous as these fires are so strong and are fueled by droughts, high temperatures, low humidity, and high winds.

I mentioned before that in July, I was in Greenland. I was there with 10 senators and Dr. Richard Alley, an expert on ice from Penn State, who accompanied us on the trip. It was amazing to see this whole situation with him at my side. What I learned from him is Greenland's ice is melting faster than anyone thought. In some places, the glacier ice is moving so quickly, if you stand there you can actually observe it moving. In the past year, new islands were discovered that were previously connected to the main mass of ice. The Greenland ice sheet holds enough ice to raise sea levels globally by 23 feet. Think about 23 feet. Sea level increases of only a few feet will cause major disruptions.

I wish to talk about public health. Public health officials have issued a call to action. We had a hearing the other day and we heard from the Director of the Centers for Disease Control and Prevention. Unfortunately, her testimony was heavily edited by the White House. I am working very hard, with other colleagues, to get her original draft. Let me tell you, we are not going to rest until we get that. But the fact is the public has a right to know everything about global warming and the threat it poses to their families and to their communities.

At the same hearing where we heard from Dr. Gerberding, the Commissioner of the Tennessee Department of Health presented the committee with a position statement from the Association of State and Territorial Health Officials on Climate Change and Public Health. Their statement was adopted unanimously.

According to the IPCC, climate change has already altered the distribution of some infectious disease vectors and the seasonal distribution of some allergenic pollen and increased heat wave-related deaths. We are already seeing and we are already feeling the difference. If trends continue, we could see increased malnutrition and related disorders, including those related to child growth and development. We will see increases in the number of people suffering from disease, injury, and death because of heat waves and because of droughts and fires and all the things we mentioned.

The World Health Organization has estimated that human-induced changes in the Earth's climate lead to at least 5 million cases of illness and more than 150,000 deaths every year already. We saw the European heat wave which caused countless numbers of illnesses and claimed 35,000 lives. That is accurate—35,000 lives were lost.

We are beginning to see right here in America what happens when the water warms. The Associated Press reported on September 27 that a 14-year-old boy died from an infection caused by an amoeba after swimming in Lake Havasu [Arizona]. According to a CDC official, these amebas thrive in warm water and as water temperatures continue to rise, we can expect to see more cases of these amoeba infections.

We are going to see an increase of ground-level ozone or smog because that is formed at higher temperatures. We know smog damages lungs and can cause asthma in our kids. We already have asthma as the leading cause of school absences in my state. We have major problems with dangerous smog days.

We know about wildlife. We know, as I said, that 40 percent of the species are at risk of extinction if we do nothing to reduce global warming. The U.S. Fish and Wildlife Service concluded that shrinking sea ice is the primary cause for the decline in polar bear populations. Senator Inhofe comes down and says the polar bears are doing great: Wrong. False information. Listen to your own administration's U.S. Fish and Wildlife Service. The shrinking sea ice is the primary cause for the decline in polar bear populations.

This [the Bush] administration—because it was threatened by a lawsuit—proposed listing the polar bear as threatened under the Endangered Species Act. So come down here and show pictures of those magnificent polar bears, saying everything is fine—that is wrong. It is wrong by every measure, by every scientific account, by our own U.S. Fish and Wildlife Service.

Global warming is a national security issue, as I mentioned before. People are telling me this current humanitarian catastrophe in Darfur is already linked to the extended drought in the region. The Secretary General of the United Nations said the Darfur conflict began as an ecological crisis, arising at least in part from climate change. This is happening right under our nose. The Senate and the House have been asleep at the wheel—until recently.

A report commissioned by the Department of Defense found the impacts of global warming would cause the United States to "find itself in a world where Europe would be struggling." Projected global warming "poses a serious threat to America's national security" and "acts as a threat multiplier for instability." This is all from retired admirals and generals. Projected global warming poses a serious threat to America's national security.

The United States, they said, could more frequently be drawn into situations of conflict "to help provide stability before conditions worsen and are exploited by extremists." Such missions could be long and require the United States to remain for "stability and reconstruction efforts . . . to avert further disaster."

That report also warns of "extreme weather events, drought, flooding, sea level rise, retreating glaciers, habitat shifts, the increased spread of life-threatening diseases" and increased scarcity of clean water that could "result in multiple chronic conditions" and "foster the conditions for internal conflicts, extremism, and movement toward increased authoritarianism and radical ideologies."

I have never seen an issue such as this, where we have such a unanimous call for action, a unanimous call for action—from the business community, from environmental organizations, from admirals and generals, from the Department of Defense, from the Wildlife Service—from all over the world. As yet we are nowhere, but we hope to change that.

Addressing global warming has major benefits. I wanted you to hear the truth about the dangers of global warming. Now I want to tell you what gives me hope. When we step up to the plate, we are going to benefit. We cannot only prevent the most dangerous effects of climate change, but we are going to be better off for it. I already mentioned Sir Nicholas Stern, former chief economist of the World Bank. He said: Spend a dollar now, save $5 later. So people are going to come on the floor and they are going to say: Oh my God, they are spending money on this. No, we are going to save money, because if we can avert the worst problems of global warming—you can't build a flood protection tall enough unless we do something now. Do you know what it costs to build that flood protection? We know because we passed the Water Resources Protection Act and we kept our promises to the people of New Orleans and the others from [hurricanes] Katrina and Rita who suffered so much.

Since 1990, Britain has reduced its greenhouse gas emissions by 15 percent. [Meanwhile,] Britain's economy has grown 40 percent. Britain's environmental industries are the fastest growing sector of the country's economy. I was just there a couple of months ago. Their environmental jobs grew to 500,000 from 135,000 in just the last 5 years.

There is a study at University of California, Berkeley [that says] in California, the gross State product, by 2020 will be up by as much as $74 billion, with 89,000 new jobs created because of our work on global warming and our laws. Sun Microsystems is already reaping the benefits of greater efficiency. They made some simple changes in the way they cool their computer servers. They have been able to cut their electrical consumption in half.

Tesla Motors, I would urge all of you to follow that company. They are producing an all-electric car with performance that rivals or even exceeds the world's best sports cars. It is exciting. It is in production. It is all-electric. There is another company, Bloom Energy, in San Jose. They are creating the next generation of fuel cell electrical generation systems. I visited there and the scientists were explaining how all of this works. I can tell you this technology has the potential to revolutionize the way that electricity is generated. It holds the potential to bring clean electricity to parts of the world that have no electricity now.

So what are the benefits, the benefits of new technology? New jobs, cleaner air as we reduce the pollution that causes global warming, by increasing our use of clean, renewable energy sources such as wind and solar, driving more efficiently, less polluting cars and trucks, and increasing efficiency.

We will reduce other forms of air population too: sulfur dioxide, nitrogen oxides, mercury. Those pollutants will be reduced as we cut global warming pollution. And that means cleaner, healthier air for us all to breathe. The IPCC also concluded that household benefits from reduced air pollution as a result of action to reduce greenhouse gas emissions can be substantial. So when I say: I meet this crisis with hope, not fear, I mean it. I think it is going to create jobs. I think it is going to make our communities healthier. I think it is going to make our air healthier. I think it is going to reduce our dependence on foreign countries to supply oil, which is now up to $90 a barrel.

We know oil is a critical strategic interest of America. Our reliance on oil-rich rogue states and unstable regimes has been at the heart of wars and interventions in the Middle East. As we develop these clean, renewable sources of energy, which is all going to be done by the private sector, my venture capitalists at home cannot wait to make these investments, but they will not make them unless we take the lead on a strong anti-global-warming bill.

I also want to express the moral imperative that was really brought to me by the religious community. The most vulnerable here and around the world have to be protected. I know we have colleagues who continue to say we have to do it, and they are absolutely right.

There is no time to waste because the longer we wait, the harder it will be to achieve the goals we have to achieve—before we find we are spending a fortune on flood control and we are spending a fortune to try to mitigate the terrible ravages that global warming will bring.

In every great issues debate, you always have a few people who stand outside the mainstream, and I respect that. I absolutely give the folks who have that point of view all the time they want to express themselves. Some will say this is not an urgent problem. Do nothing. Some have tried to argue that we should not act now.

I say there is no time to waste. Right now, there is unprecedented momentum for change. We must harness that momentum to pass strong global warming legislation. We have a small window of time to get started down this path. The longer we wait to get started, the harder it will be to achieve the emissions reductions we know we need to reach. Starting now will send a signal to the world and the business community as they make their future plans that the United States is serious about its leadership role.

I have a vision for my 11-year-old grandson and for my new grandson who was born a few months ago. My vision is that these children and yours will grow up and be able to know the gifts of nature that we saved for them, that they will understand we made the right choice for them—we protected the planet that is their home—that because of our action they will not be shackled into fighting wars over the last drops of water or oil or remaining acres of arable cropland. They will not have to spend their last treasure building higher floodwalls, bigger levees, and fortified cities to escape rising seas and angrier hurricanes. Their cars will run on clean renewable fuels that do not pollute the air they breathe. The United States will lead in exporting clean technologies and products that are the engine of a new green economy. We will lead the world in showing the way to live well, in a way that respects the Earth. To make this vision a reality, we must face our challenge in a way that overcomes our differences and that defies our party affiliations.

POSTSCRIPT

Are Warnings About Global Warming Unduly Alarmist?

The debate over the causes, extent, and impact of global warming is momentous. Then there is the question of what, if anything, to do about global warming. A first international step was the UN-sponsored treaty called the Kyoto Protocol in 1997. It requires the industrialized countries to significantly cut their CO_2 emissions but does not impose limits on developing countries including China and India. Almost every country but the Untied States ratified the treaty. The Bush administration objected that evidence of global warming was insufficient to warrant major changes that would be costly and disrupt Americans' lifestyle. Bush also argued that unless China, India, and other developing countries also had to adopt restrictions, cutbacks by the United States and other developed countries would make little long-term difference.

With the limits set by the Kyoto Protocol extending only through 2012, an international conference gathered in 2009, in Copenhagen, Denmark, to try to establish a few round of reductions. The resulting Copenhagen Accord adopted new limits, but was still adjudged a failure by many analysts because none of the limits was binding. Furthermore, many countries did not agree to cut emission below currently known levels. Instead, the cuts were below future projected levels. For example, the two largest emitters of CO_2, the United States and China, agreed to cut their emissions by 2020 to below projected 2025 levels. Moreover, none of the targets is mandatory. During the years under the Kyoto Protocol, some countries made reductions, but the overall growth of global emissions continued to increase sharply. Unless countries get much more serious about meeting their voluntary goals, the increases will continue. Indeed, even if the Copenhagen targets are met, they will only slow down the growth.

Adding to the dismay of those who favor a strong effort to curb emission, questions about the scientific evidence behind global warming erupted while the conference was in session. E-mails and other documents revealed after hackers retrieved them from the servers of a British university involved heavily in climatology purportedly showed that research about global warming was being manipulated by those favoring a strong response. In the end, reviews found most of the charges baseless, but skeptics further charged that the reviews were as biased as the original studies.

An overview of the issues involved in this debate is found in Andrew Dessler and Edward A. Parson, *The Science and Politics of Global Climate Change: A Guide to the Debate* (Cambridge University Press, 2010). The U.S. Environmental Protection Agency has a good site on global warming at http://epa.gov/climatechange/index.html. Also excellent is the UN's entry site global warming information at http://www.un.org/wcm/content/site/climatechange/gateway. An Internet site that takes a skeptical view of the alarm over global warming can be found at http://www.globalwarming.org/. Taking the opposite view is the Environmental Defense Fund at http://www.fightglobalwarming.com/, a site that includes the ability to engage your individual impact on global warming at http://www.ucsusa.org/.

Questions for Critical Thinking and Reflection

1. What has been your perceived experience from global warming?
2. There has been a tendency among Americans, at least, to support restraints on CO_2 emissions and other steps to curb global warming but to resist paying the lifestyle or economic price to implement many of the steps such as higher gasoline taxes to suppress use. How far would you be willing to go to support such steps?
3. How would you feel about paying a "global energy tax" of one-half of 1 percent of your income with the funds going to help poorer countries that cannot afford clean energy equipment and alternative sources?

Contributors to This Volume

EDITOR

JOHN T. ROURKE, Ph.D., is a professor of political science at the University of Connecticut. He has written numerous articles, book chapters, and papers, and is also the author of *Congress, the Executive, and U.S. Foreign Policymaking* (Westview Press, 1985); *International Relations on the World Stage*, 12th edition (McGraw-Hill, 1987–2008); *Making Foreign Policy: United States, Soviet Union, China* (Brooks/Cole, 1990); and *Presidential War and American Democracy: Rally Round the Chief* (Paragon House, 1993). Professor Rourke is the co-author of *Direct Democracy and International Politics: Deciding International Issues Through Referendums*, with Richard Hiskes and Cyrus E. Zirakzadeh (Lynne Rienner Publisher, 1992); *Making American Foreign Policy*, with Ralph Carter and Mark Boyer, 2nd edition (Brown & Benchmark, 1994, 1996); *International Politics on the World Stage: Brief Edition*, with Mark Boyer, 8th edition (McGraw-Hill, 1996–2009); and *American Politics: Globalization and Diversity* (Paradigm 2001). In addition to this 15th edition of *Taking Sides: Clashing Views in World Politics* (McGraw Hill, 1987–2007), he is the editor of *Taking Sides: Clashing Views on Controversial Issues in American Foreign Policy*, 2nd edition (Dushkin Publishing Group, 2000, 2002) and *You Decide: Current Debates in American Politics*, 8th edition (Longman, 2004–2011). A long career in both the academic and applied sides of politics has convinced the author that politics impacts everyone and that those who become knowledgeable and get active to promote what they believe in, whether that is based on self-interest or altruism, are the single most important driving force in the ultimate contest: politics.

AUTHORS

WALDEN BELLO is the president of the Freedom from Debt Coalition, a senior analyst at Focus on the Global South, and a columnist for Foreign Policy In Focus. He is also a professor of sociology and public administration at the University of the Philippines Diliman and a member of the Philippines' House of Representatives. He has a Ph.D. in sociology from Princeton University. In March 2008, the International Studies Association awarded Bellow its Outstanding Public Scholar for 2008.

C. FRED BERGSTEN has been director of the Peterson Institute for International Economics since its creation in 1981. He has served as assistant secretary of the Treasury for International Affairs (1977–1981) and as assistant for International Economic Affairs to the National Security Council (1969–1971). He has been a fellow at the Brookings Institution, the Carnegie Endowment for International Peace, and the Council on Foreign Relations. He also served as chairman of the international economic Competitiveness Policy Council created by the Congress (1991–1995). He earned a Ph.D. from the Fletcher School of Law and Diplomacy.

PATRICIA BERLYN writes on Israelite history and culture and is a former associate editor for the *Jewish Bible Quarterly* in Jerusalem. She has also worked for the Council on Foreign Relations, as well as its journal, *Foreign Affairs*.

SAMUEL A. BLEICHER is currently a principal in his consulting firm, The Strategic Path LLC. From 2001 to 2007, he served as chief strategist for new initiatives in the Overseas Buildings Operations Bureau of the U.S. State Department. He has a J.D. from Harvard University.

PIETER BOTTELIER is a nonresident scholar in Carnegie's International Economics Program and senior adjunct professor of China studies at the School of Advanced International Studies (SAIS) at Johns Hopkins University. He has held numerous positions at the World Bank including senior adviser to the vice president for East Asia, chief of the resident mission in Beijing, and director for Latin America.

BARBARA BOXER is a Democratic member of the U.S. Senate from California. She chairs the Senate's Committee on Environment and Public Works. Earlier she served five terms in the U.S. House of Representatives.

BARRY R. CHISWICK is UIC distinguished professor in and head of the Department of Economics, University of Illinois at Chicago and director of the UIC Center for Economic Education. He holds a Ph.D. in economics from Columbia University.

ARIEL COHEN is a senior research fellow in Russian and Eurasian studies and international energy policy in the Douglas and Sarah Allison Center for Foreign Policy Studies, a division of the Kathryn and Shelby Cullom Davis Institute for International Studies, at The Heritage Foundation. He holds a Ph.D. from the Fletcher School of Law and Diplomacy at Tufts University.

URI DADUSH is a senior associate in and the director of the International Economics Program at the Carnegie Endowment of International Peace. His former posts at the World Bank have included director of international trade and director of economic policy. He holds a Ph.D. in business economics from Harvard University.

ALAN W. DOWD was at the time of his article a senior fellow at the Sagamore Institute for Policy Research in Indianapolis. He has since become a senior fellow for defense and security research at the Fraser Institute in Vancouver, Canada. He is also a contributing editor for the *American Legion* magazine. He holds a B.A. with high honors in political science from Butler University and an M.A. in philanthropic studies from Indiana University.

WILLIAM J. DURCH is a senior associate at the Henry L. Stimson Center. He has served in the U.S. Arms Control and Disarmament Agency, as a research fellow at the Harvard Center for Science and International Affairs, and as assistant director of the Defense and Arms Control Studies program at the Massachusetts Institute of Technology. He holds a Ph.D. from the Massachusetts Institute of Technology.

JONATHAN F. FANTON is president of the John D. and Catherine T. MacArthur Foundation. He has also served as president of the New School for Social Research and vice president for Planning at the University of Chicago. He has a Ph.D. in American history from Yale University.

ROBERT FARLEY is an assistant professor at the University of Kentucky's Patterson School of Diplomacy and International Commerce. He received his Ph.D. in political science from the University of Washington.

STEVEN GROVES is Bernard and Barbara Lomas fellow in the Margaret Thatcher Center for Freedom, a division of the Kathryn and Shelby Cullom Davis Institute for International Studies, The Heritage Foundation. He has served as senior counsel to the U.S. Senate Permanent Subcommittee on Investigations and as an assistant attorney general for the state of Florida. Groves received his law degree from Ohio Northern University.

CHRISTOPHER HEMMER is a professor in and deputy chair in the Department of International Security Studies at the Air War College at Maxwell Air Force Base, Montgomery, Alabama. He has also taught at Cornell University and Colgate University. He has a Ph.D. in government from Cornell University.

JOHN L. HENNESSY is the president of Stanford University. As a faculty member, he was the Willard and Inez Kerr Bell endowed professor of electrical engineering and computer science. Hennessy co-chaired, along with former U.S. National Security Adviser General Brent Scowcroft, the Committee on Science, Security, and Prosperity in a Changing World of the National Academies, which is made up of the National Academy of Sciences, the National Academy of Engineering, the Institute of Medicine, and the National Research Council. Hennessy has a Ph.D. in computer science from the State University of New York at Stony Brook.

JAMES INHOFE is a Republican member of the U.S. Senate from Oklahoma. He has chaired the Senate's Committee on Environment and Public Works. He has also been a member of the U.S. House of Representatives, Mayor of Tulsa, Oklahoma, a member of both houses of the Oklahoma legislature, and was president of the Quaker Life Insurance Company.

HAROLD HONGJU KOH was at the time of his testimony the Gerard C. and Bernice Latrobe Smith professor of international law the Yale Law School. Thereafter he became dean of the law school and in 2009 the legal advisor to the U.S. Department of State. He has also served as assistant secretary of state for democracy, human rights, and labor (1988–2001). He has a J.D. from Harvard University and clerked for Associate Justice Harry Blackmun on the U.S. Supreme Court (1981–1982).

DENNIS KUCINICH has since 1996 been a Democratic member of the U.S. House of Representatives from the Tenth Congressional District, encompassing western Cleveland and its suburbs. He unsuccessfully sought the Democratic presidential nomination in 2004 and 2008. He also served as the mayor of Cleveland (1977–1979).

CHRISTOPHER LAYNE holds the Robert M. Gates chair in national security at Texas A&M's George H. W. Bush School of Government & Public Service. Among his other publications is *The Peace of Illusions: American Grand Strategy from 1940 to the Present* (Cornell University Press, 2006). He has a Ph.D. from the University of California at Berkeley and a J.D. from University of Southern California.

PHILIPPE LEGRAIN is a chief economist of Britain in Europe. He was previously special adviser to the director-general of the World Trade Organization and the trade and economics correspondent for *The Economist*. He has also written for *The Financial Times, The Wall Street Journal Europe, The Times, The Guardian, The Independent, New Statesman, Prospect,* and *The Ecologist,* as well as *The New Republic, Foreign Policy,* and *The Chronicle Review*. He has a master's degree in economics from the London School of Economics.

MICHAEL LEWIS is a professor of law at Ohio Northern University's Pettit College of Law, where he teaches and writes in the fields of international law and the law of armed conflict. He has served as a U.S. Navy fighter pilot and holds a J.D. from Harvard University.

GRACE SMITH MELTON is an associate for social issues at the United Nations with the Richard and Helen DeVos Center for Religion and Civil Society at The Heritage Foundation.

BARACK OBAMA is the forty-fourth president of the United States. He has served in the U.S. Senate (2005–2009) and in the Illinois State Senate (1997–2004). He holds a J.D. from Harvard University.

MARY ELLEN O'CONNELL is the research professor of international dispute resolution at the Kroc Institute for International Peace Studies, the University of Notre Dame, and also the Robert and Marion Short professor of law at the university's law school. Among her publications is *The Power and Purpose of International Law* (Ohio State University Press, 2008). She earned her J.D. from Columbia University.

NORMAN PODHORETZ is the editor-at-large of *Commentary* and widely acknowledged as one of the most influential conservative thinkers of his time. He was awarded the Presidential Medal of Freedom by George W. Bush in 2004.

WILLIAM C. POTTER is the founding director of the James Martin Center for Nonproliferation Studies at the Monterey Institute of International Studies. He also is Sam Nunn and Richard Lugar Professor of Nonproliferation Studies at the Monterey Institute. He has served on the UN Secretary-General's Advisory Board on Disarmament Matters and the Board of Trustees of the UN Institute for Disarmament Research. He has a Ph.D. in political science from the University of Michigan.

RAVINDER RENA is an associate professor of economics at the Eritrea Institute of Technology. He earned a Ph.D. in economics at Osmania University, India.

OTTO J. REICH is the president of Otto Reich Associates, LLC, an international consulting firm, and a former U.S. assistant secretary of state for the Western Hemisphere (2002–2004). He has also served as the president's special envoy for the Western Hemisphere, as U.S. Ambassador to Venezuela, and as assistant administrator of the US Agency for International Development.

DANI RODRIK is a professor of political economy at Harvard University's John F. Kennedy School of Government. He is a recipient of the Social Science Research Council's Albert O. Hirschman Prize and the Leontief Award for Advancing the Frontiers of Economic Thought. His latest book is *Globalization Paradox* (Norton, 2011). Rodrik holds a Ph.D. in economics from Princeton University and an honorary doctorate from the University of Antwerp, The Netherlands.

DAVID SATTER is senior fellow, Hudson Institute Fellow, Foreign Policy Institute, Johns Hopkins University, School of Advanced International Studies. He has worked as the Moscow correspondent of the London *Financial Times* and as a special correspondent on Soviet affairs for *The Wall Street Journal*. Additionally, Satter has been a fellow at the Foreign Policy Research Institute in Philadelphia and at the Hoover Institution.

BRETT D. SCHAEFER is the Jay Kingham Fellow in International Regulatory Affairs at the Heritage Foundation. He has an M.A. degree in international development economics from the School of International Service at American University. He has recently published an edited book, *ConUNdrum: The Limits of the United Nations and the Search for Alternatives* (Rowman & Littlefield, 2009).

ROSEMARY E. SHINKO is a member of the political science faculty at Bucknell University and former coordinator of academic services at the Stamford Campus of the University of Connecticut. She holds a Ph.D. in political science from the University of Connecticut.